THE SOCIOLOGY OF WORK

THE SOCIOLOGY OF

WORK

BY THEODORE CAPLOW

GREENWOOD PRESS, PUBLISHERS
WESTPORT, CONNECTICUT

Library of Congress Cataloging in Publication Data

Caplow, Theodore.
   The sociology of work.

      Reprint of the ed. published by University of
   Minnesota Press, Minneapolis.
      Bibliography: p.
      Includes index.
      1. Occupations. 2. Socialogy. 3. Social
   classes. I. Title.
   [HM211.C3 1978]   301.5'5   77-18112
   ISBN 0-313-20111-0

Reprinted with the permission of The University of
Minnesota Press

Reprinted in 1978 by Greenwood Press, Inc.
51 Riverside Avenue, Westport, CT 06880

Printed in the United States of America

TO BARBARA

PREFACE

THIS book was originally intended as a description of occupational institutions, but it has gradually turned into an essay on the division of labor.

The division of labor is a curiously neglected topic. It is difficult for a sociologist to read the works of Adam Smith, lately professor of moral philosophy in the University of Glasgow, without regretting that nineteenth-century scholars spent untold effort on the embellishment of Smith's model of the self-adjusting market, but saw nothing interesting in his lucid analysis of occupational institutions. Something of the same sort happened a hundred years later when Emile Durkheim undertook a doctoral dissertation on the division of *social* labor, and made a very fair start toward answering the tremendous question "What holds society together?" Yet that study is remembered for certain methodological innovations, and for an invalid proof that ethical principles can be scientifically verified.

Happily, there has been a great deal of careful research on the causes and consequences of occupational differentiation. Much of it is incidental to some other study—of educational placement, of manpower utilization, of industrial relations, or of annuity schedules—but this does not necessarily detract from its sociological relevance, as the following pages will illustrate many times.

The most compelling reason for studying the sociology of work is that no description of the human landscape is possible without taking into account the productive activities to which most adults give most of their time, and the principles which govern the allocation of social rewards and deprivations. As Everett Hughes wrote in introducing a special issue of the *American Journal of Sociology* on the Sociology of Work: "In our particular society, work organization looms so large as a separate and specialized system of things, and work experience is so fateful a part of

THE SOCIOLOGY OF WORK

every man's life, that we cannot make much headway as students of society and of social psychology without using work as one of our main laboratories."

ACKNOWLEDGMENTS ARE DUE

To Drs. Clifford Kirkpatrick, F. Stuart Chapin, James Lewis Morrill, Robert Merton, Wilbert E. Moore, Herbert Blumer, Robert Dubin, Jean Stoetzel, Georges Friedmann, René Koenig, Delbert Miller, and Reuben Hill. If there are any ideas in this volume which appear both original and sound, they are likely to have been borrowed from one of these scholars.

To Elmer Hankes, of Engineers Northwest, Incorporated, without whose encouragement this book would never have been undertaken.

To Reba McIntosh, Reece McGee, and Arlene Gable, for patient and thoughtful help with the manuscript.

To the editors of the *Scientific American,* E. P. Dutton and Company, Routledge and Kegan Paul, Ltd., the editors of the *Journal of Educational and Psychological Measurement,* and of *Minnesota Medicine,* Alfred A. Knopf, Inc., the Wharton School of Finance, Random House, and Mr. R. K. Barnhard of the Monsanto Chemical Company, for permission to reproduce material quoted in the text.

T. C.

March 1954

CONTENTS

	INTRODUCTION	3
1	THE ASSIGNMENT OF WORK	9
2	THE MEASUREMENT OF OCCUPATIONAL STATUS	30
3	VERTICAL MOBILITY	59
4	OTHER MOBILITIES	82
5	OCCUPATIONAL INSTITUTIONS	100
6	OCCUPATIONAL IDEOLOGIES	124
7	SOCIOLOGY OF THE LABOR MARKET	142
8	THE LABOR UNION AS AN OCCUPATIONAL ASSOCIATION	181
9	VOCATIONAL CHOICE	214
10	OCCUPATIONS OF WOMEN	230
11	OCCUPATION AND FAMILY	248
12	WORKING CONDITIONS	281
	APPENDIX. A BRIEF STATISTICAL DESCRIPTION OF THE AMERICAN LABOR FORCE	293
	BIBLIOGRAPHY	303
	INDEX OF OCCUPATIONS	323
	GENERAL INDEX	326

THE SOCIOLOGY OF WORK

INTRODUCTION

"In the progress of society, philosophy or speculation becomes, like every other employment, the principal or sole trade and occupation of a particular class of citizens. Like every other employment too, it is subdivided into a great number of different branches, each of which affords occupation to a peculiar tribe or class of philosophers, and this subdivision of employment in philosophy, as well as in every other business, improves dexterity, and saves time."   ADAM SMITH

THE subject matter of sociology is sometimes said to be group interaction—the range of phenomena created by the interplay of social aggregates with each other and with their members. In practice, the peculiar tribe or class of philosophers called sociologists is concerned with only certain forms of interaction. The actual subject matter of investigation falls between psychology and related subjects on the one hand, which deal with *individual* and *organic* aspects of human behavior, and economics and political science on the other, which have to do with particular *systems* of interaction.

These lines are not tightly drawn and should not be. Most social scientists share the faith that a science of human relations (comparable in validity and ultimate effectiveness to the laboratory sciences) is possible and desirable. While progress toward this hypothetical science has been halting, the effort to bring it into being has had important consequences. Through the application of scientific methods, enormous contributions have been made to what used to be known as "political arithmetic," the detailed description of society. Rough adherence to the canons of objectivity and emphasis upon the use of quantitative observations have given us far more knowledge about the workings of our own institutions than has ever before been available anywhere in the world.

Historically, the first concern of sociology was social evolution, but its *raison d'être* and the means by which it was erected into a respectable academic subject was the study of social problems—vice, crime, and misery. Out of this narrow field came the study of institutional life, the family, community organization, race relations, rural-urban adjustments, patterns of settlement, characteristics of populations, the interplay of custom and technology, and the effects of social change. Recently, and with some misgivings, the students of society have turned increasingly to the central institutions which regulate our industrial society, and have begun to investigate the distribution of power, the criteria of rank, the conflicts of organized groups, and the ordering of hierarchies.

Curiously enough, this interest involves a revived concern with the general principles of social evolution. All of modern social science is, in a sense, derived from the armchair theorists of the late nineteenth century, and it is upon the work of one of the greatest of these, Emile Durkheim, that the present attempt to outline the field of occupational sociology leans most heavily.

The underlying assumption of this book, drawn from Durkheim's doctoral thesis on the division of labor, may be stated in a highly simplified form as follows:

While early societies are held together by custom, similarity, and the authority of the elders, the complex society is maintained by the mutual dependence of highly specialized and differentiated occupational groups.

In the chapters that follow, the sociology of work will be treated primarily as *the study of those social roles which arise from the classification of men by the work they do.* That this is by no means the only approach to the division of labor is obvious from the massive literature which has accumulated in half a dozen special fields.

As early as the eighteenth century, political economists were concerned with a number of problems arising from the division of labor and the occupational distribution of the population. So much can be seen from the title of Book I, Volume I, of *Wealth of Nations*: "Of the Causes of Improvement in the productive Powers of Labour, and of the Order according to which its Produce is naturally distributed among the different Ranks of the People." Although most of this material was neglected in the nineteenth century in favor of mechanical models of market situations, it was returned to the forefront with the institutional economics of the Austrian School, and of Commons, Veblen, and their followers in the United States.[1] Somewhat later came the systematic investigation of the labor market and of technological and cyclical unemployment. More recently still, the field of labor relations has developed around the organized conflicts of labor and management, and several general theories of occupational mobility have been presented.[2]

Since the turn of the century, when the German notion of folk history was introduced into this country by James Harvey Robinson, the flourishing specialty of economic history has documented such phenomena as the agrarian revolution, the influence of frontiers, the displacement of local economies, and the development of regional and international markets, in terms of their over-all social consequences. Somewhat outside of regular academic channels, the works of Patrick Geddes and his disciple, Lewis Mumford, offer a broad interpretation of the social and aesthetic implications of economic change.

The psychological study of occupational differences begins with Francis Galton's attempt to explain occupational inheritance in terms of natural ability. Since his time, an enormous mass of information has accumulated on the individual differences and occupational variations in performance and reward. Vocational guidance on the basis of test results has become a well-established technic in industry and government. The measurement of aptitudes, skills, capacities, interests, attitudes, kinetic reactions, and almost any other discoverable characteristic of individuals is taken for granted in most educational institutions and large enterprises. Although most of these testing methods were designed to estimate the eligibility of individual candidates for training, employment, or promotion, they furnish indirectly a mass of information on the characteristics of occupational groups and on the selective mechanisms which distribute the population into occupational pigeonholes. It has also been occasionally suggested that the existence of objective and impersonal technics for matching workers and jobs is itself a major factor in the immobilization of society. We shall have occasion to examine this point of view later on in this volume.

The study of work in terms of motivation, persistence, fatigue, and other attributes of performance has led to the development of industrial psychology. Since these researches are limited for the most part to the large-scale mechanized factory, the validity of some of them is now under question. Nevertheless, industrial psychology is still the cornerstone of the very active art known as scientific management.

Vocational guidance and scientific management are only two of the fields of application which have developed from the occupational aspects of economics and psychology. There are also personnel management, production engineering, time-study, occupational classification, vocational rehabilitation, employment forecasting, and as many more.

One of the most significant of these newer fields is industrial sociology. Although initiated by professors, it has been thought of from the beginning in terms of practical application, and enjoys a limited but growing prestige among industrial managers. As a field of investigation, it arose almost accidentally out of a routine study of the relation between shop conditions and output undertaken at the Hawthorne plant of the Western Electric Company more than twenty years ago. Careful control of such variables as lighting and rest periods resulted in the discovery that the human relations in the working situation were the most significant determinants of output. Although industrial sociology has been sharply criticized for managerial bias, it is probably less partial to the special viewpoint of the industrial executive than are the older fields of scientific management and personnel work. As we shall presently see, it has cast more light upon behavior in the work situation than did the previous literature, although most of the findings refer to large factories and cannot yet be applied to the work situation of the farmer, the architect, or the peddler.

Still more recently, political scientists have extended their interest in power relationships from formal government into occupational and industrial life. They have already produced a number of cogent researches into the functioning of bureaucracies, professional associations, and occupational hierarchies as systems of power. Moreover, there appears to be an increasing awareness of the influence of occupational groupings on the ordinary movements of public opinion and a specific concern with the occupational association as a pressure group.

The systematic study of legal forms occupies a borderline area roughly bounded by history, economics, sociology, and political science. There is a substantial, though isolated, research literature on such matters as occupational monopoly, statutory control of working conditions, employer liability, the responsibility of occupational associations, and the legal standing of the wage bargain. Regrettably, the possibilities of quantitative research in jurisprudence tend to be overlooked, although Durkheim set a notable precedent in using the ratio of punitive to restitutive law as his primary index of social complexity.

Anthropology touches the study of occupations at a number of widely separated points. Archaeologists and prehistorians have busied themselves at some length demolishing the neat ladders of occupational evolution developed by early theorists from Morgan to Sumner, and replacing them with more useful formulations. The ethnologists (who are distinguished from sociologists only by their special interest in the isolated tribe and by their familiarity with primitive artifacts) have made two major contributions. They have published a few highly detailed studies of economic life among preliterate peoples. These provide an insight into the elementary consequences of the division of labor which cannot be derived from an examination of our own society alone. The ethnologists' theoretical interest in social functionalism has also resulted in a number of studies which relate the working role of the individual to his familial, religious, and political roles. Slowly but surely, studies of this latter type are defining the limits of social and cultural variation.

In sociology itself, the family, the church, the school, and the community have long been the central areas of interest. Nevertheless, the importance of occupations as a means of social classification has always been recognized. The matter is given considerable attention in the long series of community studies which begins with the Lynds' *Middletown*. In the last decade, occupational sociology has acquired a background of theory and a mass of new data. Every postwar volume of the three leading sociological journals carries many pages on the sociology of work. Yet the field continues to lack a unique identity and is often confounded with industrial sociology.

Strictly speaking, the posing of problems is as essential a scientific operation as their solution. The reader is therefore invited to make the acquaintance of some typical problems for which occupational sociology seeks an answer. For example:

1. What social processes determine the evolution of occupational groupings and the distribution of population among them?
2. How is the relative rank of each occupation in the social hierarchy determined?
3. Why do we find variations among occupational groups in political attitudes, life expectancy, interests, intelligence, insanity, reading tastes, family size, and standards of conduct? What consequences do these differences have for the community?
4. To what extent are occupations inherited from father to son? How much movement up the occupational ladder is possible? Is there a trend in the occupational structure toward greater rigidity?
5. What is the effect of occupational characteristics upon the devel-

opment of such associations as labor unions and professional societies?

6. How are the social roles appropriate to each occupation created and sustained? What are the devices by which apprentices and novices are trained to conform to the personality pattern of their callings?

7. How do working situations differ from one occupation to another? To what extent does each occupation set its own rules?

8. What are the typical forms of occupational segregation, and what are the effects of such segregation upon the general society?

9. What are the occupational functions of an educational system? Why does education tend to displace other forms of vocational placement?

10. What are the effects of working conditions, rewards, and habits upon the institution of the family? How are the occupational positions of women and children determined?

11. What yardsticks can there be for the occupational adjustment of an entire society? What long-range expectations are supported by the dominant technological trends?

The succeeding chapters attempt to summarize some of what is now known or surmised about these matters.

NOTES

[1] The work of Commons' students was especially notable. Fitch's monumental study of the steel workers, which appeared as part of the Pittsburgh Survey in 1911, analyzes the major steel-making trades in terms of their social and ethnic characteristics and in terms of the structure of each working situation. It includes data on community participation, worker morale, living standards, and the effect of working conditions upon family life. John A. Fitch, *The Steel Workers* (New York: Charities Publication Committee, 1910), part of The Pittsburgh Survey, edited by Paul Underwood Kellogg for the Russell Sage Foundation.

[2] Insofar as Marxian theory assumes specific relationships between status and occupation, it touches the same area. Engels in his *Condition of the Working Class in England in 1844* combined a political tract with a detailed study of factory conditions, housing, occupational hazards, and the effects of female and child labor. Marx presented similar material for a later period in *Das Kapital*. Few of their followers, however, have maintained this interest in specific occupational situations.

CHAPTER 1

THE ASSIGNMENT OF WORK

"The old tribal and local organization of life is everywhere in process of dissolution, but a new and different social and moral order based upon occupational association and interest is coming into existence."

ROBERT E. PARK

ALL societies, even the simplest, must maintain themselves through functional skills transmitted from each generation to the next. While the amount of labor required to sustain group life varies according to resources and climate, there appear to be certain principles which govern the assignment of work functions even before the division of labor has assumed any notable importance.

In any society, there is always a *labor force* distinct from the total population. The very young and the very old are normally excluded from the working population. Adolescents, pregnant women, cripples, chiefs, prisoners, and strangers are often excluded too. In the nature of the case, the proportion of the population found in the labor force will fluctuate from time to time. Quantitative studies are rare, but it is probable that societies on a low technical level do not exceed civilized groups in the proportion of the population "gainfully employed." The proportion which the labor force formed of the total population between the world wars was about 50 per cent for the United States, 53 per cent for France, 51 per cent for Germany,[1] and 51 per cent for Tikopia, an isolated island community of 1300 persons in the northern Solomons.[2] The lower occupational requirements of the simpler group must be balanced against its smaller proportion of healthy adults.

DIVISION OF LABOR IN PRE-INDUSTRIAL SOCIETIES

Even among those communities bound together by "mechanical solidarity" in Durkheim's sense, certain basic occupational distinctions are invariably found. These arise from the division of labor between the sexes, among the several age groups, and among different orders of skill.

9

The most important is the distinction between the work of men and the work of women, which Thurnwald calls the "primary division of labor." [3] Sometimes this distinction extends so far as to leave agriculture entirely in the hands of women or to restrict traditional handicrafts to one sex. The division of labor by sex is so pronounced a characteristic of the simpler human societies that some historians of culture explain the development of new levels of economic activity like pastoral or agricultural in terms of this observed differentiation. Thurnwald goes so far as to suggest that the form of family organization depends primarily upon the prosperity of women's work compared to men's. A typical division for a moderately advanced group is shown in the following list, which gives the division of labor between the sexes among the Maori of New Zealand as described by Firth.[4] Note that even in the case of the joint occupations, such as fishing and planting, men and women avoid doing the same work in the same way.

DIVISION OF LABOR AMONG THE MAORI

Men's Work	Women's Work	Joint Occupations
Bird spearing and snaring	Bird preserving (occasional snaring)	Fowling
Rat trapping	Preserving rats	
Climbing forest trees for fruit	Collecting forest foods from ground	Collecting forest foods
Sea fishing	Cleaning fish	Fishing
Diving for *paua* (Haliotis)	Gathering shellfish	
Fresh-water fishing	Fresh-water fishing (certain species)	
	Procuring crayfish	
	Drying and preserving fish	
Building eel-weirs, making pots, traps, nets		
Breaking up ground for cultivation	Breaking up clods	Agriculture
	Weeding	
	Carrying of gravel	
Planting	Planting (some districts only)	
Harvesting crops	Harvesting crops (some districts only)	
Digging fern-root	Collecting dug roots	
Felling trees		
Building houses		
Making canoes		
Carving		

THE ASSIGNMENT OF WORK

Men's Work	Women's Work	Joint Occupations
Making tools and implements, including weapons, working in stone and nephrite	Making twine, needles, etc., for own crafts	
Making ornaments of wood, bone, nephrite		
Tattooing		
Making dogskin or *kiwi* feather cloaks, *taniko* work	Weaving of garments and plaiting of mats, etc., including dogskin, feather cloaks, and most of the *taniko* work.	
Manufacture of musical instruments		
Preparation of pigments, dyes, and oils	Preparation of scents, dyes, sachets, etc.	
Preserving human heads		
	Cooking	
	Making food baskets	
	Serving food	
	Gathering and breaking firewood	
	Carrying water	
Performance of economic magic	Care of the house	

The age-grading of jobs may be very simple or very elaborate. At one extreme are societies which set a minimum age for the performance of adult work, define senility, and make no further distinctions. At the other extreme are numerous societies in which the life cycle is minutely defined and the worker assumes a series of precisely described functions with advancing age. The Maori represent an intermediate situation:

The children assisted their relatives in many technical occupations, and so helped to get their training. For instance, in the sawing of greenstone, youngsters were often enlisted to feed sand-grit and water to the cut, while the men sawed with their flint blades. They also took a subsidiary part in communal work. They collected soft mud in kits and smeared it on the skids when a canoe was being hauled over a portage, and in preparation for a feast, as I was told by a Kawhia native, they were sent off to collect dry branches for firewood. Being largely free from the irksome restrictions of the *tapu*, which were not imposed upon them till riper years, their sphere of activity was much less sharply defined than that of adults. At the same time they were quick to learn the ordinary observances of economic life . . .

11

Old people who were past the prime of life did not remain in idleness, but occupied themselves in work requiring no great expenditure of energy. Old women plaited baskets and aged persons of both sexes made twine and cordage of all kinds for net and snares. Besides grinding and fitting stone implements, old men spend much time in rubbing down greenstone into adzes and ornaments. Such work was monotonous, but not heavy; it gave them occupation, soothed their nerves, and had this advantage, that they could cease and begin again whenever they felt so inclined.[5]

Even where the local technology includes only a few special skills, the rise of specialties and specialists is practically inevitable. The midwife, the medicine man, and the weapons-maker tend to enjoy a well-marked social position in every stage of social life. Referring once again to the Maori, we note that even where handicraft skills are the common pride of most adults, the master workman retains some function in coordinating the work, training apprentices, or working on objects of special character.

Certain other features of occupational distribution, while not universal, are found in the vast majority of human communities.

The relationship between occupational status and social rank (what the modern investigator calls general socioeconomic status) is fairly complex. They are never quite identical. On the other hand, few class or caste structures lack a set of rules for converting one to the other by assigning occupations on the basis of rank and by awarding rank on the basis of economic achievement. Thus, the limitation of certain favored occupations to persons of high family status is a common practice, while at the same time family status is invariably associated with particular occupations. Both aspects of the situation are illustrated by the Crow warrior, the medieval knight, or the modern industrialist.

In almost every society, there are special occupational roles reserved for the stranger. Weber, Becker,[6] and many others have pointed out the intimate connection between large-scale commerce and the social role of the outsider. There are many historical instances of occupations monopolized by strangers, including judges (in medieval Italy), weavers and lacemakers (in Restoration England), administrators and soldiers (in Poland), and tinkers (throughout western Europe). Despite such examples as the podesta and the soldier of fortune, strangers are met with most frequently either in servile occupations or as merchants. From the chicle merchant of Yucatan to the sewing-machine salesman in Iraq, alien merchants are agents of cultural contact and social change.

Perhaps the most spectacular forms of what Hiller calls the commodity-mediated status are found in the early stages of mercantile development. The following description of a station of the Hanseatic League at Bergen in the late Middle Ages illustrates the critical importance of the stranger's role within a recently colonized economy.

The merchant quarters was divided into twenty-five courts . . . Each was isolated and fortified, and guarded by mastiffs and watchmen. Each communicated by a bridge with the sea, and each contained, first of all, a huge building, on the ground floor of which were the warehouses and shops, and on the first floor the lodgings of the merchants . . .

In these courts lived about 3,000 inhabitants, divided into "families." But they were all men or boys, clerks, sailors, or apprentices; women were excluded as troublesome and indiscreet. These merchant-monks were condemned to forced celibacy. They were forbidden to marry the women of the country, or to spend a night outside the courts where they were interned. But it must not be concluded that life was therefore exemplary in these commercial monasteries. The men who were shut up at night found compensation during the day in the Norwegian quarter, for they were rich and very popular with women.

The merchants who consented to this confinement undertook to trade for the benefit of the Hanseatic League for ten years. Since they were in the position of a garrison in a conquered country, they imposed severe tests to try the courage and strength of newcomers . . .

The two following facts give some idea of their supremacy. The Norwegians were not allowed to buy fish until the German colony was provided for. Again, one day the Germans persued one of their enemies, a Norwegian, and killed him in the heart of the convent where he had taken refuge, and the convent itself was burnt during the tumult. They were, however, defended against popular fury by the Archbishop of Drontheim, who urged the services which they rendered to the state. It was they who stimulated agriculture by opening markets for its produce, and encouraged trade by making money plentiful and preserving the country from pirates.[7]

The reader familiar with modern colonial administration will recognize many parallels in the foregoing account. Even within an advanced and integrated industrial culture, the sociological stranger retains a somewhat enigmatic significance in the occupational structure, by performing functions (commercial, criminal, religious, or artistic) which would not otherwise be performed at all.

The monopolization of skills and secrets is another aspect of occupational distribution which appears with the earliest division of labor. Whenever skills are difficult to acquire, dangerous to exercise, extraordinarily effective, or closely linked to the supernatural, they tend to be closely guarded as family or corporate possessions. Presumably, the family monopoly of an occupation preceded the occupational corporation in point of time. However, the effective control of a skill is greatly facilitated by the strength, continuity, and formal organization of a corporate body, so that family occupational monopolies survive only in those trades in which unusual dexterity is a requisite. Where this is the case, the advantage of undertaking training at a very early age seems to be conclusive. Even today, such highly "dexterous" callings as those of acrobats, glass blowers, bell casters, and croupiers tend toward a familial form of occupational organization and include a body of skills which are not in the public domain.

The occupational corporation in its most extensive sense includes priesthoods, guilds, misteries, craft unions, professions, and even occupationally specialized towns. It can exercise its monopoly through a number of coordinate devices which limit the diffusion of the skill and control the actual performance of the work. Only some appeal to the principle of limited possibilities can explain the world-wide distribution of patterns so similar that we give the name of guild to organizations which developed independently in China, Europe, Persia, Egypt, and India.

The minimum essentials of an occupational guild include a formal apprenticeship during which the lore of the trade is communicated, the power to punish members for the violation of standards and rules, and the exclusion of outsiders from participation in the trade activity. Even where the arts employed in the trade are actually familiar, the conditions under which they are communicated in a guild system, and the limitations placed on their use, convert them quickly into secrets. The development of well-known occupational technics into secrets may even be followed by their further development into a body of dogma. Situations as distantly related as the evolution of sub-castes in India and the growth of modern Freemasonry illustrate the tendency of craft secrets to develop into a way of life. Under certain circumstances, the advance of an occupation supersedes the older body of skills but cannot change the institutional framework within which they have become fixed, so that new and duplicating forms of occupational organization must be developed. Carr-Saunders, in his history of the British professions, has shown that physicians, surgeons, and apothecaries arose as distinct groups at different times for the purpose of healing with newly invented methods.[8]

In the simpler societies, the ritual and magical aspects of occupational practice are conspicuous. The inherent connection between group survival and the work of food-getting, fighting, healing, and governing may well explain why some degree of formal ritual is almost invariably found in agriculture, hunting, fishing, war, healing, and politics. Firth has analyzed the economic function of ritual among the Maori; the explanation may easily be extended to cover a range of cases in more advanced industrial systems:

It is of interest here to digress for a moment and consider briefly the relation of magic to native industry. In itself it cannot be classed as economic, for despite the beliefs of the native, it does not, from the rational standpoint, produce any direct effect upon the conditions of material welfare. Birds are not retained in the forest by spells, snares do not operate more smoothly when formulae are muttered over them, and the effect of people's thoughts is not neutralized by the waving of a green twig. Can it be said, then, that magic has any definite relation to economic activity? What is our justification for including it in the facts under consideration? There is no doubt that it has some very important indirect effects in giving a psychological backing to the native when he is engaged in any task, in imbuing him with confidence in his own skill and with certainty that his ends can be attained by the proper exercise of it. In short, it provides him with that assurance which is essential to success in any undertaking.[9]

The effect of ritual is to sacralize the occupation. We are perhaps on safer ground in restricting attention to ritual, and leaving to one side the question of magic. The fittings of the modern sales office suggest as profound a confidence in homeopathic magic as the face-painting of primitive hunters but this is hard to demonstrate objectively. Rituals are quite easy to observe and record, and are readily categorized.

Rituals of initiation include such phenomena as rites of passage, the execution and judging of a masterpiece, the taking of oaths and vows, investitures, anointments, and inaugurations. These elements appear as frequently in the assumption of status in occupations of low prestige as in such ceremonies as coronation and consecration. *Rituals of performance* include all the libations, sacrifices, auguries, processions, blessings and miscellaneous observances which accompny the building of a canoe or the repair of a temple in preliterate societies, and which assure the success of a surgical operation or a football game among ourselves. *Rituals of convocation* are public expressions of solidarity by ceremonial or partly ceremonial gatherings. They appear to be essential to any strong occupational organization. Firth has described the public gatherings and ceremonies which precede any important project among the Maori and the

15

Tikopia. The ceremonial convocations of the European guilds survived the virtual disappearance of the guilds themselves, just as the guilds originally developed from religious sodalities. The fabulous displays of the Renaissance guilds (see for example, Unwin's description of the Lord Mayor's show in sixteenth-century London [10]) have no precise counterpart in modern life; but it would be careless to overlook the ritualistic aspects of the very numerous convocations which are characteristic of the modern occupation: formal meetings of unions and professional associations, institutes, regional and national conventions, honorary elections, testimonial dinners, study groups, mass meetings, and luncheon clubs. Even such institutions as county and state fairs illustrate the combination of an occupational convocation with various practical purposes.

The development of an impressive and traditional body of ritual has a tendency to sacralize the entire occupational function. The classic instance in ethnology is the dairyman-priest of the Todas of Ceylon. Among this group, the entire social organization revolves around the elaborate ritual which accompanies the work performance of the dairyman.[11] Certain occupations—notably those associated with worship, military leadership, and healing—tend to be sacralized in all societies. It is easy to point out the survival of sacred, and even magical, attributes of these occupations in our own society.

Certain general considerations about remuneration in preliterate societies should be briefly mentioned here. The distribution of "pay" is almost always something more than the return to the individual of the product of his own labor. It is seldom fixed in direct proportion to his effort. Among the interfering factors are rights of ownership, traditional wage rates, allocations according to rank, ceremonial exchanges, reciprocities between specific objects and specific kinds of work, and many other conventional devices. In the absence of money as an abstract standard of value, exchange values tend to be specific for pairs of commodities or services. If ten fish are worth one fishhook, and ten fishhooks are worth one length of fishing cord, it by no means follows that a length of fishing cord may be obtained for 100 fish. The amount may be more or less, or may vary with the status of the persons involved, or the exchange may be impossible. Work is likely to be measured in terms of the performer rather than of the performance. Thus, among the Mayans of Yucatan described by Redfield,[12] the price of a day's work in the corn fields varies sharply, depending upon whether it is performed by a relative, a neighbor, or a stranger.

THE ASSIGNMENT OF WORK

Another factor is the function served by very complicated schemes of payment in the promotion of social unity. Thus, among the Tikopia described by Firth, the labor of a craftsman is paid for by a given quantity of goods, but since any transfer of goods must be met with some reciprocal transfer, this single payment sets up a whole series of exchanges. In this case, the craftsman comes out ahead, but there are similar transactions in which the holdings of the participants after a long series of exchanges are substantially unchanged. This system is roughly analogous to Christmas shopping and gift-giving. The net effect is to increase sentiments of solidarity and to stimulate economic activity.

It is illuminating to recall Malinowski's demonstration that among the Trobrianders, self-esteem plays a larger part than self-interest in the development of work incentives:

The most important point about this is, however, that all, or almost all the fruits of his work, and certainly any surplus which he can achieve by extra effort, goes not to the man himself, but to his relatives-in-law. Without entering into details of the system of the apportionment of the harvest, of which the sociology is rather complex and would require a preliminary account of the Trobriand kinship system and kinship ideas, it may be said that about three quarters of a man's crops go partly as tribute to the chief, partly as his due to his sister's (or mother's) husband and family.

But although he thus derives practically no personal benefit in the utilitarian sense from his harvest, the gardener receives much praise and renown from its size and quality, and that in a direct and circumstantial manner. For all the crops, after being harvested, are displayed for some time afterwards in the gardens, piled up in neat, conical heaps under small shelters made of yam vine. Each man's harvest is thus exhibited for criticism in his own plot, and parties of natives walk about from garden to garden, admiring, comparing and praising the best results. The importance of the food display can be gauged by the fact that, in olden days, when the chief's power was much more considerable than now, it was dangerous for a man who was not either of high rank himself, or working for such a one, to show crops which might compare too favourably with those of the chief.[13]

The foregoing pages give only the briefest outline of occupational differentiation in the simpler societies which have been studied. With economic as with other institutions, a systematic comparison of isolated cultures in the marginal regions of the globe demonstrates the impressive plasticity of human nature. Nevertheless, one important generalization may be drawn from this material. Even in those societies where the divi-

17

sion of labor approaches a minimum, the assignment and evaluation of occupations is based neither on the optimum nor on the simplest utilization of available labor power. Instead, we find the occupational system to be closely and reciprocally related to the composition of the population, the organization of the family and the community, the requirements of the religious culture, and the patterns of social interaction.

The problem of understanding an occupational system is therefore very similar to that of understanding a particular type of family life. Two fundamental questions can be raised in each case: In what way does the institution enable the society to maintain continuity and existence? What roles are created by the institution, and how do they affect the behavior of individuals?

In the case of the family, the first question must be answered with reference to reproduction, the care of the young, the transfer and inheritance of property, education, and social control. In the case of occupational structure, we are concerned instead with the production of necessary commodities, the transfer of skills between generations, adaptation to change, and the provision of sufficient incentive so that difficult and unpleasant tasks will be carried out.

In response to the second question as applied to the family, our attention is focused upon the exercise of domestic authority; the development of masculine and feminine identifications; the regulation of sexual intercourse; the definitions of childhood, adolescence, and maturity; the effect of family position on community participation; and the effectiveness of the family in assuring emotional security and biological continuity. Similarly, for an occupational system, we are led to examine the different roles played by employees and employers, manual and white-collar workers, craftsmen and professionals, laborers and artists; the mechanisms by which interoccupational relations are mediated; the life-cycle stages which lead from apprenticeship to retirement; the effect of occupational membership upon participation in family life and community affairs; and the effectiveness of the occupational institution in its double purpose of satisfying participants and maintaining the continuity of necessary skills.

Early students of institutional life took great satisfaction in setting up hypothetical sequences of institutional types to correspond with the various levels of economic evolution. Thus, the historical progression from root and berry gathering to agriculture was identified with the institutional progression from promiscuity to monogamy. Unhappily, when confronted with evidence from field investigations, these plausible schemes quietly collapsed, and it is now regarded as unsound to treat cultural evolution as a unilinear process.

In dealing with occupational institutions, however, we encounter behavior complexes which are very closely linked to specific technologies. Technology undoubtedly does evolve, in at least the limited sense that it tends to add new elements at a cumulative rate and to manifest a higher degree of organization with each increase in size.

DIVISION OF LABOR IN INDUSTRIAL SOCIETIES

There can be no serious question that the modern world is characterized by the increasingly minute division of labor, by an almost universal trend toward bureaucratization, and by an intricate dependence upon productive machinery. The results of those trends for occupational structure are in some cases so constant and explicit that they may reasonably be described as continuous processes. The more important of these processes have to do with the increasing size of social groups, the progressive diversification of their functions, and the increasing control which they exert over behavior. They will be described here under the general headings of Aggregation, Differentiation, and Rationalization.

AGGREGATION

The most visible effect of the Industrial Revolution upon social organization has been the increase in the sheer mass of social groups. The community and all its component organizations have now reached a scale quite unknown to previous history.

Even a century ago, the bulk of the labor force was occupied in the production of food and raw materials. Between 1840 and 1940, the urban population of the United States increased from 10.8 per cent to 56.5 per cent of the total, and the proportion of the population living in cities of 100,000 or more increased from 3.0 per cent to 28.9 per cent. At the time of the first census, 9 out of 10 persons in the labor force were engaged in agricultural production or related occupations. The proportion has now fallen to less than 1 out of 5.

The fundamental occupational trend for half-a-dozen generations has been the release of surplus manpower from farms, forests, and fisheries to factories, offices, and stores. The efficiency of production has increased rapidly enough to permit the continuous reduction of the agricultural labor force and a simultaneous increase of output even in the short run. During World War II, the number of farmers and farm laborers declined by 5 per cent, while agricultural production increased by about 15 per cent. Such recent innovations as hydroponic agriculture and yeast cultivation suggest that the agricultural labor force can be even further reduced, while the limits of agricultural production have not yet been approached. The limiting factor in the displacement of rural population into urban occupations is not the efficiency of agriculture, but the size of the rural population. There is no longer a sufficient proportion of the labor force engaged in agriculture to support a large percentage increase in the urban population.

However, the remaining rural population retains most of its traditional advantage in fertility. The proportion which the rural population forms of the total population is twice as high as the proportion of farmers in the labor force. The migrating sons and daughters of the farm still provide the population reservoir from which increases in the skilled and semi-skilled urban occupations are drawn without corresponding decreases in competing trades.

The city-building aspect of aggregation may also be examined from another standpoint: that of maximum size. Thompson points out: "We are reasonably sure that until quite recent times most of the cities that did exist were quite small. Even great cities like Rome and Peiping at the height of their power probably did not have as many as a million people, and they grew to this size only because they were the centers of great empires whose rulers could levy tribute on a great agricultural population, so that even a small surplus per capita came to a large absolute amount." [14]

It is difficult to arrive at the maximum size for existing cities, because of their decentralized and suburbanized structure; but the population of the New York metropolitan cluster may be fairly estimated at 15 million and at least 10 other urban clusters in the United States have populations of more than 1 million.

The aggregation of operating units, working groups, and voluntary associations is equally marked. The maximum number of employees in a single enterprise has risen from several hundred to several hundred thousand in a comparatively short time. The largest industrial working groups now include as many as 75,000 in the same plant and 5000 in the same shop. Such varied enterprises as department stores, railroad depots, newspaper staffs, government bureaus, university faculties, police departments, and hotel kitchens have attained a maximum size which requires impersonal and bureaucratic controls, if only because personal supervision is literally impossible.

Depending as it does upon mechanized transportation and communication, the very large working group is a phenomenon indigenous to the twentieth century. Its implications are by no means well understood. There is some scattered evidence that large units may reach a point of diminishing efficiency because of their size alone, but this must be weighed against the fact that such units usually do maintain themselves, once established.

The expansion of the working group is reciprocally related to the expansion of "horizontal" associations, such as labor unions and industrial institutes, and the integration of these associations into national and regional organizations on a still larger scale. A curious consequence is the development of identical organizational forms to serve completely dissimilar purposes. The tables of organization in large-scale units, whether they are business corporations, government agencies, educational institutions, labor unions, or philanthropic foundations, include much the same provision for line and staff functionaries, hierarchically divided, the same emphasis upon formal communications, morale devices, record-keeping, centralization of responsibility and decentralization of function, housekeeping services, and extra-mural liaison. The technics of management which have been developed to meet the problems of large-scale organization as such are freely transferred from one area of activity to another. Meanwhile, the tremendous inertia of these large organizations has become a force which ramifies through every phase of social life.

DIFFERENTIATION

Quite aside from the general implications of human organization on this unprecedented scale, the enormous cities have developed occupational differentiation to the furthermost point so far reached. This may be seen both in the development of thousands of specializations and in the almost incredible subdivision of existing trades and professions, where the number of practitioners is large enough to permit the growth of specialties in tree surgery, barbering, and chimney sweeping.

Theoretically, the best index of differentiation is the number of occupations. The detailed occupational classification of the census of Great Britain in 1841 listed 431 occupations. Exactly a century later, the Occupational Dictionary compiled by the United States Census Bureau provided for the coding of about 25,000 occupational titles. Since the number of occupations distinguished depends on the classification used, it is perhaps more illuminating to note the subdivision and ramification of specific occupations. It is noteworthy that the trend toward increasing differentiation is observable on all occupational levels from the casual laborer to the advanced professional worker. It can be seen in the familiar image of the machine tender tightening the same belt hour after hour on the assembly line, and in the scientist spending a lifetime of research in an obscure corner of an obscure problem.

Within any large and growing organization, the process of differentiation is to a considerable extent the result of organizational requirements and the necessity of coping with larger and larger aggregations of people, things, functions, and relationships. The technical aspect of the division of labor—the increase of speed and skill which is obtained by subdividing a technical operation—has been familiar since the eighteenth century and Adam Smith's analysis of pin-making. The related social aspect has not been explored in as much detail. We may note the tendency of general managerial functions to be dispersed among such staff departments as personnel, accounting, engineering, planning, purchasing, quality control, market analysis, labor relations, advertising, internal security, and field inspection and to be performed by increasingly limited specialists. But the consequences, though analogous to the subdividing of a technical process, are not identical. In the division of labor among functionaries who deal primarily with symbols and relationships, the process and its results are substantially altered, much as if the division of labor in pin-making produced, instead of pins, some very complicated locking device whose uses were not clearly understood.

The specialization which occurs within large organizations is designed to improve internal communication; an unintended consequence is the development of barriers to communication in the general society. One of the more interesting findings of the Western Electric study [15] was the discovery that some of the newer positions in that large organization did not carry appropriate prestige in the community because they were completely unfamiliar to anyone outside the plant. In professional pursuits, the minute breakdown of specialties (as reflected, for example, in the titles of academic dissertations) is often a matter for amusement. Where the Renaissance man of knowledge might take the entire area of philosophy and science for his domain, the modern scholar is more likely to restrict himself so severely that neither the technics nor the ultimate significance of his work can even be explained to the layman.[16]

This phenomenon is not entirely peculiar to the modern era. It should be remembered that the word *mistery* originally referred to membership in a craft guild, and the secret understandings which such membership implied. But while the barriers to interoccupational communication were formerly erected with deliberation and defended with difficulty, they now arise spontaneously out of a high degree of differentiation and a rapid rate of occupational change. Eventually, the mutual incomprehensibility of occupational "languages," the increasingly rigid organization of occupational interest groups, and the barrier between working environments combine to create a situation for which there is no close historic parallel, where the habits, customs, and standards of a neighbor's occupational world may be no more familiar than those of the Australian aborigines.

The process of differentiation has other implications than the separation of the worker in one field from the worker in another. It tends at the same time to introduce sharper distinctions between the worker and the nonworker, the supervisor and the supervisee, and work itself from play, leisure, or casual interaction. As the family loses the last vestiges of its functions as a productive unit, active engagement in production is increasingly limited to qualified adults. More and more of the population is found in such nonoccupational categories as school attendance, vocational training, home leisure, unemployment, and retirement. The line between the labor force and the remainder of the population becomes increasingly distinct.

The segregation of supervisory levels is also implicit in the development of organization on the modern scale. The historians of the Industrial Revolution have dwelt in detail upon the transition from the master craftsman toiling among his journeymen and apprentices to the old-fashioned industrialist who had his glass-enclosed office just off the shop floor and addressed each workman by his first name to the giant manufacturing corporation with its top management completely removed from the factory in time, space, and point of view. The students of bureaucracy have called attention to the close relationship between rationalization of work and the creation of new and finer divisions of authority. While the overriding distinction between men who work with things and men who work with symbols loses none of its importance with the passage of time, the internal distinctions between operating "levels" become characteristically more significant, and such terms as "junior management" and "intermediate policy level" denote very sharp differentations among the members of occupational groups who are ostensibly engaged in a single kind of activity.

RATIONALIZATION

Here again, as with aggregation and differentiation, we may talk of a general process because of trends which are apparent at many levels and in a wide variety of situations.

Rationalization is essentially the substitution of the formal control of behavior for the informal, personal, and spontaneous devices which regulate human activity in unplanned social situations. It leads to a more precise specification of how, when, and by whom work should be done. It also leads to the standardization of the working environment and the substitution of impersonal judgments for the relationships which evolve out of close personal contact.

There can be no serious doubt of two facts which modern industrial organization demonstrates at every point. Rationalization is disturbing to the individual in that it replaces the relatively free interplay of human personalities with a set of fixed formulas to which conformity is enforced. Rationalization is effective in that it allows for greater predictability of work results and, consequently, for more efficient allocation of resources.

Personal relationships continue to form the essential kernel of experience in the family, the clique, the school, the church, and the neighborhood. But increasingly, personal relationships in occupational situations are undermined by the rational specifications for behavior which are imposed. The identifications between employer and employee, client and practitioner, citizen and public functionary, become weaker and less spontaneous.

The informal organization of the work group, which recent studies in industrial sociology have "discovered," exists as a marginal and almost furtive adjunct to the official scheme of organization. Where a strong informal organization, based upon personal qualities, exists, it will generally have as its chief function the subverting of those rational ends for which the formal organization is designed, as in the limitation of daily output to a socially acceptable quantity. In the long run, these informal organizations do no more than soften the impact of rationalization.

Similarly, occupational selection and adjustment are facilitated by the use of ability and personality tests in placement, the dependence upon objective rating systems, analytical job classification, formal systems of upgrading and promotion, and the elaboration of specific experience and training requirements for employment.[17] Again, the effect is to decrease the range of individual choice and to weaken the effect of personal relationships in the job situation. The rigidity of an occupational structure which includes these elements may be traced back to the rational end of adjusting the man to the job, rather than allowing the man to determine the scope and manner of the job.

Throughout the occupational structure, the expression of personal idiosyncrasy is sharply limited by fixed specifications and by the progressive reduction of social contacts. The assembly line displays both of these tendencies in an extreme degree, but the essential quality of rationalization is better illustrated by the training now given to canvassers,[18] store clerks, and filling-station attendants, in which the content of casual conversations to be held with customers is specified, including suitable comments on the weather and prefabricated personal reminiscences.

NONOCCUPATIONAL TRENDS

Nothing in the foregoing pages is especially novel. Indeed, the crucial importance of these processes for occupational sociology can only be understood by close attention to the contrast which they introduce between occupational and nonoccupational life. As Simmel first suggested, a generation ago:

In the Middle Ages . . . the guild did not only regulate the trade activities of its members; it regulated their whole lives. The apprentice was not only a vocational student of his master; he was one of his family. The different aspects of life were intimately integrated, and if the emotional and political life centered around the vocational life, regulation of the latter implied and included regulation of the former.

In modern times the different sides of the individual's life have become more clearly differentiated, and he expresses each of these sides in separate associations and relationships. This differentiation has been due to a large extent to the division of labor. The division of labor has led to a type of activity which becomes on the one hand increasingly mechanical, but which on the other hand absorbs much less of the total personality, and allows other interests to assert themselves more freely. Besides, the increasing professional differentiation must show that similar life-interests can be combined with different professions.[19]

Since Simmel's time, students of modern society have documented a series of changes in the "private life" of modern man which at first glance represent almost a complete reversal of the occupational processes just described.

In contrast to aggregation, note the gradual diminution of cultural differences between city and country. The modern city dweller shows an unmistakable preference for a style of living (single family dwellings in sparsely settled neighborhoods, primary group interaction with neighbors, and a variety of outdoor activities) patterned after the more dispersed settlements of earlier times. The disappearance of the extended family is another decentralizing tendency, together with the redefinition of the family as an atomistic and inwardly focused unit of two generations.

In contrast to occupational differentiation, there is massive evidence of reduced differentiation in other areas of life. The emancipation of women and the partial emancipation of children have blurred the sex-grading and age-grading systems. The instruments of mass communication are slowly ironing out the major differences in habits, manners, values, and tastes which once distinguished social classes so clearly. The wide diffusion, first, of literacy and, recently, of higher education has had the same effect. Such differences as exist among classes, ethnic groups, and regions with regard to the spoken language, drinking habits, the conduct of church services, or the expression of political sentiments are all less marked today than they were a generation ago.

Against the rationalization of occupational duties, we must balance the flourishing of the romantic cult as a norm for relations between the sexes, the freedom of clique formation in urban society, the emphasis on congeniality and fellowship characteristic of nonoccupational associations, and, above all, the intense concern with the quality of personal relationships which is the chief theme of our literature and of our more important neuroses.

Occupational and nonoccupational life are still so closely entwined in actual experience that these opposite tendencies are not always clearly visible. Nevertheless, they conform to the theoretical expectation that increasing functional interdependence will be associated with decreasing individual differences.

This discussion has an immediate bearing on certain contradictory assertions which are put forth with confidence whenever the question of work satisfaction arises. It is often said, for example,

That modern industry reduces its workers to mindless robots,	or	That modern industry encourages the development of new skills and the substitution of brain for brawn.
That present forms of organization are unable to elicit cooperation,	or	That large enterprises exemplify cooperation developed to an unprecedented degree.
That mobility is progressively restricted by undue specialization,	or	That mobility is the prime characteristic of the modern industrial worker.

At the root of these contradictions, there lie a number of genuine paradoxes. It is obvious that differentiation and rationalization reduce the individual's competence while at the same time increasing his productivity. The modern urban dweller is perhaps the first man in history who would starve if placed in a fertile wilderness with appropriate tools. Even the expert, with some skill developed to a superlative degree, does not control any major fraction of current technology. Modern generals do not lead charges, and many a modern architect would be unable to construct a sturdy shed. Yet the speed and precision of thousands of human operations have been developed to an extent which would once have been regarded as humanly impossible.

Moreover, as the differentiation of occupational functions proceeds to extremes, the mastery of a trade becomes increasingly irrelevant to the performance of a particular job. As the work becomes increasingly specific, there is a shift away from apprenticeship to general education. It becomes impossible or useless to learn the details of a calling in advance. Required instead are literacy, familiarity with the number system, and an acquaintance with technological theory. In somewhat different forms, this trend is equally apparent in machine tending and in professional pursuits.

The second paradox is of a different species. The word *cooperation* has two distinct meanings. Despite the romantic yearning of efficiency experts for the warmth and comradeship of the medieval workshop, modern organization is unmistakably bent toward the elimination of cooperation as a moral and emotional element in work, so that cooperation as a technical coordination of resources may be enhanced. In the former case, cooperation is something which may be freely given or withheld; in the latter, it is an abstract quality of a productive system in which necessary functions are appropriately interlocked. In neither case should cooperativeness be confused with morale. It is possible that morale is higher in voluntary enterprises than in those with a fixed organization, but large-scale operation seldom permits organization on a voluntary basis.[20]

Permanence, stability, predictability, and fixed relationships among the human participants are inherent components of all highly aggregated and rationalized systems. The satisfactions which once arose from the free interplay of personality in the working situation are either derived from other areas of activity or elicited from the working situation in defiance of its formal rules.

The paradox of mobility is a more complex matter and will be reserved for discussion in a later chapter. Here it may be remarked that there are a number of factors operating to produce contrary results. Aggregation and differentiation increase the number of social ranks and lengthen the status scale. The rationalization of career patterns sets strict limits on individual advancement. On the other hand, the effect of the nonrational factors which have traditionally governed the distribution of prestige (birth, property, and chance) is weakened by the introduction of objective methods of occupational selection and rational evaluation of occupational performance. Since these processes do not operate in a vacuum, it is rather difficult to disentangle the effect of occupational trends from such historical factors as the availability of natural resources, political ideologies, and the legal structure. It is precisely the interrelation of such historical factors with the more or less predictable consequences of the division of labor which constitutes the core of our problem.

NOTES

[1] *Encyclopedia of the Social Sciences*, Vol. II, p. 432.

[2] Raymond Firth, *Primitive Polynesian Economy* (London: George Routledge & Sons, 1939), and *We, the Tikopia* (London: George Allen & Unwin, 1936).

[3] Richard Thurnwald, *Economics in Primitive Communities* (London: Oxford University Press, 1932).

[4] Raymond Firth, *Primitive Economics of the New Zealand Maori* (New York: E. P. Dutton & Co., 1929), p. 195. For a further account of the sex division of labor in preliterate societies, see Melville J. Herskovitz, *Economic Anthropology* (New York: Alfred A. Knopf, 1952), Chapter 7.

[5] Firth, *Primitive Economics of the New Zealand Maori*, p. 200.

[6] Max Weber, *Das Antique Judentum*, Vol. III in *Gesammelte Aufsätze zur Religionssoziologie* (Tübingen: Mohr, 1923). Howard Becker, "Constructive

Typology," in *Contemporary Social Theory*, edited by H. E. Barnes and H. Becker (New York: Appleton-Century, 1940).

[7] G. Renard and G. Weulersse, *Life and Work in Modern Europe* (New York: Alfred A. Knopf, 1926), pp. 317–19.

[8] A. M. Carr-Saunders and P. A. Wilson, *The Professions* (Oxford: Clarendon Press, 1941).

[9] Raymond Firth, *Primitive Economics of the New Zealand Maori*, p. 146.

[10] George Unwin, *The Gilds and Companies of London* (London: George Allen & Unwin, 1938), pp. 267–92.

[11] George P. Murdock, *Our Primitive Contemporaries* (New York: The Macmillan Company, 1926), pp. 129–32.

[12] Robert Redfield, *The Folk Culture of Yucatan* (Chicago: University of Chicago Press, 1941).

[13] Bronislaw Malinowski, *Argonauts of the Western Pacific* (London: George Routledge & Sons, 1932).

[14] Warren S. Thompson, "It Was Not Always So," in *Cities Are Abnormal*, edited by Elmer T. Peterson (Norman, Okla.: University of Oklahoma Press, 1946), p. 55.

[15] F. J. Roethlisberger and William J. Dickson, *Management and the Worker* (Cambridge, Mass.: Harvard University Press, 1950).

[16] Even in sociology, titles like the following are found: "A Literal Replication of a Sociometric Study of Informal Social Participation in a Homogeneous Neighborhood" by Kenneth Shimota (Unpublished M.A. thesis in sociology, University of Minnesota, 1953).

[17] Perhaps the furthest development of rationalized selection technics was the wartime assessment program of the Office of Strategic Services. An account of the dramatic, ingenious, and sometimes ruthless procedures employed is found in OSS Assessment Staff, *Assessment of Men* (New York: Rinehart & Company, 1948).

[18] The following is taken from a set of mimeographed instructions distributed to door-to-door salesmen of an appliance dealer: ". . . when the party answers the door, the salesman gives a big hearty smile, greets the person by his or her name if possible, then he takes one step backward. The prospect's initial impulse was to get ready to resist an invasion. By doing just the opposite of what had been expected, your man gains a momentary advantage by having surprised and disarmed him. He also implies to the homeowner that the expected thing for him to do is to open the screen or storm door. The salesman has already stepped back to suggest that the door might swing open for him any second. In many cases, the prospect will then at least stick his head out the door in sheer curiosity. Another successful maneuver is for the salesman to remove his rubbers at the prospect's door. This is an obvious indication to the prospect that the salesman expects to be invited into the house."

[19] Quoted in Nicholas J. Spykman, *The Social Theory of Georg Simmel* (Chicago: University of Chicago Press, 1925).

[20] For a very thorough and detailed discussion of this question, see Morris S. Viteles, *Motivation and Morale in Industry* (New York: W. W. Norton & Company, 1953).

CHAPTER 2

THE MEASUREMENT
OF OCCUPATIONAL STATUS

Hucksters
Hunters
Hypnotists
THREE CONSECUTIVE ITEMS ON AN
OCCUPATIONAL SCALE

OCCUPATIONAL position is an important factor in the determination of individual prestige and in the allocation of social privileges. There appears to be a consistent tendency for occupational identification to displace such other status-fixing attributes as ancestry, religious office, political affiliation, and personal character. Each of the three general trends which can be discerned in modern industrial society (aggregation, differentiation, rationalization) seems to lead toward increasing emphasis on the importance of the occupational label.

One of the consequences of *aggregation* is the substitution of formal organizations for informal groupings, and the substitution of regulatory mechanisms for the voluntary coordination of human activities. The village type of community, in which most human history has been enacted, identifies individuals in terms of their total life histories, which in turn form part of larger family histories. In the village community, status is always hereditary to some extent, and all the segments of an individual's personality enter into the definition of his role. The metropolitan community is driven by its own complexity to associate each status with a particular economic function. The urban dweller tends to define his own relationship to his fellows in functional terms, since other means of identification with the community are attenuated. Then too, the separation of home from workplace and the necessity for casual interaction with many unrelated people require various shorthand methods for recognizing others, of which occupational designations are the most convenient, after sex, age, and race.

The large working unit presents a parallel situation, also characterized by anonymity and impersonality. Thus bureaucratic structures come to rely more and more upon formal position. The uniform, not the man, is saluted; duties are ascribed to the office rather than the officeholder, and people are designated by position rather than by name.

Differentiation narrows the scope of the individual's activity and introduces complexities into the social order which are hidden from the view of all but the specialists concerned. The requirements of each occupation, the importance or responsibility of its functions, and the evaluation of performance come to be more and more esoteric. The layman cannot judge the competence of a physician or of a coremaker, and is therefore forced to respond primarily to an occupational label rather than to a set of individual characteristics.

Both *aggregation* and *differentiation* destroy the continuity of the individual's life history, as seen by his fellows. The shift from a status system based upon family background and personal history to one based upon occupational function is inevitable. Private histories evaporate in the mobile and impersonal urban environment.

Moreover, as *rationalization* proceeds and the assignment of occupational functions becomes "scientific," "appropriate," and "efficient," it comes to be assumed that the occupational label is a fair index of intelligence, ability, character, and personal acceptability. The modern reliance upon occupation as the measure of a man takes for granted the existence of high correlations between occupational position and all other attributes. That these correlations are probably exaggerated is beside the point; the general belief in their existence is a pervasive element in social interaction.

The construction of scales and other classification systems to measure the relative social rank of occupations has been a vigorous branch of social research for several decades. In 1897, William C. Hunt, working for the Bureau of the Census, grouped all gainful workers into four categories: the proprietor class, the clerical class, skilled workers, and the laboring class. This may be regarded as the first of a long series of socioeconomic occupational scales, designed to show the distribution of general status for the entire population in terms of occupational groups.

In 1921, R. M. Yerkes [1] and his associates presented the results of the intelligence tests which they had administered to thousands of army recruits during World War I. They were able to give the average scores on the Army Alpha Test achieved by soldiers coming from 55 civilian occupations. Since that time, research on the psychometric aspects of the occupational ladder has been continuous and extensive. Dozens of psychometric scales have been constructed for various purposes, and the relationship between ability and vocational selection is now fairly well understood.

In 1925, George S. Counts published the first prestige scale, which contained 45 familiar occupations ranked in order by a sample of teachers and students. Various forms of this instrument have been used in many different studies, and in recent years, occupational prestige ratings have been extensively used in the study of stratification systems in American communities.

Needless to say, these three types of scales are not absolutely distinct, nor has the research on one type of scale failed to influence the assumptions and methods used in another. Along the general lines suggested by these pioneering studies, hundreds of specific investigations have been carried out, and there now exists a real technology of occupational classification. The discussion which follows is by no means a complete review of this broad field, but it is focused on certain dilemmas of classification, which themselves cast considerable light on the nature of occupational status.

Most of these dilemmas are related to a particular type of scale and will be treated in that connection, but there are two problems which appear in every consideration of the subject.

First, there are a number of callings which cover too wide a range of status to be conveniently assigned to any single point in a hierarchy. Among these are salesmen, retail proprietors, criminals, and farmers. Farm owners are found in every social stratum, but most scales classify the hungry Ozark mountaineer and the millionaire Texas rancher in the same way. Salesmen are not often found below the semiskilled level, but they are represented in every higher group. Like the retail proprietors, they are more readily classified by income and influence than by the work they do.

Second, it is a plain fact, often awkward to the classifier, that occupations differ in definiteness. The learned professions, the organized crafts, and certain other trades like policeman, janitor, butler, or bootblack are readily defined and easily recognized. Opposed to these are a variety of callings, at every status level, which are either too unfamiliar or too amorphous to be identified with any certainty. Such occupations as key punch operator, counterman, or vitrifier are too little known to be clearly separated from other clerical or mechanical jobs of a similar kind. The duties of opinion analysts, administrative consultants, or traffic managers are equally obscure to the general public, and vary sharply from one organization to another.

These two considerations suggest that any occupational scale, however accurate, will involve a respectable number of marginal or doubtful cases. They do not bear directly, however, on the central question raised by all such scales: Is there a single occupational hierarchy? In other words, is there enough consistency in the data to make possible the construction of a single scale which will indicate the relative standing of all occupations from highest to lowest, and which will correlate closely with such other social indicators as standard of living, wealth, education, class membership, and power? Each type of scale needs to be examined separately with this dominating question in mind.

SOCIOECONOMIC SCALES

The work of Hunt and of Carroll D. Wright was carried forward for many years at the Bureau of the Census by Alba Edwards, who is chiefly responsible for the general occupational classification used in the censuses of 1940 and 1950. With a minimum of rearrangement, the categories of the census classification can be divided into six hierarchical groups, described as "social-economic classes":

1. Unskilled workers
   - 1-a   Farm laborers
   - 1-b,c Laborers, except farm
   - 1-d   Servant classes
2. Semiskilled workers.
3. Skilled workers and foremen
4. Clerks and kindred workers
5. Proprietors, managers, and officials
   - 5-a Farmers (owners and tenants)
   - 5-b Wholesale and retail dealers
   - 5-c Other proprietors, managers, and officials
6. Professional persons

Edwards characterizes these groups in the following terms: "It is evident that each of these groups represents not only a major segment of the Nation's labor force, but, also, a large population group with a somewhat distinct standard of life, economically, and, to a considerable extent, intellectually and socially. In some measure, also, each group has characteristic interests and convictions as to numerous public questions—social, economic, and political. Each of them is thus a really distinct and highly significant social-economic group." [2]

An alternative classification of the census categories was devised by Beckman, who groups them into five occupational grades or ranks:

Grade 1. Unskilled manual occupations
Grade 2. Semiskilled occupations
Grade 3. (a) Skilled manual occupations
　　　　　(b) Skilled white-collar occupations
Grade 4. (a) Subprofessional occupations
　　　　　(b) Business occupations
　　　　　(c) Minor supervisory occupations
Grade 5. (a) Professional (linguistic) occupations
　　　　　(b) Professional (scientific) occupations
　　　　　(c) Managerial and executive occupations

This scale, which varies sharply from the previous one, was set up in a somewhat different fashion. According to Beckman, "What seemed to be needed under the circumstances was some grouping which would readily indicate the rank of any occupation on the basis of the intelligence, capacity or skill, education and training required for its pursuit. Such a scale should also reflect the socio-economic prestige attached to a given occupation . . ." [3]

Another classification of census categories was developed at about the same time by Kefauver, Noll, and Drake. This was described as a socio-economic scale and divided the population into only five groups: Unskilled, Semiskilled, Skilled, Semiprofessional, and Professional. It is more exhaustive than the Beckman classification, but far less sophisticated. For example, sign painters, typists, and steamship captains are found together in the skilled group; bankers, brokers, chemists, and librarians are included in both the professional and the semiprofessional classifications; auctioneers, hotel chefs, servants, and county sheriffs are all considered to be semiskilled; and aviators are found in the same group as canvassers.

The most careful and elaborate classification of occupations by socio-economic rank is the Minnesota Occupational Scale, devised by Goodenough and Anderson on the basis of 1920 census occupations, and since revised by their students. [4] Because of its great importance in educational research this scale warrants some detailed analysis. The occupations included in the original form of the scale are divided into seven groups:

Group I. Professional
Group II. Semiprofessional and managerial

Group III. Clerical, skilled trades, and retail business

Group IV. Farmers

Group V. Semiskilled occupations, minor clerical positions, and minor business

Group VI. Slightly skilled trades and other occupations requiring little training or ability

Group VII. Day laborers of all classes

The construction of the scale was influenced by Barr's estimates of occupational intelligence requirements, so that of all socioeconomic scales it is most favorable toward the learned professions, which are unequivocally rated higher than all types of managerial work, and toward those occupations with predominantly verbal functions. Thus, schoolteachers are considered to have a higher socioeconomic rank than bankers, and librarians to enjoy more prestige than manufacturers. Similarly, reporters are included as professional workers, but musicians as semiprofessional, and actors as merely skilled.

A special problem in a scale devised primarily for the rating of urban middle-class families is the distribution of retail dealers. In the Minnesota Occupational Scale, these are ranked not by size of enterprise but by the type of commodity handled, and are found in several groups. For example, book and fur dealers are classified in Group VI; the operators of shoestores and stationery shops in Group III; milk and grocery dealers in Group IV; restaurant owners and paint dealers in Group V. Thus, the median ranking of all retail dealers will vary violently from one community to another.

The opposite predicament occurs in the classification of farmers, ranchers, nurserymen, and florists—none of whom are classified higher than Group IV in the Minnesota Occupational Scale, so that all pawnbrokers, carpenters, and ticket agents (Group III) are made to outrank the entire agricultural population.

There appears to be a general bias in the Minnesota scale against work which is dirty or strenuous, even when it is highly paid and skilled. For instance, while theater ushers and waiters are found in Group V, mine foremen and steel ladlers are relegated to Group VI. Blacksmiths and stonemasons are one step lower than electricians and machinists.

Certain puritanical biases can also be detected in the scale ratings. Jailkeepers are classified in Group I (Professional), but the keepers of pleasure resorts have been demoted all the way to Group V, and hypnotists even further to Group VI.

The public-opinion analysts and market-research investigators have devised another group of a priori scales to meet their needs; that of Centers [5] is especially comprehensive, but it encounters some of the familiar difficulties:

1. *Business Executives:*
Consists of persons owning or managing banks, factories, wholesale businesses, the larger retail businesses, etc.
2. *Professionals:*
Includes persons such as teachers, professors, lawyers, engineers, artists, writers, editors, and physicians.
3. *Small Business:*
Represents owners and managers of smaller retail, service, and repair enterprises, contractors, and nonfarm proprietors of almost every other sort.
4. *White-Collar Workers:*
Are a large heterogeneous category of clerical and technical workers, such as stenographers, bookkeepers, typists, draftsmen, salespeople, and others whose work is primarily managerial and nonmanual.
5. *Skilled Manual Workers:*
Are those such as bricklayers, plumbers, machinists, locomotive engineers, printers, as well as all foremen, and skilled service workers, such as cooks and barbers.
6. *Semiskilled Manual Workers:*
Are truck drivers, machine operators, service-station attendants, waiters, countermen, and others whose work is primarily manual and involves a minor degree of skill.
7. *Unskilled Manual Workers:*
Are the lowest grade workers in point of skill and responsibility: sweepers, porters, janitors, cleaners, construction laborers, bootblacks, and other workers of similar character.

This scale probably comes closer to measuring level of living than any preceding one. Note the omission of rural occupations, the preference given to business executives over professionals and to small businessmen over salesmen, and the very high rating of skilled service workers.

PSYCHOMETRIC SCALES

Yerkes' discovery that occupational groups, when arrayed in order of average scores made by recruits on the Army Alpha Test, were distributed over a very broad range and in a consistent fashion was enthusiastically received as evidence for the importance of individual differences. The data seem to have been quite valid, but were widely misinterpreted. They do show that occupations of higher status are generally characterized by higher average intelligence, as measured by a paper-and-pencil test. They do not tell us whether the differences are innate or acquired, and they do not indicate that the occupational order is in perfect harmony with the distribution of natural ability, as some scholars hastily concluded. Indeed, simple arithmetic suffices to show that while the lower ranking occupational groups show much lower average scores, they include — because of their greater size — a clear majority of the intellectually superior members of the population.

The first psychometric scale for the classification of all occupations was designed by Barr,[6] who "drew up a list of 121 representative occupations, each definitely and concretely described, and had 20 judges rate them on a scale of 0 to 100 according to the grade of intelligence which each was believed to demand." His scale values (expressed in terms of P.E. transmuted) therefore express a composite opinion of the intelligence which each occupation demands for ordinary success. The characteristics of the judges are nowhere described in the literature. It may be assumed that their rankings were made from the vantage point of the more literate occupations, and that not all of them were familiar with either the personnel or the work involved in each of the 121 occupations. How many of the rankings are really based upon statistical estimates of the minimum intelligence required for success, and how many are only prestige ratings, is difficult to determine. Terman further comments, "In the use of the scale it is only necessary to compare the occupation which is to be rated, with the occupations whose scale values are known, and to assign it the value possessed by the scaled occupations which it most nearly matches."

Strictly speaking, the Barr scale includes a mixture of occupations (e.g., butcher), positions (educational administrator, superintendent, city 2000–5000, college or normal graduate), and personalities (inventive genius, Edison type). In many cases, the description given indicates the degree of success more accurately than the occupation pursued (musician, successful player or singer in good company; dairy owner and manager, small dairy, 50–100 cows). By assuming a priori that a given degree of success is associated with a particular minimum intelligence, the author neatly begs the question of whether occupations vary in the intelligence required for success. A further difficulty in evaluating this scale is the method used in setting up the scale values. It is impossible to ascertain how much difference in measured intelligence is implied by a given difference in scale value.

The results are nevertheless of interest. The skilled manual trades are found scattered through an enormous range from general repairman at 7.05 to master mechanic at 13.29. The professional occupations cover an equal range from librarian at 12.02 to surgeon at 19.73. There are some curious juxtapositions, so that chef and editor, salesman and tailor, primary teacher and landscape gardener, are found in adjacent ranks. It is difficult to say whether the finer divisions of the scale are more than random ratings.

Some evidence along this line is available from the testing of army recruits. As early as 1922, Fryer[7] published standard scores on the Army Alpha Test for a list of selected occupations. In 1942 Lorge and Blau[8] compared the Barr scores with the Army Alpha scores reported by Fryer for 44 occupations which were interpreted as common to both lists. The correlation was +.76, indicating only a fair degree of correspondence.

Studies of civilian populations by Pond[9] and others[10] have generally given quite comparable results, with a tendency for sharper differences to appear than can be found among the young and vocationally mobile recruits tested in the army studies.

Some detailed evidence on occupational intelligence standards is available from the A.G.C.T. scores of World War II soldiers, classified by their civilian occupations. A study by Harrell and Harrell[11] reports the scores by civilian occupations of 18,782 white enlisted men in the Army Air Forces; and Christensen[12] has given the 1 per cent confidence interval for each of the means listed in 74 occupations. If we assume that the mean scores were derived from representative and randomly selected samples, intelligence differences found between occupations whose confidence intervals do not overlap are statistically significant. Examining the figures, we find that such differences do exist but only between widely separated occupational levels. Thus the five occupations of accountant, pharmacist, watchmaker, carpenter, and farmer represent a genuine rank order in A.G.C.T. scores, and cover the range from 82.7 to 128.1 with only a few small gaps. On the other hand, none of the adjacent pairs of occupations in the list can be significantly differentiated.

The general question of the validity of intelligence tests is beyond the scope of this discussion, but it should be noted in passing that both Fryer and the Harrells show much higher scores for urban occupations than for comparable rural occupations. Most clerical functions also show surprisingly high scores. Tabulating-machine operators in the Harrell study have a larger mean score than production managers and purchasing agents, and a significantly higher score than store managers. Stenographers rank high on both rank orders, and general clerks outdo all the skilled manual trades. It seems evident that the measured intelligence, in such cases, has been affected by experience in manipulating symbols.

PRESTIGE SCALES

The third group of occupational scales are those which attempt to establish the prestige of occupations empirically, either by the mass rating of occupations or by the judgment of an informed expert. In the sociological literature, prestige is not exactly the same thing as status or social position, and may perhaps best be said to represent the subjective value granted to the perceived cluster of habits, objects, and expectations associated with the statuses of a given position. It is certain, however, that the respondents to occupational prestige questionnaires do not make these distinctions, and that the public-opinion investigator who uses such a scale is merely seeking a general expression of socioeconomic status. In a sense, the prestige scales are statements about occupational preferences in raw form, without the benefit of semantic analysis.

"In most communities," wrote Counts in the directions to respondents who took part in his first study, "certain occupations are accorded a higher rating than others. There is a tendency for us to look up to persons engaged in some occupations and down on those engaged in others. We may even be ashamed or proud of our relatives because of occupations." [13] In contrast to some of the scales previously discussed, the total rank order ratings of 45 occupations by 450 students and teachers presented by Counts contained few anomalies. Moreover, a study by Deeg and Paterson [14] which duplicated Counts' investigation (except for the reduction of the list to 25 occupations) 21 years later showed a correlation of .97 (rho) between the two rank orders. Both studies showed remarkably high intercorrelations among different groups of raters.

The meaningful content of "prestige" as measured by these scales will be discussed a little later. The method of median ranks does not permit the calculation of confidence intervals, but a study by Baudler and Paterson [15] of women's occupations rated in a similar way shows standard deviations ranging from 3.28 to 6.69 in a range of 29 ranks. This suggests the existence of a good deal more inconsistency than appears on the tabulation of median ranks.

39

Another limitation is that the selection of occupations which are easily visualized has the effect of selecting the older, more universal, and less urbanized occupations. All but three or four of the occupations in Counts' list were well known and similarly defined a century ago and about half of them would have been familiar to raters in the Massachusetts Bay Colony. With the exception of "auto manufacturer," all the occupations listed would be found in a small community.

Similar studies were undertaken by Welch [16] (500 raters and 25 occupations), Anderson [17] (673 raters and 25 occupations), Menger [18] (704 raters and 35 women's occupations), Stevens [19] (150 raters and 25 occupations), Lehman and Witty [20] (26,000 school children and 200 occupations). The results are generally consistent with those of Counts.

Hartmann [21] had three groups of adults rate 25 medical specialties. He found that "the easily understood and well-recognized occupations stand either near the top or the bottom of the list," and that although the average ratings of samples of farmers, industrial workers, and graduate students were not identical, the shifts in rank were largely confined to the central part of the list.

Among other studies of this kind are those of Smith and Davis. The Smith scale [22] is very elaborate and includes 100 numbered items, ranging from professional prostitute to Supreme Court justice, but the method used is doubtful, and the confusion between occupations and positions is carried to an extreme. A suggestive study by Davis [23] tested the social attitudes of children in Soviet Russian government schools by having them rate a list of occupations adapted from the Counts scale. The children ranked farmers first, bankers among the last. Davis' suggestion that such tests be used for the intercultural comparison of status attitudes is still an interesting one.

Together with the prestige scales based on research there are a number of more informal prestige classifications which rest on the judgment of a single author. The most influential have been those of Sims,[24] who divides the occupational scale into four levels, and Taussig,[25] who characterizes his groups in the following terms: "Amid the great variety of occupations and of wages certain broad groups may be distinguished. These may be called, in the phrase introduced by Cairnes, non-competing groups; non-competing in the sense that those born or placed in a given grade or group usually remain there, and do not compete with those in other groups." Both of these scales contain some of the familiar anomalies. Sims, for example, chooses to rank clerks above artisan proprietors, foremen, and small businessmen. Taussig omits the low-level nonindustrial occupations altogether.

QUESTIONS OF CONSISTENCY

It may be inferred from the foregoing pages that there is a good deal of disagreement among the several occupational scales as to the ranking of occupations. This is true. The examples of inconsistency which have been given are not merely statistical anecdotes plucked from context.

While the scales are reasonably consistent in ranking bank presidents high and street sweepers low, they are not at all consistent in their evaluation of intermediate occupations, especially those in which self-employment is common. It is interesting to see how the application of different scales to groups of roughly similar status gives us almost all the permutations of ranking that are mathematically possible. The occupations of farmer, electrician, and insurance agent, for example, are populous and representative; their rank order on a number of familiar occupation scales varies considerably, as shown in the tabulation.

	Counts, Deeg & Paterson	Minnesota Occupational Scale	Sims	Edwards
Farmer	1	3	2	1
Electrician . . .	2	2	3	3
Insurance agent	3	1	1	2

It appears plain that the scales are not even in approximate agreement on occupations of intermediate status. There are certain inescapable dilemmas, concerning these occupations particularly, which haunt the architects of occupational scales and which have been resolved by a variety of makeshifts. For example:

1. Should professional persons or business executives be given the highest rating?

2. Should all white-collar workers be placed above all manual workers, or should the two categories overlap? If so, by how much?

3. Should an occupational scale qualify the description of each category by data on income, size of community, or property ownership?

4. Where should professional burglars, fortunetellers, ward heelers, gamblers, prostitutes, and other deviants be classed? Should they be arranged in a hierarchy of skill? How about apprentice gamblers and part-time prostitutes?

5. At what point in the scale do public employees become public officials? Should policemen, firemen, and United States Marines be classified by skill? If so, by which skill?

6. Should butlers, nursemaids, and other skilled servants be classified as unskilled because personal services are degrading? If so, why should chiropodists enjoy higher status than hairdressers?

7. What distinctions must be drawn between artisan-employees and artisan-proprietors? Is there a real distinction between foremen who are skilled in the work they supervise and those who are not?

8. Should the owner of a junkyard be considered an executive? Is a stripteaser a professional worker? If not, where should they be grouped?

9. Do rich farmers engage in the same occupation as poor farmers?

These questions are by no means frivolous. The effect of selecting one set of answers rather than another is to change the total distribution of the labor force and to alter the long-term trends beyond recognition. An analysis of occupational trends in the period from 1920 to 1950 based on Edwards' socioeconomic classification of census data will be flatly contradictory to any analysis based upon the application of the Minnesota scale to the same data.

At this point, it may be hypothesized that the construction of a single occupational scale for the simultaneous measurement of such diverse matters as prestige, skill, intelligence, and social position is in fact impossible. The distribution of each of these characteristics among the different occupations must be examined separately, and will be found to depend upon special assumptions not applicable to others. In the next few pages, we shall examine the assumptions that seem to underly occupational scales which measure socioeconomic status, minimum intelligence, and prestige. These scales are highly significant in social research, but their usefulness—as with any scientific instrument—is restricted to cases where their limitations have been taken into account.

ASSUMPTIONS UNDERLYING SCALES

SOCIOECONOMIC SCALES

The Centers scale, the Beckman classification, and the census classification itself when used as a status scale are based on a number of widely held assumptions. These are roughly defined, but extremely important. Among the assumptions are these:

1. White-collar work is superior to manual work.

2. Self-employment is superior to employment by others.
3. Clean occupations are superior to dirty ones.
4. The importance of business occupations depends upon the size of the business, but this is not true of agricultural occupations.
5. Personal service is degrading, and it is better to be employed by an enterprise than to be employed in the same work by a person.

Superiority of white-collar work. Undoubtedly, the most important of these supposed principles is that white-collar jobs are superior to blue-collar jobs. The existence of such a preference as a social fact cannot be disputed. A number of studies have shown, for example, that young women entering the labor market prefer clerical employment to factory work even when it is offered on much inferior terms. Nor can this preference be described as irrational, given the historical and cultural circumstances associated with the choice. It is undoubtedly correct to rank typists above machine operators in a general status scale. There are some situations, however, in which the assumption does not hold, and these are precisely the situations likely to be important in the study of occupational stratification.

The urban blue-collar occupations include two conspicuous groups: machine operators in factories and artisans in the conventional trades. Union activity in the United States has been centered in these two groups. Each of them presents certain characteristic problems to the scale-maker

The income of artisans is highly variable over the business cycle. At the depth of the Depression, it seldom exceeded the going minimum factory wage and the distinction between artisans and factory hands tended to blur out. Throughout the decade of the 1940s, it compared favorably both in amount and in stability with the income of the lower professional groups, and exceeded on the average the income of minor proprietors. With this increase in income level came a corresponding increase in prestige and respectability. This was something more than a reflection of disposable wages. To the extent that craft organizations were able to control recruiting and to maintain a partial monopoly of the trade, journeymen were in effect proprietors, disposing of rights and privileges readily convertible into money. Moreover, the organization of the building trades is such that there is no clear distinction between proprietors and workers. In many places, a subcontractor must, by custom or regulation, be a qualified artisan, and in many private employments, foremen are selected from the crew of artisans and maintain their union status. A substantial number of

43

small-home builders, for example, are carpenters, or journeymen of other building trades, who are permanently identified with their craft, but whose general social position reflects a high level of economic well-being and local influence.

Factory machine operators are, on the whole, the most homogeneous of the large occupational groups. With the increasing bureaucratization of the factory, there come to be a considerable number of skilled jobs which are specific to a given industry, to a given plant, or even to a given operation, and which cannot be casually classed as semiskilled without doing violence to the facts. Many of them, in inspection and quality control, for example, are literally white-collar jobs, without clerical function. The average tenure of employment in factory jobs is very short, and probably only a minority of all semiskilled industrial employees are identified with an occupation in the same sense that craftsmen or professionals are so connected. In certain industries a large proportion of all factory employees are in the marginal categories of the labor force: married women, adolescents, farmers. Since factory income is in these cases a supplementary income, classification in the semiskilled group will not correctly reflect the position of these workers in the community.

While it is undoubtedly accurate to observe that the work of the businessman is preferred to the work of the artisan under our cultural norms, it is probably misleading to think that it is preferred as such. Given a pecuniary system which controls the distribution of social rewards, it is reasonable to expect that more prestige will be attached to the manipulation of pecuniary symbols than to the manipulation of tools and materials. As a matter of fact, all cultures emphasize certain central symbols, and the occupational functions attached to these always confer a degree of power and respect. The priest, the pedagogue, the politician, and the patrician are universal dignitaries.

But manual work is not misprized as such. Indeed, there are certain elements in the American tradition which favor manual competence, and a large proportion of the hobbies of our upper classes involve the demonstration of skill with tools and materials. In the actual setting of the factory or the construction gang, it is the manual workers who despise the clerks, and this evaluation is generally accepted by the clerks as long as they exert no direct authority over the working crew. In the long run the relative prestige of office jobs, set over against shop jobs, is based on the potential upward mobility of the white-collar worker.

One other phenomenon which has baffled the scale-makers is that while occupations are rated internally by degree of skill — helper, apprentice, journeyman, master — the relative rank of manual occupations does not always depend upon the degree of skill required. It is possible to identify certain very highly skilled operations, which, because of either limited mobility or the irrelevance of the product, are given very mediocre recognition (acrobats, etchers, mail sorters, machine embroiderers, for example); while a number of occupations which demand relatively little skill (like projectionists or linotypers) are highly rewarded.

It would seem that the relative rank of manual occupations is fixed by the usual complex of factors: pecuniary value, potential upward mobility, functional status, responsibility, ascribed intelligence level, and historical connotations. Admittedly, the outcome of this calculation is generally less favorable to the manual occupations than to those which involve only the manipulation of symbols. Admittedly too, social class factors, the remnants of the ideology of a landowning aristocracy, and the conditions of industrial employment, all contribute to attach a certain negative weight to work done in overalls. The fact remains that the white-collar occupations enjoy no general and categorical superiority over the blue-collar occupations with respect to any important social index, and that blue-collar occupations cannot be easily sorted by skill.

Each of the other assumptions on which the census scales are based is also a useful half-truth, representing certain real elements in the social structure, but representing them too fancifully.

Superiority of self-employment. The popular belief that self-employment is superior to employment by others has special reference to two familiar situations: the advantageous position of the independent practitioner in the fee-taking professions of medicine, dentistry, and law; and the freedom of the small merchant as compared to others of equivalent rank. As a popular creed, the belief in self-employment has regained a good deal of the support which it lost during the Depression. Historically, the value attached to self-employment is clearly related to the experience of the farmer escaping from European or Eastern tenancy and establishing ownership on the frontier, as is the parallel American dogma of home ownership. In both cases, more attention is given to the legal formula and the images which the formula evokes than to the economic and social facts. Even for the two typical situations, the advantage of self-employment is not unequivocal. The disproportionate rewards accorded to physi-

45

cians have more to do with the monopoly position of their occupational organizations than with individual independence. Indeed, recent studies indicate [26] that a highly coercive system of promotion and status-fixing operates in many corners of the medical system. Similarly, for at least a generation, the large and highly organized law firm has steadily crowded most of the independent practitioners out of the more important and lucrative fields of practice. What appears to be the fruit of independence is more likely to be a consequence of the high interactional status enjoyed by the professions — a matter to which we will return shortly.

It is significant that the migration toward small retail business which was encouraged by veterans' legislation after World War II was directed toward a few retail fields: filling stations, grocery stores, dry-cleaning shops, and taxicabs were typical. In all four of these fields, a system of product distribution has been worked out by powerful producers and middlemen, which allows the new entrant the legal status of an owner, together with some real (although often exaggerated) chance of speculative gain, in return for a capital contribution, long hours, and the performance of services not required of employees. It would appear that in most of these fields those unit managers who function as employees are more adequately rewarded than those who function as owners. It is chiefly the recruits of the occupation who are attracted to the owner status, and few of the salaried managers aspire to independence under the terms offered. This is a curious instance of the way in which prestige may become a cause as well as an effect of occupational reward.

For the majority of the labor force, and in most modern occupations, self-employment is not a plausible alternative. Indeed, the term ceases to have much meaning on the upper levels of industrial or professional employment, where the identification of the individual and the organization is so close that he rarely thinks of himself as employed, or where — as in the case of railroad jobs — the nature of the work implies an employer.

Superiority of clean occupations. A good deal of the strength of the Hindu caste system in inhibiting interoccupational contacts apparently lies in the attachment of sentiments of disgust to the work of lower occupational groups. Wherever work involves activities or contacts which most people have been trained to shun, there will be negative connotations attached to the occupation. Street cleaners may be as well paid as policemen, or better paid, but they will not enjoy equal status. Butchers are less acceptable than grocers. Sewer technicians, coal miners, laundry workers, and junk dealers — all have less prestige than their earnings and the usefulness of their services might seem to imply. Some of the more genteel occupational scales classify the highly skilled worker who controls a blast furnace on about the same level as a day laborer.

There are two modern tendencies at work to annul this ancient form of invidious comparison. The first of these is professionalization: the deliberate remodeling of occupational structure which enables funeral directors and sanitary engineers to fill their roles without arousing the traditional prejudices. The other is the gradual disappearance of most of the filthier occupations through mechanization. Chimney sweeps and cesspool cleaners are now totally mechanized, tanners and glue-makers are not far behind, and hostlers and coal-carriers have almost passed from the scene.

Importance of size of business. The statement that the rank of business occupations depends upon the size of the business embodies a half-truth which is particularly difficult to revise into a whole truth. The size of an enterprise always has some influence on the roles of its members. This is sometimes positive and sometimes negative. Department stores are appropriately graded in order of size, but country clubs are not. The largest wheat farm and the smallest have many things in common, but owning one is not the same thing as owning the other. Any change in organizational size is likely to be accompanied by a fairly complex series of consequences, whose nature depends more upon the specific situation than upon any general principles.

We do not have adequate statistics on the origin or even on the distribution of high incomes, but it would appear that most very high incomes are derived from small enterprises, where the owner's or manager's share is not limited by bureaucratic considerations. It would also seem that the authority of a supervisor over a given number of employees is likely to bring more recognition in a relatively small company than in a very large one. On the other hand, identification with certain organizations confers advantages automatically. In communities dominated by a single company or group of companies, mere employment by them may constitute membership in a favored class.

When we add to these somewhat contradictory considerations the fact that the distribution of functions within large and small organizations is often entirely different (who corresponds to the editor of a country weekly on the staff of a metropolitan daily?), it is quite obvious that no summary generalization will cover the matter. Perhaps the most useful statement is that very small organizations (school systems or smelters will do equally well for examples) usually lack prestige, that large organizations always enjoy some prestige, but that the proudest group is likely to be middle-sized. Needless to say, this is not an easy state of affairs to scale.

Degrading nature of personal service. The last assumption to be discussed is that personal service is inherently degrading. To this there is sometimes attached the related notion that it is less honorable to be employed by an individual than to be employed in the same capacity by an organization.

The census classification of Edwards places all servants at the very bottom of the occupational heap, below farm laborers and unskilled industrial workers. The Minnesota Occupational Scale is somewhat kinder, putting most servants among the slightly skilled and butlers and waiters among the semiskilled. Curiously enough bartenders are considered less skilled than waiters—on what basis it would be interesting to determine.

The house servants present no serious complications. This group is overwhelmingly composed of housemaids, laundresses, and cleaning women, together with a small number of housekeepers (who may be common-law wives), butlers and chefs (who may be highly skilled), chauffeurs, governesses, and valets. No great harm is done by classification of domestic service as a low-status function, if only because of the limitation of personal freedom which is usually involved.

The difficulty arises when we come to apply the idea of personal service to a variety of extra-domestic occupational groups whose importance has always been considerable, and whose numbers are increasing, such as restaurant workers, barbers, beauticians, bellboys, bootblacks, practical nurses, and porters. In addition, there are a considerable number of marginal service occupations like those of chiropodists, masseurs, and taxi drivers.

One curious thing about these occupations is that they are readily professionalized. The difference between barbers and hairdressers is perhaps as wide as the difference between any two parallel trades, and the status of nurses doing approximately the same work runs from the very bottom to the very top of the occupational range for women. More curious still is the fact that some of these occupations, like those of bartenders, taxi drivers, and countermen are not markedly respectable but are nevertheless generally respected. Many an executive is on terms of equality with a bartender, although he would never confide in one of his foremen. A small-town barber often counts himself among the leading citizens. Indeed, the only work which can be depended upon to preserve its menial character is that which is consistently ill-paid or reserved to outcasts. In the last analysis, the service occupations are structured in terms of personal relations and it is profoundly misleading to attempt a classification by skill even in those cases where measurable differences of skill are involved. The menial character of personal service as such is a myth; where the situation is differently defined, as in the case of dentists and physicians, no derogation attaches to the circumstance that the service is personal.

INTELLIGENCE SCALES

Turning from the socioeconomic scales to those based on intelligence, we encounter another set of underlying assumptions. Unlike the socio-economic scales, which were mostly devised by practical men who needed a handy classification for other purposes, the Barr scale and other rankings of occupation by intelligence are viewed as research findings rather than research instruments. Since they are permeated by a single ideology, it is possible to relate them to a single major assumption: namely, that the differences in occupational status and in social reward which are observed in the labor force are founded on differences in natural ability. These differences being genetic and unalterable, it is the business of the social order to give them scope. The superiority of the professional over the sub-professional, and of the skilled worker over the semiskilled, is supposedly accounted for by a richer germ plasm.

I have already suggested several reasons why this happy conclusion is premature. A glance at Table 1, which shows the average scores of samples of 74 occupational groups on the Army General Classification Test, indicates two flaws in the stratification. First, it is notable that while minimum test intelligence declines with declining occupational status, the maximum scores remain almost unchanged throughout most of the listing. Since any large-scale status system must be more or less pyramidal, the lower rank-ing occupations are more populous. While they contain a smaller propor-tion of high intelligence, they include, in absolute numbers, a clear ma-jority of the intellectually talented. This principle now seems fairly ob-vious, but it was quite overlooked until Lehman and Stokes [27] pointed it out in 1930. Using the Army Alpha results of World War I, they were able to show that more than half of the A caliber males in the population would

49

Table 1. Range of A.G.C.T. Scores of 18,782 Army Air Force White Enlisted Men by Civilian Occupation

Occupation	N	Mean	Median	S.D.	Range
Accountant	172	128.1	128.1	11.7	94–157
Lawyer	94	127.6	126.8	10.9	96–157
Engineer	39	126.6	125.8	11.7	100–151
Public relations man	42	126.0	125.5	11.4	100–149
Auditor	62	125.9	125.5	11.2	98–151
Chemist	21	124.8	124.5	13.8	102–153
Reporter	45	124.5	125.7	11.7	100–157
Chief clerk	165	124.2	124.5	11.7	88–153
Teacher	256	122.8	123.7	12.8	76–155
Draftsman	153	122.0	121.7	12.8	74–155
Stenographer	147	121.0	121.4	12.5	66–151
Pharmacist	58	120.5	124.0	15.2	76–149
Tabulating machine operator	140	120.1	119.8	13.3	80–151
Bookkeeper	272	120.0	119.7	13.1	70–157
Manager, sales	42	119.0	120.7	11.5	90–137
Purchasing agent	98	118.7	119.2	12.9	82–153
Manager, production	34	118.1	117.0	16.0	82–153
Photographer	95	117.6	119.8	13.9	66–147
Clerk, general	496	117.5	117.9	13.0	68–155
Clerk-typist	468	116.8	117.3	12.0	80–147
Manager, miscellaneous	235	116.0	117.5	14.8	60–151
Installer-repairman, tel. and tel.	96	115.8	116.8	13.1	76–149
Cashier	111	115.8	116.8	11.9	80–145
Instrument repairman	47	115.5	115.8	11.9	82–141
Radio repairman	267	115.3	116.5	14.5	56–151
Printer, job pressman, lithographic pressman	132	115.1	116.7	14.3	60–149
Salesman	494	115.1	116.2	15.7	60–153
Artist	48	114.9	115.4	11.2	82–139
Manager, retail store	420	114.0	116.2	15.7	52–151
Laboratory assistant	128	113.4	114.0	14.6	76–147
Tool-maker	60	112.5	111.6	12.5	76–143
Inspector	358	112.3	113.1	15.7	54–147
Stock clerk	490	111.8	113.0	16.3	54–151
Receiving and shipping clerk	486	111.3	113.4	16.4	58–155
Musician	157	110.9	112.8	15.9	56–147
Machinist	456	110.1	110.8	16.1	38–153
Foreman	298	109.8	111.4	16.7	60–151
Watchmaker	56	109.8	113.0	14.7	68–147
Airplane mechanic	235	109.3	110.5	14.9	66–147
Sales clerk	492	109.2	110.4	16.3	42–149
Electrician	289	109.0	110.6	15.2	64–149
Lathe operator	172	108.5	109.4	15.5	64–147
Receiving and shipping checker	281	107.6	108.9	15.8	52–151
Sheet metal worker	498	107.5	108.1	15.3	62–153
Lineman, power and tel. and tel.	77	107.1	108.8	15.5	70–133
Assembler	498	106.3	106.6	14.6	48–145
Mechanic	421	106.3	108.3	16.0	60–155
Machine operator	486	104.8	105.7	17.1	42–151
Auto serviceman	539	104.2	105.9	16.7	30–141

Table 1. *Continued*

Occupation	N	Mean	Median	S.D.	Range
Riveter	239	104.1	105.3	15.1	50–141
Cabinetmaker	48	103.5	104.7	15.9	66–127
Upholsterer	59	103.3	105.8	14.5	68–131
Butcher	259	102.9	104.8	17.1	42–147
Plumber	128	102.7	104.8	16.0	56–139
Bartender	98	102.2	105.0	16.6	56–137
Carpenter, construction	451	102.1	104.1	19.5	42–147
Pipe fitter	72	101.9	105.2	18.0	56–139
Welder	493	101.8	103.6	16.1	48–147
Auto mechanic	466	101.3	101.8	17.0	48–151
Molder	79	101.1	105.5	20.2	48–137
Chauffeur	194	100.8	103.0	18.4	46–143
Tractor driver	354	99.5	101.6	19.1	42–147
Painter, general	440	98.3	100.1	18.7	38–147
Crane hoist operator	99	97.9	99.1	16.6	58–147
Cook and baker	436	97.2	99.5	20.8	20–147
Weaver	56	97.0	97.3	17.7	50–135
Truck driver	817	96.2	97.8	19.7	16–149
Laborer	856	95.8	97.7	20.1	26–145
Barber	103	95.3	98.1	20.5	42–141
Lumberjack	59	94.7	96.5	19.8	46–137
Farmer	700	92.7	93.4	21.8	24–147
Farmhand	817	91.4	94.0	20.7	24–141
Miner	156	90.6	92.0	20.1	42–139
Teamster	77	87.7	89.0	19.6	46–145

Source: T. W. and M. S. Harrell, "Army General Classification Test Scores for Civilian Occupations," *Educational and Psychological Measurement*, vol. 5, 1945, pp. 231–32.

be found in manual work, although fewer than 2 per cent of all manual workers scored in the A category as compared with 38 per cent of professional workers. There is good reason now to think that the Army Alpha was strongly biased in favor of the educated soldier. Even after the tremendous expansion of higher education which the last generation has witnessed, only a fraction of those who are intellectually qualified for advanced training actually complete a college education.[28]

The further down the scale we go, the larger is the standard deviation. It is nearly twice as great for the last group of occupations as for the first. In other words, while there is every reason to believe that an accountant or engineer selected at random will have better than average intelligence, there is *no* occupation whose members selected at random will be reliably subnormal.

Even if the occupational hierarchy formed a smoother statistical continuum than it does, it would still be difficult or impossible to use an intelligence scale as an index of income or prestige, or to infer the distribution of natural ability in a population from the distribution of occupational labels.

PRESTIGE SCALES

It does not appear that the occupational hierarchy is essentially a gradation of intelligence, even if intelligence is taken in its broadest sense to include trainability and skill. There are a number of other characteristics which may be derived for an occupation whose combined effect on the status of an occupation is greater than that of intelligence. We may note in the accompanying list a few examples, related to simple four-point scales for convenience of explanation.

Scale Definition	*Example*
Responsibility	
1. Responsibility affecting life and property	judge
2. Responsibility affecting property only	auditor
3. Responsibility for the avoidance of negligence	chauffeur
4. No responsibility	artist
Nature of work	
1. Manipulation of symbols	reporter
2. Manipulation of symbols with some use of tools and materials	draftsman
3. Manipulation of tools and materials, with some use of symbols	radio repairman
4. Manipulation of tools and materials	bricklayer
Formal education	
1. Higher education required	architect
2. High school education	secretary
3. Literacy required	executive
4. No formal education required	gardener
Training	
1. Long training required	musician
2. Some training required	piano tuner
3. Some training desirable	purchasing agent
4. No training required	letter carrier
Authority	
1. Large group of subordinates	orchestra conductor
2. Small group of subordinates	station agent
3. Assistants and helpers only	legislator
4. No subordinates	actor
Class attributes	
1. Conventional upper-class occupation	bond salesman
2. Conventional upper-middle-class occupation	dentist

Scale Definition	Example
3. Conventional lower-middle-class occupation...fireman	
4. Conventional lower-class occupation.........longshoreman	

Income
1. High income assured.....................physician
2. High income possible but not assured........realtor
3. Moderate income assured.................laboratory technician
4. Low income assured.....................dishwasher

By a consideration of these elements, we are led very naturally to examine the major assumption which underlies the use of prestige scales: namely, that all the familiar components of status are correlated with prestige. In Table 2, five raters have rated the 45 occupations of the original Counts scale on the elements listed above (responsibility, nature of work, formal education, training, authority, class attributes, and income). These ratings carry no particular authority since five ratings are not enough to establish a reliable average, but they are inserted here for illustrative purposes. They are based upon the raters' notion of the occupational system in a midwestern city of 50,000.

All these ratings show some association with prestige as commonly understood, but none of them is close enough to sustain the hypothesis that prestige is directly based on that element. Various averages and combinations of the five ratings will be found equally imperfect. The question remains whether prestige may be based on some other single element not yet taken into account.

As a matter of fact, it is evident that we have not included all the elements which contribute to occupational status. One such element of great importance is historical connotation, and it is almost impossible to rate. It is evident that the status of locomotive engineers is affected by the ballad of Casey Jones, and that the social position of clergymen is colored by two thousand years of church history. Another elusive element is what might be called the coefficient of isolation. In Counts' original study, those occupations that belong in one way or another to closed systems which are not familiar in the small-town environment from which the subjects were drawn suffered thereby. The man of leisure (15) would not in his own circle be considered inferior to the elementary teacher (13). The railroad conductor (27) probably outranks the electrician (22) in income, tenure, and self-esteem. The coal miner (39) is not less esteemed than the factory operative (37) in his own territory or for many miles around.

Granted the existence of still other factors which weight the total status

Table 2. Rating of the Components of Occupational Status for 45 Occupations

Occupations from Counts Scale	Re-sponsi-bility	Nature of Work	Formal Educa-tion	Train-ing	Author-ity	Class Attri-butes	In-come	Behav-ior Con-trol
1. Banker	1	1	2	2	2	1	1	1
2. College professor	1	1	1	1	3	2	3	1
3. Physician	1	2	1	1	3	2	1	1
4. Clergyman ...	1	1	2	1	3	1	3	1
5. Lawyer	1	1	1	1	3	2	2	1
6. Auto manu-facturer	2	1	2	2	1	1	1	1
7. Superintendent of schools	1	1	1	2	1	2	3	1
8. Civil engineer.	2	2	1	1	2	2	2	1
9. Army captain .	1	2	3	2	1	1	3	2
10. High school teacher	1	2	1	1	4	2	3	2
11. Foreign mis-sionary	1	1	2	2	3	2	3	2
12. Factory manager	1	1	2	2	1	2	2	2
13. Elementary teacher	1	2	1	2	4	2	3	2
14. Dry-goods merchant	1	2	2	2	2	2	2	2
15. Man of leisure	4			4		1	1	2
16. Farmer	2	3	4	2	3	3	2	3
17. Machinist	2	3	3	1	3	3	3	3
18. Traveling salesman	4	2	3	4	4	2	2	3
19. Rural school teacher	1	2	2	2	4	3	3	2
20. Grocer	3	3	2	3	2	3	2	3
21. Bookkeeper ..	3	1	2	2	3	2	3	3
22. Electrician ...	2	3	3	1	3	3	3	3
23. Locomotive engineer	2	3	3	1	3	3	3	3
24. Insurance agent	4	1	2	4	4	2	2	3
25. Policeman ...	1	2	3	3	4	4	4	2
26. Mail carrier ..	3	3	3	3	4	3	4	3
27. Railroad conductor	2	2	3	1	2	2	3	3
28. Carpenter	3	3	4	1	3	3	3	3
29. Salesman	4	2	3	4	4	3	3	3
30. Soldier	3	4	4	3	4	4	4	4
31. Typesetter ...	3	3	3	1	3	3	3	3
32. Plumber	3	3	4	1	3	4	3	3
33. Tailor	3	3	4	1	3	3	3	3
34. Motorman ...	2	4	3	3	4	4	4	3
35. Chauffeur	3	4	3	3	4	4	4	3

Table 2. *Continued*

Occupations from Counts Scale	Re-sponsi-bility	Nature of Work	Formal Educa-tion	Train-ing	Author-ity	Class Attri-butes	In-come	Behav-ior Con-trol
36. Barber	3	4	4	2	4	4	4	4
37. Factory operative	3	4	4	3	4	4	4	4
38. Blacksmith ...	3	4	4	1	3	4	4	3
39. Coal miner ...	2	4	4	1	3	4	4	4
40. Janitor	3	4	4	4	4	4	4	4
41. Waiter	4	3	3	3	4	4	2	4
42. Teamster	3	4	4	3	4	4	4	4
43. Hod carrier ..	4	4	4	4	4	4	4	4
44. Street cleaner.	4	4	4	4	4	4	4	4
45. Ditch digger ..	4	4	4	4	4	4	4	4

cluster, there is still a possibility that prestige is a unitary characteristic. Indeed, there does seem to be one property of an occupational position which correlates almost perfectly with the rank order of prestige ratings. I have called this element "behavior control" and it is shown in the last column of Table 2 in terms of the average judgment of the five raters.[29] What this element represents is the status of the individual in the typical situations elicited by his occupational role, vis-à-vis his clients, customers, subordinates, superiors, pupils, passengers, or indeed whatever other persons he normally meets in the course of his occupational duties.

There is in all occupations, without obvious exception, an element of behavior control. In the administrative occupations, the control of behavior may constitute the entire purpose of the work. But even in such an occupation as ditch digger or janitor, the manner by which the behavior of the incumbent is controlled is of major importance and—as advocates of slavery since Aristotle have delighted to point out—the most servile subordination inevitably involves some control of the superior's actions.

It would be absurd to suggest that no other element enters into the determination of occupational prestige. Nevertheless, it is worthy of note that the position of the subject with respect to the control of other people's behavior, and their control of his, appears to conform rather well to what is reported as occupational prestige. Thus, the first five occupations involve their incumbents in frequent and important relations with adults of all statuses, in the course of which it is they who control the situation. The

55

banker and the physician are perhaps the only persons whose role in interaction with other citizens of high status is consistently authoritative, and in the more recent prestige studies they occupy an uncontested summit of prestige.

The next four occupations are also characterized by control of the behavior of adults, but in these cases the adults are limited to a special group of employees and subordinates. The four occupations from high school teacher to elementary teacher involve control of the behavior of low-status persons like students, natives, and factory workers. The next six occupations (excluding rural school teacher, which is really a variant of elementary teacher previously rated) involve coordinate relationships with persons of all statuses, characterized by relatively little control of behavior. Similarly, it will be seen that none of the last eighteen occupations (carpenter to ditch digger) allows any important control of the behavior of others, while in the last six occupations the incumbent is under the strict control of persons of low status. In general terms, this explanation appears to provide a fair explanation of the prestige ratings. It does not completely account for the distribution of ratings in the middle of the range. There seem to be other cultural values which explain why electricians are rated far above carpenters and insurance agents far below traveling salesmen.

The last inconsistency is removed in the re-rating of the Deeg and Paterson study, and it may be that the departures of the prestige rating from a simple rating of interactional status are for the most part errors of comprehension or judgment. This possibility is suggested by the obvious relationship between the parenthesized descriptions of each occupation and the way they were rated. Thus it happened that an electrician was described as one who "wires houses for electricity" but a carpenter as one who "works for a building contractor."

However, Hatt has shown in a brilliant study that even where a prestige continuum may be developed by rating technics of this kind, there is serious doubt whether it holds together and constitutes a "real" scale. Using the Guttman scaling technic, Hatt and his associates analyzed the scalability of a prestige scale developed on a very large sample by the National Opinion Research Center:

Three different samples of twenty-five, sixteen, and twelve occupations were analyzed by this method, but none of these yield even a "quasi-scale," nor was there reason to believe that empirical manipulation would substantially improve scalability. This result made it necessary to reconsider the nature of the prestige continuum as constructed in this study and the addition of a new hypothesis. This hypothesis is that, although the full series does not scale, there are subgroupings which do scale. That is, these are subgroupings within which individuals are consistent, not only in their gross prestige judgments, but also in maintaining constant and precise differences of prestige ratings.[30]

He proceeded, by a priori judgments, to develop such subgroupings (called *situses*, and further subdivided into occupational families) and discovered a high degree of scalability for the occupational families. Each of the eight situses (political, professional, business, recreation and aesthetics, agriculture, manual work, military, and service) includes only jobs and occupations which can be compared consistently by most people.

The Hatt analysis presents us with quantitative proof for the conclusion suggested by our examination of the various occupational scales — that no single-dimensional rating of occupational status will satisfactorily rank the major occupations. In other words, we are confronted with the empirical problem that although occupational designation is at once a major indicator of general social position, and a source of such other social indicators as income, honorific esteem, group participation, and ecological location, the system is neither unequivocal, nor generally recognized, nor unitary. We may tentatively consider that the approach to the study of mobility and of social structure must use a more complicated group of indices than the rating of a simple occupational label will provide and, even with these aids, must be centered upon the study of specific occupational groupings embedded in particular communities.

NOTES

[1] R. M. Yerkes, Editor, "Psychological Examining in the U.S. Army," *Memoirs of the National Academy of Science,* vol. 15, 1921.

[2] Alba M. Edwards, *Comparative Occupational Statistics for the United States, 1870–1940* (Washington, D.C.: Government Printing Office, 1943), p. 179.

[3] R. O. Beckman, "A New Scale for Gauging Occupational Rank," *Personnel Journal,* vol. 13, September 1934, pp. 1–16.

[4] Originally presented in F. L. Goodenough and J. E. Anderson, *Experimental Child Study* (New York: Century Company, 1931). I have used the 1948 revision by Katherine Nikolaisen and others, issued in mimeographed form.

[5] Richard Centers, *The Psychology of Social Classes* (Princeton, N.J.: Princeton University Press, 1949), pp. 76–101.

[6] See L. M. Terman and others, *Genetic Studies of Genius,* Vol. 1 (Stanford, Calif.: Stanford University Press, 1925), pp. 66ff.

[7] Douglas Fryer, "Occupational-Intelligence Standards," *School and Society,* vol. 16, 1922.

[8] Irving Lorge and Ralph Blau, "Broad Occupational Groupings by Intelligence Levels," *Occupations,* vol. 20, March 1942.

[9] M. Pond, "Occupations, Intelligence, Age and Schooling," *Personnel Journal,* vol. 11, 1933.

[10] See Donald Super, *Appraising Vocational Fitness* (New York: Harper and Brothers, 1949).

[11] T. W. and M. S. Harrell, "Army General Classification Test Scores for Civilian Occupations," *Educational and Psychological Measurement,* vol. 5, 1945.

[12] T. E. Christensen, "The Dictionary Classification of AGCT Scores for Selected Civilian Occupations," *Occupations,* vol. 25, no. 2, November 1946.

[13] G. S. Counts, "The Social Status of Occupations: A problem in Vocational Guidance," *School Review,* vol. 33, January 1925.

[14] M. E. Deeg and D. G. Paterson, "Changes in Social Status of Occupations," *Occupations,* vol. 25, January 1947.

[15] Lucille Baudler and D. G. Paterson, "Social Status of Women's Occupations," *Occupations,* vol. 26, April 1948.

[16] M. K. Welch, "The Ranking of Occupations on the Basis of Social Status," *Occupations,* vol. 26, January 1949.

[17] W. A. Anderson, "The Occupational Attitudes of College Men," *Journal of Social Psychology,* vol. 5, 1934.

[18] C. Menger, "The Social Status of Occupations for Women," *Teachers College Record,* vol. 33, 1932.

[19] R. B. Stevens, "The Attitudes of College Women toward Women's Vocations," *Journal of Applied Psychology,* vol. 24, 1940.

[20] H. C. Lehman and P. A. Witty, "Further Study of the Social Status of Occupations," *Journal of Educational Sociology,* vol. 5, 1931.

[21] G. W. Hartmann, "The Relative Social Prestige of Representative Medical Specialties," *Journal of Applied Psychology,* vol. 20, 1936.

[22] Mapheus Smith, "An Empirical Scale of Prestige Status of Occupations," *American Sociological Review,* vol. 8, April 1943.

[23] Jerome Davis, "Testing the Social Attitudes of Children in the Government Schools in Russia," *American Journal of Sociology,* vol. 32, May 1927.

[24] V. M. Sims, *The Measurement of Socio-Economic Status* (Bloomington, Ill.: Public School Publishing, 1928).

[25] F. W. Taussig, *Principles of Economics* (New York: The Macmillan Company, 1939), Vol. 2, Chapter 52.

[26] Oswald Hall, "The Stages of a Medical Career," *American Journal of Sociology,* vol. 53, 1948.

[27] Harvey C. Lehman and Stuart M. Stoke, "Occupational Intelligence in the Army: A Postscript," *American Journal of Sociology,* vol. 36, 1930.

[28] For detailed evidence see the report of the President's Commission on Higher Education, *op. cit.*; and Dael Wolfle, "Intellectual Resources," *Scientific American,* vol. 185, no. 3, September 1951.

[29] The reader is invited, however, to substitute his own rating in any of these columns.

[30] Paul K. Hatt, "Occupation and Social Stratifications," *American Journal of Sociology,* vol. 55, May 1950.

CHAPTER 3

VERTICAL MOBILITY

"It takes very special circumstances to back up a belief in the close connection between virtue and success." MARGARET MEAD

IT IS customary to discuss the dynamics of occupational change in the terms first used by Pitirim Sorokin [1] — horizontal and vertical mobility, the former signifying a change in function and the latter a change in rank. *Mobility* is one of the most frequently used words in the sociological vocabulary, and one of the most confusing, so that it will be valuable to examine the theory upon which this usage rests.

The position of an individual in any social system may be described by his rank in a hierarchical scheme of relationships, his functions as a participant in group life, and his location in space and time. A significant occupational change may be a promotion or demotion, an alteration of function, or a change in residence or workplace. The spatial model on which these movements are traced may be conveniently visualized as a three-dimensional graph of which one horizontal axis represents function, the intersecting horizontal axis represents distance, and the vertical axis is a status scale.

If we are to avoid the confusion which leads some competent scholars to discuss the diminishing opportunities for mobility in our society at the same time that others are deploring the consequences of increased mobility, we must analyze in some detail the kind of events that may be represented on such a graph.

Vertical mobility is a movement of the individual upward or downward, with a gain or loss in social rank. This may occur in several different ways:

1. The simplest kind of vertical mobility is a change of occupation which involves a change in social position, as when a waiter becomes a businessman, or an unsuccessful accountant goes to work in a factory.

2. A different form of mobility involves promotion or demotion within an occupational group, as when a naval officer receives command of a ship, or a locomotive fireman becomes an engineer.

59

THE SOCIOLOGY OF WORK

3. Another form of vertical mobility within the occupational group is incidental to aging. Each occupational level displays certain characteristic career curves; and in addition, the mere accumulation of seniority represents a significant change in status.

4. A fourth type of vertical mobility is the change in occupational assignment from one generation to another, usually studied as the correlation between the occupations of fathers and sons.

There is still another kind of vertical mobility which is not included in this discussion. It involves the ascent or descent of an entire occupational group — the increasing dignity of nurses or the diminishing prestige of midwives may serve equally well as examples. This is a phenomenon of primary importance but is more conveniently considered as an aspect of occupational change.

Horizontal mobility is a change in function, including both the technical and the social functions which arise from group membership. Here too, it is necessary to distinguish a number of distinct forms:

1. Horizontal mobility of the simplest type involves a change in employment within the same occupation, as when a general practitioner becomes a medical specialist, or an executive is transferred from the production division to the transportation division of the same company.

2. A change in occupation which involves new and different activities is the second type of horizontal mobility. The punch-press operator who becomes a lineman or the toymaker who undertakes to sell insurance are examples.

3. Again, the succession of generations introduces a distinct category of horizontal mobility, in which comparisons must be made between parents and children, rather than between successive states of the individual career.

Ecological mobility may be visualized on the other horizontal axis of our three-dimensional model, and involves two major phenomena:

1. Migration is, strictly speaking, a change of residence and need not necessarily involve any change of occupation, but it is closely associated with occupational shifts of one kind or another. The principal directions of migration are illustrated by the more or less continuous movements from rural areas toward the city, from areas of stable population toward centers of industrial or commercial opportunity, from more densely settled countries toward less densely settled countries, from the center of cities to their suburbs, and (in the United States) from south to north and east to west.

2. There is quite another type of spatial mobility which must be considered among the salient characteristics of any occupation: the amount of travel and the changes in residence or in workplace which are entailed by the occupation itself. All high-status and many low-status occupations are relatively mobile in this sense, and there are a number of callings which are marked by an extreme degree of spatial detachment, such as diplomats, dance-band musicians, and railroad workers.

The reader will have already observed that these nine subtypes of mobility are by no means independent and exclusive; he may have remarked that most job changes involve some change in social status or that vertical mobility between generations implies horizontal mobility as a matter of course, while rural-urban migration invariably involves multiple alterations in the individual's activities.

Each type of mobility may be usefully analyzed by itself.

VERTICAL MOBILITY: CHANGE OF OCCUPATION

In the United States, and to a somewhat lesser extent in other industrialized countries, the beginning of the individual's work history is marked by a period of preliminary and tentative employment, described by Davidson and Anderson [2] as the floundering period and by Miller and Form [3] as the initial work period. In all classes, it is normal for the adolescent to accept a series of low-level jobs (often supplementary to high school or college attendance) which may or may not be connected with his eventual choice of a permanent occupation. The floundering period is partly a trial-and-error experience in which different sorts of employment are sampled. In some instances this period is terminated at the end of an educational curriculum, which confers the qualifications necessary for skilled or professional work. In other cases it may continue for several years; but the typical career pattern includes at least one gratifying ascent from casual work to consequential employment.

Davidson and Anderson, in their first study of the occupational histories of the labor force in San Jose noted above, discovered that for their subjects the median number of permanent occupations (those followed for more than three years consecutively) was 3.1. The median number of jobs held was, of course, very much higher. Confirmatory evidence is found in the work of Miller and Form and others.

While the movement is greatest between related occupations, and ascent or descent to an adjacent level is most frequent, this limitation is by no means absolute. In their comparatively small samples, both of the studies cited found instances of movement across broad ranges of the occupational scale — from lawyer to factory operative, from servant to manufacturer. No combination of occupations in the individual career seems impossible, even those which involve separate courses of apprenticeship. It is not uncommon to discover artisans who have qualified in two quite different skilled trades.

The stability presented by the occupational hierarchy when observed at any given moment is contradicted by the presence of a substantial number of people who follow two or three occupations simultaneously. Certain of these are conventional combinations and are adapted to seasonal conditions: farmer and factory worker, typist and shop clerk. A great many others, however, represent unexpected combinations of talent and opportunity: dentists who play in professional orchestras, grocers who run assay offices, laboratory technicians with secondary jobs as night watchmen, policemen who raise chickens, and draftsmen who supplement their incomes by stevedoring. Then, too, a great many salaried posts require prior qualification in a profession or trade: building inspectors may be required to be carpenters or masons and heavy-appliance salesmen may be recruited from among mechanical engineers. A great deal of vertical mobility represents a gradual change in emphasis, by which a secondary occupation or even a hobby gradually displaces a less profitable primary vocation.

It has been frequently observed that there appears to be more occupational ascent thant descent.[4] Given the conditions of an expanding economy, in which managerial and technical functions are expanding even relatively, this may well be the case. The movement from country to city, the rather low fertility of upper-income families, the increase in average educational achievement, and the progressive assimilation of wage-earning positions into the middle class — all are well-documented trends which favor upward mobility.

In the short run, however, the predominant direction of mobility depends upon the turns and twists of the business cycle. The Anderson and Davidson studies illustrate the catastrophic reductions of occupational status which were commonplace in the early years of the Great Depression. Other studies suggest that the eventual career pattern is strongly affected by the opportunities which are encountered at the outset, so that many of the persons who begin their work lives under the unfavorable auspices of large-scale unemployment never fully recover from the competitive disadvantage imposed upon them.

By far the most important controls imposed upon vertical mobility are found in the internal structure of each occupational group. As Form and Miller point out, "Occupational security is associated with white collar, skilled and foreman positions: insecurity with semi-skilled, unskilled, and personal service." [5] We may go somewhat further, and note the existence of several species of occupational involvement, each of which has different mobility implications. These categories are in some sense the key to the entire analysis of occupational mobility. For the purposes of the present discussion we may distinguish five kinds of occupational situation with respect to involvement.

First, there are the occupations which normally involve a lifetime commitment. These include the free professions — law, medicine, dentistry, architecture, the academic sciences — and certain more obscure specialties such as those of actuaries and plant pathologists. The second large group of permanent occupations are the guild-organized crafts: carpenters, masons, painters, plumbers, steamfitters, roofers, cabinetmakers, electricians, machinists, millwrights, tool and die makers, motor mechanics, and a few others.

Second are the occupations which involve a long-term career for the same employer: in such public organizations as fire departments, post offices, police forces, and civil service systems generally; in the executive levels of very large businesses; in railway employment; and in many varieties of technical engineering.

Third, there are a great many occupational groups so vague as to defy precise definition which nevertheless enjoy a considerable degree of financial security. The careers of agents and brokers (outside large business bureaucracies), small proprietors, artists and entertainers, politicians, and salesmen are characterized by relatively frequent changes of employment and of specific occupational activity, accompanied by a tendency to move between related occupations. It is within this group that the sharpest short-run changes in income and prestige take place, and that the total range of social reward is greatest. It is likely that the highest earned incomes in the United States are received by entertainers and salesmen. At the same time, it is not unusual for members of these occupations to receive zero, or even negative income. Indeed, an individual may approach the two extremes of the total range in two successive years.

Another occupational level within which the specific occupations can scarcely be defined at all is the level of semiskilled manual work and of the service trades. A somewhat greater degree of precision attaches to semiskilled white-collar work. In these cases, the normal career includes frequent changes of employment and of specific activity, with very little security and with comparatively little upward mobility.

Finally, there are the two great reservoirs of manpower: agriculture and unskilled labor, originally the major components of the labor force and still numerically important. Although by no means immobile, laborers are relatively restricted in opportunities for ascent; the two categories represent lifelong statuses for very many persons.

Form and Miller have shown that "once started on an occupational level, a worker tends to remain at that level." [6] Vertical mobility, like other forms of social change, tends to be embodied in specific institutional devices. With increasing bureaucratization and professionalization, the primary type of occupational ascent, which consists of a change to an occupation of clearly higher status, tends to become increasingly rare. The Lynds,[7] Warner,[8] and others have documented the diminishing opportunities for the machine operator to escape to a higher occupational level.

This does not necessarily mean that the total amount of opportunity — if such a quantity could be measured — has diminished. The professions, for example, have been consistently successful in discouraging easy movement into and out of the professional fold. In this sense, opportunities for vertical mobility have been sharply curtailed. On the other hand, the opportunities for advancement within each profession have been multiplied. Wilson describes in detail the elaborate mobility arrangements of university professors,[9] and Hall has analyzed types of medical careers [10] to show how long and well lighted are the paths to professional eminence. This situation, common to all the major professions, tends to be repeated in dozens of other callings, from journalism to tree surgery, which are professionalized to some degree. The relationship between restriction of entry and advancements within an occupation is thoroughly functional. The restriction of numbers is a major factor in improvement of professional status.

Then, too, the establishment of long, regular career sequences in both public and private organizations has vastly enlarged the horizons of the minor functionary. At the same time that manual, service, agricultural, and casual workers have been increasingly restricted by educational and guild barriers, there has been increasing attention given to the establishment of "opportunities for advancement" on the more favored levels. It often happens within the single enterprise that as workmen are increasingly barred from supervisory employment the promotion opportunities for minor supervisors are systematically enlarged.

Vertical mobility of the simplest type, involving a series of different occupations with rapidly increasing or decreasing status (from Ragpicker to Banker) is largely limited to the third of the groups described above — businessmen, small proprietors, some farmers, artists and entertainers, writers and journalists, politicians and salesmen.

This rather miscellaneous assortment of trades actually falls into two categories: on the one hand, those who administer the "business" system and control the exchange process through the manipulation of financial and power symbols; on the other hand, those who dominate the communication processes of society by the creation and manipulation of emotional and aesthetic symbols.

It has already been suggested that many phases of these activities have been bureaucratized: for example, in a very large business, where managerial personnel may operate under the essential conditions of civil service, or in university or government employment, where writers and entertainers may stand on the same footing as technicians. Nevertheless, there remains a very large and important area in which the "free" manipulation of symbols flourishes, and in which the opportunities for the acquisition of power or prestige are virtually unlimited. These conditions rest on certain basic characteristics of our society.

Given the right of private property, and the existence of monetary and market arrangements which enable property to be easily exchanged, stored, transferred, or converted, there is theoretically no limit to the amount of property which an individual can acquire. In the last quarter of the nineteenth century, when these conditions existed almost without qualification, individuals could and did acquire in a few years substantial fractions of the total national wealth. Since then, and particularly during the last twenty years, the manipulability of property symbols has been rather sharply curtailed through such devices as securities regulations and currency controls. The rights of property have been even more drastically affected by income, capital gains, and inheritance taxes; by the regulation of utilities, railroads, and to some extent all other industries in the details of their operation; by labor legislation and negotiation; by the competition of public and quasi-public corporations; by antitrust actions; and in general by the extension of governmental controls over economic activity.

The private concentration of economic power is equally important in limiting financial opportunity. Almost all the heavy industries are closed to new entrants by virtue of existing market arrangements and the enormous capital requirements for effective competition. Most fields of enterprise in the United States, and in the remaining capitalist countries of Europe, are marked by rather rigid power structures, whose net effect is to limit acquisition by newcomers and to strengthen the position of established firms, families, and combinations with the passage of time.

Individuals are, however, somewhat less limited. For reasons which are analyzed later, most bureaucratic structures are capped by a nonbureaucratic elite operating with greater freedom than the lower levels of the organization. Civil service systems usually recognize this explicitly by restricting the application of their rules to all posts *below* a certain rank (approximately that of a bureau chief in the federal civil service).

A certain number of highly mobile individuals move from one employment to another in the upper ranges of large-scale enterprise. But oddly enough, extremely high incomes and extreme increments of personal power are more frequently encountered in medium-scale enterprise and in marginal economic functions, where the necessary conditions persist.

The broker, the salesman, the promotor, the administrator of speculative enterprises, the developer of new products, the retail merchant, and the financial expert, all are among the predominant types of highly mobile businessmen, who normally pass through a long succession of different affiliations in the pursuit of accessible advantage. Such occupational associations as exist in this milieu are graded in terms of financial rank rather than in terms of occupational function, as may be seen by a hasty survey of the commercial associations and lunch clubs in any small city.

The conditions for unlimited vertical mobility in those occupations associated with the communication system are freedom of access to the means of large-scale communication and effective competition for the services of individuals. These conditions are realized, albeit imperfectly, in the major and minor arts, in sports and entertainment, in advertising and the more legitimate forms of journalism, and in certain other fields — such as clothes styling — where direct personal publicity plays an important part.

The "jackpot" occupations, in which immediate fame and fortune may be acquired by the merest hazard, are almost all associated with communication activities. Movie stars represent the most extreme development of this skyrocket mobility, and the mere existence of careers which surpass the Cinderella story has a symbolic importance which has been carefully outlined by the social anthropologists.

The situation of serious artists — particularly writers and musicians — is perhaps more favorable in our society than in any previous one, and for the same reasons. Given mass communication devices which enlarge the potential audience to include almost the entire population, the artist who has achieved a wide reputation through the standard media enjoys a god-like prestige which is readily convertible into cash. True enough, this fame is distributed indiscriminately to cartoonists, evangelists, vitamin faddists, infant orchestra conductors, and canasta experts, but it is none the less real. The sheer magnificence of the rewards offered in these fields, together with the important fact that they are available *immediately* to the fortunate, has attracted toward the arts, serious and trivial, a much larger proportion of the available talent than can possibly be absorbed. It has also created cults whose importance in shaping current thoughtways can scarcely be exaggerated. More than one serious student of the family believes that the major dilemma in our current mores arises from the wishful identifications which almost all adolescent females sustain with the stars of the Hollywood pantheon. Similarly, the cult of the salesman (up to and including the identification of salesmanship with Christianity, or more simply, with Western civilization) still finds a place in the official ideology of American business. The salesman, whose participation in the system of disproportionate reward is based both on mass production and on mass communication is at once a symbol of unlimited opportunity and the bearer of the mystic qualities ascribed to those individuals who can convert their "personalities" into marketable monopolized products.

Politics also involves some elements of the same situation. True enough, the normal political career is a progress through the ranks of a graded bureaucracy; but the intrusion of intensive publicity in campaigns and investigations links the political occupations closely to the media of mass communication.

Thus it happens that the groups most influential in shaping the public mind are constantly confronted in their own experience with examples of extreme vertical mobility, and with the awareness of unlimited opportunity, whereas most people live within a much narrower framework of limited advancement and closely defined possibilities. Certainly, a great deal of industrial and political conflict is the result of the fact that vice-presidents who have been presented at each stage of their careers with well-defined opportunities for promotion cannot easily sympathize with the machine operator's desire for security, and newspaper columnists, whose very presence in that calling usually depends on a series of happy accidents, cannot understand why their readers are more inclined to put their faith in large-scale government than in happy accidents.

VERTICAL MOBILITY: HIERARCHIC PROMOTION

Skyrocket mobility has enormous symbolic significance in our culture. Yet only a small proportion of the labor force is in direct contact with the milieus in which it takes place. Intraoccupational mobility — the career pattern within a single calling and often within a single hierarchy — touches almost everyone directly and includes the selective processes by which power is usually distributed. The operating leadership of any society is largely selected by hierarchic promotion. Hierarchic promotion may involve a partial change in function within an economic organization, as when stock clerks are promoted to buyers and buyers to merchandise managers. It may consist of a simple change of rank, with or without the acquisition of broader functions, as in the army, the Catholic church, or a university. Most simply, it may consist merely of a more lustrous reputation (as in the arts) or a more favorable market position (as in small business). There are many possible combinations of these elements. Each occupational milieu sets the conditions for individual advancement in terms of its own customs and its own requirements.

The essential element in hierarchic promotion is that promotion depends on the judgment, and hence on the good will, of one's superiors. Wherever merit is appraised by agencies outside the occupational framework — the market, the critics, or the record book — the judgment of superiors is of course qualified by these "objective" factors. But even objective achievement usually requires the active cooperation of occupational superiors. This is true in the competitive environment of small business,[11] and is especially marked in the free professions and the arts. In large enterprises of all kinds, hierarchic promotion always represents the principal possibility of self-advancement.

We have already noted that occupations differ sharply with respect to permanence, including some which are normally followed from adolescence to retirement and others which are seldom followed for more than a few days at a time. Similarly, an important difference among business organizations is the variation of turnover. Even within the same trade, and among enterprises of similar scale, turnover rates vary enormously. A department store, for example, may have so little recruitment and dismissal as to approach the situation of a closed bureaucracy, whereas its competitor across the street may treat even executives as temporary help.

The more serious the individual's involvement in his occupational milieu, the greater will be his dependence upon his superiors. In a permanent bureaucracy such as the army or the church, the individual is accompanied through his career by a permanent dossier, so that any offenses against group discipline are remembered forever. In a great many business jobs, and a substantial number of factory employments, skills laboriously acquired are useless outside of the particular market situation or even the particular plant in which they are learned, which again increases dependence.

The effect of this dependence is, in general, to magnify the consequences of errors and malfeasances, and to encourage a high degree of conformity to the will of superiors. This conformity need not be brutally exacted. Many industrial studies have described the exaggerated sensitivity to the boss's behavior which is characteristic of the highly organized work situation.

There have been only a few serious attempts to examine the fuctioning of hierarchic promotion systems, although good descriptions are found scattered through modern fiction, notably in the work of Lewis, Dos Passos, Tolstoi, Balzac, and Romains. This remains an area in which literary insight is far in advance of sociological analysis. The following description is a minor classic of this kind:

Captain Eugene Bidon, of the Engineers, had nothing aggressive or fantastic about him. He had never read Jomini, or Clausewitz, or Moltke, or von der Goltz, or Dragomirov, or Napoleon. He was unfamiliar with the maxim of Foch: "Being disciplined does not mean being silent, avoiding participation, or undertaking only whatever carries no risk of being compromised, nor does it mean the art of evading responsibilities, but rather *acting* to carry out the spirit of the orders received, and finding in oneself by training and reflection the possibility of carrying out these orders." He was a punctual officer, modestly decorative, without imagination or personal opinions, who avoided taking the initiative like the plague. He might have had an equally successful career in civilian life as an accountant, a draftsman, a cashier, or fiscal agent. But, by entering the army, he had by-passed the risks of a civilian career. His employers would not go bankrupt, he would never be laid off, he would have a pension. Besides, his advancement would proceed regularly, without any strenuous activity on his part.

As a subaltern, the captain had learned to respect slightly obsolete material (it delighted him, for example, that a certain type of wagon had been practically unchanged since the time of Napoleon, and that the same old ponton-bridges were still favored for crossing rivers). In the same way, he preferred to cling to theories confirmed in the older wars, telling himself that the army — one of the last bastions of French tradition — had no need of novelties, which undermined the good old teachings, never sufficiently observed, whose spirit one absorbs in twenty years of barracks or office life. Thus, he inspired confidence in his superiors who, as his seniors, were the natural enemies of innovation, and more and more so as they approached retirement age. The old chiefs had the same unfavorable prejudices about modern methods as they held about the young women of the rising generation; they preferred their girl friends of a bygone era, better designed as to breast and haunch.

With Bidon, they said in the Engineers Corps of Grenoble, there's nothing to worry about. Never any trouble.

It was a favorable rating, the best perhaps, and guaranteed Captain Bidon his chance of finishing his career as a high ranking officer in a good branch, even though he was known to write unwillingly. But this difficulty — like a stammering of his pen — had the compensation that he never overwhelmed people with reports and that his activities left only the minimum traces in writing. His superiors were grateful for the assurance that everything would go according to the rules, and would be suitably covered.

At each stage of his career, Capain Bidon had been marvelously the man of his rank, without any vain desire to shine, or any intention to annoy his comrades by advancing too rapidly. Before a superior, he held himself back, as if stricken before the grandeur and the power of the other, and everything in his attitudes expressed the most absolute admiration and approval. It is relevant that an inspector-general had been able to say of him to his colonel:

"He's pretty good, this Lieutenant Bidon. Keeps his mouth shut! Intelligent! Good record?"

"A very good record, General," the colonel answered eagerly, having never noticed Lieutenant Bidon.

"Might be promoted," said the general. "Good material for the cadres."

Lieutenant Bidon's third stripe was the result of this episode, the colonel not being inclined to displease the general. The general, by the way, whose attention was dispersed over a broad population, had completely forgotten Lieutenant Bidon when he wrote "approved" on the colonel's recommendation.

Thus Captain Bidon personified marvelously a type of officer-functionary who prevailed in an army drowsing on its laurels and losing sight of military efficiency, so strongly did it hold the opinion that no enemy would dare to challenge its evident power. He spared nothing to his subordinates of what was necessary to assure his own security, but above that did not require anything but a prudent application of the regulations. For he applied the regulations literally, distrusting imaginative interpretations which rarely accord with the interpretations of those well placed in the hierarchy. Above all, he admired the fact that that great institution, the army, bulwark of all other institutions, rested on visible signs which defied error, of which the most inspired is that the professional intelligence of a man be inscribed on his sleeve and discernable at twenty paces: a sleeve is easier to decipher than a physiognomy. Civilian life mixes persons in a dangerous anonymity, which favors imposture. Nothing of the kind in military life, where a five-strip intelligence cannot possibly be confounded with a two-, three-, or four-stripe intelligence. It is one of the great superiorities of the army to have known how to create simple syntheses, which remain obvious even in the confusion of battle and the hurly-burly of assaults.

Captain Bidon experienced a peaceful satisfaction in sensing in himself the operation of a three-stripe intelligence, after having thought, acted, and obeyed, during long years by means of a one- or two-stripe intelligence. He reflected that his intelligence would increase even more with seniority, and that is another advantage of military over civilian life, where intelligence tends to diminish with age.[12]

The official ideology of any hierarchy necessarily includes the insistence that all promotions are determined by merit and achievement. Popular insight counters with the wistful or derisory observation that all promotions are nepotistic. Both positions are necessarily correct. A functioning hierarchy which wishes to stay in business must necessarily consider the talent of candidates in making its selections. But, even under the most rigorous civil service controls, any such hierarchy will also evaluate the candidate as a potential in-group member, and will therefore give special attention to his congeniality in the broadest sense — a factor which depends upon his ability to conform to the habits and standards of the elders, and also upon the quality of his ancestors, his relatives, and his friends.

The essential reasons for this condition seem to lie in the psychology of group life. As Homans has shown,[13] the mere existence of a face-to-face group presupposes the establishment of group standards, and the continuity of a group depends upon its ability to enforce its standards upon its members. At each hierarchical level certain secondary qualities determine which of a number of equally intelligent or equally efficient candidates for promotion shall be favored. They are by no means the same for all occupations or even for all similar occupations, but general trends can always be discerned. For many centuries, most positions implied or required membership in a particular social class. Even after the disappearance of legally recognized class distinctions in the eighteenth century, historical or imputed membership continued to influence the hierarchical acceptability of individuals. This is still noticeable in certain very specialized institutions — the State Department and investment houses, for example — but for the most part ancestry now figures among the secondary qualities, either as ancestral association with a particular occupation, enterprise, or region (modern corporations take an enormous pride in third-generation employees, and in modern armies, they constitute a caste within a caste),[14] or as nonmembership in certain critical ethnic groups. There are even some occupations, notably the arts, where ancestral distinction is believed to be a hindrance to individual achievement. With the increasing impersonality which marks the modern large-scale organization, the direct inheritance of positions becomes increasingly rare, although by no means insignificant.

Other secondary qualities which typically figure in hierarchic promotion are appearance, skills of sociability (including sexual attractiveness), religious and athletic affiliations, participation in formal and informal associations, miscellaneous talents for oratory, poker, or golf, and judiciously conspicuous consumption.

The most important selective elements, however, are those which have to do with the workings of the hierarchical system itself. Thus, the elders are inclined to select those who are like themselves in general appearance, and who, in addition, have demonstrated specific ability to conform to hierarchic expectations, to render personal services to their sponsors, to conduct themselves prudently in internecine conflicts, and to maintain the interests of the group against all outsiders.

These are relatively simple ends to achieve in a situation where expectations are carefully defined, and so it often occurs that hierarchic candidates compete in terms of neither ability nor secondary qualities, but in terms of sheer volume of work. It is usually in those business organizations which are most stable and least vulnerable to crisis that the lights burn latest in the offices.

The net effect of hierarchical organization is to bring to the fore persons who have carefully shaped themselves to conform precisely to group norms imposed by authority — including such very delicate nuances as the proper choice of ties and the use of appropriate inflections in conversation. Again, the novelists have given us more detail on the workings of this process than other investigators. Such persons will be exceedingly conservative, will hesitate to take unprecedented actions, and will, in general, reserve their heaviest condemnation for those who violate the fraternity rules of their own group. It is precisely in those segments of the society which are dominated by systems of hierarchical promotion that a general indifference to social issues is combined with a defense of group interests so passionate as to mystify the outsider. It may well be that the internal stability of the hierarchical group is achieved, in some sense, at the expense of the larger society. Whether this is the case or not, some effort is usually made to conceal the workings of the hierarchy from the vulgar.

VERTICAL MOBILITY: THE REWARDS OF SENIORITY

It is sometimes difficult to distinguish promotion within a well-established hierarchy from the third type of vertical mobility, that which is incident to the process of aging.

One of the major structural changes in American industry within recent years has been the development of seniority rights on a hitherto unknown scale. This development has given seniority a connotation which is quite new. The modern concept of seniority developed first in those industries — especially railroads and coal mining — where employment is sporadic, with frequent layoffs, but where most of the working force is permanently involved in specific occupations.

Of course, it must be recognized that there are elements of seniority in every system of work organization, and that the predominance of the active elders is characteristic of almost all human groups. On the other hand, seniority as a vested right carries with it a number of novel implications.

The first of these, and the one which presents itself most conspicuously to class-conscious employers, is the fact that a contractually recognized seniority right is an enforceable priority, and hence, in the broadest sense, a property right in the job. Thus, employees have established an indirect form of ownership in industries in which seniority rights determine jobs, hours, wages, and working conditions.

This close tie to a particular job is not an unmixed advantage to the employee, and it is significant that the strongest of the craft unions are able to abandon seniority in prosperous times. Seniority rights are always specific to a given industry, usually to a particular establishment in the industry, and often to a single job. Since he cannot take his seniority rights with him, the worker's mobility is sharply diminished by the existence of a strong seniority system. More accurately, the margin of comparative advantage

73

necessary for a change of employment is widened. For a broad range of semiskilled occupations, seniority rights have become a major deterrent to that kind of horizontal mobility which is otherwise encouraged by the flexibility of the occupational structure on the semiskilled level.

To the extent that the industrial structure discourages individual advancement by promotion, there is a tendency — often conscious — to make the seniority system compensate for the absence of vertical channels. Thus, in the mass-employment heavy industries, which always have severe problems of employee turnover, there is a very steady tendency to increase seniority privileges and also, insofar as it lies within management's power, the prestige of long service. For it is plain that with the acceptance of the fact that factory workers have very little chance of advancement to supervisory positions, attitudes develop which accord genuine respect to seniority, and even to such expressions of managerial motives as the long-service pin.

The question of seniority in a hierarchic system is much more complicated. In the formal study of administration (which is almost always concerned with bureaucracies) there is a generally recognized opposition between "seniority" and "merit." All organizations of this type are likely to confer special privileges on members of long standing, and it is generally felt by administrative experts that seniority is a threat to the effectiveness of a bureaucracy. Thus Moore writes: "The more highly developed is bureaucratic specialization, the more prevalent is trained incapacity, and the less reasonable is a system of promotion by seniority." [15]

But this is to focus attention exclusively on the efficiency of the bureaucracy in day-to-day operation, and to forget that bureaucracies have a legitimate function of maintaining internal stability and continuity. The distinction is important. The most efficient government agencies are by no means the most durable or even the most effective in accomplishing their stated purposes. Many hierarchic systems, including government and educational and business establishments, are able to secure highly skilled labor at a discount by guaranteeing job tenure, which is a special case of seniority right.

Over and beyond any formal system of seniority is the fact that aging is itself a change of status. Even in a loosely organized occupation, there will be a normal career pattern to which the individual's status position is referred for comparison. The same rank held at different ages may carry completely different status implications. It is one thing to be a foreman at 25, and quite another to achieve the post at 60.

The normal career curve is of great significance, even though it is always distorted by the economic and political oscillations which occur during a given span of time. Differences among occupational levels in social reward are most clearly reflected by differences in career curves.

The first curve of this kind was traced half a century ago by Rountree, who constructed a life cycle for the English workman, with three periods of meager subsistence (childhood, early maturity, and old age) separated by two eras of relative prosperity (youth and middle age).[16] There has been very little continuity of investigation, however, and current empirical work is limited to a handful of studies.[17]

All the careers which involve permanent commitments can be represented by an earnings curve which starts at a fairly low level, rises to a peak, and thereafter declines. The higher the status of the group, however, the later in life the peak occurs, and the greater the range from low point to high point. These are differences of a very large order, as social phenomena go. For unskilled labor, the peak is reached in the early twenties, and represents an advantage of less than 50 per cent over the low point. For the learned professions, the peak occurs after the age of sixty, and average earnings at the high point may be ten to twenty times more than those of the low point. Thus the laborer may enter the declining phase of his career before the professional man of the same age has even begun his life work. The extent to which low-status groups are at a disadvantage in their working lives is much better indicated by curves of life earnings than by any direct comparisons of income, which tend to minimize the enormous differences in comfort, convenience, satisfaction, and security that are represented by intervals on the occupational scale.

VERTICAL MOBILITY: BETWEEN GENERATIONS

We have still to consider the type of vertical mobility most often referred to in Sorokin's original discussion and in most subsequent discussions of trends in opportunity: the changes of occupational status which occur from one generation to the next.

It is widely believed that before the Industrial Revolution occupations were smoothly handed down from father to son, and that since that complicated event, each individual has selected his own calling in the light of his own inclinations. A parallel belief is held about the selection of marital partners. Neither opinion is very accurate but, for a number of reasons, the historical study of occupational selection is more difficult than that of marital selection.

In the first place, the grandfathers of most of today's urban workers were farmers. This is so not only because 75 per cent of the population was rural as recently as 1870, but also because of the much higher fertility of farm populations and the perennial replacement of urban "stock" by rural migrants. It is practically impossible to fix the relative status of farmers at a distance of 70 or 80 years, even if there were not a tendency to glorify the social position of one's progenitors. In the United States, this difficulty is compounded by the very large proportion of foreign-born ancestors belonging to different and imperfectly understood agricultural systems.

Secondly, many studies of occupational inheritance have dealt with the father's occupation without taking any notice of the fact that most persons follow several occupations during the course of their lives. A partial solution would be to determine the father's occupation at the same age as the age of the respondent, but this leaves a number of variables uncontrolled, and slurs over the fact that the father's occupation at the time the son chooses his occupation has a more direct significance.

Thirdly, the data on this matter which can be obtained from questionnaires, life histories, or documents are simply not very good. Reports by children on their parents' histories prior to their own maturity are notoriously inaccurate, and it is almost impossible to find data about grandparents worth tabulating. When the ineradicable tendency to exaggerate family status is also taken into account, it is easy to see why so little is known about occupational inheritance.

The occupation which is most frequently inherited is farming, in which the inheritance of property, the usefulness of childhood training, and the immersion of the occupation in a well-defined local culture, all contribute to facilitate the gradual assumption of the parental role. The number of farmers not raised on farms is small; and the number with an urban background is negligible. The same considerations apply, although with less force, to such other rural occupations as fishing and lumbering.

We have already had occasion to mention the small group of strictly hereditary occupations, in which an assortment of very special skills are passed down from generation to generation as family secrets: bell casters, circus performers, croupiers, and chefs, for example. In all these, very early training is essential and the total market is sharply limited.

The most significant of directly inherited urban occupations are those which have a proprietarial element. Retail stores, service enterprises, small factories, sales agencies, truck companies, commercial schools, and similar establishments are very frequently passed from parent to child. Such enterprises typically demand personal supervision and derive much of their value from personal contact. They cannot easily be sold for a price proportionate to their profitability. In addition, the skills required to operate them are relatively specific and best acquired by experience.

Inheritance of professional, craft, and service occupations seems to depend on the extent to which they include a proprietarial element. Occupational inheritance is much more frequent among the children of physicians, who can take over their father's practice intact, than among the children of architects, who cannot. Direct inheritance of crafts is most conspicuous where the children of union members are admitted on specially favorable terms to a partly monopolized occupation.

It may be predicted that wherever a proprietarial element appears, together with the possibility of childhood training or at least early immersion in the occupational culture, the probability of specific inheritance is fairly great. However, it is generally agreed that the more important side of the matter is the inheritance not of specific occupations but of occupational level. Here we find a considerable mass of evidence.

It has long been known that eminent achievement is largely restricted to the children of persons in the higher occupational categories, and it was on such findings that Galton and his numerous followers have founded the case for what might be called the natural selection of elites. Visher [18] studied the occupations of the fathers of persons listed in *Who's Who,* and reported that more than two thirds of them had been in professional or business occupations, while fewer than one half of 1 per cent were unskilled. Schneider obtained similar results in a study of English men of genius and concluded that "the relative number of eminent men a given social class does produce over a period of years must be expressed as a function of the interaction of the forces which lead to permanent stratification and those which compel change in the mode of life of an entire population in time." [19] Form and Miller, in the important study previously referred to, arrive at an even more startling conclusion, although it is based on too small a sample to be accepted without further support. They find that there is a strong tendency for the children of white-collar workers to inherit their father's occupational level or to climb above it, whereas children of manual workers tend to inherit their father's occupational level or fall below it.

The question usually raised is how much of this consistency between generations is attributable to biological differences in capacity, and how much of it is due to differential opportunity. This question is really several separate questions, which need to be approached separately.

It may be asked whether the distribution of ability, as measured by intelligence tests, school achievement, and aptitude inventories, is correlated with parents' occupational status, and if so, how closely. If such a correlation is established, we are faced with the further question of the extent to which such differences are the result of heredity, rather than of home environment. Finally, it remains to be established whether the superior opportunities open to the college-educated, and to the middle class generally, are responsible for the status correlations between generations, and how much must be referred back to native ability.

A variety of studies have demonstrated the correlation between parent's occupation and the intellectual abilities of children. One of the earliest and best of these was incidental to Terman's well-known investigation of a thousand gifted children.[20] The fathers of his subjects had a mean of 12.77 on the Barr scale, corresponding to a primary teacher or a small-town librarian. According to Terman the general population from which the gifted children were drawn had a mean of 7.92, the level of bakers, plasterers, and metal finishers.

Taken together, these studies establish an unequivocal relationship between parental status and scholastic aptitude. However, the effect of these correlations (none of which are extremely high when applied to the population as a whole) is to locate the majority of superior children on the lower occupational levels, where most of them are destined to remain. How much of this difference in intelligence is due to differential heredity and how much to environment is a question too complex (and possibly too meaningless) to consider here.

As to the later association between parents' status and the occupational choices of their children, it would be flying in the face of social reality to deny a phenomenon so easily observed. A curious bit of evidence is furnished by Thorndike's[21] study in the prediction of vocational success. He found that when the analysis of initiatory career patterns was restricted to high school graduates (with the economically privileged college population excluded) there was little or no influence of parental status upon occupational success. Indeed, despite the many instances in which occupational functions are directly inherited, and the numerous circumstances which enable parents to facilitate the placement of their children in advantageous positions, the principal mechanism for the inheritance of occupational level appears to be the educational system.

In a later chapter, we shall examine in detail the ways in which education has displaced birth, marriage, and property-holding, as a determinant of status. Here, it is sufficient to notice that each occupation which adopts definite educational qualifications for admission is thereby removed from the scale of direct vertical mobility. Such occupations, ranging from anesthetist to zoo keeper, are now numbered by the hundreds, and as part of a general trend toward professionalization, many new sequences of required vocational preparation are devised each year.

To the extent that such an educational course involves serious effort, and is impersonally administered, the occupation will be increasingly "open." This system of occupational selection has many historical precedents. The famous Chinese system of examination for the mandarinate, though often corrupted, established a channel of free access to the ruling class which functioned for many centuries. Similarly, the priesthood in the Middle Ages offered striking opportunities for individual mobility in the midst of a rigorously stratified society, although the net effect was minimized by the celibacy of the clergy.

There can be no serious doubt that within the last half-century, formal education has become the principal channel of upward mobility in the Western world. The distribution of educational opportunities thus becomes a crucial factor in determining how much movement between social classes will be permitted.[22] The distribution of these opportunities is still far from being egalitarian. In 1947, the President's Commission on Higher Education found that, "For the great majority of our boys and girls, the kind and amount of education they may hope to attain depends, not on their own abilities, but on the family or community into which they happened to be born or, worse still, on the color of their skin or the religion of their parents."[23]

The commission went on to suggest that a major revision of the existing procedures for financing higher education will be required if higher education is ever to be distributed on a merit basis. There appears to be some general movement in that direction. The G.I. Bill of Rights, for example, introduced en masse into the colleges entire social groups who had been virtually excluded before. The development of junior colleges has had a parallel effect. It is curious to note that while the unequal distribution of educational opportunities is often defended on the basis of an assumed

THE SOCIOLOGY OF WORK

correspondence between biological worth and social rank, each enlargement of opportunity has disclosed a new population of students, fully as competent as those who were educated before.

NOTES

[1] Pitirim A. Sorokin, *Society, Culture and Personality: Their Structure and Dynamics* (New York: Harper and Brothers, 1947).

[2] Percy E. Davidson and Dewey Anderson, *Ballots and the Democratic Class Struggle: A Study in the Background of Political Education* (Stanford, Calif.: Stanford University Press, 1943).

[3] Delbert C. Miller and William H. Form, *Industrial Sociology: An Introduction to the Sociology of Work Relations* (New York: Harper and Brothers, 1951); Form and Miller, "Occupational Career Pattern as a Sociological Instrument," *American Journal of Sociology*, vol. 54, January 1949.

[4] Lewis and Maude, however, have recently described the British occupational structure largely in terms of descent. Roy Lewis and Angus Maude, *The English Middle Classes* (New York: Alfred A. Knopf, 1950).

[5] Form and Miller, "Occupational Career Pattern as a Sociological Instrument," p. 319.

[6] *Ibid.*, p. 328.

[7] Robert S. and Helen M. Lynd, *Middletown* (New York: Harcourt, Brace & Company, 1929).

[8] W. Lloyd Warner, Robert J. Havighurst, and Martin B. Loeb, *Who Shall Be Educated?* (New York: Harper and Brothers, 1944).

[9] Logan Wilson, *The Academic Man: A Study in the Sociology of a Profession* (New York: Oxford University Press, 1942).

[10] Oswald Hall, "The Informal Organization of the Medical Profession," *Canadian Journal of Economics and Political Science*, vol. 12, 1946; "Types of Medical Careers," *American Journal of Sociology*, vol. 55, November 1949; "The Stages of a Medical Career," *American Journal of Sociology*, vol. 53, January 1948.

[11] See the masterly description of Babbitt's relationship to William Washington Eathorne in Sinclair Lewis' *Babbitt* (New York: Harcourt, Brace & Company, 1922).

[12] Gabriel Chevallier, *Les Héritiers Euffe* (Paris: Presses Universitaires de France, 1945), pp. 167–171. My translation.

[13] George C. Homans, *The Human Group* (New York: Harper and Brothers, 1951).

[14] Hugh Mullan, "The Regular Service Myth," *American Journal of Sociology*, vol. 53, January 1948.

[15] Wilbert E. Moore, *Industrial Relations and the Social Order* (New York: The Macmillan Company, 1946), p. 157.

[16] B. S. Rountree, *Poverty: A Study of Town Life* (London: The Macmillan Company, 1901), p. 137, "Diagram Showing Alternate Periods of Want and Comparative Plenty in the Life of a Laborer."

[17] Louis I. Dublin and Alfred J. Lotka, *The Money Value of a Man* (rev. ed.; New York: The Ronald Press Company, 1946).

[18] Stephen S. Visher, "Occupations as Shown in Who's Who," *American Journal of Sociology*, vol. 30, March 1925; "Environmental Backgrounds of Leading American Scientists," *American Sociological Review*, vol. 13, February 1948.

[19] Joseph Schneider, "The Definition of Eminence and the Social Origins of Famous English Men of Genius," *American Sociological Review*, vol. 3, December 1938.

[20] Lewis M. Terman, *Genetic Studies of Genius,* Vol. 1, *Mental and Physical Traits of a Thousand Gifted Children,* by Lewis M. Terman and others (2nd ed.; Stanford, Calif.: Stanford University Press, 1926). See also Mapheus Smith, "University Student Intelligence and Occupation of Father," *American Sociological Review,* vol. 7, December 1942; Martin L. Reymert and John Frings, "Children's Intelligence in Relation to Occupation of Father," *American Journal of Sociology,* vol. 41, November 1936.

[21] Edward L. Thorndike and others, *Prediction of Vocational Success* (New York: The Commonwealth Fund, 1934).

[22] Warner, Havighurst, and Loeb, *Who Shall Be Educated?*

[23] President's Commission on Higher Education, *Higher Education for American Democracy* (New York: Harper and Brothers, 1947), p. 27.

CHAPTER 4

OTHER MOBILITIES

Let us honor if we can
The vertical man
Though we value none
But the horizontal one.

W. H. AUDEN

HORIZONTAL MOBILITY

IN AN excellent volume of autobiographies collected by the Federal Writers' Project is the life story of a man, then in his thirties, who had started his career as a sweeper in a cotton mill just before the age of 11.[1]Thereafter, he held this series of jobs:

Doffer boy: A mill job — taking off full quills and putting on empty ones.

Spinner: Operating spinning machines.

Inspector: Inspecting finished cloth.

Calendar man: Recording the quantity of cloth produced — a white-collar job on the shop floor.

Furniture salesman: In a small department store.

Assistant undertaker: Learning the trade of embalming .

Soda clerk: In a drugstore.

Electrician's helper: Working for a contractor on the installation of conduits.

Evangelist's chauffeur: Assisting an Episcopal revivalist.

Student, lay-reader, Sunday school teacher: A systematic preparation for the ministry which was never completed.

Candy-maker: In a booth at Coney Island.

Salesman: Selling newspaper subscriptions, candy, and furniture polish, each under a different arrangement.

Candy-maker: In a small factory.

Contact man: Locating business for an insurance broker.

Reporter: And general factotum on a small, unsuccessful weekly newspaper.

Dry-cleaning solicitor: Door-to-door canvassing.

Battery filler: Back in the mill, winding thread.
Insurance agent: Selling insurance on commission.
Cloth doffer: Back to the same mill again.
Timekeeper: Promoted in the mill.
Learner-weaver: Demoted for union activity.
Stores clerk: Works Project Administration.

This career is not unusual. Anyone who has examined personnel files and social agency records, or interviewed candidates for semiskilled employment, is aware of the vast amount of mobility in the occupational histories of those who never find their calling. The record presented here illustrates very aptly several of the elements which characterize horizontal mobility.

One question which presents itself is whether such a history reflects personal disorganization. Employment offices, credit departments, social workers, and the police are inclined to look askance at the mobile individual. But in the absence of any evidence about our subject's possible neurotic traits, the history given above may represent a genuine effort to escape from the narrow conditions of a millhand's life. In a more prosperous era, or merely with better luck, the attempt might well have succeeded.

The narrator was himself aware of this question: "You notice every time I quit one job and went to another one I gotta raise. Maybe that's one reason I quit so many. Of course the accusation might be raised that if I'd stuck to one job I would have made more of a success." [2]

There is such a thing as pathological mobility. The "floater" or the "drifter" who moves from job to job under the pressure of his own restlessness is a familiar figure everywhere, and sometimes appears in responsible positions. The floater is often a rural migrant who never established very deep roots in the city. He is often an alcoholic. The records of transient shelters reveal the existence of a considerable population of middle-aged men who have not had a fixed residence or a definite occupation since their youth.

When this wanderlust is not too acute, it is hardly to be distinguished from the restlessness of the pioneer and the curiosity of the settler. The drifter is often not clearly different from the ambitious man who wanders in search of opportunity.

To classify any given degree of horizontal mobility as normal or abnormal is very difficult. We would need to know the normal rate of job change for a given class and region before attempting anything of the sort. Even then, it would be far more useful to regard as pathologically mobile only those in whose histories the abandonment of job after job is clearly a self-destructive device.

The determination of a normal or average rate of job change depends on the classification of moves within the same general field. Although the personnel men classify a hundred-odd positions in a cotton mill, it is unrealistic to suppose that each of them is a separate occupation. The dynamics of circulation from one job to another within the same establishment are properly viewed as part of the working situation; they do not affect the occupational environment — that of a millhand — or the basic relationship to the world outside.

Most workers who move rapidly through a variety of occupations may be identified in terms of a basic trade, at which they have acquired considerable skill, and to which they may return from time to time when other alternatives are lacking. In this the history cited above is typical of the general American pattern of horizontal mobility. It is probable that in the subsequent occupational history of our subject, he was again employed as a mill operative, and very likely as a candy-maker too.

There is still another way in which the career sequence we have been discussing is illustrative. The white-collar occupations open to the untrained include a very large number of activities. This broad fringe of unstandardized occupations, with its salesmen, dealers, and small enterprisers, is marked by rapid mobility — both horizontal and vertical. Important changes of occupational level are very likely to involve a preliminary sojourn in this commercial shadowland, where the printing of a business card is the purchase of a lottery ticket for those attempting to escape from a marginal position.

In considering horizontal mobility, as in the previous discussion of vertical mobility, we are again confronted with a set of occupational conditions based partly on custom and partly on technical requirements.

Near the midpoint of the occupational status scale, where white-collar and manual levels overlap, there are a vast number of employments which are usually called "semiskilled." As a matter of fact, most of them cannot be readily evaluated in terms of skill. Their common characteristic is that no lengthy experience is required to perform the work, and that movement from one occupation to another is easy and frequent. Indeed, the mark of a semiskilled occupation is its vagueness. Unlike the higher and lower portions of the scale, this great central cluster of factory and office jobs is not clearly compartmentalized. Lifetime involvement in a job is rare. Men and women perform comparable work under comparable conditions. Job titles do not correspond to organized social groupings; and each occupation merges into many others. All these factors together contribute to the very high and sustained rate of horizontal mobility which is characteristic of semiskilled workers.

Although very little training is required, most semiskilled jobs do call for some aptitude and for a fairly high level of general education. As Thorstein Veblen pointed out in *The Instinct of Workmanship*: "In the new era the stress falls rather more decidedly on general intelligence and information, as contrasted with detail mastery of the minutiae of a trade; so that familiarity with the commonplace technological knowledge of the time is rather more imperative a requirement under the machine technology than under that of handicraft." [3]

Increasingly, a high school diploma is the prerequisite for admission to semiskilled work. The characteristic jobs of machine operators in modern factories, of clerical workers in large offices, and of sales clerks, inspectors, and other minor functionaries require a general familiarity with technical and commercial operations, together with a minimum command of the number system, the written language, and the technic of operating such devices as automobiles and cash registers. Although the emphasis upon mechanical insight and manual dexterity is greater in the factory trades than in the office jobs, the two broad branches of semiskilled work tend to become increasingly alike in many ways. Movement from one to the other takes place very readily. Tests carefully devised to measure clerical aptitude sometimes turn out to be better indicators of mechanical aptitude, and vice versa.[4] This is apparently explained by the fact that the tests are patterned after operations actually required in typical jobs, and that the operations required in machine production and clerical work are often very similar.

The modern technics of job classification and personnel selection, developed in connection with large-scale production, are designed above all to facilitate the interchangeability of personnel. One method of ensuring interchangeability is to reduce each complex operation to a series of simple operations which require no extraordinary ability. When this is done, an automatic effect is to standardize output throughout the series of related operations at a point well below the maximum output of which individual workers might be capable. At the same time, the formal qualifications required for employment are standardized by the educational process, so that there are comparatively few differences that matter between one worker and another.

Under these circumstances, the few differentiating factors which do affect the individual's career assume a special importance. Aside from age, sex, race, ethnic affiliation, and union membership, whose weighting depends upon the local industrial environment, the most important differentiating factors arise out of personal relationships.

Because most semiskilled work is sufficiently routinized to become partly or wholly autonomic, and because it is usually performed in a group which comes to control the output as well as the attitudes of its members, personal relationships will tend to dominate the working situation. Friendships and enmities, conversation and play, make up the positive content of the working day. The individual's chances for advancement, or for the good opinion of his fellows, depend much more upon his personal relationships than upon his work performance, whose variability is strictly limited. There are no virtuosi on the automatic sewing machine. Even where the design of the machinery permits outstanding performance, the design of the social system does not. A long series of studies by industrial sociologists has disclosed that the informal limitation on output by the work group is a normal aspect of mass production.

Personal relationships, although always important, are not always effective means of adjustment to office or factory. Most semiskilled operations are performed in large establishments where close ties between employee and supervisor are inhibited by the sheer mass of the organization, and the stability of the work group is continually threatened by changes in the processes of production. Even the union may be a large-scale organization of forbidding impersonality as seen from the shop floor. Katherine Archibald has given us a vivid picture of the social jungle created when these typical conditions were carried to an extreme in the wartime shipyard where she worked.[5]

It is this very lack of opportunity which makes possible, and indeed encourages, a high rate of horizontal mobility. In many kinds of semiskilled employment in factories, shops, and offices, it is almost impossible for the individual employee to acquire a vested interest in remaining where he is. He is too easily replaceable to be highly valued; but by the same token he will be equally valuable across the street or in California.

OTHER MOBILITIES

There are some other reasons why the semiskilled worker is predisposed to change jobs on slight provocation or none at all. Much of the work he does is overpoweringly monotonous so that a change of scene is welcomed. The emphasis on personal relationships often develops considerable frustration on the part of those rejected or excluded from a group. The opportunities will seldom be the same in one plant as in another at the same time.

No one has ever computed a national employment turnover rate, but the available statistics are suggestive. Turnover rates as high as 200 per cent per year are not uncommon in heavy industry. The monthly separation rates for all manufacturing industries, as computed by the Bureau of Labor Statistics, have ranged in recent years from a high of 17.9 per cent in August 1945 to a low of 2.8 per cent in April 1950. In the long run, the number of voluntary terminations is slightly greater than the number of layoffs. In 1950, which had the lowest turnover rates in many years, the cumulative total percentage of separations for manufacturing industries was 41.6 per cent, of which 13.1 per cent were layoffs.[6]

The personnel office of an American company may require twenty interviewers, while a European plant of the same size and type would not be able to keep any full-time interviewers occupied. A single large corporation in the electrical industry, with a history of fairly stable labor relations, estimates its hiring rate as one factory or office employee per minute throughout the working year. Among the technical and executive personnel of this same company, the cumulative rate of voluntary termination is less than 2 per cent per year. The sociology of organization presents no stranger spectacle than the cooperation of the executive and semiskilled employees of this company within a common enterprise. The members of one group are almost as firmly committed to a lifetime affiliation as the members of a monastic order. Most of them eventually retire after thirty to forty years of consecutive employment with the company. The other group is a stream of casual passers-by, who average fewer than 200 days of consecutive employment.

A considerable proportion of terminations continue to be involuntary. Semiskilled employees, although somewhat better protected than formerly against dismissal, are mostly liable to layoff on short notice. Since the advent of union grievance agreements, very few of these layoffs are disciplinary. They arise from the routine exigencies of the business: a shutdown for repairs, a fall in orders, the slack season, or an economy drive at the

87

end of the fiscal year. Such a procedure tends to disrupt whatever stable working relationships have formed within the organization, and to emphasize the transitory and impersonal connection of the employee with the firm. Whether the right of casual layoff is advantageous to management or not is debatable, but it is generally thought to be.

SPATIAL MOBILITY

The third dimension of occupational mobility is sometimes denoted as spatial mobility, and includes two quite different things: the mobility involved in migration from place to place, and the mobility involved in the performance of work which is not attached to a single work site. The first of these subjects can be treated under the general heading of Migration and the second under the general heading of Transiency, although neither term is absolutely precise. There is an impressive body of accurate data available on both matters. Indeed the study of migration is probably as far advanced as any other branch of the social sciences.

MIGRATION

Certain constants may be observed at once wherever migration occurs. The tide of migration tends to flow from areas of high fertility to areas of low fertility, and in the direction of economic opportunity. The most systematic reflections on this subject are found in two classic studies: Ravenstein's investigation of population movements in England and Wales in the 1880s [7] and Stouffer's study of residential movement in Cleveland, published in 1940. [8] Ravenstein enunciated seven laws (we should probably call them trends today) that described his data, of which the most important are these: that migration proceeds principally by small steps (the leapfrog principle); that each main current of migration produces an important countercurrent so that a very large total movement is necessary to produce significant changes in the distribution of population; that inhabitants of towns are less migrant than those of the country; that the male is less migrant than the female; and that long-distance migrants go by preference to the great metropolitan centers.

Stouffer's hypothesis, which he calls the law of intervening opportunities, is expressed by the formula $M = I/D$ which states that the number of migrants between any two points is inversely proportional to the distance and directly proportional to the number of intervening opportunities. The formula has been several times tested and appears to conform reasonably well to the observed facts. Its chief limitation is obvious; the measurement of "opportunities" is not easy.

These principles and their more detailed extensions account for the location of migratory movements. They do not tell us very much about the amount of migration that will take place. To do this, it is necessary to take into account basic attitudes and values which are exceedingly complex. Thus, even with extreme conditions of population pressure (Push) and availability of resources (Pull) the Japanese government was unable to promote any large-scale migration to the undeveloped colonial territories it acquired between 1900 and 1941. Similarly, although France sustained much greater damage during World War II than the United States, it is still possible to use the French census of 1936 for sampling purposes in 1954, while because of internal migration, the United States census of 1940 was mostly of historic interest by 1943.

The findings about migration in the United States cannot therefore be generalized to include other countries, or even other highly industrialized countries. A very high degree of spatial mobility is part of our folkways, and the arrangements which permit and encourage frequent changes of residence are incorporated in our legal and commercial systems.

Nearly two thirds of the American population changed residence between April 1935 and April 1940. More than 15 million families moved from one county to another in these five years of relative stability. It is also estimated that 15 million families moved from one county to another in the two years 1942–1943, and that interstate migration in the decade 1940–1950 involved nearly a third of the total population.

These figures are particularly striking because it has often been assumed that the era of large-scale migration came to an end with the final disappearance of the agricultural frontier. It now appears, on the contrary, that the cultural set in the United States is still so favorable to migration that comparatively small differentials in opportunity may provoke major population movements. Rural–urban migration and east–west migration are continuing processes which have been going on steadily, although at fluctuating rates, since the early settlement of the Atlantic Seaboard. Within these broad tendencies, each period develops local movements, such as the migration of rural southern Negroes to New York and Chicago which began in the early 1920s and still continues at a reduced rate, the rural depopulation of the Great Plains in the thirties, and the movement of midwestern urban workers to the boom cities of Texas and the Pacific Coast in the forties.

Some direct consequences of migration may be observed by comparing the occupational distributions of metropolitan centers which have been gaining population rapidly with those which have been losing. These differences are illuminating, but less extensive than might have been expected. There are several reasons why migration does not affect the occupational structure more drastically. In the first place, a very large proportion of migrants are young people who have not yet established an occupational identification. In the second place, migration now occurs so quickly after the opportunity is perceived that differential opportunities do not last long enough to create any permanent changes in occupational patterns. Finally, the economic cultures created in the new centers have not differed very significantly from those left behind. Recent migration has been related to such background factors as the southern segregation system, the increasing mechanization of agriculture, the dispersal of war plants for security reasons, the development of hydroelectric power, and shortages of housing, rather than to the growth of new kinds of production.

In general, the propensity to long-distance migration is inversely correlated with occupational status. There is nothing mysterious about this phenomenon. The people most likely to migrate are those whose status is least dependent upon their ties in the local community, who can do so with the minimum of inconvenience and the least settlement of affairs, who have universally salable skills and no immovable property. This brings us back to the two large groups of factory operatives and clerical workers, and as a matter of fact it is they who predominate in large population shifts.

It is partly because of the resistance to migration in other occupational groups that rapidly growing centers tend to be inadequately provided with professional and personal services, underdeveloped commercially, and especially short of skilled workmen and technicians. Many of the cities which attracted migration in the early forties retained for several years afterward some of the atmosphere of temporary bivouacs, with genuine problems of health, government, education, protection, and assimilation.

Aside from these general aspects of migration, there is some reason to think that a well-defined system of purposive migration forms an important part of the institutional structure for many occupations which are ordinarily envisaged as stable. Thus, Rodehaver and Smith found a high incidence of migration among clergymen, but noted that it was higher in congregational denominations than in those having an episcopal hierarchy, and that the objective result of success-seeking migration was very frequently the achievement of the projected goal.[9] Unfortunately, there is not yet enough evidence on this kind of migration to support any generalizations.

TRANSIENCY

The migratory laborer, variously known as the hobo, tramp, transient, bum, or stiff, represents a special case of spatial mobility. The migratory laborer is a wanderer, following a definite traverse. Unlike the ordinary migrant, who detaches himself from one community only to join another, the migratory laborer follows a way of life which bars him from membership in any community.

This is a very ancient phenomenon. Most settled societies recognize the professional wanderer. The Romany gypsies have been a wandering caste throughout Europe for centuries. The more stable the host society, the more clearly differentiated the migratory population tends to become. Homelessness has always been a legitimate status in the United States, and the hobo has a long history and a distinctive culture pattern. During lean years, the rather precarious institutions of Hobohemia — as Nels Anderson called it — have always been able to accommodate an enormous number of newcomers, driven by poverty and unemployment to seek a limited fortune on the road. As it could be described in 1940, freight-riding was still a large-scale phenomenon: Between ten and twenty thousand illegal train riders were apprehended daily on American railroads. Between two and three thousand were killed every year between 1920 and 1940, and a somewhat greater number were injured. Estimates of the total population varied from 300,000 to 3,000,000.[10]

This isolated world, with its special attitudes toward organized society, has been explored by many writers at different periods. Most of them have underlined the misery of the wanderer and the harsh treatment he receives as an outcast. Yet Hobohemia, with its flophouses, cheap restaurants, ten-cent saloons, pawnshops, burlesque shows, all-night movies, second-hand stores, fundamentalist missions, railroad routes, recruiting offices, jungles, park benches, and barber schools, represents something more than a simple reaction to poverty. It is linked to an economic need which has now persisted for many decades, and which has enabled it to serve successively such diverse clients as the old-time lumberjacks, the bindle-stiffs of the Dakota wheatfields, the railroad laborers of the twenties, the boy and girl tramps of the early thirties, Steinbeck's Oakies, soldiers on war-time leave, and the social security pensioners who make up the bulk of its permanent population today.

Historically, Hobohemia has sheltered four distinct populations and its continued existence suggests that these have by no means disappeared. Before the mechanization of grain harvesting and handling, tens of thousands of bindle-stiffs followed the wheat harvests north and west from Illinois. The labor requirements so far exceeded the resources of the local population that, except in the worst years, migratory labor enjoyed a favorable market; wages were high and working conditions fairly good — at least to the extent that the harvester's meals have become legendary. Some vestiges of this great annual circuit persist today on a scale just sufficient to afford strenuous employment to college athletes during the summer vacations. A similar migratory circuit connects the canneries up and down the Pacific Coast, particularly those which handle such highly seasonal products as the salmon catch. Heavy concentrations of migratory labor are found in the orchards and vineyards of California and Oregon, and in the irrigated fields of the dry Southwest. McWilliams [11] and other careful observers have documented the plight of these unhappy people and there is a huge literature ranging from the poetic to the bureaucratic about the million and a half families who represent the most harshly exploited sector of the national labor force.

The second group of occupations represented in Hobohemia are those which are highly seasonal without being continuously migratory. The classic example was that of the old-time lumberman, whose work stopped with the first snow, and who then went down to the city to winter up. Farming is to some extent such an occupation, and there still remain some farm-hands who hire out only for the growing months. A great deal of road and bridge construction, strip mining, reforestation, and urban construction falls into this same category.

The third group are the travelers. Given the great area of the United States, the maintenance of mobility at the levels indicated previously requires many alternate varieties of transportation, and tourist accommodations to suit all purses, even those completely empty. An extraordinary number of social devices to facilitate low-cost travel have been developed, and the importance of these has never been properly recognized. It is significant that those credentials which facilitate individual mobility (diplomas, degrees, apprenticeship certificates, social security cards, veterans' papers, etc.) are generally transferable from one state to another without formality, whereas those negative credentials which in other countries hinder mobility (police records, social agency files, and credit ratings) are generally nontransferable except in extreme cases.

There are a variety of transportation alternatives ranging from first-class airline tickets down through day coaches, unapproved bus lines, share-the-ride arrangements, hitchhiking, and freight-riding. Since a temporary fall to the status of hobo involves no ear-cropping or other permanent disadvantage, a great many persons for whom migration would otherwise be prohibitively expensive avail themselves of the accommodations offered by Hobohemia, and the corresponding modes of transportation.

Finally, there are the unemployed, 'the unemployable, and the partially unemployable. None of these categories is absolute. The unemployable include the superannuated, the physically and mentally handicapped, and a large number of alcoholics. The partially unemployable include the very young, the illiterates, the emotionally unstable, members of minority groups, and those whose trade is closed to them in the locality in which they are residing.

During periods of large-scale unemployment, a very large proportion of the labor force becomes at least partly unemployable. A few years ago, the superannuation of factory workers who had not yet reached early middle age aroused national concern. Many firms adopted maximum hiring ages as low as 35, while others, in a frenzy of nervous self-interest, began superannuation layoffs twenty years before the normal age of retirement. The situation reflected the enormous surplus of labor then in the market. On the other hand, even chronic alcoholics, whose unsteady attendance is likely to produce a negative employment record, become highly employable when labor is in short supply.

There is no clear line of demarcation between the partly and the totally unemployable. Those who are far beyond the usual working age, acutely and chronically alcoholic, or very severely handicapped tend in time to be institutionalized, so that they are never more than a small proportion of this marginal group. In most parts of the country, it is the partly employable who provide the reservoir of casual day labor. There is usually an area which serves as a rendezvous for employers and workers, employment is normally for one day, and payment is made at quitting time. The work consists of clean-up jobs, large-scale moving, ditching and landscaping, and the like. It is these marginal groups, rather than Edwards' "servant

93

classes," or the "unskilled laborers" of other occupational scales, who stand on the bottom rung of the ladder.

A labor force which is active only part of the year represents a diseconomy. The conflict of interest between employers and their workers will be especially sharp, since in sharply seasonal activities, the employer may be forced to pay premium wages to attract the labor he needs for a brief period, whereas the worker may not be employed for a large enough part of the year to assure his bare subsistence. It is not surprising that the only frankly revolutionary labor movement in American history, the I.W.W., found most of its strength among migratory workers.

Under favorable circumstances, working conditions may be fair. In the early days of the wheat circuit, almost optimum conditions obtained. The work was sufficiently muscular to exclude women and children, and, if not skilled, at least required strength and alertness. The circuit was long, and there was no attempt to coerce the harvest hands either by force or by quasi-legal pretext.

Given the fundamentally acute conflict of interest which usually exists, however, and the absence of moderating social ties between employers and workers in this field, the question of bargaining power is crucial. It is illuminating to examine the elements which alter bargaining power, and then to apply the findings to the situation of migratory agricultural laborers in the West and Southwest. From the power standpoint, workers are at a disadvantage in any situation where men can be replaced — even at a lower efficiency — by women. Women will accept lower wages, are less amenable to organization (for reasons which are examined more closely in a later chapter), are more likely to accept authority as embodied in foremen and supervisors, and are usually in long supply in the locality. Thus, cannery workers have traditionally been somewhat underpaid and underprivileged.

Where children may also substitute for adults, all these considerations apply with redoubled force. In addition, family groups enjoy much less freedom of action than single individuals. Their requirements for food, shelter, and other facilities are less elastic, their logistics are more complicated, and their needs more urgent. Family groups are not well qualified to take risks when separated from a local community.

It may therefore be safely predicted that any migratory labor force consisting of families will be in a specially vulnerable position. Such a group may be additionally weakened by increasing their separation from civil society. This may be assured by the selection of a population who by race, assumed race, nationality, language, religion, or a combination of these are barred from forming close ties with the resident community. When to this general disadvantage are added special devices like legal segregation, and punitive action by the police, it is easy to see why the situation of the Californian fieldhand has varied from miserable to desperate.

Migratory farm labor as it exists in the West and Southwest is in a sense an anachronism. There has been no shortage of industrial employment for more than a decade and the going industrial wage is intended to support the wage earner and his family. There is thus no motive for the migratory fruit picker to continue as a fruit picker unless, like the Mexican, he is liable to expulsion from the country or, like the Filipino, is barred by preju- dice — partly contrived for this purpose — from work in the factory. With the passage of time, it has been necessary to look further and further afield for new recruits. Yet it would appear that this last of the great agricultural circuits must give way before the forces now in operation and change its technology sufficiently to operate with a resident labor force.

The case of the partly unemployable is quite different. In an industrial economy there will probably always be a considerable population of per- sons marginal to the labor force. Many of these will be homeless, or at least unattached to a family or community. For the economic system as a whole, the situation is in reasonable balance. The demand for casual labor is per- ennial, and has been fairly well matched to the supply, so that the market rate for casual labor has not been far from the average hourly factory wage. Nevertheless, this balance has certain aspects which are socially patho- logical. The most serious of these problems is currently that of the social security pensioners. The accident of inflation has reduced the subsistence income provided for retirement under social security to a level where sub- sistence is only possible in Hobohemia. Moreover, although on a more modest scale than before, involuntary superannuation still occurs, as when industrial employees over fifty are unable to find new employment.

Needless to say, these economically marginal occupations are character- ized by a high degree of transiency with respect to social identification. It is difficult to disentangle the consequences of transiency from the conse- quences of poverty, dependence, old age, and isolation. It will therefore be more instructive to examine a number of occupations of moderately high status which also are transient but are economically secure. Among the extreme cases are dance-band musicians, journeymen potters, professional thieves, and railroad men.[12] The professional thieves are not included here for amusement, but because they represent a particularly high degree of marginality, sharing the fundamental values of the society, but centering their lives around antisocial acts. If Sutherland's analysis is to be taken seriously, the thieves are a fundamentally orderly population.

In all these occupations, almost everyone is certain of *not* remaining in the same community for any length of time. In all four examples, perhaps by coincidence, the work itself requires an abnormal distribution of time, being largely performed at night. In each case the nature of the work requires interaction with a great many unrelated strangers, and with a certain number of unacquainted colleagues.

The transient railroad men studied by Cottrell [13] do not usually buy their houses; they therefore do not spend their incomes on home furnishings. They do not seem to live as well as their neighbors. But since their incomes are fairly high, they dress better and travel more than their neighbors; their children have more expensive toys. Their style of life, as expressed in consumption, separates them from the community.

They work late hours, and irregularly, so that participation in community organizations — parents' associations, welfare leagues, political clubs, or even pool halls — is difficult for them. If they do participate, it is impracticable for them to guarantee regular attendance, so that they do not hold office or assume continuous functions.

Even if it were feasible for these families to associate more closely with the local community, it is not certain that they would want to do so. In the first place, there is hardly any question for them of lifelong ties, except at great cost. A man who wants to get ahead must move from town to. town and from one division to another. Because they travel more, know more people, and live on a different time-scale than those in other occupations, their ideas are not small-town ideas, and their attitudes are less fixed.

Finally, it is significant that railroad people accord a higher prestige to their own occupation than other people do. This is an almost universal tendency, of course, but it seems to be more marked in psychologically mobile occupations. Railroading is something more than an occupation. Like thieving and music, it is a world by itself, with its own literature and mythology, with an irrational system of status which is unintelligible to the outsider, and a complicated rule book for distributing responsibilities and rewards. Like any transportation network, the railroads live by communication — both formal and informal — and there is a great deal for a man to hear. Railroad people often find railroad people more interesting than anyone else.

Even from this hasty summary, it will be seen how different are horizontal mobility between occupations and transiency as an occupational characteristic. While horizontal mobility tends to destroy occupational identifications and to substitute new ones, the necessity of close and continuous communication in an established transient occupation leads to a remarkably coherent and even rigid occupational structure, in which the following elements are generally present:

1. A considerable degree of in-group solidarity, which includes pride in the métier, readiness to band together for common interest or common defense, and a corresponding disinclination to associate with outsiders. This is hardly more marked for the professional thieves than for the railroaders, journeymen potters, and dance-band musicians.

2. A well-defined status system, interior to the occupation, relatively unfamiliar to outsiders, and marked by a good deal of gratuitous elaboration. There are several reasons why this is so. In the first place, the members of these groups have less-than-normal participation in the society at large. They are therefore driven back upon the resources of their subculture. Then, too, the privileges and the occupational intimacy extended to peers imply a system of identification which is fairly precise. It is essential to have a set of recognition signs which cannot be easily counterfeited. Finally, all these occupations require frequent choices of partners, companions, employees, and associates. The formal expression of preference for a particular partner has long been one of the conspicuous singularities of work assignment on the railroads. Such choices are vastly facilitated by an exact and even arbitrary stratification.

3. The remarkable development of internal communication is similarly explained. All the occupations cited have developed a grapevine which functions exceedingly well and is constantly reinforced by accurate gossip. In addition, the shoptalk vocabularies are far more extensive than those of sedentary occupations. The jazz-band musicians may almost be considered as having an occupational dialect.

4. It follows from the social isolation of such groups, taken together with their usual prosperity, their irregular working schedules, and the great importance of the occupational subculture, that they tend to develop a family system at variance with the general society.[14] Indeed, the very existence of a family group, which is necessarily attached to a local com-

munity for housing and other services at least part of the time, sets up a certain pressure which is justly felt to be a threat to the spirit of the occupational group. All psychologically mobile occupations — thieves, jazz musicians, symphony musicians, potters, railroad men, diplomats — contain an unusually high proportion of single persons, and the number of children in married households is likely to be small.

There are certain other consequences of the contradiction which is perceived between family norms and occupational norms. The sexual mores of such groups are typically far less strict than those found in settled groups of equivalent status. There is a marked tendency for wives to be selected from the daughters or other female relatives of colleagues. Finally, the upbringing of children is often directed with an eye to their eventual inheritance of the occupation or, in the case of daughters, to their marriage within the group. All these tendencies might be expected to lead to the development of a partial caste. In fact, they do so, although the low rate of natural increase, the pressure upon aging members to adopt a nonmobile occupation, and the requirement of special aptitudes are factors tending in the opposite direction.

The examples cited are relatively "pure" cases of transient occupations. Many other occupations share these characteristics to a lesser degree. All the callings which involve a great deal of travel — from archaeology to night club entertaining — will show some development of an isolated, deviant, and highly communicative private world.

It will be seen from this limited discussion why the analysis of horizontal mobility is so difficult, and why, in contrast to the many excellent discussions of vertical mobility that are available to us, there are hardly any systematic treatments of horizontal mobility. Much as we owe to the original geometric model, which presented vertical and horizontal mobility as perpendicular to each other, even a cursory examination of the facts suggests that this model is far too simple. It compels us, for example, to equate the isolation of the casual laborer with the intense immersion of the traveling musician in his special culture. In the present state of knowledge, the separate varieties of occupational mobility need to be considered separately if the concept of mobility is to remain meaningful.

NOTES

[1] Federal Writers' Project, *These Are Our Lives* (Chapel Hill, N.C.: University of North Carolina Press, 1939), pp. 380–410.
[2] *Ibid.*, p. 392.

OTHER MOBILITIES

[8] Thorstein Veblen, *The Instinct of Workmanship* (New York: The Macmillan Company, 1914), p. 307.

[4] Edward L. Thorndike and others, *Prediction of Vocational Success* (New York: The Commonwealth Fund, 1934).

[5] Katherine Archibald, *Wartime Shipyard: A Study in Social Disunity* (Berkeley, Calif.: University of California Press, 1947).

[6] Bureau of Labor Statistics, *Handbook of Labor Statistics* (Washington, D.C.: Government Printing Office, 1950), Table B-1, p. 40.

[7] E. G. Ravenstein, "The Laws of Migration," *Journal of the Royal Statistical Society*, vol. 52, June 1889.

[8] Samuel A. Stouffer, "Intervening Opportunities: A Theory Relating Mobility and Distance," *American Sociological Review*, vol. 5, December 1940.

[9] Myles W. Rodehaver and Luke M. Smith, "Migration and Occupational Structure: The Clergy," *Social Forces*, vol. 29, no. 4, May 1951.

[10] Theodore Caplow, "Transiency as a Cultural Pattern," *American Sociological Review*, vol. 5, October 1940, p. 731.

[11] Carey McWilliams, *Factories in the Field: The Story of Migratory Farm Labor in California* (Boston: Little, Brown & Company, 1939).

[12] The two best studies of transient occupations are probably W. Fred Cottrell, *The Railroader* (Stanford, Calif.: Stanford University Press, 1940), and Edwin H. Sutherland, editor, *The Professional Thief, by a Professional Thief* (Chicago: University of Chicago Press, 1937).

[13] Not all railroad employees belong to transient occupational groups, although mobility exerts a powerful influence on the common occupational culture.

[14] Becker writes of jazz musicians: "Musicians tend to feel that the imperatives of their work must take precedence over those of their families, and they act accordingly. . . . Marriage is likely to turn into a continuing struggle over this issue; the outcome of the struggle determines whether the man's musical career will be cut short or will continue. . . . For other men who feel their family responsibilities more strongly the situation is not so simple. The economic insecurity of the music business makes it difficult to be a good provider, and may force the individual to leave the profession, one of the typical patterns of response to this situation. . . . Even if the career is not cut off completely in this fashion, the demands of marriage exert a very strong pressure that pushes the musician toward 'going commercial.' . . . The family then, as an institution which demands that the musician behave conventionally, creates problems for him of conflicting pressures, loyalties and self-conceptions. The individual's response to these problems has a decisive effect, in terms of duration and direction, on the development of his career." Howard S. Becker, "Some Contingencies of the Professional Dance Musician's Career," *Human Organization*, vol. 12, no. 1, Spring 1953, p. 26.

99

CHAPTER 5

OCCUPATIONAL INSTITUTIONS

"THIS INDENTURE WITNESSETH that Stephen D. Maillory of the Borough of Pottstown in the County of Montgomery and State of Pennsylvania hath put himselve and by these presents doth voluntarily and of his own free will and accord, put himselve apprentice to Daniel S. Glackens of the said Borough, County & State Printer to learn his Art, Trade and Mystery . . . During all which term, the apprentice his said master faithfully shall serve, his secrets keep, his lawful commands every where gladly obey, he shall do no damage to his said master nor see it done by others, without letting or giving notice thereof to his said master, he shall not waste his said master's goods, nor lend them unlawfully to any. With his own goods nor the goods of others, without license from his said master he shall neither buy nor sell, he shall not absent him day nor night from his said master's service, without his leave; nor haunt ale-houses, taverns or play-houses, but in all things behave him as a faithful apprentice ought to do, during the said term. And the said master shall use the utmost of his endeavors to teach, or cause to be taught or instructed, the said apprentice in the trade or mystery of a Printer the said master is to give his said apprentice two pair of new shoes in each year and sixty two and half cents each week payable weekly . . . and procure and provide for him sufficient meat, drink, apparel, lodging and washing, fitting for an apprentice . . . [1833]

POTTSTOWN, PENNSYLVANIA

THE term *occupational institutions* is usually thought to refer either to the protective associations and pressure groups which are created to advance the common interests of an occupation, or to the business, governmental, and eleemosynary establishments which provide employment. These will be discussed respectively in the chapters on Occupational Ideologies and on the Sociology of the Labor Market. What we are concerned with here is simpler, but less familiar.

The occupational milieu is best defined, not by the bylaws of unions or the personnel policies of corporations, but by a set of institutions which reflect the occupational culture. It is the nature of these institutions, the conditions from which they develop, and the attitudes which they encourage that fix the character of each occupation and determine its effect upon other aspects of life. It may seem confusing to the reader to describe as an institution the network of circumstances within each occupation which determine the roles of its members. But, as E. C. Hughes writes in discussing occupations: "Conscious fulfilling of formally defined offices distinguishes institutions from elementary collective behavior." [1] Hughes also notes that each occupation "tends to have its peculiar realm of sacred and secular objects. The sacred objects are its interests and prerogatives. Its secular objects are within the realm of its technique."

The occupational characteristics considered in job analysis (skill, dexterity, responsibility, required education, size of working group, etc.) pertain to the "secular" part of the occupational culture and arise more or less spontaneously out of its realm of technic. They are somewhat less important for the study of occupational institutions than the "interests and prerogatives" which are embodied in historical associations, mythologies, codes of ethics, occupational secrets, special titles, rituals, distinctive costumes, special gestures, private argots, and, in addition, the whole number of subtle controls which in the name of respectability, dignity, or conformity are exerted by the occupational group over the nonoccupational lives of its members.

As we have already seen, there is great variability among these occupational cultures. At one extreme are those of the learned professions, some of whose elements are a thousand years old. At the other are functions so new and so casual as almost to defy classification. Except in the professions and crafts, and certain occupations (policeman, waitress, coal miner) which chance to be precisely delineated, it is often very difficult to determine which group should be taken as the essential unit. Shall we discuss stenographers as a separate occupational group, or include them among female clerical workers, or regard them as forming part of a huge population of submanagerial office employees? In practice, we are likely to use all three categories, losing something in precision, and gaining something in generality, as we move up the scale. This flexible usage is possible because all three groups are sufficiently well defined to have social reality for both members and outsiders.

If we analyze any such group carefully we find a unique configuration of institutional traits, arising from the interaction of social roles and technical functions within an established framework. Close attention to the reinforcement of these structures by specialization and differentiation led

101

Durkheim,[2] and later Park,[3] to suggest that occupational associations might ultimately become the basic political units of an industrial society.

It is impossible to discuss all the dimensions of a single occupational milieu within the frame of a single chapter, nor is it easy to enumerate all the types of occupational institutions. The present discussion will therefore be limited to certain of the principal dimensions which are important in all institutions of this kind, and to a brief discussion of these dimensions in four groups of occupations, each of which has a distinctive situation. These are (1) independent, fee-taking professionals (lawyers, physicians, dentists, or architects); (2) building craftsmen (carpenters, masons, electricians, or steamfitters); (3) semiskilled machine-tending factory workers (employed in the manufacture of shoes, automobiles, appliances, or paper); and (4) small retail merchants (grocers, butchers, hardware dealers, or filling-station operators).

Among the structural characteristics of occupational institutions which will be considered in this and the following chapter are these: the manner of recruiting, the evaluation of seniority, the evaluation of merit, the control of occupational behavior, the control of extra-occupational behavior, the formation of occupational attitudes, the occupational culture or internal ethos, the occupational stereotypes or external ethos, and the rate of growth or decline.

THE MANNER OF RECRUITING

We note at the outset that the manner of recruiting is entirely different in each of the four occupational settings.

In the independent professions the entire recruiting process, from the initial choice of candidates for training to the bestowal of honors at retirement, is under the close control of the professional group itself. Although the right to practice is generally conferred by a governmental board, this agency normally represents the profession and has usually been kept free from "political interference," i.e., the intervention of laymen. In the case of the independent professions, the violation of the occupational monopoly is punishable as a crime. These circumstances comprise the essential strength of professional organization, and explain the yearning for professionalization which besets almost all technical, service, and business occupations.

Recruiting in the building crafts is equally formal and still bears many marks of guild ritual. As in the case of professions, the rights and duties of candidates are specified with precision at each stage of their advancement, and the power of the state is often invoked to prevent outsiders from practicing the occupation. The most important differences are that the ultimate judges of competence are members of "higher" occupations, such as engineering, and that governmental authority cannot be overtly exercised by the occupational association. The control of recruiting is seldom complete—apprenticeship has partly given way to trade schooling organized by outsiders; effective occupational monopoly is usually limited to a local community and ceases abruptly at the urban limits; and the penalties for violation are nominal, unless they are reinforced by personal violence or by agreements with employers and suppliers.

Recruiting for factory workers is largely controlled by the employer, who was formerly able to establish whatever qualifications he pleased. The most important criteria are those which favor men over women in most industries and women over men in certain others, establish minimum and maximum ages and minimum educational level, prescribe family status and exclude Negroes and other ethnic minorities. Public authority is invoked only to increase the supply of recruits — by manpower campaigns and by training courses — in times of labor shortage. In recent years, closed shops or union shops have given a limited jurisdiction to unions in the matter of recruiting to the occupation. Indeed, this has been established practice in a few industries since before the turn of the century. It is not unusual for factory unions to exclude women or minorities from membership but such action usually requires more or less active cooperation from employers. The chief influence exerted by factory unions over recruiting still lies in the prevention of sudden increases in the available labor force.

In the retail trades there are few or no formal controls over recruiting, but there are a variety of informal limitations. In the first place, the capital required for the establishment of a retail business, although small, places an effective bar upon entry. It would appear that the vast majority of retail businesses are established on borrowed capital, and it is certain that a retail operation normally depends upon the extensive use of commercial credit. In many communities, this implies a close dependence upon local banks. In large cities, the more impersonal agencies of credit exchanges and rating services restrict eligibility. In some instances, such as the retail gasoline business, credit and planning services are furnished by the supplier, who is thus able to recruit filling-station operators very much as if they were employees. It often happens that local merchants, related in one way or another to one of these controlling agencies, are able to limit the number of competitors admitted. Over and beyond these financial elements are the various factors which favor recruiting by inheritance — the importance of early familiarity with the business, the inheritability of good will, the practice of using family members as part-time helpers. On the other hand, enterprises of this sort are so small, numerous, and mobile that the retail occupations remain fairly open and are important channels to middle-class status.

The limitation of entry to an occupation has a double function wherever it occurs: first, the maintenance of standards of performance, both in the public interest and in the interest of those concerned; second, the maintenance of standards of remuneration, both by the limitation of supply and by the selection of candidates with socially favored characteristics. It is usually argued by the spokesmen for successfully restricted occupations (which may lie as far apart as bricklaying and editorial writing) that high standards of performance can only be maintained by establishing a high rate of remuneration to attract superior recruits.

The more or less perennial conflicts associated with this phase of occupational organization arise from the circumstance that the balancing of quality against cost is a delicate and often indeterminate calculation. In the long run, there is probably a tendency for an occupational group to overestimate the level of remuneration necessary for maintaining satisfac · tory performance, and thereby to restrict admission to the point where the function itself is jeopardized. This is especially likely because, as Clark has shown,[4] every occupation tends to underestimate its average earnings in comparison with others and is thus almost certain to develop an elaborate myth about its relatively unfavorable rewards.[5]

On the other hand, as soon as limitation of entry has produced a disproportionately favorable situation for a group of practitioners, some outside pressure will be felt to nullify the restrictions and to open the occupation more widely. This has often occurred in the weaker crafts and even occasionally in the professions, with the effect of lowering wages and possibly standards of performance.

A stock situation in modern industry is that in which an occupation has been simplified by additional mechanization, so that many of the old skills are obsolete and entrance standards tend to fall sharply. In such a case, the efforts made to retain occupational restrictions will tend to restrict production directly. The ensuing struggle will probably be the more bitter for lack of a clear-cut justification. This has been going on, as a corollary to technical improvement, ever since the Lancaster weavers attacked the first mechanical looms in the eighteenth century.

As has been shown, the control of recruiting may be formal or informal, direct or indirect. It may be exerted by the occupational group, by outsiders, by governmental agencies, or very frequently by a combination of all three.

The formal control of recruiting may be illustrated by apprenticeship, the requirement of a specified course of schooling, articleship, or internship — in general, the passage through predefined preparatory stages, each carrying an appropriate status. Informal control also involves a series of related statuses to which some importance is attached but which tend to be casual, covert, and undefined by written specifications. Thus, nepotism, the informal designation of institutional successors, the relationships established by admission to a clique or acceptance as a disciple, all illustrate informal control.

Direct control occurs when there is a definite procedure which applicants must undergo to emerge either fully qualified or definitely rejected, as in bar examinations, trade licensing, and civil service appointments. Indirect control occurs when access to required training or the acquisition of necessary previous experience is used to limit the number of candidates. Most newcomers in the open job market, reading the want ads, are puzzled by the number of occupations in which no one will be employed without previous experience, but in which it appears impossible to acquire experience without being employed. The theater is a traditional ground for this form of indirect control.

Needless to say, formal, informal, direct, and indirect controls may all exist together. Wherever an occupation is professionalized, and its members in addition form a coherent and intimate circle, all four kinds of control are certain to be found coordinately — as in the peacetime careers of army officers.

Some distinction should be made here between controls based primarily upon technical considerations and those founded only on group interest. In many highly specialized callings, experience is essential to any successful performance at all, as in production engineering. Here, indirect control is based upon technical necessity. In other instances, where the element of pure monopoly is more marked, and where persons may be excluded from an occupation without regard to their technical qualifications (e.g., un-licensed motion picture projectionists and immigrant physicians), it is more convenient to rely on the direct control embodied in a refusal of certification. Still other occupations (e.g., teaching) involve work which is essentially social in nature and cannot be detached from the status and personality of the practitioner, so that there can be no clear separation of social and technical considerations.

Finally, it should be noted that the greater the rewards offered by an occupation, the more rigorous the control over recruiting which may be expected. We must leave open for the present the question of whether this relationship is reciprocal. Clark and Pancoast,[6] in their theory of occupa-tional mobility, maintain that high occupational rewards are due *solely* to the restriction of entry in the favored occupations. While this appears to be a sweeping overstatement, it is obvious at first glance that the strength of occupational control over recruiting is a partly independent variable in the determination of occupational reward and, eventually, of occupational status.

THE EVALUATION OF SENIORITY

We have previously noted that the shape of the career curve is markedly different for the various occupational levels. Clark's study of lifetime earn-ings in selected occupations, and the trend information provided by Dublin and Lotka in *The Money Value of a Man*,[7] show how these variations in the career curve sharpen the differences in fortune which appear in any income distribution. Variations in degree of involvement also need to be taken into account when comparing occupations of similar level. It remains to be considered how these two elements — seniority and involvement — are expressed in the occupational institution.

The independent professions anticipate lifelong involvement as a matter of course. They are embarked upon with great expense, great ceremony, and the taking of oaths. Within the last two generations the structure of each profession has been modified by an extreme lengthening of the period of preparation. One unexpected consequence is that those who fail in the profession are no longer expected to leave it, unless their failure is touched with criminal intent. So strong is this tendency that the ex-lawyer or ex-physician is likely to be regarded rather like an unfrocked priest, as a per-son who has proved unworthy of great responsibilities. The number of persons who permanently quit the major professions is therefore very small; the more usual course for the dissatisfied is to assume a salaried function for which the professional qualification is a prerequisite, although the work is essentially different. For example, public-health physicians, architectural engineers, and tax experts are drawn quite often from among those who might, in an earlier day, have abandoned their profession.

It is largely because of this lifetime involvement that the career curve continues upward nearly to the age of retirement, having its sharpest slope in the early years of practice, and for the very successful, another sharp slope in the later years.

Professional progress comes to be measured not in absolute terms, but rather like an I.Q., as a ratio of achievement at a given age to expected achievement at that age. It should be remarked that achievement is evaluated only by members of the profession, any systematic kind of rating by outsiders being sharply disapproved. Because of the upward career curve, these evaluations are largely in the hands of senior colleagues, who control the distribution of prestige tokens and are thereby enabled to "normalize" the career patterns of their juniors.[8] Since prestige tokens (titles, honors, and affiliations) may be more reliably controlled than income, which depends partly upon the reaction of a clientele, there are often gross disparities between relative status and relative income. In general, fewer limitations are placed upon rapid advancement in earnings, so that conscientious professional men are often made aware of a choice between professional progress and the maximization of income.

In the building trades, lifetime involvement is taken for granted to the extent that there is little voluntary movement to other trades involving other apprenticeships, nor is there any motive for permanently retreating to a manual trade of inferior skill. Except for certain occupational hazards (principally lead poisoning among painters, lung ailments among plasterers and masons, and a variety of ailments interfering with work on ladders and stages) there is nothing to prevent active work to an advanced age, and the structure of the craft includes all the known devices for inhibiting technological change which might cheapen skills. However, the strength of the individual's involvement in a craft is very much less than in a profession, and for two good reasons. Because of the general superiority attributed to white-collar employments, there is a tendency for craftsmen to seek upward channels to business and supervisory positions. Then, the building trades are highly seasonal and also subject to violent alternations of prosperity and stagnation. It is normal for the craftsman to turn his hand to other employments at various times in his career, just as it is normal for him to preserve a permanent identification with his trade. These same fluctuations have induced the crafts to limit accreditation as narrowly as possible, and craftsmen who migrate sometimes find it impossible to re-establish themselves in a new area.

The normal career pattern in the crafts involves progress through apprenticeship to the journeyman stage some years after the completion of general schooling. There follows a period of progressive improvement in status and security, accompanied by only slight increases in income, to a high point reached in middle life. Normally, there will be no advancement in occupational classification or in general prestige thereafter.

There are, however, a number of mobility channels within the craft itself which are important, and which do not ordinarily become accessible until about the middle of the individual's career. Most craft unions recognize various classifications of "masters," who may be salaried foremen, subcontractors, inspectors, or jobber-dealers. All these positions are closely related to the craft training and the union affiliation; indeed in some respects, the modern craft union has compromised more successfully than the ancient guild with the problem of retaining employer-capitalists inside the craft organization.

These mobility channels, though relatively accessible, are not the normal career termination. The high point of the career pattern may still be said to occur in middle life. What the occupational institution does achieve is a set of attitudes which favor seniority in itself and allow a large measure of respect to the old-timer.

For the factory hand, the evaluation of seniority is entirely outside of the occupation. Increasing age is likely to bring increasing insecurity of employment, except to the extent that the employer recognizes and encourages long tenure of employment. Thus, for all practical purposes, seniority within the occupation is meaningless, although seniority in a particular job may have considerable importance. The development of union strength in the mass industries has in no way changed this situation. The career curve may still be seen to reach its peak very early in life, and to decline steadily thereafter. Similarly, the concept of involvement is less definite in the machine-tending trades. It may be applied to continued employment by a particular establishment, or to long-term involvement in an industry, but it carries no major advantages. The occupational institutions do not discourage the very high degree of horizontal mobility which is characteristic of factory workers.

OCCUPATIONAL INSTITUTIONS

When we consider retail business, we are confronted with still another kind of situation which bears little resemblance to the three just described. For the owner-operator of a small enterprise, the duration of involvement is linked to the financial fate of the business. As numerous studies have shown, the average life of a small business is very short. Only a negligible proportion of those founded survive for as much as five years. Since repeated failures damage the credit rating which is essential to success, each subsequent effort is less likely to succeed than the original one. Success or failure does not depend upon the organized consensus of one's fellows, and age scarcely enters the picture except as an index of prudence or of physical condition. However, amid the debris of millions of abortive ventures, there is a solid core of small enterprises which not only persist but tend, in the long run, to expand. It is among their operators that the skeleton of an occupational organization begins to emerge. Yet we cannot meaningfully discuss the evaluation of seniority in this field, except to note that it has little significance.

It is evident at this point that we are dealing with a variety of career characteristics which are closely linked and intertwined. The most important of these are the shape of the career curve, the degree of involvement, and the strength of the occupational association. The stronger the association, the more easily will it be able to secure such permanent advantages to its members as will make most of them unwilling to change occupations. As we have already seen, a strong and relatively autonomous occupational association will have several motives for lengthening the period of preparation and increasing the expense and effort required for admission. This will further tend to discourage mobility, and in extreme cases will make lifetime involvement the norm. Such a situation inevitably favors the elders, in part because of the continuity of the group's membership and experience, in part because of their direct control of organizations. The greater the involvement, therefore, the later in life will the peak of the career curve be found. This is a self-reinforcing situation. The deferment of reward to the later years of a career has much the same effect as lengthening the period of preparation. It results in the loss of important deferred rewards by anyone who quits the occupation before retirement, and therefore tends to increase the degree of involvement, which in turn gives additional weight to seniority.

One further point should be clarified here. The autonomy of an occupational association is at least as important in this regard as its political power. The large industrial unions currently enjoy considerable political influence, but as we have seen, they have very little discretion in the selection of recruits, the limitation of their numbers, or the *differential* distribution of income and prestige. On the other hand, an occupational in-group which is not even formally defined and which never sets up bylaws or holds business meetings may have all the characteristics of a powerful association. This is the case for almost all long-established bureaucracies whether they are in government, industry, religion, education, or research.[9] Perhaps the most striking illustration is found within the managerial groups of certain large corporations, where salaries are fixed with reference to a curve of expected earnings at given ages and given seniority and where the last promotion ordinarily occurs at the time of retirement. As might be expected, these strata are also characterized by extremely selective recruiting and by extraordinarily low turnover.

THE EVALUATION OF MERIT

The prevailing ideologies of "success" tend to obscure the very different meanings which must be attached to either success or failure in dissimilar occupational environments. As we shall see later in analyzing the labor market, a consideration of the various ways in which merit is evaluated is essential to an understanding of differential remuneration. The questions to be asked are very simple. Who evaluates? How? What is evaluated?

In the free professions, the determination of merit is entirely in the hands of fellow-professionals, at least in principle. In practice, the judgment of clients and, in the case of lawyers and architects, of the general public needs also to be taken into account. The professional society is therefore required to evolve special devices for limiting the effect of these outside judgments. This is precisely the function of the rules which limit the participation of architects in the construction business, which oppose the popular election of the higher judiciary, and which restrict the access of physicians to public hospitals.

The modes of evaluation are numerous. They are subject to the qualification that the fundamental right to practice, which is essential to the structure of the profession, must not be seriously impaired. Among the formal devices are honorific titles, membership in institutes, the right to specialize, office in the controlling professional societies, and the right to practice in other areas. But equally important are the functions of gossip, the allocation of partnerships, and the prevailing systems of consultation and referral.

What is evaluated is a kind of skill, but conceived so broadly as to include the practitioner's personality, creativeness, and social contacts. It is assumed, first, that any practitioner is perfectly qualified to perform any of the ordinary duties of the profession, and that the restriction of the client's choice does him no essential harm (as in referral to medical specialists, assignment of a public defender, or required inspection of buildings). It is assumed, secondly, that professionals are, like poets or sculptors, perfectly noninterchangeable, the work of each being a free creation of his personality. It follows from this that the work cannot be accurately valued in money (since no exact substitute is obtainable) and that the monetary equivalent should be based largely on the client's ability to pay. In the case of salaried professionals, particularly teachers and ministers, the same assumption leads to the parallel formulation that remuneration is intended merely to provide decent subsistence and is unrelated to the value of the work, which is performed as a public service.

In theory the evaluation of merit among craftsmen is also performed by their fellows. In practice, there is likely to be a good deal of direct evaluation by employers and by engineers and other experts. Again in theory, evaluation of skill is limited to the apprenticeship, and to the occasions of passage from apprentice to journeyman or from journeyman to master. Indeed, the entire institution is designed to reduce comparisons among equals to a minimum.

It is assumed, therefore, that all passed craftsmen in the same craft are perfectly interchangeable, that any journeyman, put to a given job, will perform the same quantity of work of the same quality as another. Where the craft organization is strong, this is not very far from the fact. It is made possible in part by the restriction of a standard day's work to much less than the maximum which could be performed by a craftsman of average ability, and in part by the standardization of tools, materials, and technics. These practices, often attacked by outsiders as "stalling" and "featherbedding," are really essential to the occupational institutions. By making it impossible for the employer to develop a rational preference for one employee over another, they enable the craft to maintain a degree of internal control which would otherwise be impossible. It is still reasonable, of course, for the employer to choose craftsmen for their personal qualities, but very strong unions also succeed in assuming disciplinary functions, either directly or by the designation of eligible foremen. Where the system is well developed, therefore, the distribution of work may be almost entirely in the hands of the union, which assigns the men for each job. It is assumed that this works no injustice to the employer, who buys a certain number of standard work units at a standard price — merit having been substantially equalized for all qualified craftsmen.

In the machine-tending occupations, evaluation by one's fellows is of importance in many situations where, as Roethlisberger and Dickson first showed,[10] the group determines how much skill each member may be allowed to demonstrate. Officially, evaluation is entirely in the hands of superiors, principally foremen and straw bosses. Moreover, this evaluation tends to be directed at personal characteristics, including especially congeniality and reliability, since skill is either standardized (as on an assembly-line operation) or directly remunerated by piece rates.

Factory hands are interchangeable, not only between jobs, but between industries. This is assumed to be true even when, as often occurs, a particular machine-tending job comes to require a highly specialized skill. Where a skill is neither recognized nor protected, it tends to be disregarded as an element in the evaluation of the individual, except in periods of severe labor shortage. In the typical factory situation, with very limited opportunities for promotion on the basis of work performance, the evaluation of merit is often a negligible item in the determination of the individual's career, being much outweighed by seniority, union activity, personal relations, and schooling.

In the retail business, it is the public which plays the principal part in the evaluation of merit. This process is supplemented in important ways by the judgments of bankers, suppliers, and competitors. This evaluation is very precise and rational, being expressed in the short run by the balance sheet of the business, and in the long run by its growth or its disappearance. Yet merit is not quite the same thing as in the three previous examples. It applies to the business taken as a whole, rather than to the performance of the individual, and it gives a heavy weight to two factors only remotely related to proprietarial skill: the size of the original capital and the selection of a location. Moreover, the fate of the business is also dependent upon the great swings of the business cycle, the activities of large competitors, and other sizable events entirely beyond individual control.

After all this is taken into account, there does remain a conventionalized situation in which the proprietor of a neighborhood business, with only family or part-time help, finds his fate determined by the prudence with which he keeps his accounts and inventories and his standing with the local householders. Under these conditions, his annual income is likely to be a very close reflection of his work performance as compared to that of his competitors.

In the simplified apology for free enterprise which is presented to the public through advertising there is a tendency to treat any corporate enterprise as if it closely resembled the corner grocery, and at the same time, to confuse the situation of the industrial employee with that of the same corner grocer, whereas in fact one of the principal social problems of a free enterprise society is to reconcile the startlingly different rules governing advancement in different occupations with some common principle of equity.

Generally speaking, we must distinguish most clearly among those occupations where the individual is judged by his peers, those in which he is subject to the evaluation of hierarchical superiors, and those in which he reports to the public at large or to some special fraction of it. In none of these cases will he be rated entirely on skill. We may suppose, in advance of further analysis, that competence will be most heavily weighted by one's fellows, that personal relations will assume great importance in a hierarchy, and that in those occupations which are subject to evaluation by the public the rating of individual merit will be least predictable. We may also suppose that in all occupations such nonoccupational characteristics as ancestry, appearance, and age will condition even the most objective judgments. The smaller the group of "judges," the greater will be the influence of these extraneous factors.

Finally, it should be observed that the chances of advancement are least where interchangeability is greatest. This principle operates not only between different occupations on the same status level, but also within occupations, and helps to explain the modern tendency to carry occupational specialization far beyond the point indicated by technical considerations.

THE CONTROL OF OCCUPATIONAL BEHAVIOR

The specifications for the control of behavior in a well-organized occupation are exceedingly numerous. Indeed training for such an occupation as policeman or locomotive engineer consists principally in learning the rules governing the exercise of a function, rather than in rehearsing the function itself. We will usually find that these rules are of two sorts: those designed to protect outsiders from incompetence and abuse; and those designed to safeguard the socioeconomic position of insiders.

113

In the professions, the most important of these specifications are set down at length in codes of ethics. Others are embodied in bylaws, administrative regulations, licensing rules, statutes, technical manuals, and custom. But the importance of the code of ethics itself as a cultural trait should not be ignored. The general acceptance of such a code has the effect of establishing in advance a whole series of contractual relations between practitioners and clients, among practitioners themselves, and between practitioners and the state.

The most ancient and famous of these statements is the Oath of Hippocrates which, incredibly ancient, embodies all the essential elements of a professional code more succinctly than some codes drafted yesterday.[11] These are:

1. The prohibition of certain acts by which the practitioner abuses the client for his own advantage.
2. The prohibition of certain other acts considered antisocial in themselves.
3. The prohibition of business procedures which give the practitioner a permanent advantage in competition with his fellows. Often, but not invariably, specification of a minimum fee or wage.
4. Specification of the rules of eligibility and ineligibility, together with the interdiction of activities capable of weakening the professional monopoly.
5. The claim to whatever legal exemptions are necessary to accomplish the foregoing purposes, among these being professional confidence and the right to refuse to divulge information; immunity from prosecution in the event of various accidents; and the corporate privileges of the professional society.

In addition to the codes, there are a whole series of supplementary rules which are not set down, because they are regarded as self-evident, or as not entirely legitimate, or as of local application. An example of the first situation is the obligation of a lawyer to accept an assignment as defense counsel for a pauper. The second may be illustrated by the understanding that physicians do not testify against each other in malpractice suits, and the third by the subtle rules governing architectural plagiarism.

In the case of the building trades, the rules may sometimes be found set down in a manual, which often preserves the terminology of the guild system. They are sometimes found in union bylaws, or in the licensing regulations prepared by an examining board. Within the last two decades, master contracts have come into use in many urban areas. These are usually negotiated by an employers' association with the union and govern the wages and working conditions of all craftsmen in the area whether or not their employers are signatory to the agreement. Taken together, these various specifications are popularly known as the Rule Book, and include the following essential elements:

1. Specification of a standard hourly wage (which serves as both a minimum and a maximum) and of standard rates for overtime, waiting, hazard, and other special conditions.

2. Specification of the rules of eligibility and ineligibility, together with rules limiting the number and defining the working conditions of apprentices.

3. Specification of hiring procedures and seniority rights.

4. Provision of penalties for a variety of activities tending to weaken the occupational monopoly.

5. Specification of acceptable tools and methods.

6. Specification of safety rules.

7. Specification of what shall constitute a fair day's work.

This last item is sometimes not set down in writing, because of the public resentment it evokes, but it will usually be familiar to employers and others having to do with the trade.

For the factory trades, the written rules and regulations are chiefly those imposed by management. Unlike union contracts developed for the crafts, the contracts between factory unions and management do not have much effect upon the performance of the individual workman, except as they concern the handling of grievances and thereby interpose a check upon disciplinary regulations.

These rules and regulations, as found in most plants, fall into several categories:

1. Rules prescribing the length of the working week and day, and the time allowable for lunch and rest periods, usually accompanied by specific penalties for absenteeism, lateness, and loitering.

2. Rules restricting freedom of activity in the shop, including prohibitions on smoking, conversation, leaving machines, and entering other parts of the plant.

3. Safety rules, typically emphasizing the use of guards and similar devices, and often prescribing the dress of employees: helmets, goggles, metal-toed shoes, and hairnets. It was nominally as a safety rule that certain war plants prohibited female employees from wearing sweaters, and it is by a parallel extension of the meaning of safety that the privilege of wearing a white collar is often restricted.

4. Rules defining responsibility with respect to company property, including the care of machines, tools, and materials, and financial responsibility for items drawn from stock.

5. Rules defining the authority of foremen and other supervisors.

6. Formal definitions of the role of shop stewards and other union agents, together with contractual agreements specifying the kind of union activities that will be allowed on company property.

These categories are represented in the rules of almost all industrial establishments. Their impact upon the workmen, however, depends on the general atmosphere of the plant and is notably modified by the presence of a strong union. Under extremely authoritarian conditions, the rules for conduct in a manufacturing shop may not differ significantly from those in a penitentiary: No Talking, No Smoking, No Leaving Machines. Even under more enlightened supervision, the coercion exercised upon the individual during his working hours is always very much greater than in the professions or crafts.

One of the major findings of research in industrial sociology has been the discovery of another set of rules with coercive force, which are evolved by the working group itself, usually in covert opposition to the factory management. These are always unwritten, but are nevertheless explicit. The function of these rules is to restrict output, and this is done for two reasons: first, to prevent a speed-up, in which the output rises while wage rates and employment are diminished; second, to equalize earnings and to adjust earnings to the relative status of group members. Thus, in the Bank Wiring Room at Western Electric:

Among the employees in the observation room there was a notion of a proper day's work. They felt that if they had wired two equipments a day they had done about the right amount. Most of the work was done in the morning. As soon as the employees felt sure of being about to finish what they considered enough for the day, they slacked off. This slacking off was naturally more marked among the faster than among the slower workmen.

As a result, the output graph from week to week tended to be a straight line. The employees resorted to two further practices in order to make sure that it should remain so. They reported more or less output than they performed and they claimed more day work allowances than they were entitled to . . .

They shared a common body of sentiments. A person should not turn out too much work. If he did, he was a "rate-buster." The theory was that if an excessive amount of work was turned out, the management would lower the piecework rate so that the employees would be in the position of doing more work for approximately the same pay. On the other hand, a person should not turn out too little work. If he did, he was a "chiseler"; that is, he was getting paid for work he did not do. A person should say nothing which would injure a fellow member of the group. If he did, he was a "squealer." Finally, no member of the group should act officiously. The working group had also developed methods of enforcing respect for its attitudes.[12]

Evidently, the regulations which will be evolved in a working crew depend upon the details of the situation. Other studies have demonstrated that the informal rules of the factory group may take quite different forms. But it seems certain that some such development will take place inevitably in a factory group.

It is not at all certain whether these findings can be generalized to other types of working situation. As we have seen, the factory worker is subject to much heavier coercion than most other employees. The function of the rules evolved by the working group is, in large measure, to relieve the psychological pressure created by this coercion. We are accustomed to similar phenomena wherever direct coercion is exerted by outsiders — upon enlisted men, prisoners, students, and minority groups, for example. There is every reason to suppose that they are incidental to the exercise of power, rather than to the common performance of work.

In the retail trades, the control of occupational behavior is entirely different, being at once much wider and much more diffuse. Indeed, it is the popular belief that self-employment in a small business carries with it freedom from personal coercion which constitutes the prinicipal appeal of retail trade, just as it is often the impact of impersonal coercion which subsequently disillusions the neophyte proprietor.

We may distinguish three sets of rules: those enforced by the government, those imposed by creditors, and those evolved by customers.

The control of the state (typically exerted through the local municipality) over the small retailer is a very ancient phenomenon. In fact, Pirenne and other scholars [13] have sought the origin of modern law in the market regulations of medieval towns. In the regulated markets of the Middle Ages municipal jurisdiction extended to the inspection of weights and measures, the enforcement of sanitary precautions, the fixing of prices, and the assignment of locations. In European countries where the public market has had an uninterrupted history, many of these administrative practices still survive in their original form. In the United States, they are mostly of recent origin, and form part of an administrative patchwork which varies from one locality to another. The most important elements are these:

1. Provision for standardization of weights, measures, and labels, the inspection of scales, and the correct identification of products.
2. Regulations and ordinances specifying sanitary measures and providing for periodic sanitary inspection.
3. Statutes restricting the sale of poison and adulterants.
4. Regulations providing for compulsory labeling, minimum quality, or both. (The required use of official U.S. grades in the sale of meat and the ban on the sale of electric appliances not approved by underwriters illustrate these practices.)
5. The licensing of premises or of proprietors before sale of a commodity is permitted, as frequently in the case of beer, milk products, meat, gasoline, and patent medicines.
6. The fixing of maximum prices as a feature of planning the national economy during periods of emergency. This may or may not be accompanied by rationing and by regulations forbidding preferential treatment of customers.

With the advent of packaged foods identified by brand — and parallel innovations in other retail fields — much of this regulatory activity has been shifted back to the wholesaler, the processor, or even the original producer. Yet there remain so many regulations directly applicable to the retailer that he often finds it difficult to keep track of them.

The standard of enforcement is typically low. The elimination of short measure in the sale of foods has been an insoluble problem for centuries. Experts in price control regard 80 per cent enforcement at the retail level as highly successful. There are a number of reasons why this is so: the great number of retailers and their mobility; the absence of occupational bodies concerned with enforcement; the scattered agencies which originate the regulations; and the difficulty of surveillance. Perhaps the principal factor, which has always operated in situations of this type, is that evasion may bring considerable profit to the merchant without causing any serious loss to the individual customer. Yet, taken together, the regulations exert a considerable influence upon the conduct of the occupation.

The rules enforced by suppliers and other creditors are much more categorical and cannot be violated without serious risk. These have to do with the following:

1. Promptness in the discharge of financial obligations, with the loss of discount and credit facilities as the penalty for violation.

2. Trade practices which determine the retailer's purchases by forbidding him to stock competitive brands, by minimum orders and quantity discounts, by tie-in sales, and by the assignment of exclusive territories.

3. Rules prescribing the handling, display, and advertising of merchandise supplied.

4. The fixing of minimum retail prices by the supplier.

This last practice, which removes from the retailer his major competitive recourse of price competition was long regarded as a monopolistic abuse. With the increasing concentration of economic power among suppliers, and the increasing importance of brand identification, it has become respectable. Since 1940, most states have reinforced the fixing of minimum prices by means of fair trade acts which give the supplier's price determination the force of law.

Compared to this rigid system, the control which the customer exerts upon the occupational comportment of the merchant is very informal. It is none the less important. Particularly since the restriction of price and quality competition, personal relations with customers are often the decisive factor in the history of a retail business.

The "rules" are essentially these:

1. The merchant is expected to minimize his status and exaggerate that of the customer by exaggerated forms of deference, by yielding in minor arguments, by expressing more interest in the customer's personal affairs than the customer is expected to show in his, and by small personal services.

2. Under this ritual, it becomes essential that the habits of the customer be identified and protected. A strain is thus produced on the merchant to maintain nearly absolute consistency in his manners, his purchasing routines, and his hours of work.

Thus, one way or another, the worker is closely constrained by the rules of his occupational environment in these four types of work. Indeed, in all but a few vagrant or ornamental callings, the individual at work finds himself governed by a complex system of regulation. But this finding needs to be tempered by certain considerations which arise from the nature of social control.

It may be useful to visualize the general problem in terms of a physical analogy. Social control may be thought of as a "force" impelling men in a given direction. The amount of force depends upon the energy allocated by the social group, and powerful controls will normally be expressed through correspondingly massive institutional devices. But the work done by the force (plus the friction produced, to run the analogy into the ground) can only be determined by taking account of the resistance offered. "Work" in this sense — the propulsion of the individual against a given resistance — is known as coercion.

It will be noted that coercion depends not only upon the force exerted, but upon the resistance to be overcome. Returning to more reasonable language, we may say that the fact of coercion, and the psychological frustrations which invariably accompany coercion, arise from a collision of motives. It is always misleading to assume that the degree of coercion is proportional to the control exerted, or that maximum frustration is encountered under conditions of maximum control.

This principle has some rather general applications. It helps to explain, for example, why stable folk societies, in which all behavior is prescribed minutely, are less aware of coercion than mobile societies which offer a wide range of choices. In the folk society — where rules and regulations are felt as part of the natural order — resistance is relatively slight. In the mobile society where the individual is bound by conflicting and inconsistent codes, conformity of any kind is accompanied by some degree of resistance.

In the control of occupational behavior, the application of the distinction between control and coercion resolves a whole series of apparent paradoxes, the most important of which is that the members of tightly organized occupational hierarchies are usually less aware of coercion than those who work in mobile environments. Thus of our four examples, the professions and crafts are usually thought to offer more "freedom" than factory work or retail trade. Practically speaking, the decrease of resistance in the two former groups is brought about in the following ways:

1. The longer the period of occupational formation, the more completely are the rules assimilated and internalized as habits, and at the same time the greater will be the participant's self-identification with the occupational group. In the end, he may cease to feel the rules as something imposed from outside, and will regard them as his own motives.

2. The greater the individual's identification with the agency which imposes the rules, the less will be his resistance to them. (This is, after all, the fundamental justification for democracy.) In the case of the professions, this identification is well-nigh complete, even where the professional association is actually manipulated by a closed clique.

3. The more uniform and unchanging the rules, the less resistance will

they encounter. This has several important consequences, one of which is that resistance to personalized authority (despite the wistful yearnings of some scholars for the patriarchal factory owner of 1850) is usually greater than the resistance to impersonal authority. Then too, the wider the area in which the rules are applicable, the more easily will they be observed. In this respect, the professions have a singular advantage over the crafts. The extreme conservatism of hierarchically organized occupations rests in part upon the practical advantages of avoiding changes in the rules.

4. The more unified the agencies of control, the easier will it be to follow the rules. In the protests of the factory worker and the storekeeper against coercion, the objection to inconsistent authorities is always conspicuous. Industrial sociologists have been repeatedly struck by the fact that the worker's attitude toward the union — in mass industry — is not much friendlier than toward management, even where the union is effective and commands a deep loyalty. It would not be far amiss to regard the whole structure of the professions and the trades, as well as of military, political, and industrial bureaucracies, as designed to limit the impact of outside authorities, even at the cost of developing tyrannical controls inside the working group.

Coercion and resistance to coercion have enormous consequences in themselves, as socio-psychological phenomena. But in addition, they react back upon the occupational structure out of which they arise. Thus, it may be proposed as a hypothesis that the smaller the degree of coercion in proportion to the control exerted, the wider will be the area of control. This rather esoteric formulation will be tested in the next chapter.

NOTES

[1] Everett C. Hughes, "Institutional Office and the Person," *American Journal of Sociology,* vol. 43, November 1937, pp. 404–13.

[2] Emile Durkheim, *On the Division of Labor in Society,* translated by George Simpson (New York: The Macmillan Company, 1933).

[3] Robert E. Park, Introduction to Frances R. Donovan, *The Saleslady* (Chicago: University of Chicago Press, 1929).

[4] Harold F. Clark, *Economic Theory and Correct Occupational Distribution* (New York: Bureau of Publications, Teachers College, Columbia University, 1931), and *Life Earnings in Selected Occupations in the United States* (New York: Harper and Brothers, 1937).

[5] An article in the *Journal of the American Medical Association* for April 1950, illustrates the extent to which this illusion may be developed:

"First, consider the cost of becoming a physician. The prospective physician typically spends at least three years in premedical training and four years in a medical college — a total of seven years. Almost all graduating doctors of medicine today spend a year in internship. During this year the physician receives board and room and sometimes a nominal salary. The year of internship, or eighth year of training, is thus one of zero income but no cost. The previous seven years were years of cost and years of zero income. The physician who wishes to specialize, in addition to his year of internship, must serve one or more years — depending, in part, on the field he has chosen — as a resident in an approved hospital. As a resident he will receive board and room and a nominal salary. At about age 28, then, our typical physician may begin to earn an income.

"During the seven years before graduation from medical school our physician spent about $3,500 for tuition, books and the like — exclusive of board, room and clothing. During his two years of internship and residency he was presumably self sustaining on his small salary. But the money he might reasonably have earned throughout the entire nine years of training, in addition to the value of the perquisites and small salary of his internship and residency, must be added to the $3,500 expenses incurred in school. This income would have been roughly $26,500 for the nine years. Thus his out-of-pocket expense plus his lost income is approximately $30,000. When interest is accumulated on this amount the nine year training period has cost the young man entering the practice of medicine at age 28 roughly $35,000. He must amortize that investment — pay it off in annual installments — before it can be truly said that he is even with another man of the same age who started to earn after leaving high school at age 18.

"An endowment policy for $35,000 in force from age 28 to age 65 — the traditional age of retirement — and payable in full at age 65 or death, whichever is earlier, would require a premium of about $800 per year. An additional $1,400 per year, the 4 per cent interest on a $35,000 capital investment, must also be recovered. Thus a physician must earn $2,200 per year after paying the expenses of operating his office and after paying taxes on his income just to amortize the cost of his training. The operating expenses (office rent, personnel, supplies) of a physician in private practice generally run about two fifths of his gross income. His income taxes, depending on his income bracket, may be any one of numerous possible amounts. Nevertheless, considering expenses and taxes, it is reasonable to estimate $5,000 per year as the minimum allowance in terms of gross income necessary to amortize a capital cost of $35,000. Hence the first $5,000 of gross income for the physician should be excluded in making comparisons with the earnings of a person whose earning period started at age 18."

⁶ Harold F. Clark and Omar Pancoast, Jr., *Occupational Mobility* (New York: Columbia University Press, 1941).

⁷ Louis I. Dublin and Alfred J. Lotka, *The Money Value of a Man* (rev. ed.; New York: The Ronald Press, 1946).

⁸ See, for example, Oswald Hall, "The Stages of a Medical Career," *American Journal of Sociology,* vol. 53, January 1948.

⁹ Theodore Caplow, "The Criteria of Organizational Success," *Social Forces,* vol. 32, October 1953.

¹⁰ F. J. Roethlisberger and William J. Dickson, assisted by H. A. Wright, *Management and the Worker* (Cambridge, Mass.: Harvard University Press, 1946).

¹¹ The following translation is taken from Blakiston's *New Gould Medical Dictionary,* 1949. The numbers in brackets identify the appearance of the five indispensable elements of a professional code, as listed in the text:

"I swear by Apollo the physician, and Asclepius, and Health, and All-heal, and all the gods and goddesses, that, according to my ability and judgment, I will keep this oath and this stipulation — to reckon him who taught me this Art equally dear to me as my parents [4], to share my substance with him, and relieve his necessities if required; to look upon his offspring in the same footing as my own brothers and to teach them this art, if they shall wish to learn it, without fee or stipulation [4]; and that by precept, lecture, and every other mode of instruction I will impart a knowledge of the Art to my own sons, and those of my teachers, and to disciples bound by a stipulation and oath according to the law of medicine but to none others [4].

"I will follow that system of regimen which, according to my ability and judgment, I consider for the benefit of my patients, and abstain from whatever is deleterious and mischievous [2]. I will give no deadly medicine to any one if asked [2], nor suggest any such counsel; and in like manner I will not give to a woman a pessary to produce abortion [2]. With purity and with holiness I will pass my life and practice my art.

"I will not cut persons labouring under the stone, but will leave this to be done by men who are practitioners of this work [3]. Into whatever houses I enter, I will go into them for the benefit of the sick, and will abstain from every voluntary act of mischief and corruption [1]; and further, from the seduction of females or males, of freemen, and slaves [1].

"Whatever, in connexion with my professional practice, or not in connexion with it, I see or hear, in the life of men which ought not to be spoken of abroad, I will not divulge, as reckoning that all such should be kept secret [5]. While I continue to keep this Oath unviolated, may it be granted to me to enjoy life and the practice of the art, respected by all men, in all times [5]! But should I trespass and violate this Oath, may the reverse be my lot!"

[12] George C. Homans, *The Human Group* (New York: Harper and Brothers, 1951).

[13] Henri Pirenne, *Medieval Cities: Their Origins and the Revival of Trade* (Princeton, N. J.: Princeton University Press, 1925); Cecil Stewart, *A Prospect of Cities* (New York: Longmans, Green & Company, 1953).

CHAPTER 6

OCCUPATIONAL IDEOLOGIES

". . . the very different genius which appears to distinguish men of different professions, when grown up to maturity, is not upon many occasions so much the cause, as the effect of the division of labor. The difference between the most dissimilar characters, between a philosopher and a common street porter, for example, seems to arise, not so much from nature, as from habit, custom, and education." ADAM SMITH

THE influence of a calling on the lives of those who follow it does not cease with the five o'clock whistle, but extends beyond the shop or office to every aspect of existence. The few thorough studies of occupational milieus which extend to family life and social participation are amazingly rich in insights, and provide us with an understanding of certain social mechanisms which no studies of the general class structure are likely to distinguish. Such studies have been made of railroad men, professors, steelworkers, newspaper correspondents, actors, beggars, physicians, shipyard workers, hoboes, taxi-dancers, schoolteachers, waitresses, lumberjacks, naval officers, government officials, farmers, boxers, musicians, pharmacists, diplomats and thieves.[1]

These inquiries, while hardly complete, cover a range from very high to very low status, and from high to low stability. In all of them, the shaping of extra-occupational life by occupational influences appears to be extensive and complex. This out-of-hours influence usually has two major components. First, there are the customs and folkways which arise out of the nature of the occupation, or out of the traditions of the occupational group. Second, there are the standards of conduct which are enforced because of the real or supposed effects which their violation would have on the performance of the job.

OCCUPATIONAL FOLKWAYS

In the professions, the distinctiveness of occupational folkways depends on the size of the community. Only in metropolitan centers are the members of any one profession sufficiently numerous to form a closed community. In smaller communities, the standards of a professional group are replaced by certain norms which apply to the entire professional class, or to an even larger group of middle-class functionaries.

The usual professional folkways include the following elements:

1. Standards of consumption, including appropriate expenditures for housing, house furnishings, clothing, and automobiles; appropriate sports and patterns of recreation, institutional memberships, and civic participation.

2. Rough adherence to the financial folkways, which allow a considerable margin for tax evasion and slow payment of bills, but prohibit fraud and the receipt of earned income from unprofessional activities.

3. Adherence to the family mores, which prohibit polygamy, open concubinage, miscegenation, nonsupport, cruelty to children, and neglect.

4. Standards of dress, including the specification of a special costume for certain functions (i.e., the white coat) and of the general costume of respectability in most others.

5. Standards of decorum, including dignified carriage, inconspicuous table manners, a degree of aloofness, and avoidance of violent language and of public daytime intoxication.

This, of course, is the mere skeleton of a system, which in its full development may be sufficiently precise to control the choice of a children's school and the selection of neckties. In addition to these general obligations, local environments include much more specific rules such as total abstinence or obligatory hard drinking, residence in a particular neighborhood, or the expression in stereotyped form of certain approved political opinions. Here again, current fiction is rich in insights:

It was amusing but not ridiculous to observe that all the minor executives in the Stuyvesant, as well as the more ambitious clerks, wore conservative double-breasted suits like Tony Burton's, at the same time allowing undue rigidity to break out into pin stripes and herringbones, just like Tony Burton's. They all visited the barber once a week. They all had taken up golf, whether they liked it or not, and most of them wore the same square type of wrist watch and the same stainless-steel strap. They had adopted Tony Burton's posture and his brisk, quick step and even the gently vibrant inflection of his voice. In fact once at one of those annual dinners for officers and junior executives when everyone said a few words and got off a few local jokes about the bank, Charles had brought the matter up when he had been called upon to speak. Speaking was always an unpleasant ordeal with which he had finally learned to cope successfully largely from imitating Tony. He remembered standing up and waiting for silence, just as Tony waited, with the same faint smile and the same deliberate gaze.

"I should like to drink a toast," he had said, "not to our president but to everyone who tries to look like him. When I walk, I always walk like Tony, because Tony knows just how to walk; and when I talk, I always talk like Tony, because Tony knows just how to talk; and when I dress, I always dress like Tony, in a double-breasted suit. But no matter how I try, I cannot be like Tony. I can never make myself sufficiently astute." [2]

It should be noted too that this conformity tends to arise out of direct imitation of superiors, as much as group pressure. The predominant influence of the elders in the hierarchic structure of the professions has already been noted. Thus, young and even middle-aged professionals typically stand in a quasi-filial relationship to older men who guide and sponsor them, and who set the standards of personal as well as professional conduct.

The concept of responsibility plays a great part here. It may be regarded as the summary expression of the personal qualities required to maintain a given personal authority. In the professions, where the legal right to practice confers a certificate of minimum competence, the evaluation of responsibility is often more significant than the evaluation of merit. On these levels, responsibility is measured in terms of such qualities as punctuality, discretion, conformity, and nervous endurance; all of which increase the predictability of the subject's future behavior and, more specifically, guarantee the continuity of his career pattern. These are matters which are far more important to the professional elders than to patients and clients, and this circumstance creates some conflict and may encourage the further isolation of the professional group. Especially among physicians and lawyers, isolation may be carried to the point where any serious extra-occupational interests are disapproved, and where sociable contacts with laymen are consciously held to a minimum.

In the crafts, the folkways are somewhat less exacting. A definitive status is achieved at a much earlier age and, as previously noted, the possibilities of advancement are limited. In the United States — as nowhere else — craftsmen are typically middle class. Indeed, it is as manual workers who are also "bourgeois" that they occupy a distinctive position. Given the extreme fluctuations to which craft employment is subject, this position is nevertheless marginal, and most of the occupational folkways are designed to reinforce it and to confirm respectability.

Standards of consumption are as important as in the professions, but less elaborated; more importance is attached to the possession of property than to its conspicuous display. Thus it is for this group that home owner-ship has its greatest symbolic value, and in times of prosperity becomes almost mandatory. The possession of late-model automobiles, of such heavy appliances as refrigerators, television sets, and automatic washing machines, of real property, and of life insurance, all have more emotional significance here than elsewhere in the general society. Conspicuous con-sumption — lavish expenditure on food or entertainment for example — is likely to be disapproved as interfering with the orderly accumulation of property.

For similar reasons, conformity to conventional family mores — mo-nogamy, assortative mating, an equitable division of income, protection of children and the assumption of responsibility for their acts, observance of family rituals, and the rigorous division of labor between the sexes and between generations — is strongly marked. But sexual activities and atti-tudes which do not have a direct influence upon status are partially ex-cluded from the scope of this control.

Over and beyond these two generic characteristics, there is the usual pat-tern of differential folkways applied in one community or another. As a rule, we may suppose that whatever behavior is most strongly encouraged by the group — religious participation or union solidarity or financial re-liability — will be well calculated, in each local setting, to confirm the middle-class status of the craftsmen.

While the folkways of the crafts tend to minimize variations in social status, the standards of individual conduct which define responsibility are highly personal. Not only does the craft organization, when intact, guaran-tee competence and standardize output; it also ensures a roughly equal dis-tribution of opportunity, so that the only uncontrolled area is that having to do with personal relationships on the job. The craftsman comes to be evaluated very precisely in terms of his habits and personality traits. Those which are disapproved are the ones which interfere with the smooth func-tioning of the working group: pugnacity, carelessness, ill humour, taci-turnity, nervousness, dishonesty, self-pity, and the like. In a sense, the rules of comportment which are applied are extensions of the tacit rules encountered in the "normal" family. Under favorable circumstances, the environment of the crafts may be less disorganizing than almost any other occupational milieu.

In the factory trades, as in all mobile occupations, control of extra-vocational behavior is relatively weak. In fact, it may be misleading to discuss folkways at all in this connection, since, in most instances, the occupational group is something of an abstraction outside of the factory gates, and not nearly as significant as the family, locality, religious, ethnic, and congeniality groups in which the worker is involved. This tends to hold even when a factory working force is recruited from a relatively homogeneous population, as in a southern mill village or in the ethnic settlements of South Chicago.

Evidently, all the mechanisms which exist in more highly organized milieus are present here, but they are attenuated by the limitation of social rewards. The factory hand cannot ordinarily establish a secure economic status, or even achieve the credit privileges of the higher economic groups. Conspicuous consumption tends to be tailored to the possibilities. Clothing rather than housing, and the automobile rather than the insurance policy, are the effective symbols of achievement.

Responsibility tends to be more narrowly defined for the same reasons. The only personal qualities which are invariably relevant in the working situation are those summed up under the heading of "reliability": punctuality, regular attendance, immobility, attention, and abstinence from heavy drinking — a factor of great importance in the evaluation of semiskilled workers. This is a very limited set of norms compared to the vast elaboration of standards on other levels.[3]

For the professional man, long identification with a single establishment may be an indifferent or even negative factor in the personnel record. For the craftsman, it is of minor importance. But for the machine tender, stability (as an index of reliability) is often the only kind of personal achievement which can be made a part of his reputation.

For the shopkeeper, the control of nonoccupational behavior is conditioned by three factors: first, the absence of strong occupational organizations; second, his passionate identification with the role of businessman; third, the fact that his personal characteristics and his style of living affect his business.

The separation of the shopkeeper's residence from his shop is a fairly recent occurrence and has been more complete in the United States than elsewhere. The codes of symbols developed by Bardet[4] for the systematic study of European communities use a single symbol to indicate both the shop and the shopkeeper's home, which are ordinarily found in the same building. One basic motive for separation is that the norms of deference imposed on the shopkeeper prevent him from displaying a distinctly higher

status than his customers, while his aspirations toward the role of businessman impel him to do so.

The most conspicuous element in the folkways of this group is the
double status imposed by circumstances: on the one hand, the attempt to
achieve full business-class status by an appropriate style of living and by
intensive participation in business-class associations; on the other, the
concealment of this status during the working day. Thus it comes about
that when the retail business expands to the point of obvious prosperity,
the owner usually retreats into anonymity and no longer wishes to be
identified by all his customers.

The legal device of incorporation offers an opportunity to make this
separation explicit, by divorcing the behavior of the business from that of
its owner. The divorce is nullified to some extent by the network of credit
information facilities which continues to present the essential facts of
ownership to potential lenders and suppliers. Nevertheless, the most striking element in the social organization of retail merchants is their withdrawal from traditional identifications.

Social conformity, in the sense of adherence to community standards,
is one of the most complex correlates of an occupational position. As related to status, it is subject to two principles which, while not contradictory, work in opposite directions. The first is that personal freedom and
a degree of immunity from moral sanctions is one of the definite perquisites
of high status in any system of stratification. The second is that occupations closely associated with sacred elements, or especially charged with
social responsibility, require their practitioners to function as models and
examples. In the United States, the matter is further complicated by the
anonymity of metropolitan life, by the diffusion of middle-class patterns,
and by specific limitations on the occupational freedom of women.

Other things being equal, we should expect to find the strictest control
of nonoccupational behavior attached to those occupations which have
important role-setting obligations, are identified with sacred symbols, and
have relatively low status. We should expect least control in connection
with those occupations which enjoy high status without the involvement of
sacred elements.

This seems to be the case. Teaching is perhaps the best illustration of the
former situation. Hundreds of communities still allow schoolteachers less
freedom than any other adults, often forbidding them to smoke, to marry,
or to choose their own friends. Examples of the other extreme may be

readily found in the more mobile branches of engineering, in such quasi-professions as advertising and sales management, and in a few highly skilled industrial trades.

There are some apparent exceptions too. Considerable license is accorded to movie actors, who do have a role-setting function, and to journalists, whose social responsibility is conspicuous, but as Rosten's studies of both these groups show,[5] the norms which actually regulate conduct in Hollywood and Washington differ considerably from those of less specialized communities.

THE FORMATION OF OCCUPATIONAL ATTITUDES

It is by consensus and by the sharing of attitudes that occupational groups on the large scale become sociologically meaningful. These common values and understandings are not limited to the working situation but touch every corner of human activity. For the purpose of analysis, a distinction can be drawn between occupational attitudes and extra-occupational attitudes associated with a particular occupation, but in practice this distinction is difficult, and probably unnecessary.

It is by means of attitudinal formulas, expressed in a set manner, that men and women describe the problems posed by human interaction during the working day. Even the most loosely organized occupational group will share certain attitudes toward the evaluation of its own status; the definition of appropriate work; the measurement of effort; the motives of the public; and the motives of competing and related groups.

In closely organized occupational systems, there will also be found a range of political, religious, recreational, and economic values, which cannot be easily summarized by the outside observer, precisely because it is the full appreciation of their nuances which constitutes membership. The aspiring bank cashier learns to choose the appropriate haberdashery for each stage of his career, just as the young instructor in philosophy knows to a hair's breadth the effect of a given metaphysical theory on his chances of promotion. In the course of these conditionings, each of them learns to think sufficiently like his elders, so that even if they should later choose to assert a difference on some particular issue, their general orientation to the world which surrounds them will follow the prescribed pattern.

It would be quite impossible to set down a full description of occupational attitudes, because of their number and variety. Nevertheless, a brief review of our four occupational types may be useful. Certain themes well worth noting emerge in each case.

As we have seen before, the world of the professional is a fairly tight enclosure. The development of common attitudes is reinforced at many points: by the essential distinction which must be drawn between co-professionals and laymen in every working situation, by the concentration of attention which marks the professional career, by the long period of formation, and by the informal association out of working hours which is tacitly required.

Each of the major professions tends to award itself a higher status than outsiders would be willing to concede, and to underestimate its relative rewards. Of course, disproportions between the relative prestige and the relative earnings of a professional group may exist, but the degree of disproportion is invariably exaggerated. This mild paranoia serves as a constant support for the militancy of professional organizations in promoting their economic interests.

A similar mechanism prevents the various professions from forming a single class. It is chiefly in comparison with other professions that each professional group exaggerates its own importance and deprecates its own rewards, so that interprofessional cooperation is sporadic at best. The few studies of interprofessional attitudes [6] show unexpectedly great social distance between professional groups of similar status.

Another circumstance which tends toward attitudinal isolation is the development of superordinate and specialized attitudes (bedside manner, judicial calm, etc.) toward patients and clients, which come to be inappropriately transferred to other situations involving laymen, so that social interaction with them is hampered.

In the crafts, the most distinctive attitudes are those which revolve around contractual obligations, implicit or explicit, which specify the rights and duties of each in relation to all. These attitudes, which define a day's work, a fair wage, a good shop, a bad foreman, the right tools, a reasonable order, a one-man job, or the jurisdiction of a craft, are essentially moral. They contain a principle of justice drawn from two important sources: the medieval idea of the "just price" and the early modern theory that society is founded by a free contract.

The attitudes of factory workers are less standardized; indeed the findings of industrial research suggest that occupational attitudes are a function of the structure of the informal group in which the worker finds himself. The element which has been most carefully studied is the informal group's orientation toward management. Even in the same plant, this may range from docile acquiescence to open hostility. There are many other elements as well. It would appear that many factory groups are organized around ethnic conflict, that others contain a sort of spontaneous craft organization, and that some are oriented to outside activities.

The American factory worker can still be legitimately differentiated from factory workers in other countries by the lack of a systematic class identification. Yet, like the enlisted man in the armed forces, the factory worker is inevitably aware of his disadvantaged position in the social structure and of his subjection to a hierarchy of authority from which he is excluded. Lack of class consciousness does not mean that this situation goes unnoticed; but only that it does not lead to definite political beliefs or to consistent identification with others in the same position. Nevertheless, as Jones [7] and others have shown, the political attitudes of industrial workers are sharply differentiated from those of managers and white-collar employees. It is probable that informal attitudes on property and respectability differ even more sharply, but being unrelated to any specific creed, they do not have predictable political consequences.

The shopkeeper, as we have seen, is partially isolated from his confreres. His occupation is not characterized by the day-by-day exchange of opinion and gossip which shapes common attitudes. On the other hand, his role as a small businessman is defined with extraordinary precision by all the agencies of mass communication.

This places the shopkeeper squarely in the middle of one of the major ideological conflicts of our society: he is committed on the one hand to oppose "government interference" and the constantly enlarging network of social controls which interfere with the businessman's liberty of action, but he is constrained by the facts of economic concentration to oppose the specific measures taken by large-scale business to diminish competition and to increase its control over him.

Over and beyond the attitudes formed in the working situation, and the attitudes toward current social issues developed in an occupational milieu, is the more fundamental question of attitudes toward work itself.

In his quasi-historical study of what work has meant to men through the ages, Tilgher [8] points out that Western civilization inherits a number of inconsistent theories on the significance of work: the Greek derogation of all labor as servile, the medieval view of work as the penalty of Adam's fall, the exaltation of work as a means of self-discipline and a visible token of grace in the Calvinist ethic, and the modern identification of work with conscious creativity, most clearly expressed by Henri Bergson. All these influences survive together in the ensemble of modern culture. The contempt for manual labor is associated with the cult of physical exercise. The Marxist deification of the toiling masses and the universal ideal of early retirement are no more inconsistent than the imposition of work as a privilege in our schools and as a penalty in our prisons.

The differences between occupational levels in this respect are very significant. We may note, in passing, that work tends to be regarded as an end in itself precisely in those spheres where it is highly rewarded, and as a painful necessity wherever it is meanly paid. There is nothing very obscure in this situation. Its importance is seen in the scale of differential values which extends from the lower end of the occupational scale, where work offers few psychic rewards and is justified only by the necessity of eating, to certain specialized positions at the upper end, where work is its own sufficient goal, to which all other life activities are more or less subordinated.

The empirical studies of job satisfaction undertaken by Hoppock and others, although so far very limited, provide a surprisingly clear picture. In Hoppock's study of New Hope,[9] the curve of job satisfaction is heavily skewed toward satisfaction; indeed, it resembles very closely the distribution of happiness in marriage as reported in numerous investigations of marital adjustment. This should occasion no surprise. The survival of any set of social institutions implies a reasonable degree of satisfaction. The fact is easily forgotten by those who study the problems generated by these same institutions, but it should never be left out of account in an interpretation. Another finding of the same order is that occupational satisfaction increases sharply and regularly with higher occupational status.

These attitudes toward work are seldom the worker's personal reaction to an environment. The norm of occupational satisfaction seems to be rather exactly defined in each occupational group: policemen are expected to be better satisfied than are post office clerks, and scholars more than manufacturers. The origin of these norms has been at least partly explained by researches in industrial sociology to which we will return later. For the moment, it is important to note that there is no simple correlation between the objective conditions presented by an occupation and the relative satisfaction of its members.

THE SOCIOLOGY OF WORK

THE OCCUPATIONAL STEREOTYPE

The description of an occupation is not complete when we have measured it in terms of prestige, remuneration, and mobility, described its internal organization, and examined the ways in which it shapes the behavior of its members. There remains another set of occupational attributes: a sort of subculture composed of the manners and mores and folkways peculiar to the calling, the legends grown up about it, and the symbols which it displays.

The sheer age of an occupation has important consequences for its stereotype. To be a cook, a philosopher, a sailor, or a carpenter is to be qualitatively different from oil-well gun perforators, group dynamicists, seismic observers, or acid chambermen. The former, being universally recognized, and each having a very long history, are universally credited with certain moral and personal characteristics. The member of a highly familiar occupation is continuously aware of his definite role as defined by tradition. He can predict with reasonable accuracy the manner in which he will be received in any company, and the status which will be accorded to him. Where the expectations are very definite, he will even be likely to assume the appropriate personality traits. It is probable that professors are more absent-minded, reporters more cynical, chefs more excitable, and policemen more brutal, than an examination of their Rorschach scores would suggest.

There is, in this matter, the usual relationship between behavior and role. The stereotype is based on certain "real" elements in the working situation. Whyte's study of the restaurant kitchen as a working group shows some factors which predispose chefs to emotional excitability.[10] Wilson shows how the professorial job encourages an appearance of impracticality and unworldliness.[11] However, the stereotype is itself the most important agent for the conditioning of roles.

Most occupations today are relatively unfamiliar, which means that communication between the working situation and the general society is seriously hampered. Achievements on the job cannot be easily exchanged for social prestige. The small coinage of daily experience at work has no currency outside the plant, and the individual is continually subjected to misidentifications. Roethlisberger notes that the unfamiliarity of technical jobs at Western Electric left their holders at a disadvantage in the community.[12]

Not only are thousands of modern occupations unfamiliar; but many others are readily confused. Rural postmen, who are independent contractors, resent identification with urban postmen, who are merely employees. Automobile mechanics are often confused with filling-station attendants, power-house engineers with janitors, and accountants with clerks. Pretentiousness in occupational titles (consulting sales engineer, for example) is often a device to prevent misidentification. Indeed, one of the strongest factors making for professionalization is the attempt to escape an unfavorable stereotype by transmuting undertakers into morticians, bill collectors into credit representatives, and reporters into journalists.

Nevertheless, the very distinctness of the professional stereotype raises certain characteristic problems. In the first place, each of the major professions is engaged in a continuous struggle against interlopers who assume its style and titles. Carr-Saunders [13] has described the desperate efforts of professional engineers in Great Britain to prevent locomotive drivers, furnace tenders, blueprinters, caretakers, millwrights, and others from describing themselves as engineers. In the United States, a similar effort has been even less successful, and the title of engineer is lightheartedly claimed by tree surgeons, shoe salesmen, and snowplow drivers.

A quite different problem is presented by the unfavorable popular stereotypes which have attached for centuries to lawyers, physicians, dentists, teachers, and the clergy. The situation of a professional group is, after all, somewhat vulnerable. Highly visible, moderately privileged, partially isolated, and responsible in the exercise of their authority for some of the major woes of their fellow men, professional men are logical targets for popular aggression. In the case of physicians, an intensive propaganda has somewhat dissipated this sentiment, but no study of professional groups should overlook the fact that they are usually highly aware of the unfavorable stereotypes of shyster, quack, butcher, pedant, sissy, and the like, which, in spite of full-page, full-color ads, keep them slightly on the defensive.

In the crafts, the stereotypes serve the interest of the occupational organization more directly. Particularly where the monopoly of the building trades has been effectively preserved, the tendency of the stereotype is to exaggerate the skill of the craftsman and to present him in the part of one who practices a mystery.

Although the craft-organized occupations are among the very oldest which can be distinctly identified, the uniformity of their practices has the effect of mixing them together in a single popular image, which does not distinguish clearly between carpenters and painters, masons and brick-layers. Inside the occupational milieu, these distinctions tend to be made very sharp, and the brash, reckless character attributed to electricians is quite different from the surly cynicism of plumbers or the stoical gaiety of swing-stage painters. How much these collective representations differ from place to place and from time to time it is, in the absence of research evidence, quite impossible to guess.

In the factory trades, the most conspicuous aspect of this process is the conflict which takes place among contradictory social images. The stereo-typed image of the Right-Thinking American Workman is perhaps about as current as that of the Militant Member of the Toiling Masses. In between lie a variety of highly differentiated roles which have only local significance.

Indeed, the principal difference between the United States and the rest of the industrialized Occident with respect to industrial relations is the absence so far of any coherent image of the American working man and woman. While Labor is clearly conceptualized, and becomes for the more prosperous classes a highly charged symbol, the attribution of personality traits to workmen is relatively feeble. It is rather curious, given the general tendency in the United States to exaggerate spurious ethnic and class characteristics, that the industrial worker is less clearly stereotyped than almost any other occupational group. The principal explanation must be sought in the facts of mobility.

By contrast, the retail trades appear to have preserved a good deal of their distinctive characters, based in part upon historical associations, and in part upon current differences in economic organization. Thus, it was the butcher who became the symbolic figure of the oppressive merchant under price control, and examination of the popular literature suggests that this involved the blending of elements drawn from his ancient func-tion of slaughtering and dressing and from his contemporary uniqueness as the supplier of an unpackaged and unmarked commodity.

Here again, only certain crude outlines of the situation can be sketched, since we lack the studies on which an adequate analysis would rest. The richness of the folklore concerning the retail merchant is easily explained in terms of the familiarity of the situations in which he figures, and the degree to which they are patterned by objective circumstances. Most of the elements which enter into occupational status generally are represented in the formation of these images: differences of sex, age, skill, wealth; the negative weights attached to personal service and manual labor; the hostility to ethnic groups disproportionately represented in some commercial categories; the highly inflected distinctions which are drawn between hard goods and soft goods, necessities and luxuries, perishables and nonperishables, commodities and services. In the end, the differences created, for example, between the lewd half-comic stereotype of the iceman and the arch-respectability of the hardware merchant are sufficient to erase the formal identity which places them in the same category on an occupational scale.

CHANGES IN OCCUPATIONAL INSTITUTIONS

The principal changes in occupational institutions are the result of, first, the numerical growth or decline of the occupation and, second, the strengthening or weakening of its internal organization.

The characteristic syndrome of a declining occupation (for example, linotyping, baking, railroading) is well marked. There is a tendency for status to decline somewhat in advance of the decline in employment opportunities and for the number of recruits and marginal practitioners to fall off very rapidly. At the same time, the defensive efforts made by the union or professional association, whether or not successful, tend to increase its influence and thereby strengthen its monopoly. The average age of members increases as younger men find another trade and as it becomes easier to restrict numbers. This movement sometimes has the net effect of raising standards and thereby raising productivity. Given an initially strong association, it may also happen that the occupational monopoly is tightened by the restriction of numbers to the point where wages rise and productivity falls. This appears to have been characteristic of railroad employment for several decades. Nevertheless, as Cottrell has shown, the patterning of nonoccupational behavior becomes fainter with each decline in status, and it is in occupations of this type that dissatisfaction is likely to be general.

It should be noted, in passing, that even an occupation which has declined very far (such as shiprigging) is not necessarily doomed to extinction, but may be revived or even changed into an expanding occupation by the run of circumstances. Under these conditions, the combination of effective monopoly and a real scarcity of skill creates a highly privileged situation for some time. Beyond a certain point of decline (for example, in bottle-making) the occupational structure disappears, and the survival of a small remnant — either very specialized or very isolated — must be explained in terms of family or personal histories.

The same tendency for changes in status to outrun changes in trend is seen in the case of expanding occupations. The number of recruits attracted is usually disproportionately great. Thus it was at one time estimated that the number of students in schools of journalism in the United States approached the number of employed journalists, and the number of those trained for personnel work under the G.I. Bill of Rights alone was said to exceed the number of active positions in the field. The perennially attractive occupations (entertainment, aviation, certain civil service categories) can never accept more than a small fraction of those available.

Whether and how quickly an expanding occupation will be swamped by this acceleration of recruiting depends on the time and expense of training and on the control exerted by unions or associations. As wartime experience illustrated, the number of workers in simple trades could be multiplied by ten or twenty in a few months, and a number of trades formerly considered to be highly skilled could, by subdivision, be subjected to expansion on the same scale.

So it comes about that the position of the individual in an expanding occupation, threatened at once by the acceleration of recruiting and the increased competition of marginal practitioners, is often more precarious than it would be in a declining occupation. But an effective organization is capable of arresting these tendencies, or even reversing them. Thus the motion picture projectionists were able to reduce recruiting in an occupation prepared for rapid expansion. In the most spectacular and important instance, an exceptionally powerful association has been able to reduce the proportionate number of physicians, in the face of an enormously increased demand for medical services.

We should expect, therefore, to find that expanding occupations are characterized, in the case of manual work, by a strong impulse toward the development of craft organization, and in the case of white-collar work, by an effort toward professionalization. There are, however, several reasons why craft organization is not easily developed in these times; especially important among these are the difficulty of creating apprenticeship systems and the tendency for new occupational functions to be rationalized and supervised by the managerial employees who create them. In spite of certain exceptions (sailors, broadcasting technicians, furriers), the creation of new craft organizations is relatively rare. Professionalization, on the other hand, is of great significance in any consideration of occupational trends.

Indeed, it may be asserted that virtually all non-routine white-collar functions are in the process of being professionalized to some extent. The nature of the economy gives most such functions the character of expanding occupations (through its progressive shift of manpower from direct production to distribution, communication, and control). At the same time, the growth of facilities for secondary and higher education, as well as the pragmatic bias which adds more and more vocational training to the educational curriculum, assures a steady oversupply of recruits. Finally, the increasing degree of economic concentration in the economy reduces the possibility of speculative profits based on a business type of organization (e.g., for accountants and architects) while at the same time widening the opportunities for personal earnings.

The steps involved in professionalization are quite definite, and even the sequence is explicit, so that we may illustrate it with equal facility from the example of newspaper reporters (journalists), real estate agents (realtors), undertakers (morticians), junk dealers (salvage consultants), or laboratory technicians (medical technologists).[14]

The first step is the establishment of a professional association, with definite membership criteria designed to keep out the unqualified.

The second step is the change of name, which serves the multiple function of reducing identification with the previous occupational status, asserting a technological monopoly, and providing a title which can be monopolized, the former one being usually in the public domain.

The third step is the development and promulgation of a code of ethics which asserts the social utility of the occupation, sets up public welfare rationale, and develops rules which serve as further criteria to eliminate the unqualified and unscrupulous (see Chapter 5). The adoption of a code of ethics, despite certain hypocrisies, imposes a real and permanent limitation on internal competition.

The fourth step is a prolonged political agitation, whose object it is to obtain the support of the public power for the maintenance of the new occupational barriers. In practice this usually proceeds by stages from the limitation of a specialized title to those who have passed an examination (registered engineer, certified public accountant) to the final stage at which the mere doing of the acts reserved to the profession is a crime.

Concurrently with this activity, which may extend over a very long period of time, goes the development of training facilities directly or indirectly controlled by the professional society, particularly with respect to admission and to final qualification; the establishment through legal action of certain privileges of confidence and inviolability, the elaboration of the rules of decorum found in the code, and the establishment — after conflict — of working relations with related professional groups.

It is difficult to exaggerate the importance of this general phenomenon for the structure of the economy. So powerful are the motives conducing to professionalization that it may be observed under way in occupations once considered entirely commercial (banking, advertising), in occupations which never involve independent work (drafting, photographic processing), and in those which used to be thought of as quite removed from the economic arena (philanthropy and the research sciences). Even pure management is perhaps in the process of being professionalized, and it is not farfetched to suppose that the professional society may eventually be counted among the major social institutions.

NOTES

[1] See the studies cited in the Bibliography for this chapter.

[2] John P. Marquand, *Point of No Return* (New York: Bantam Books, 1952), p. 81.

[3] Davis has studied the reactions of underprivileged workers for whom even these limited norms are nonoperative, because of their failure to lead to reward in the slum environment. Allison Davis, "The Motivation of the Underprivileged Worker," *ETC*, vol. 3, no. 4, Summer 1946.

[4] Gaston Bardet, *Le Nouvel Urbanisme* (Paris: V. Freal, 1948).

[5] Leo C. Rosten, *Hollywood: The Movie Colony, the Movie Makers* (New York: Harcourt, Brace & Company, 1941) and *The Washington Correspondents* (New York: Harcourt, Brace & Company, 1937).

[6] Arthur E. Briggs, "Social Distance between Lawyers and Doctors," *Sociology and Social Research*, vol. 13, November–December 1928.

[7] Alfred Winslow Jones, *Life, Liberty, and Property* (Philadelphia: J. B. Lippincott Company, 1941).

[8] Adriano Tilgher, *Work: What It Has Meant to Men through the Ages*, translated from *Homo Faber* by Dorothy Canfield Fisher (New York: Harcourt, Brace & Company, 1930).

[9] Robert Hoppock, *Job Satisfaction* (New York: Harper and Brothers, 1935).

[10] William Foote Whyte, *Human Relations in the Restaurant Industry* (New York: McGraw-Hill Book Company, 1948).

[11] Logan Wilson, *The Academic Man: A Study in the Sociology of a Profession* (New York: Oxford University Press, 1942).

[12] F. J. Roethlisberger, *Management and Morale* (Cambridge, Mass.: Harvard University Press, 1941).

[13] A. M. Carr-Saunders and P. A. Wilson, *The Professions* (Oxford: Clarendon Press, 1933).

[14] Note the following very typical sequence of events, reported in an editorial in *Minnesota Medicine,* vol. 35, April 1952:

"A new profession — Medical Technology — has rather rapidly come into existence.

"Prior to 1928, the qualifications of the laboratory technician were vague. That year the American Society of Clinical Pathologists, under the direction of Dr. Kano Ikeda of Saint Paul, set up a national registry of clinical laboratory technicians and established preschool and training standards for students. At first, high school graduates were admitted to the laboratory schools. Later, one year of college and then two years were required. Today most matriculates are college graduates.

"Likewise, the American Society of Clinical Pathologists undertook the standardization of the training schools. Later, this was done in co-operation with the Council of Medical Education and Hospitals of the American Medical Association, and in 1935 the Council took over entirely.

"The registered technicians organized as the American Society of Clinical Laboratory Technicians at a meeting held in Chicago in June, 1933. The next year the society's first publication, known as *The Bulletin of the American Society of Clinical Laboratory Technicians,* appeared. In 1936 the name was changed to *The American Journal of Medical Technology.*

"With the increase in preschool requirements and better technical training, the term technologist was adopted instead of technician. The national society became the American Society of Medical Technologists. The purpose of the Society is self betterment and the encouragement of mutual understanding between members and other medical and scientific organizations. Membership is restricted to those registered by the American Society of Clinical Pathologists.

"An attempt was made to obtain the exclusive right to the letters M.T. to designate a Medical Technologist registered by the American Society of Clinical Pathologists. That having failed, the designation M.T. (ASCP) was adopted.

"The standards of the Registry have been approved by the American Medical Association, the American College of Surgeons and the American Hospital Association. The AMA and the ACS, in their inspection and standardization of hospitals, stress the necessity of having registered (ASCP) laboratory personnel.

"The American Society of Medical Technology is composed of numerous state societies. It holds annual meetings which until 1947 were held in conjunction with the annual ASCP meetings. With the increase in membership (about 5,000 in 1951), the Society has met independently since 1947.

"Many commercial schools for the training of laboratory technicians have been established throughout the country to meet the growing demand. The graduates of these unrecognized schools are not qualified for registration with the American Society of Clinical Pathologists, nor are they eligible for membership in the American Society of Medical Technology."

CHAPTER 7

SOCIOLOGY OF THE LABOR MARKET

"The workmen desire to get as much as possible, the masters to give as little as possible. The former are disposed to combine in order to raise, the latter in order to lower the wages of labour." ADAM SMITH

THE labor market — the central mechanism of social distribution in modern societies — is something of an enigma. The theory, or rather the conflicting theories, of its operation are familiar to the point of banality, yet until recent years very little was known about its actual workings, and there are still important gaps to be filled before even an elementary description can be completed. All that will be attempted here is a sketch of the main outlines. This is nothing more than a continuation of the subject of occupational institutions; but the institutions which frame the sale and purchase of services enjoy a special importance.

Historically, wage theory has addressed itself to the question "What determines the level of wages?" and has emerged with two contradictory answers. Curiously enough, no clear distinction can be drawn between classical and Marxian economics on this point. The first answer is that wages are in the long run determined by the cost of subsistence and tend to approach the minimum compatible with the survival of the laborer. This assumption was first formulated by Malthus in the *Essay on Population*.[1] It provided the basis for Ricardo's Iron Law, which justified starvation wages in terms of the inexorable workings of supply and demand, and also for Marx's theory of surplus value, which holds that under capitalism the difference between the cost of subsistence and the worker's productivity will always be diverted to the exploiter. As has often been pointed out, the early English textile industries, which both the classical economists and the communist theorists took as a model, did for a long time pay wages which approximated the minimum cost of subsistence.[2]

The second answer, evolved by a long line of theorists from Marshall through the Austrian School to Keynes, is that in general wages tend to be determined by marginal net productivity: the value of the work of the least productive worker. This theory has the advantage of explaining the secular changes in the wage level but the disadvantage of requiring a number of rigid assumptions, such as perfect mobility of labor, and the absence of those inevitable combinations to which Adam Smith referred. Another difficulty is that, while the minimum cost of subsistence can be roughly measured, marginal productivity is an abstract concept except in small-scale situations.

The course of events has not been kind to either of these explanations. Contrary to prediction, real wages have risen in most industrialized countries during the last century. At the same time, the functions of unions, employer associations, and government agencies restricting the free play of economic forces have expanded steadily and continue to do so.

More and more, the theory of the labor market has come to seem archaic. With increasing knowledge of income distributions, it becomes evident that "the level of wages" is very nearly a meaningless concept. It is the differences among "levels of wages" which call insistently for explanation. Why, for example, do some industries consistently pay nearly twice as much for unskilled labor as other industries in the same area? Why are some especially disagreeable occupations well paid, and others poorly? Why do construction carpenters receive much higher wages than cabinet-makers, who represent a more skilled branch of the same occupation? Why do locomotive salesmen, with a large dollar volume of sales, earn so much less than toy salesmen? Why do the average earnings in certain occupations rise during depressions and fall during booms, while others remain nearly stable? Although such differentials seem inequitable to participants and observers alike, the few efforts which have been made to state a principle of equitable distribution have not been notably successful.

The most coherent (and perhaps least successful) effort to describe an ideal wage distribution is that of Clark, who holds that "the income of the country is a maximum when the marginal net return is equal in each occupation," [3] and that "occupational distribution is correct when people of equal ability receive equal wages in all occupations." [4] By ability, he apparently means native ability, as measured by intelligence tests and similar devices. Unfortunately, native ability is known not to correlate very highly with performance even within a single occupation, being far outweighed by the combination of such factors as interest, experience, motivation, role, and specific talent. The problem of equating the native abilities of a copyreader and a pastry cook in any logical way is probably insoluble.

There is also a more fundamental objection which can be raised. Unless the scale of ability is identical in all occupations, which is manifestly absurd, the only condition which would satisfy the condition that people of equal ability receive equal wages would be a single uniform wage for all wage earners. But this hypothetical arrangement would contradict the other requirement that marginal net return be equal in all occupations.

Another sort of norm can be derived empirically from the administrative technique of job evaluation. As personnel technicians explain it, in an industrial manual: "A job-evaluation rating scale is usually constructed on a logical direct-ratio basis. Equal increments of skill, effort, and responsibility required by the job result in equal increments of job-rating value . . . In theory, the wage curve for a group of jobs, arranged equally distant along a base line according to their importance to the company, should be a straight line rising evenly from a low base (usually the legal minimum) to the highest rates the community can pay for its most skilled workers."

Such a system, generalized to a substantial segment of the community, does provide a system which approaches objectivity in that each job is evaluated by comparison with those which are most similar to it. The scale is thus built up out of a series of very small differentials which command agreement. Nevertheless, it must be recognized that the minimum and maximum points which fix the slope of the curve are quite arbitrary when applied to a whole community, and that the equal rating intervals which determine its shape are merely a statistical convenience.

At various times in the past a number of very general principles have been proposed. Of these, the most important is the medieval notion of the Just Price, which, as will be shown a little further on, may still be found operative in some of our current practices. The Just Price, applied to wages, derives the wage distribution from a pre-established status distribution, so that a fair wage is that which enables the recipient to "maintain the station into which he hath been called." When the status distribution is supported by a system of occupational inheritance, and further reinforced by sumptuary legislation which fixes the standard of living at each level, the determination of wages in this way is perfectly practicable. Morris gives numerous illustrations of the application of these devices in the early American colonies.[5] A system of customary wages demands stability in the status scale on which it is based, and a slow enough rate of social change to allow specific wage rates to take on a traditional character.

Two other criteria which figured prominently in the ideological ferment of the nineteenth century deserve mention. Both of them owe a good deal to Jeremy Bentham, and the pleasure-pain principle of the utilitarianists. The first is to correlate wages with disagreeableness, the best paid occupations being those which are least attractive or most dangerous. The other — which would likewise have the effect of turning existing income distributions upside down — is to price services in proportion to their social utility.

Indeed, the fact that the disagreeable and the hazardous occupations are among the worst paid has long been something of a puzzle in labor market analysis.[6] Supply and demand, in the classical sense, should assign a high wage to these occupations — if it is assumed that the unattractiveness of the work would restrict the supply of labor without any corresponding restriction of demand. In practice, it seems to work the other way around. The only candidates for jobs as sewer cleaners and lead miners are those who have few other occupational choices. Their number is sufficiently large so that the supply is not restricted. The reciprocal influence of status and remuneration being most marked at the extremes of the social scale, the low status which attaches to such employments tends to set a ceiling on the wage level. Further, the pyramidal structure of the labor force makes it intrinsically unlikely that any low-status occupation will experience a serious restriction of supply, except for brief periods when there is a general labor shortage. It should be noted that occupations which are *extremely* dangerous, such as driving dynamite trucks, or extremely disagreeable, such as preparing cadavers for laboratory dissection, do command high wages, especially where a certain measure of skill is required.

The pricing of services according to their social utility involves a similar paradox. It is precisely in the primary productive activities — those most essential to society — that interchangeability is highest, as we have previously noted. In general, the more indispensable the function, the less indispensable are the particular individuals performing it. Here again, the numerical implications are important. The most essential activities are those which engage labor on a large scale — agriculture, manufacturing, and transportation. Any rise in the price of this labor involves very large costs, and a limit (set by the productivity of the economic system as a whole) is soon reached. The least essential activities, the arts and sciences perhaps, employ a small fraction of the labor force and, within reasonable limits, may take as much income as they are able to secure without seriously disturbing the balance of the system. Managerial groups are in the same position, with the additional consideration that they themselves are charged with wage-setting, and that the marginal productivity of managerial services is likely to be reckoned high.

Strangely enough, the literature of socialism has not contributed very much to the question, even though one of the mainsprings of socialism has always been the unequal and inequitable distribution of income. Socialists of all colors are agreed on the elimination of unearned income from productive property, but the larger problem of allocating wages has scarcely been discussed. Fourier and other forerunners of socialism advocated what is perhaps the only coherent theoretical solution — equality of wages. The Soviet economy, on the other hand, has leaned very heavily on the incentive principle[7] and the disproportion between minimum and maximum wages is greater, on the average, in Russian industry than in our own. In Britain, the raising of minimum wages by legislation and the lowering of maximum wages by taxation have developed the shortest income ladder ever known in an industrialized economy.

The theory behind this policy is the original socialist ideal of equality modified by the necessity that superior status be reflected somewhat by the standard of living. It is eloquently expressed by Tawney in *The Acquisitive Society*:

No one has any business to expect to be paid "what he is worth" for what he is worth is a matter between his own soul and God. What he has a right to demand and what it concerns his fellow-men to see that he gets is enough to enable him to perform his work. When industry is organized on a basis of function, that, and no more than that, is what he will be paid. To do the managers of industry justice, this whining for more money is a vice to which they (as distinct from their shareholders) are not particularly prone. There is no reason why they should be. If a man has important work, and enough leisure and income to enable him to do it properly, he is in possession of as much happiness as is good for any of the children of Adam.[8]

In the United States, where belief in the Economic Man dies hard, the problem of distributing income is often identified with the problem of maximizing incentive, so that the ideal distribution of wages is conceived to be that which results in the greatest total product by providing appropriate incentives at all points. There is a tendency to confuse productivity and individual effort and to regard financial incentive as the sole spring of individual effort. Hence, the long quest for an ideal piecework plan whose results would match these assumptions, and the development of hundreds of piecework plans, ranging from a simple fixed price per piece produced to progressive formulas so complicated that the cost of computing the payroll becomes a major item in the production budget.

For skilled, professional, technical, and managerial functions, whose productivity cannot be precisely measured, a similar theory tends to regard the market value of an individual as the best approximation to his productivity. Market value in this case is not the intersection of supply and demand curves, since only one individual is being considered. It is the salary he can command when changing positions which represents a collective estimate by potential employers of the value of his services.

This appears to be the fundamental, or Horatio Alger, theory of incentive wage determination. In practice, it is usually applied in combination with other standards which are inconsistent with it.

In the first place, the principle of a minimum legal wage capable of sustaining a meager, but not miserable, standard of living has come to be generally accepted as appropriate to the economy of abundance. The minimum wage is variously justified on the grounds of fairness, of increased purchasing power, of child protection, of the reduction of social conflict, and of political expediency, but the reasons for its introduction must be sought in the events of the Great Depression. Once established, a legal minimum is unlikely to be abandoned. Quite aside from its welfare aspect, it offers the business community a valuable guarantee against the cutthroat competition of marginal producers.

The progressive income tax has the effect of setting limits at the other end of the earnings scale. This limitation is much less effective than is generally supposed. Rosten's study of the tax payments of Hollywood stars and directors illustrates what is common knowledge among tax accountants and lawyers: that the rates on even the highest earned incomes, after all the legitimate loopholes have been used, are far from confiscatory.[9]

Very high incomes have a special significance in American culture. Mead and other social anthropologists have discussed the jackpot principle: the general belief in luck and opportunity which is sustained by conspicuous cases of "striking it rich." The most powerful objection to the proposals for an absolute income ceiling put forth in recent years seems to have been the value attached to the possibility of becoming a millionaire rapidly. While this supplementary incentive does not touch most of the population at all, it is felt to justify and validate some of the prevailing inequities at lower income levels.

Finally, it should be noted that a growing proportion of the labor force is employed in public or private bureaucracies which by their very structure set up other goals in the place of financial incentives, and in which it is, assumed that earnings should be proportionate to status rather than vice versa.

One reason why the theory of earnings has not been further developed is that there have been comparatively few studies of differential wages and the available data are deficient in several ways. In the first place, it is almost impossible to determine the incomes of the self-employed, of those employed in family enterprises, of those in illicit occupations, of salesmen, brokers, and agents, or of managers whose earnings are taken partly in dividends. In the case of the self-employed and of certain others, it is practically — and perhaps theoretically — impossible to disentangle earnings from capital returns. How much of a pharmacist's income should be attributed to his professional service, how much to the professional franchise which reserves him the right to operate a drugstore, and how much to his invested capital — this is a more or less insoluble calculation.

Second, it is very difficult to determine a cash value for perquisites and payments in kind. The salary of an admiral is comparatively modest but he enjoys about the same level of living as the wealthiest of civilians. What cash value should be allowed for the rent of the suite he occupies on his flagship? At the other end of the scale, farmhands and servants are usually paid in part by the provision of food and lodging, and often by clothing, medical service, and other incidentals. A formidable statistical technique has been evolved in the mass industries to calculate the cash value of retirement credits, vacation, sick leave, and other benefits. Although these are much more easily reckoned than payments in goods and services, it is notable that union and management are seldom agreed in any particular case on the cash value of a given program.

Third, a large part of the labor force is engaged in systematic concealment of supplementary income. The fine distinction between tax evasion, which is criminal, and tax escape, which is legitimate, has made the matter of income very delicate. Those who use questionnaires in social research are aware of the fact that it is often more difficult to elicit responses to questions dealing with income than to those concerned with the violation of the sexual mores.

Over and above these practical difficulties is the extraordinary complication presented by time series having to do with earnings. No single unit of working time will serve for the analysis of the entire labor force. An hourly basis is grotesquely inapplicable to concert pianists or auctioneers; a monthly basis distorts the earnings of all those occupations, from fishing to dry cleaning, which are in any way seasonal; an annual basis is confusing when applied to those who change occupations during the year. For some purposes, the most satisfactory measure is a calculation of lifetime earnings, but this again excludes from reasonable consideration those mobile occupations which are seldom pursued throughout a lifetime. Then too, the monetary units in which earnings are expressed fluctuate in value from year to year. The reduction of these to some such standard unit as 1923 dollars or 1939 pounds, aside from being laborious, introduces errors of sufficient magnitude to destroy much of the value of the original data.

Indeed, it is questionable whether the statistical comparison of earnings between occupational groups or occupational levels can be useful at all, without a thorough understanding of the structural differences among the various systems of wage determination. In other words, it is the organization of the several labor markets rather than the prices quoted in them at any given time which commands our first attention.

The brief descriptions of specific markets which are given below do not by any means cover the entire field of labor market arrangements, nor are the descriptions complete, but taken together they may serve to suggest the general outlines of the system.

THE BUREAUCRATIC LABOR MARKET

Essentially, a bureaucracy is an organized hierarchy of social positions which, at least in principle, is complete in itself without reference to the characteristics of the individuals who occupy the positions at a given moment.[10] The key words which identify bureaucracy are rationality and impersonality. The usual form of bureaucracy in the United States is a "civil service" system, in which all or most positions are classified in a scale of rank, salary, and perquisites. This scale is intended to correspond to degrees of responsibility, skill, and seniority. The requirements for each position are predefined to ensure the rational selection of candidates.

It is difficult to estimate what proportion of the American labor force is employed in bureaucratic systems; civil service principles are applied not only in federal, state, and municipal employments, but also in many private companies. A large number of such bureaucracies are incomplete in that they include only part of the employees of an enterprise, or that the governing rules of civil service are only applied in part. It is not unusual in industry for managerial, technical, and clerical employees to be covered by civil service arrangements, while the conditions of employment for manual workers are determined by a system of collective bargaining. It is normal, too, for the highest few levels of appointment — even in government service — to be placed outside of the bureaucratic system. A reasonable estimate of the number of bureaucratic employees in the civilian labor force is 15 million, while perhaps 20 million are covered by collective bargaining.

The important peculiarities of the bureaucratic labor market are the restriction of supply, the peculiar nature of demand, and the dominance of nonmonetary considerations.

Supply is restricted initially by the definition of specific qualifications for each position. This is the first and most important element in civil service since it is the only way in which formal rationality in selection can be guaranteed. The classification of a civil service position will therefore include a statement of the qualifications required. These fall into the three categories of training, experience, and social status. It is customary for training to include both a minimum general education, certified by the proper diplomas and degrees, and a particular kind of training or schooling. Experience is usually measured in terms of both duration and rank. Seniority in the organization is always given some weight, and it is comparatively simple to exclude outsiders altogether by defining as relevant only the experience accumulated within the organization. Social status is usually referred to as character. It usually includes the possession of a record free from criminal associations, alcoholism, mental illness, public scandal, and financial irresponsibility, but may also involve all sorts of other attributes: sex, race and religion, residence in a particular community or willingness to travel, war service, minimum and maximum ages, absence of family relation with other employees, and so forth.

Training beyond the minimum may be allowed as a substitute for some of the required experience, and vice versa, but there usually remains an irreducible minimum in both categories. The effect of the educational requirement is to restrict employment to those who have followed a certain course of formal instruction. This fact — taken together with the recent growth of such systems — has had an enormous influence in enlarging the institutions of higher education, and in establishing the educational system as an increasingly important channel of vertical mobility. The effect of the

SOCIOLOGY OF THE LABOR MARKET

experience requirement is to restrict employment to those already within the bureaucratic circle; "promotion from within" is always a meaningful slogan to bureaucrats. There is some evidence that privately owned organizations tend to be even more closed, when organized on civil service lines, than government agencies, which are legally forbidden to discriminate explicitly between insiders and outsiders.

It comes about as a matter of course that the crucial market situations have to do with promotions and transfers rather than with initial recruiting. Recruits entering the organization at a low level seldom intend to retain their initial position; they are attracted by an offer of long-range opportunities. Hence, most well-established bureaucracies have no problem of labor supply, and are even able to pay less than the going rate for newcomers to the labor force. Moreover, since the recruits represent a comparatively small proportion of the payroll, it is usually possible for the organization to maintain the supply of recruits in times of labor shortage by increases in beginning salaries, which are not very costly to the organization.

Of the nonmonetary incentives offered, the most important is tenure. The only organizations capable of establishing bureaucratic systems are those which enjoy a degree of permanence, and which are therefore able to offer security of employment. In addition, the principle of rationality demands that in any reduction of personnel the selection of those to be released must be calculated by a prearranged formula, which is almost invariably based on seniority. Since sharp reductions are infrequent, the typical bureaucratic employee enjoys a security of tenure which becomes more and more definite with length of service. This tends to limit the number of resignations above the beginning level and assures the internal labor supply even during periods of severe labor shortage.

This internal labor supply is stabilized in quite another way. With a few special exceptions, all bureaucratic hierarchies are pyramidal: that is, the number of employees at a given rank is smaller than in the rank immediately below and larger than in the rank above. At the same time, mobility is normally upward; security of tenure prevents demotions except under extraordinary circumstances. It is arithmetically unlikely that any general shortages will develop in the internal labor supply, since the population of potential candidates is always larger than the number of posts to be filled. Certainly, it happens often enough that none of the applicants for a position are considered suitable, but their unsuitability is usually based on personal grounds rather than on their lack of the formal qualifications.

For similar reasons, a general oversupply of labor is also unlikely, so long as the successive strata remain in a fixed relation to each other. It occurs only when the organization itself sustains a major crisis. This is most likely during a depression and at such times, though the opportunities for promotion are diminished, the advantages of security are enhanced.

As far as supply and demand of labor are concerned, the closed bureaucracy is to some extent a self-regulating mechanism. For this very reason, supply and demand do not determine bureaucratic wages in any clear fashion. The process is quite complicated. In the long run, the pressure of a rise in the cost of living will be expressed within a bureaucracy by a demand for general wage increases. Most public bureaucracies are partially unionized, and private bureaucracies have evolved methods for making their demands felt. Nevertheless, the economic isolation of each system goes far toward cushioning such demands and there is typically a lag between a rise in the cost of living and a rise in bureaucratic wages.

The problem is usually presented as an administrative issue rather than as a political question. Administratively, there is a good deal of resistance to wage increases because the one-way mobility which permits promotion but not demotion carries over into the determination of wages, and it becomes difficult to make subsequent wage reductions without administering a severe shock to the organization. To avoid this dilemma, many bureaucracies have adopted a system of basic wage rates plus cost-of-living bonuses, which fluctuate freely with the index of the Bureau of Labor Statistics or some other impartial indicator of consumer prices. In this way, at least the illusion of a fixed and permanent wage structure can be maintained throughout the business cycle.

Bureaucratic wages also lag behind the cost of living on a downward trend. In a bureaucracy many of those charged with policy decisions, including the formulation of wage policies, are paid under the same system as their subordinates. While they can be specially rewarded in a period of rising prices by reclassification of high-level positions, it is difficult for them to avoid the personal impact of a wage reduction. In general, the evidence indicates that trends in bureaucratic wages lag far behind trends in the general price level and that the lag is even greater on the downturns. In several cases, bureaucratic wages continued to rise from 1929 to 1932 and quite commonly they remained unchanged from 1939 to 1942.

Nevertheless, the problem of wage determination in this economic environment can never be simply resolved. The setting of differential wages *within* the system is perhaps the principal source of internal conflict in such organizations.

The establishment and maintenance of the job classification system is a staff function, which is usually entrusted to a special office staffed by personnel experts, whose work is based on certain rational assumptions. However, no personnel office ever starts with a clean slate. The job classification system is normally superimposed upon whatever wage structure existed before its introduction. Even in the case of a brand-new establishment, created *ad hoc* in the manner of certain wartime agencies, the sheer necessities of the situation require that the initial classification of positions be based on that of a comparable establishment, rather than created afresh. Job classification is a sort of labor of Sisyphus, involving a continuous effort to iron out inequities, in the course of which new inequities are brought about.

To see why this is so, it is necessary to return for a moment to the statement of formal qualifications which is the essential part of a job description. The elements included under social status may be disregarded; they serve merely to exclude candidates whose respectability or appropriateness is questionable, or those against whom the organization wishes to discriminate. But the elements included under training and experience are specifically related to a position, and beyond that to a range of positions. Since they are expressed in quantitative terms, they are capable of being ranked (two years of graduate study above one year, seven years as a foreman above seven years as a sub-foreman). It is the first principle of rational job classification that the rank order of wages must follow this rank order of training and experience,[11] and that a position must never pay more than another position which requires a greater degree of education and experience.

A second rational principle is that status and wages be perfectly correlated. A supervisor should invariably receive higher wages than any of his subordinates. The increment between any two successive grades should not be grossly disproportionate to the increment between any other two. New employees should never be paid more than employees with seniority already working in identical positions. And so forth.

A third principle is that both the qualifications and the remuneration for positions involving similar work with similar responsibility be the same. Otherwise, it will inevitably come about that different names lead to dissimilar classifications for identical jobs.

To these three principles are added certain useful rules of thumb. It is generally believed that the bureaucratic wages for a particular type of work should correspond to the average wages paid for comparable work in the community. Since there is ordinarily no way of determining marginal productivity in bureaucracies, this rule is the slender link which connects the whole structure of bureaucratic wages to the general labor market. Practically speaking, allowance is often made for security and other benefits and an effort is made to have the bureaucratic wage correspond to the community average minus 10 or 20 per cent. To pay less, it is believed, would place the organization at a disadvantage in hiring; to pay more would be to incur an unjustifiable expense.

Finally, it is thought necessary to provide financial incentives to balance the slothfulness encouraged by job security, and to reward seniority directly. This is accomplished by increments of pay within each grade which, in theory, are given for special merit, as an alternative to promotion. In practice, such increases usually become automatic and therefore amount to a simple bonus for seniority.

It is apparent at first glance that the principles on which sound job classification is based will come into conflict with each other at many points, so that any bureaucratic wage structure will require continuous and unending revision.

In the absence of any accounting procedure for assessing the value of a position in terms of productivity, the personnel expert is forced to use its market value, as expressed by the going wage paid in the community. This is a very weak reed on which to lean. Some of the occupations in a given bureaucratic system will not be found anywhere else in the community, and some will be found only in other bureaucracies. It is commonplace to see each of the large public and private employers of clerical personnel in a local area basing their rates on wage surveys taken among the others. In such a circular process, chance plays a larger role than the market. An incidental effect of wage surveys is to import into the supposedly rational bureaucratic wage structure some of the inequities which political pressure, occupational monopoly, or historical accident have produced in the community at large. Thus, it is not unusual for the civil service wage rates of building craftsmen to be fixed at a rate two or three times as high as that of comparably skilled artisans, whose general market situation is less favorable.

The requirement that differences in qualifications be recognized by differences in pay also has interesting consequences. In general, the minimum and maximum rates paid in a bureaucratic system are fixed with reasonable precision; in the case of government employment, such limits may be established by law. The gap between successive pay grades must be broad enough to allow room for merit increase above the beginning level of each grade. In occupations which are by their nature subject to numerous divisions, there will seldom be enough room between the minimum and the maximum rates to allow for the distinctions of status, responsibility, or skill which actually exist. In other occupations where only a few subdivisions are distinguished, it will be difficult to place them with any precision along the range. A typical conflict occurs whenever an intermediate level of such an occupation is found to be out of line with the comparable level of a finely subdivided occupation. It is not possible to lower either position without strong protest; and it is impossible to raise a single level of the finely subdivided occupation without creating a host of new problems.

It is probably impossible for a bureaucracy to maintain a consistent internal structure and at the same time establish parity with a market based on short-run supply and demand factors. Thus, the less isolated a bureaucratic system becomes, the more disorganized its wage system is apt to appear. When the organization is in the course of expansion, the usual compromise is to "hold the line" for the sake of internal consistency, and to satisfy protesting individuals by a generous promotion policy. When the organization is stable or declining, the only workable device by which the wage structure can be protected is the multiplication of nonmonetary rewards: honorific distinctions, comforts, reduction of working hours, increase of vacation and sick leave, or a general relaxation of discipline. In some instances — Dreyfuss presents a documentation for German business in the 1920s [12] — competition comes to be diverted almost entirely toward such nonmonetary symbols as double-pedestal desks, offices with carpets, and access to executive washrooms. The accompanying chart, in spite of its burlesque elements, has some relation to the realities of life in the great corporations.

In spite of the assumptions of permanence and stability on which a bureaucratic system operates, it is only by complete isolation (i.e., a turnover rate approaching zero) or by steady expansion that a bureaucracy can maintain its rational wage structure in the face of the contradictions imposed by its own complexity.

A SYSTEM OF STATUS SYMBOLS

Visible Appurtenances	Top Dogs	V.I.P.'s	Brass	No. 2s	Eager Beavers	Hoi Polloi
BRIEF CASES	None — they ask the questions	Use backs of envelopes	Someone goes along to carry theirs	Carry their own — empty	Daily carry their own — filled with work	Too poor to own one
DESKS, Office	Custom made (to order)	Executive Style (to order)	Type A "Director"	Type B "Manager"	Cast-offs from No. 2s	Yellow Oak — or cast-offs from Eager Beavers
TABLES, Office	Coffee tables	End or decorative wall tables	Matching tables Type A	Matching tables Type B	Plain work table	None — lucky to have own desk
CARPETING	Nylon — 1 inch pile	Nylon — 1 inch pile	Wool-Twist (with pad)	Wool-Twist (without pad)	Used wool pieces — sewed	Asphalt tile
PLANT STANDS	Several — kept filled with strange exotic plants		Two — repotted whenever they take a trip	One medium-sized; repotted annually during vacation	Small; repotted when plant dies	May have one in the department or bring their own from home
VACUUM WATER BOTTLES	Silver	Silver	Chromium	Plain painted	Coke machine	Water fountains
LIBRARY	Private Collection	Autographed or complimentary books and reports	Selected references	Impressive titles on covers	Books everywhere	Dictionary
SHOE SHINE SERVICE	Every morning at 10:00	Every morning at 10:15	Every day at 9:00 or 11:00	Every other day	Once a week	Shine their own
PARKING SPACE	Private in front of office	In plant garage	In company garage — if enough seniority	In company properties — somewhere	On the parking lot	Anywhere they can find a space — if they can afford a car
LUNCHEON MENU	Cream Cheese on Whole Wheat Buttermilk and Indigestion Tablets	Cream of Celery Soup Chicken Sandwich (White Meat) Milk	Fruit Cup — Spinach Lamb Chop — Peas Ice Cream — Tea	Orange Juice Minute Steak French Fries — Salad Fruit Cup — Coffee	Tomato Juice Chicken Croquettes Mashed Potatoes Peas — Bread Chocolate Cream Pie — Coffee	Clam Chowder Frankfurter and Beans Rolls and Butter Raisin Pie à la Mode — Two Cups of Coffee

Source: Monsanto Chemical Company Exec-Chart: A Ready Guide for Evaluating Executives. Reprinted by permission.

THE INDUSTRIAL LABOR MARKET

There are a number of differently organized markets for industrial labor but the one to be discussed here is the market for semiskilled manual labor in industries which are not highly specialized technically and regionally.[13] The working force whose services are offered in this market does not include more than a fourth of the total labor force, yet because of its susceptibility to economic fluctuations, it has a special influence on other labor markets.

The supply of industrial labor is determined, in the first instance, by the size of the population in each local area and by the competition of other employment opportunities. There continue to be great migrations and employment rushes in the United States: to the shipyards, the dams, the tank factories. Yet, in the day-to-day run of events, the geographical mobility of industrial labor is not markedly greater than the geographical mobility of other occupational groups.

The principal factors which affect the market situation of the factory hand are the existence of a reserve labor force which expands and contracts very easily; the organization of collective bargaining on a regional or national basis; and the right of casual layoff which factory managers still exercise.

The reserve labor force is made up of women, who can be attracted from housekeeping or from school with relative ease; of the partly employed; of the partly employable; and of racial minorities. There are very sharp differences among American communities with respect to the proportion of women in the population, and the proportion of married women with children, so that the reserve of employable women in a New England textile town may be three times as great as in a midwestern community of the same size. In addition, there are important differences of industrial tradition. In communities which are heavily industrialized, the intermittent entry of women and adolescents into the factory world is taken for granted.

The organization of collective bargaining in a broader arena than that of the local community is a fairly recent development; it did not become typical until the early days of the New Deal, when the unionization of the heavy mass-production industries took place. Whereas the local labor supply was once the first element to be ascertained in any study of wage determination, it has now become nearly irrelevant in many industrial areas. Even where collective bargaining is on a local basis, negotiations tend to follow the pattern set in certain crucial power centers. Harbison and Dubin [14] have shown in detail how the local negotiations in automobile plants follow the pattern set by General Motors and the United Automobile Workers in Detroit. To a lesser extent, all employment in manufacturing is influenced by the pattern created through negotiation in certain key areas: notably the steel, automobile, electrical, and chemical industries.

The practice of mass layoffs on short notice is a curiously archaic survival in an industrial order which has become obsessed with old-age security, hospitalization funds, unemployment insurance, and other safeguards against the interruption of earnings. Despite a good deal of discussion of guaranteed annual wages, and a certain amount of experimentation by fortunately situated companies such as Hershey and Hormel, the question of job continuity has not been very conspicuous in the union-management discussions of the last twenty years. The reason must be sought in the historical circumstances which made guaranteed employment a hopeless mirage in the first half of that period, and a secondary form of protection in the second.

The effect of mass layoffs is to create in most local labor markets a violently irregular curve for factory labor. The beginning of a layoff may increase the number of "unemployed seeking work" from a few dozen to a few thousand, and the termination of a layoff by a single large employer may create a general shortage of manpower. One factor which has helped to release wages from close dependence on supply and demand has been the expectation of employment managers, union officials, and others in close touch with local markets that the supply of industrial labor would fluctuate unpredictably from week to week, especially in periods of full employment where there is no standing army of unemployed to offset the effects of hiring and firing en masse.

How, then, are wages fixed? As one text points out, "Many of those who have regarded the question of wage determination superficially or by reference to some isolated or personal experience have frequently concluded that wage rates are simply set by employers at whatever rate they are willing to pay." [15] Yet, curiously enough, the literature of wage theory tends to understate the considerable margin of freedom allowed to the employer in fixing wages. True, the legal minimum wage fixes a wage floor (not infrequently disregarded) in the underprivileged branches of industry, and union contracts tend directly or indirectly to establish basic minimum wages for each industry. At the other end of the range, the "going wage" paid by competitors establishes an approximate ceiling. But within these limits, there is often room for considerable fluctuation, which may or may not be based on rational considerations. Rationally, the highest wages might be expected in industries where labor cost is a small proportion of the total cost of the product, where machinery or raw materials are valuable and easily damaged, or where interruptions to production are especially costly. Within a given industry the lowest wages should be paid by marginal firms who are not securely enough established to look to the long-range stability of their labor force, and to whom the immediate reduction of out-of-pocket expense is a dominant motive.

Under the conditions of modern hiring, it is usually true that labor for factory operations may be secured at a range of prices: that is, that no single supply curve can be traced. In the short run, there may be no conspicuous difference in the quality of labor available at various prices.

Thus, between the broad limits set by legal, social, and economic influences, the employer has a certain amount of discretion in fixing wages for factory work. This discretion he may exercise either rationally, as a well-behaved economic man, or as often occurs, on the basis of personal inclination.

The factor which has been somewhat neglected in the discussion of industrial wage determination we may call, for want of a more precise term, custom. There are two ways in which this factor operates. Whenever wages are altered — either by administrative determination or negotiation — the new figure is determined by reference to the wages previously paid for that kind of work. Indeed, it is usual to express the change in percentages, which represent increased or decreased costs to management and an increase or decrease in income to employees. Even if all industries employing semiskilled labor were to start from the same basic wage level, the differences in their subsequent fortunes, and in the history of their wage negotiations, would soon introduce considerable differentials between industries. But in fact they do not start from the same point. Besides the elements already cited as influencing managerial decision, there are some others which are equally significant. The higher the proportion of women, the lower the average age of the working force; the smaller the community, the lower in general will be the wage level. The larger the working force, the further north the plant (in the United States); the smaller the proportion of the population in industrial employment, the higher will average industrial wages be. Those industries with a declining market almost invariably pay less than those with an expanding market; the heavier industries tend to pay more than the light industries; those employing foreigners or Negroes in large numbers tend to pay less than others; and highly seasonal industries are characterized by both exceptionally low and exceptionally high wages.

The other way in which custom affects wage rates is in the determination of differentials between jobs within the same plant. Warner and Low [16] have shown very lucidly in their study of shoe manufacturing in Yankeetown that wages are roughly correlated with the degree of skill *assumed* necessary for each job. On close analysis these assumptions are often found to be spurious. The rank order of skill attached to jobs is a derivation from the original rank order which existed in the days when the boot and shoe industry was on a handicraft basis, but intervening events have stripped it of all validity.

Summing this up, we may say that industrial wages are determined either by managerial decision, or by negotiation, or by both, within a range. The theoretical lower limit of this range is fixed by the demand curve. It is possible to offer wages so low that no one can be hired, but this rarely occurs because the minimum wages established by law, contract, or public opinion are usually higher than the economic minimum. The upper limit of the range can be theoretically determined as the point beyond which production would entail a net loss. This does not figure largely in practical calculation either, since the raising of wages is usually arrested at a point considerably below this by the formal or informal agreement of employers.

Within this range, employers will be influenced by a variety of considerations. In general, they will be more willing to pay high wages whenever the effect on unit labor cost is small. This may come about either because the labor in question is a small component of total cost, or because increased productivity results from higher wages. Hence, the perennial appeal of piecework plans. In general, management will be willing to pay higher wages to the extent that the good labor relations and low personnel turnover are important to particular operations, and to the extent that good relations are correlated, or are believed to be correlated, with wages. On the other hand, because of the large number of intangibles involved, sheer predisposition often plays an important part in the situation. It may become part of the managerial tradition of the firm to pay consistently more or less than the "going rate."

The willingness of employees to accept a particular wage will depend primarily on the social composition of the working force, with continual reference to the larger industrial situation in which they are placed. A working force composed of family heads will insist on higher remuneration than one made up of women and boys, and public opinion will support this demand. Wherever there are conspicuous alternatives available, as in any large city, the pressure for higher wages will be more consistent than in one-industry settlements. To the extent that workers have inferior political and social status — immigrants, Negroes, wanderers, poor whites, or the like — they will be less disposed to demand increases. Finally, it should be recognized that the general market situation may have less influence upon workers than the special aspects of the market to which they happen to be exposed. Two factories located side by side will invariably influence each other's wage rates, even if one manufactures biscuits and the other airplanes. A sharp rise in the cost of living will be more acutely felt than a gradual rise of the same magnitude. Wage negotiations conducted at a time when neighboring firms have laid off men will not have the same outcome as those which take place during a period of local labor stringency.

In the short run, the differentials between jobs in the same industry are scarcely affected by the processes of union-management negotiation. Such negotiations are almost invariably directed to securing percentage changes in existing wage rates, and they are governed by a variety of strategic considerations, like any situation of formalized conflict. In the mass industries, a whole array of social devices have been worked out, of which only the essentials will be mentioned here. It has come to be accepted that any conspicuous changes in the general cost of living, the profit position of the great corporations, or the individual productivity of the worker require an alteration of wage rates. The limits within which such alteration is possible are roughly determined either by the change in the cost of living or by the change in the ability of the employer to pay, and are usually expressed by the first offers and counteroffers. The actual outcome is affected, among other things, by the willingness of either side to sustain a strike, the solidarity of the union organization contrasted with the solidarity of the employers' associations, the attitude of the courts and the public, the economic arguments advanced on both sides, and the ideological importance attached to the occasion. Strictly speaking, the prediction of the wage bargain resulting from full-fledged negotiations is impossible. The theoretical model which fits the negotiating table appears to be the two-player situation presented by Von Neumann and Morganstern in their *Theory of Games*.[17]

On the other hand, a pattern has emerged very clearly in recent years by which the results of single negotiations are generalized to include other firms and other industries. It has come to be assumed that wage-level changes in any of the major mass-production industries — steel, automobiles, electrical, communications, rubber, chemical, petroleum — require corresponding (but not exactly equivalent) changes in the others. Indeed, there has come to be a recognized order by which crucial negotiations in industries making producers' goods set a pattern for industries producing directly for the consumer, and in which the percentage increase set by negotiation in the "heaviest" industries (steel and automobile, especially) is acknowledged as a standard — or at least as a point of departure — by all others. Within a single industry, there is a similar tendency for the most powerful firm and the most powerful union to establish the standard bargain to which all other negotiating parties will more or less conform.

This system is relatively new. It dates essentially from the organization of the mass-production industries undertaken by the C.I.O. after 1934. Except for the recession of 1937–38, in which the pattern was only beginning to evolve, the entire period has been one of rising prices, productivity, profits, and wages. It is thus rather difficult to anticipate how this system of bargaining at the crucial points would function in case of general deflation.

It must be remembered, too, that not all the industrial labor force is included within this system. At least a third of industrial workers were not unionized in 1950, and a considerable fraction of established unions are ineffectual. Even before the great increase in union activity inspired by the Depression and encouraged by the Wagner Act, the wages of unionized workers were markedly higher than those of the nonunionized. The present system of large-scale unionism has accentuated this advantage by providing that contract wages can be quickly brought into line with rises in the cost of living or in the productivity of the whole system. This also tends to raise wages in the nonunionized sectors of the economy by increasing the inducement of the nonunionized worker to move to a unionized industry. However, this tendency operates only in the long run, and the "going wage" for nonunionized employees lags far behind when wages are increasing, and may even lead when wages are decreasing, as seems to have been the case in the temporary deflationary movement of 1946.

All this touches wage differentials within a particular structure very little or not at all. In a sense, the entire occupational hierarchy operates on an invalid but powerful assumption: that variations of skill are apparent and easily classified. This is nowhere more marked than in the mechanized factory. It is not extravagant to maintain that wherever a wage differential exists between two jobs, the holders of the more highly paid job (at least) will assume that it requires superior skill. It seems only common justice that they should be paid more, and any alteration of the differential will be strongly resented, even if it involves no loss of income to anyone. Sayles and Strauss present a typical example:

The union had won unusually loose (i.e., lucrative) incentive rates for labor pool jobs at the bottom of the plant promotional ladder. As a result unskilled workers obtained earnings nearly double those of skilled workers in the same plant. These skilled workers felt embarrassment when weekly pay checks were compared in the shop and outside the plant. Realizing that under the contract they had no chance of increasing their own earnings, they insisted that the union try to "tighten" those of the labor pool. Of course, the men in the pool argued that their higher earnings were entirely the result of hard work rather than faulty rate setting.

Union leaders were in a quandary. If they were a party to reducing the earnings of the men in the labor pool, they would be accused of playing management's game. On the other hand, the skilled day workers were protesting that the union was "just run for the benefit of those unskilled piece-workers." [18]

It is a bold management that tampers lightly with wage differentials, and unions have even less interest in doing so. Indeed, one of the principal problems at the negotiating table is how to distribute wage increases without affecting existing differentials; arithmetically, a percentage increase gives the highest paid employees the largest raises, which seems inequitable. On the other hand, an increase expressed in cents per hour gives a much larger proportionate raise to the poorly paid. In practice, a percentage increase is usually preferred because of the ease of calculating its cost, and the "appearance" of equity. The net effect is to widen the differentials in the wage structure.

Wage differentials are not as permanent and rigid as all this might seem to suggest. Even though they are almost unaffected by the labor market in ordinary times, there are other ways in which they are modified. In the first place, wherever piecework systems are used, it is impossible to state with precision what the wage corresponding to a job really is. When changes are made in piece rates, they usually occasion disturbance among the workers directly concerned, but are less likely to be made the basis of invidious comparison. Then, too, the continuous rationalization which is typical of many industrial processes introduces many new jobs, and changes many old ones. These are usually, but not always, classified by reference to comparable jobs and, in this way, substantial changes are introduced in the structure of differentials. Yet, the striking characteristic of these variations in the price of labor is that they are almost entirely independent of the market and even — except by accident — of the negotiating table. It is the operation of the job classification system, and the minor alterations of technological processes, which most affect the price differences between one kind of labor and another in the same plant.

Within any plant, there is likely to be considerable internal mobility as men shift, or are shifted, from one department to another, and from one job to another. When these shifts are voluntary or are made in recognition of merit, they are usually in the direction of higher wage rates. One unexpected consequence is that in many plants, the jobs with high wage rates are occupied almost entirely by employees with considerable seniority, and it may easily happen that the structure of wages shows a much closer association with seniority than with skill. This is especially marked in well-established industries with continuity of operation. Thus, even in the highly mobile world of factory employment, the tendency toward bureaucratization may be expressed by the high wages paid to those with the greatest length of service. This is especially true when the manufacturing process is technically complicated, so that familiarity with the workings of a particular plant becomes a kind of substitute for individual skill.

THE CRAFTSMAN'S MARKET

The term *craft* is most frequently applied to the occupations involved in building construction and maintenance (bricklayers, carpenters, electricians, stationary engineers, painters, plasterers, plumbers, steamfitters, roofers, masons, and some others) and to certain others which, for historical reasons, have evolved a comparable organization (potters, engravers, printers, linotypers, dry cleaners, cutters in some textile industries, various heavy machinery operators, millwrights, certain millers, stagehands, boilermakers). There are also a number of manually skilled white-collar occupations (cameramen, orchestra musicians, radio operators) which somewhat resemble the crafts.

Recruiting to the crafts has been discussed in a previous chapter. It will be remembered that the essential elements include apprenticeship, certification, and continuous union membership. Entry to the craft is to some extent controlled by the craft organization and is likely to be extended over several years.

In theory, then, the supply of craft labor is fixed, and there is no question of attracting additional labor by higher wages or of reducing an oversupply by a reduction of the wage rate. How closely the reality conforms to these expectations depends upon local circumstances. Many of the craft-monopolized operations are fairly simple; in the building trades they must usually be performed in public. It is thus impossible to keep them secret, and there is always a supply of amateur or marginal painters who will undertake to paint the side of a barn as well as the next man. The union, on its side, has recourse to a number of familiar devices to preserve its monopoly. Employers who hire nonunion labor for craft work may be permanently boycotted by all the crafts. Personal violence against these competitors is not unheard of. The most effective controls are embodied in local ordinances and agreements, so that in many cities building permits, permits to operate machinery, and other necessary licenses will be revoked if inspection discloses the use of nonunion labor. While this control often ceases at the city limits, it is sufficiently effective in most communities to restrict the use of nonunion labor on craft work to small projects of no economic importance. There are, of course, some conspicuous exceptions in either direction: entire villages have been built by large-scale contractors with nonunion labor; while in other places, private householders have been effectively prevented from doing plumbing or wiring on their own premises.

The demand for labor in the building trades is highly variable. The work is by nature seasonal. Cold winter weather makes construction work difficult and expensive; soft ground in the spring and heavy rain at any time of the year are major handicaps. In many of the northern states, building activity is concentrated in the period from May to October. Seasonality varies from trade to trade, being sharper for masons and roofers than for electricians and sheet-metal workers, but it is always an element. Moreover as Colean [19] and others have shown in detail, the construction industry is essentially disorganized. The financial weakness of the building firms and the speculative character of their activity induces violent fluctuations in the rate of construction activity.

165

Similar considerations apply to the other industries where craft organization is conspicuous. As will be presently shown, the craft system presupposes the financial weakness of employers and sharp oscillations in the condition of the trade. Dry cleaning is highly seasonal, and orchestra work is not only seasonal but normally insecure.

The market for craft labor thus presents a fixed supply of labor and a highly variable demand. It remains to be ascertained how the price of labor is determined.

Before we examine this question, it is useful to recall the similarities between the modern unionized craft and the medieval craft guild. These similarities are overtly recognized in the preservation of medieval terminology (brother, journeyman, master) and the imitation of medieval forms (apprenticeship and oaths). They rest upon certain real identities of social structure.

Both the ancient and the modern crafts are founded upon the monopolization of a trade whose performance is socially essential. In both cases, the clients for services are very numerous and economically weak, so that the workman's identification is with his calling rather than with a particular job or a particular establishment. All the crafts are universal: that is, they are required everywhere and can be performed anywhere. None of them require heavy fixed capital. All involve determinate operations which, once learned, are not much affected by individual talent. (This is probably because the services of a craft are essential and need to be standardized. In nonessential work of a similar nature, there is always a tendency for standardization to give way to individual expression, and for the craft to become an art.) Once standardized, the technology of the craft becomes relatively rigid. The advantages of large-scale production are minimized and the process of rationalization is slowed down. This contributes, in turn, to the maintenance of the original situation, in which clients are numerous and employers weak.

The medieval craft in its full development minimized the distinction between employer and employee. The master was a workman who had the right to hire other workmen to assist him; this right was deliberately restricted in order to prevent the growth of large enterprise, and when the restrictions were evaded in those crafts producing exportable commodities, the guild system came to an end. The modern occupations which preserve a craft organization also discourage large-scale employment, and allow an easy transition from employer to employee status. As a matter of fact, it is just this condition which gives the building industry its unique character.

From the point of view of the craftsman, a wage rate fixed either by the free action of the market or by bargaining has several disadvantages. Given the fixed supply and the highly variable demand, the wage rate under pure market conditions would approach zero in slack seasons, and would rise so high during peak periods as to provoke a reaction aimed at the destruction of the craft. As a matter of fact, something like this happens at extreme points of the business cycle. Wage rates in the building trades in 1933 did approach zero, and during the housing shortage of 1946 rose so high as to lead to public action, such as the subsidy of prefabrication. Wage rates fixed by bargaining would be no more satisfactory; the clients of a craft are numerous and unorganized, and many of the direct employers are themselves workmen paid at the going rate before they take their profit. Individual bargaining would shortly lead to cutthroat competition, in view of the insecurity of employment in the crafts. Collective bargaining is often impossible for want of a responsible entity to represent the employers.

Looked at in another perspective, the problem of the craft union — where it functions effectively — is the same as that of any monopolist selling a standard product: the maximization of total return. This is only slightly complicated by the corollary problem of equitable distribution of the total return among the craft members. The medieval answer to this puzzle was the formula — eventually promoted to philosophical dignity by St. Thomas Aquinas — of the Just Price, a customary price which enables the workman to maintain himself and his family at the customary level without driving the customers who stand in need of the service out of the market. The modern slogan of "fair wages" still carries the ethical implications attached to the Just Price, but no customary price will stay adjusted to rapidly changing price levels.

The maximum price at the height of the business cycle will tend instead to be the highest price at which full employment of craftsmen can be maintained. The lowest acceptable price at the depth of a depression will be that which ensures subsistence to all active craftsmen when the available work is evenly distributed.

Adjustment to either the maximum or the minimum implies control by the craft of the distribution of work. Where the system is fully developed, the employer hires directly from the union, and the union assigns and reassigns its members to equalize the distribution of wages. From the union standpoint, this has the further advantages of making the employer-employee relation exceedingly tenuous and of giving the union considerable powers over both employers and its own members.

These arrangements, of course, are always inconsistent with bureaucratic and industrial hiring systems. Yet, a considerable proportion of craft work — particularly the indoor maintenance work which is done off-season — is performed for establishments which are bureaucratic or industrial or both. Various compromises have been worked out. In many civil service systems, union craftsmen are placed in a special category where they do not enjoy civil service rights but are paid union wages. In some cases, they are offered the choice of remaining in the craft, or of giving up their union cards and taking civil service status. In industry, men are sometimes permanently employed with the understanding that they will be paid union wages but will not enjoy other union privileges. A fairly common device is to hire foremen as permanent employees (many unions provide for some such classification as "nonworking master" which permits the individuals to resume their journeyman status at will) and to allow the foremen to hire their crews on an hourly basis without other employment formalities.

The power of the union to distribute work depends upon local and even upon individual circumstances. The craftsman does not normally anticipate a full year's work, and his habits are based on the expectation that he will be unemployed during part of the slack season. Many craftsmen have supplementary trades or business activities to which they turn when not working in the craft.

The high wage rates of the crafts are not necessarily reflected in a high annual income. However, extreme situations are common in these occupations. During periods of strong demand, the unions may come to govern the activities of employers by favoring some and neglecting others. Under these conditions, they will be able to impose unilateral wage increases without the slightest difficulty. During times of low employment, the craft may become so disorganized that its devices for distributing employment are reduced to "each man for himself."

Even more striking than union control of wage rates is union control of what might be called the conditions of sale for labor. Sociologically, the function of these controls is to preserve the system of selling labor in standardized units by preventing the employer from modifying either the organization or the attractiveness of the work. These craft regulations are generally of three kinds: (1) those which set bonus pay (time and a half, double time, straight bonus) for work done after hours, on Sundays or holidays, at night, or under hazardous conditions; (2) those which regulate the union affiliations of foremen and of co-workers, provide for the sympathetic boycott of employers in difficulty with other crafts, prescribe the allowable number of apprentices and the required number of foremen; and (3) the technological restrictions — often unwritten — which define a day's work and prohibit the use of unauthorized tools, materials, and methods.

One of the peculiarities of the craftsmen's market is its local circumscription. Wage rates are nicely adjusted to a local situation. In view of the variations in demand from one locality to another, it would be difficult or impossible to establish a wage rate over a broad area which would serve the purposes of the craft as well. Nevertheless, this local circumscription poses a number of problems. To allow free mobility of craftsmen from one area to another would seriously weaken the locally centered craft; but to prohibit it entirely would prevent craftsmen from taking advantage of the universality of their skill. It is customary to allow a limited mobility by means of permits, which give the visiting craftsman the right to work for a limited time in another area but not to establish himself permanently. This mobility is sufficient to keep wage rates for the same craft roughly parallel in adjacent areas, but not great enough to make them identical.

Another peculiarity of the craftsmen's market is that the demand for any particular kind of craft work normally varies with that for the others. This is especially true in the building trades where any major construction normally requires the cooperation of all the building trades. It is normal, therefore, for craft unions in the same area to act in close concert on wage questions. In spite of this, there are variations — sometimes as great as 30 per cent — between the wage rates of comparable crafts in the same locality. These are not easily explained. To some extent, they rest on customary status: steamfitters are often paid more than plumbers. To some extent, they reflect the difference between an expanding trade like the electrician's and a declining one like the mason's. There is also some tendency for the more highly seasonal trades to claim higher rates than those which have enough inside work to fill the slack season. Yet, when all this is admitted, there seems left a considerable margin to be accounted for by chance, and the strength of local union administration.[20]

THE MARKET FOR PROFESSIONAL SERVICES

It is perhaps misleading to discuss the market for professional services without emphasizing the fact that a large proportion of professional persons are the salaried employees of bureaucratic organizations. Among the salaried professionals, a systematic distinction must be made between those who perform a technical function for nonprofessional superiors, like industrial chemists or accountants, and those who form part of a bureaucracy under professional leadership — hospital residents, university professors, and social workers, for example.

Even among the "purest" professions, notably law and medicine, there is a considerable proportion of full-time salaried employees. Nevertheless, the independent practitioner remains the most typical of professional men, and the market in which he sells his services has a major influence on the level of remuneration for his salaried colleagues. Moreover, the special features of the professional market provide us with a number of clues as to the nature of the special markets for other types of individualized service.

The supply of professional practitioners is, in the short run, unchangeable. What is more surprising is the tendency of the supply to *decrease* in the presence of increased demand. An increase in the demand for professional service tends to strengthen the entire system of professional controls. One of the first consequences is the elimination of substandard training centers, and the tightening of eligibility requirements for professional candidates. Given the autonomy of the well-established profession which, unlike the craft, need not share its supervision of recruiting with outside authorities, there is a tendency to restrict further and further the supply of new practitioners.

The demand for professional services has never been adequately charted, but it is subject to sharp variations. There is comparatively little relationship between psychological demand and economic demand. It is probable that the psychological demand for the services provided by all the major professions far outruns the effective demand. The provision of complete medical and dental service to the American population is still a distant dream; the majority of legal transactions are accomplished without legal assistance; and only a very small proportion of dwellings owe their design to an architect's drawing board.

In general, the effective demand for professional services follows the business cycle, with varying elasticities. For example, architectural services are probably more dispensable than either legal or medical services.

Over and beyond these market considerations, the pricing of professional labor is subject to a special ideology. Professionals are, in theory, perfectly noninterchangeable. The work of each is considered to be his individual expression, not capable of direct substitution. By this assumption, it is specious to talk — except in the most general way — of either supply or demand. Professional services cannot be summed up.

Thus, in the professions, the value of a unit of work is theoretically unmeasurable. It is assumed as a matter of course that the service is unique; where it touches matters of life, property, and general welfare it is thought to be charged with intangible values not convertible into money.

The fixed supply in the face of a varying demand allows the professions, like the crafts, to fix within limits the price of their services. The professional ethic, with its emphasis on intangibles, discourages any attempt to standardize prices. The only remaining basis for payment, therefore, is what the market will bear, or more precisely, the client's ability to pay.

Wherever a system of simple fee payments exists, it will be based, at least in part, on the economic status of the client. This is conspicuously true of surgery and of fiduciary functions in law, where the same amount of work may cost the richer client a hundred times as much. In another form, the fee may be expressed as a fixed percentage of a total expenditure, as in architecture, engineering, or contingent legal fees. It is generally thought proper that remuneration be based on the wealth of clients rather than on differences in the services rendered. On the other hand, this same professional ethic carries an obligation to render the same quality of service regardless of the fee paid, and in some cases, to render the service even when no fee is forthcoming.

It would hardly be practical to apply so delicate a criterion to all the multifarious business of the professions. Thus the price of minor services comes to be standardized to all comers, and the more expensive practitioner gives over the performance of such routine chores to his assistants.

The chief concerns of the profession as an organized interest group are, first, to establish minimum prices and, second, to restrict price competition. Neither of these matters represents major concerns for the main body of practitioners, but they will have an indirect effect upon the social position of the profession. At both extremes of the business cycle, professional services will become flatly unavailable to large segments of the population.

When demand is very low, the maintenance of a minimum will keep many clients from seeking professional services and at the same time reduce professional incomes very sharply. Where demand is high, the limitation of the number of practitioners may cause them to discontinue the less remunerative branches of practice. Thus, after 1945, many sizable communities in the United States found themselves without any medical service, and many urban physicians discontinued the practice of home visits entirely.

In between these extremes, the pricing mechanism assures a fairly high basic wage to most practitioners, and the possibility of very large incomes to a few, since the price of services is not limited by the number of hours at the practitioner's disposal.[21] Yet, the impossibility of adjusting supply to demand at any point remains a crucial problem in the relations of the professional bodies to the public, and leads to minor but perennial crises.

In the case of medicine or dentistry, there have been numerous proposals that the government assume the distribution of the limited supply of professional personnel and standardize the prices. In the case of law and architecture, there has been an increasing tendency to abandon the system of independent practice for a system of semi-commercial firms which are large enough to develop a stable clientele on a continuous basis.

The principal peculiarity of this market is the dependence of remuneration upon the financial position of the clientele, rather than upon the services rendered. Mobility will normally tend to move the more competent practitioners in the direction of the more lucrative areas of practice, but this is a secondary effect, and there is a strong tendency for admission to an "area of practice" to depend more closely upon personal relationships and extra-occupational characteristics than upon technical qualifications.[22]

THE MARKET FOR COMMON LABOR

Although most occupational categories include a category of the unskilled, it is difficult to attach any precise meaning to the term. It is only careless usage which regards freight-handlers and farmhands in regular employment as less qualified than punch-press operators, and it is sheer snobbery that leads certain of the occupational classifiers to group all household servants as unskilled.

A more accurate criterion with which to identify the least privileged class of urban workers is regularity of employment. Industry, retail commerce, and even the private household maintain a continuous demand for "hands," hired on a day-to-day basis for clean-up jobs, moving, heavy construction, snow removal, digging, carrying, hewing of wood, and drawing of water. The exact size of this population is not known; of all the labor markets, this is the least studied, and employment is so casual that personnel records are scanty or nonexistent. It is certainly a market of considerable extent. It is not at all unusual in a city of moderate size — with a total labor force of perhaps 100,000 — for a single firm to recruit 2,000 men from this market, or for hundreds to be hired on a few hours' notice after a snowstorm.

The casual labor force is of strikingly mixed composition. In addition to the partly retired, the pensioners, and the partly unemployable, the drifters and drunks, the physically and mentally handicapped, there are those who normally belong to higher occupational categories but have been temporarily laid off or are waiting out a strike or an off-season, together with the migratory farm workers, the stranded travelers, the part-time students, the part-time criminals, and many others.

The supply of this sort of labor is highly variable in the long run. In the days of the Works Progress Administration, somewhere between 10 and 20 million persons were available, and most of the 6 million employees of that enterprise were used as common labor. During the war years, on the other hand, it sometimes happened that the supply reached zero in expanding production centers. Even in the short run, there are distinct variations from day to day, based on changes in the weather as well as changes in demand.

The demand for common labor varies seasonally. It probably increases somewhat in periods of prosperity, because much of the work for which common labor is used is marginal work which is likely to be deferred unless conditions are favorable. Nevertheless, the bulk of the work is in maintenance, clean-up jobs, or the handling of a seasonal rush (as in canning, department store wrapping, or ice-cutting), and is much more predictable than the supply of labor. In the short run, the demand is more variable, especially in situations where a few large employers intermittently take enormous crews for short periods.

Finally, it should be noted that both supply and demand are markedly elastic. Since the labor force is largely composed of marginal workers, it can always be somewhat expanded by a rise in the wage rate. Conversely, much of the demand for common labor arises from marginal projects, which can be deferred or simply not carried out. Thus, in the typical case of snow removal, if men are not available in sufficient numbers, the snow is left to melt on the streets.

It will be seen that the conditions of the classical market are approached more closely here than in any of the other situations we have so far considered. There is even likely to be a "marketplace" — some street corner or public square where, by usage, potential employers look for potential employees in the early morning hours. The procedure is simplicity itself, even currently. The employer or his agent drives up with a truck, announces the pay and conditions, bargains if necessary, loads the truck with his new employees, and proceeds forthwith to the work site. This is one of the usual hiring procedures. The other involves a card pasted in a window, or pinned to a stake outside the plant door, announcing the need for men and the price offered.

Even in this simple situation, the special nature of the commodity leads to certain results which would not be anticipated on a stock exchange or at a cotton auction. In the first place, public opinion opposes the use of a continuous price range and insists that prices be quoted in round figures: 50¢, 75¢, $1.00, more rarely 90¢ or $1.10. This insistence is founded upon the prejudice that labor quoted at 92¢ or 93½¢ *is* being regarded as a commodity and upon the just perception that since each employer is operating on a relatively small scale in this market, the extra expense of coming up to the round figure is not great compared to the added convenience in reckoning and paying. Readers of Steinbeck's *Grapes of Wrath* will remember that for the Oakies, utterly at the mercy of their employers, prices were quoted to half-cents, which seems to be characteristic of a market in which labor is offered at an extraordinary disadvantage.

In theory, the market for common labor provides the opportunity for good communication — both buyers and sellers can acquaint themselves with current transactions, since these are public and highly localized. But buyers are often disinclined to do so, and sellers are likely to be heavily influenced by nonmonetary considerations and to prefer some employments to others even at a monetary loss. In other words, neither of the parties in the market is willing to conform to "rationality" beyond certain limits. Taken together with the preference for certain prices, this leads to a situation which only roughly approximates the model of the pure market. The going wage rate is usually a round figure; once established, it tends to persist for a very long period of time. If it is an especially round figure like

One Dollar, it may remain unaltered for years. Employers with pressing needs or with special requirements may offer bonuses over this figure, up to a maximum of perhaps $1.20. Those who arrive early in the market, or who have time to wait, may offer less than the going rate by a like amount. The workman claims the same privilege. He may take 80¢ an hour if he passes a sign at the factory gate a block from his home; he may require $1.20 if he is not especially eager to work. None of these day-to-day fluctuations shake the market price, until general trends force it up or down to another round number.

OTHER TYPES OF LABOR MARKET

This brief survey by no means exhausts the classification of labor markets but enough has been said, perhaps, to indicate how closely the determination of remuneration is tied to the occupational structure, and how different are the mechanisms which govern the different markets.

Some mention should be made of a number of specialized markets, which differ from all the foregoing and which present interesting problems.

The markets for unique services are found in entertainment, sports, journalism, politics, advertising, and certain areas of management. What is offered in these instances is the personality, the individual talent, or merely the name of someone who commands a special claim to attention from the general public or from some limited business public. The value of these individualized qualities is usually speculative: no one can say with certainty what profits will accrue from the presence of a particular pair of legs in a motion picture or a gifted first baseman in a pennant race, but because they appeal to a wide audience, their potential productivity is very great. Considerations of supply cannot determine wages in this case; strictly speaking, the supply of one public personality is absolutely fixed. Marginal productivity is equally beside the point, and absolute productivity is not often determinable. Under these conditions, wages are fixed by individual bargain and are determined by actual bidding. Where the bargaining skill of the individual concerned (or that of his agent) is equal to the situation, the bidding process may result in some of the highest earned incomes known. At the same time, an active public personality may be unable to secure employment, since he cannot accept remuneration below a minimum level without destroying his peculiar status, and in the temporary absence of bidders may have no market value at all.

The market for middlemen's services is another which offers wages out of any apparent proportion to the individual's talent or skill. The important components of the labor force in this market are commission salesmen and sales managers, whose remuneration is usually based on a percentage of the value of their sales and in the case of costly commodities is almost unlimited. This despite the fact that the occupation is ordinarily open — at least at the lower levels — to anyone who commands a clean shirt and the means of transportation. The practice of a fixed percentage is based on a variety of circumstances: the impossibility of predicting productivity, the desirability of determining sales cost as a proportion of total unit cost in advance of sale, the provision of incentive in a field of activity where personal incentive is regarded as the crucial element in performance, and the basic bookkeeping fact that most profit is taken on the last items sold, after fixed costs have been met. Perhaps the strategic element is to be found in the nature of the salesman's activity, which is fundamentally the cultivation of good personal relations. The resulting advantages can easily be transferred to a competing product. In the case of weak enterprises, the threat of desertion by the successful salesman may be so effective that commissions are higher on sales above normal quotas. Very strong companies, on the other hand, are often able to reduce their salesmen to the status of salaried employees.

The market for domestic services and the market for farm hands, although not usually considered together, are parallel in many ways. Both are unusual in that remuneration is largely in kind, workers are unorganized and isolated from each other, the wages are usually computed on a monthly rather than an hourly basis, and the employer-employee relationship is very close. As in the market for common labor, a going wage tends to be established at a round figure and to be maintained for a long time. However, because of the preferences developed for particular individuals, wages two or three times as high as the going rate are not unheard of; and because of the exploitability of both domestic servants and farm hands, wages sometimes approach zero, and occasional cases of slavery are still reported in the newspapers. In this chaotic situation, it is particularly easy for the market to go out of balance, and it happens without reference to the general economic situation that domestic servants are for a time unobtainable in a locality, or that no jobs are available at any wage. Because personal relationships are usually tested on a trial-and-error basis, there is a great deal of short-range mobility in both these occupations. In the absence of organization, the only coercive measure which can be taken against employers is abrupt resignation, and a great many jobs are quitted after a few days or weeks. On the other hand, where the relationship is successfully established, the same job is often held for a lifetime. How the immobile members of these occupations compare in wages to the mobile is not precisely known, but it is probable that the trend of their wage rate lags somewhat behind that of the going rate in the market.

THE FORM OF WAGES

Reference has been previously made to the difficulty of taking into account the payments in services, perquisites, or kind, which are so conspicuous at the two extremes of the occupational scale. If we restrict our attention to cash remuneration, we find again that the form of remuneration has distinct social importance.

In general, wages, salaries, and fees represent ascending levels of prestige. The denotation of payment as salary rather than as wage may in fact be a form of intangible compensation and is often prized by office workers even where it involves the loss of overtime and double-time payments.

Wages may be paid by the hour, the day, or the week (time rates) or by the work unit (piece rates) or in any one of innumerable combinations. The questions of time of payment and of payment in script, which once gave rise to widespread discussion, are now somewhat obsolete. It is customary to pay by check, at intervals of not more than two weeks, and to pay off discharged workers almost immediately. These have been made legal requirements in many states.

The principal element which distinguishes wages from salaries, fees, commissions, and other forms of compensation is that wages are paid for a specific amount of work, as measured either by pieces produced or by time spent on the job. Thus, the wage earner's lack of property rights in his job is implicit in the form of compensation.

Salaries may be paid by the week, month, quarter, or year — this again on an ascending scale of status. For ritualistic reasons, salaries are almost never paid in cash, or at intervals shorter than two weeks. In theory, a salary is paid for fulfilling a function, or "holding a position," and this implies certain rights of tenure. Even where the growth of unionism among manual workers has left the salaried clerk in a more insecure position than the wage earner, these rights are generally recognized. The principal practical consequence is that employment cannot be terminated without advance notice, and usually creates some obligation of severance pay.

177

THE SOCIOLOGY OF WORK

Moreover, by this implicit definition, the earnings of salaried workers cannot be reduced by working them only a few hours a day or for two or three days a week in slack seasons. This distinction is abetted by the technological facts: the peaks and dips in the flow of clerical work are rarely as marked as in the manual operations to which they relate.

In the case of fees or commissions, remuneration is for a specific achievement, and the time basis is abandoned altogether. Indeed, a great deal of special ritual surrounds the payment of fees. In Britain, the custom of reckoning fees in a special currency — the guinea — is still preserved. The use of such terms as *honorarium,* and the classic practice of enclosing the check in a sealed envelope, impart the same delicate touch to fee payment in the United States.

These are pure and simple marks of stratification. What is more important is the distinction, which exists at every income level, between regular and irregular earnings. Regularity of earnings is one of the principal reasons why clerical work may be preferred to factory work, or a bureaucratic position to independent professional practice. It seems evident that pronounced irregularity of earnings must have important consequences for family life and for social participation in general, and this is confirmed by the few studies of occupational groups in which irregularity of earnings is conspicuous.

NOTES

[1] Thomas Robert Malthus, *First Essay on Population* (London, 1798): "It may at first appear strange, but I believe it is true, that I cannot by means of money raise a poor man, and enable him to live much better than he did before, without proportionably depressing others in the same class." Chapter V.

[2] Economists usually distinguish the wage-fund theory, formulated by John Stuart Mill, as distinct from the subsistence theory, but the difference may be disregarded here since the implications of the two theories are nearly identical.

[3] Harold F. Clark, *Economic Theory and Correct Occupational Distribution* (New York: Bureau of Publications, Teachers College, Columbia University, 1931), p. 1.

[4] *Ibid.,* p. 57.

[5] Richard B. Morris, *Government and Labor in Early America* (New York: Columbia University Press, 1946).

[6] See F. W. Taussig, *Principles of Economics* (3rd ed.; New York: The Macmillan Company, 1930), Vol. 2, pp. 132ff.

[7] C. Arnold Anderson, "Soviet Russia and the Nature of Society," *Southwestern Social Science Quarterly,* vol. 33, September 1952.

[8] Richard H. Tawney, *The Acquisitive Society* (New York: Harcourt, Brace & Company, 1920), pp. 178–79.

[9] Note the widespread popular belief that at certain income levels, the addition of

a dollar to income means the addition of more than a dollar in surtaxes. While there are no circumstances under which this can occur, the myth has a certain importance in itself, and has perhaps contributed to the shortening of the income range.

[10] See, for example, Talcott Parsons, *Structure of Social Action* (New York: McGraw-Hill Book Company, 1937); Robert K. Merton, "Bureaucratic Structure and Personality," *American Journal of Sociology,* 1945, and "Role of the Intellectual in Public Bureaucracy," *Social Forces,* 1945; Chester I. Barnard, *Functions of the Executive* (Cambridge, Mass.: Harvard University Press, 1938), and "Functions and Pathology of Status Systems in Formal Organizations," in W. F. Whyte, editor, *Industry and Society* (New York: McGraw-Hill Book Company, 1946); Reinhard Bendix, "Bureaucracy: The Problem and Its Setting," *American Sociological Review,* vol. 12, October 1947; Philip Selznick, "An Approach to a Theory of Bureaucracy," *American Sociological Review,* vol. 8, February 1943; Philip Selznick, "Foundations of the Theory of Organization," *American Sociological Review,* vol. 13, February 1948; Wilbert E. Moore, *Industrial Relations and the Social Order* (New York: The Macmillan Company, 1946 and 1951).

[11] This does not mean that the individual's wages are determined by his training and experience. Job classification is a classification of positions, not of people. It is always possible that the individual will have much higher qualifications than those required for the position he holds.

[12] Carl Dreyfuss, *Occupation and Ideology of the Salaried Employee,* Vol. 1, translated by Eva Abramovitch (mimeographed; New York: WPA and Department of Social Science, Columbia University, 1938).

[13] This distinction is made because an industry which is specialized both technically and regionally is likely to develop a separate and somewhat immobile labor force. Coal mining and the garment trades are two examples of this situation.

[14] Frederick H. Harbison and Robert Dubin, *Patterns of Union-Management Relations* (Chicago: Science Research Associates, 1947).

[15] Dale Yoder, *Manpower Economics and Labor Problems* (New York: McGraw-Hill Book Company, 1939), p. 202.

[16] W. Lloyd Warner and J. O. Low, *The Social System of the Modern Factory,* subtitled *The Strike: A Social Analysis,* Vol. IV, Yankee City Series (New Haven, Conn.: Yale University Press, 1947).

[17] John Von Neumann and Oskar Morganstern, *Theory of Games and Economic Behavior* (Princeton, N.J.: Princeton University Press, 1947).

[18] Leonard R. Sayles and George Strauss, "Conflicts within the Local Union," *Harvard Business Review,* vol. 30, no. 6, November–December 1952, p. 85.

[19] Miles Colean, *American Housing: Problems and Prospects* (New York: The Twentieth Century Fund, 1944).

[20] The degree of this intercraft variation may be illustrated by the rates and hours in the building construction crafts in the Twin Cities in January 1952 (*Occupational Wage Survey,* Minneapolis–St. Paul, Minnesota, Bulletin No. 1068, November 1952):

Classification	Rate per Hour	Hours per Week
Bricklayers	$2.900	40
Carpenters	2.400	40
Electricians	2.650	40
Painters	2.255	40
Plasterers	2.750	40
Plumbers	2.550	40
Building laborers	1.670	40

179

[21] *Survey of Current Business:* "Incomes of Physicians, Dentists and Lawyers," July 1952; "Income of Physicians," July 1951; "Income of Lawyers," August 1949. See also C. D. Long, "Professors' Salaries and Inflation," *Bulletin of the American Association of University Professors,* vol. 38, no. 4, Winter 1952–53.

[22] Oswald Hall: "The Informal Organization of the Medical Profession," *Canadian Journal of Economics and Political Science,* vol. 12, February 1946, pp. 30–44; "The Stages of a Medical Career," *American Journal of Sociology,* vol. 53, January 1948, pp. 327–36; "Types of Medical Careers," *American Journal of Sociology,* vol. 55, no. 3, November 1949, pp. 243–53.

CHAPTER 8

THE LABOR UNION AS AN
OCCUPATIONAL ASSOCIATION

"The disputes which matter are not caused by a misunderstanding of identity of interest, but by a better understanding of diversity of interests."   RICHARD TAWNEY

THE first strike to be analyzed in an American sociological journal was a week-long strike of the Journeymen Horseshoers Local No. 6 of Philadelphia against the Master Horseshoers Protective Association Local No. 23, in June 1902. Horseshoeing was a closed-shop trade with a union stamp on every shoe. The masters were graduated journeymen, or their widows, and a four-year apprenticeship was required. The journeymen, who received a minimum wage of $3.00 per day, demanded a nine-hour day with a half-holiday on Saturday during the hot months, 50 cents an hour for overtime, and one day a year for an outing. After a week, the masters gave in.[1]

This archaic affair occurred only fifty years ago. The emergence of strong occupational associations in the Western world is a recent phenomenon, and it is more recent in the United States than in Europe. During World War I, when American unions numbered fewer than 5 million members, there was talk of labor dominating the government; after World War II, it was a general belief among businessmen that the unions had come to be the controlling influence in public affairs. Yet, even at their height, unions have never included more than about 25 per cent of the labor force, and all types of occupational association taken together account for fewer than half of those employed.

No one would seriously suggest that the present role of unions and of professional societies is insignificant; the developments of the last two decades alone have permanently altered many aspects of our economy. Moreover, the trend throughout Europe has been toward more and more intensive occupational organization. The British Labour Party is scarcely

181

distinguishable from the federation of trade unions on which its strength is based. In France, occupational organizations cover all classes of industrial and agricultural employees, and even retail trade, small business, and managerial occupations are solidly organized. The various forms of European fascism all relied heavily on state-directed occupational corporations, and a form of compulsory organization is part of the Soviet economy.

It should not be assumed, however, that an increasing degree of occupational organization is inevitable in a complex economy. The American industrial structure was almost fully developed before occupational organization became important outside of a handful of specialized industries. As a basic form of organization, occupational groupings appear to be subordinate to more fundamental affiliations based on kinship, locality, religion, property, and status. The history of occupational associations suggests that they become major elements in the general society only when one or more of these other interests are added to the occupational identification.

HISTORICAL SUMMARY

The earliest occupational associations on which there is adequate information were the Roman corporations, whose growth and decline have been analyzed in a massive study by Waltzing.[2] These were quasi-political organizations whose major function was to represent the urban trades in their relations with the bureaucratized government of the later Empire. Occupational elements are also conspicuous in the Hindu caste system, with its original categories of priests, soldiers, farmers, merchants, and laborers, and its later elaboration of thousands of sub-castes, each of which in principle is occupationally homogeneous. Strictly speaking, the Hindu caste system embodies the homogeneity of occupational *levels* rather than separate trades. Its surprising survival into the modern world may well be due to the fact that it combines in one association all the major bases of organization: kinship, common descent, location in the same territory, religious motives, economic interests, and social status.

Organizations usually described as guilds are recorded in the histories of China, Persia, Java, Japan, Syria, and medieval Russia, although not very much is known about any of them. The guild system of medieval Europe, on the other hand, has been admirably documented and has had important consequences for most of our occupational institutions and for many of the forms of modern culture.[3]

The rise and fall of the guilds is quickly recounted. They arose at the end of the Middle Ages with the decline of feudal authority and the renascence of town life, and as the towns flourished, the guilds became important institutions. They reached their height in the commercial city-states of the thirteenth and fourteenth centuries. Thereafter, they were weakened externally by the growth of the royal power and internally by the expansion of the market, which established a sharp distinction between artisan and merchant functions which had originally been combined. The merchants eventually broke away into separate trade-guilds, which dominated and partly controlled the craft-guilds of the artisans. With the Commercial Revolution of the fifteenth century, and the much greater market expansion which followed, the trade-guild proved inadequate to maintain the old collective controls against the emergent capitalism of the great merchants, while the craft-guild split into permanent factions of masters and journeymen. With the advent of mercantilist policies, directed by the trade-conscious monarchs of the seventeenth century, the whole system quietly collapsed.

In detail, the history of the guilds is much less straightforward. The world in which they arose was one of isolated settlements and poor communications. Their history as well as their constitution varied from town to town. In the Lowlands, where the feudal system was especially weak, the conditions of commerce unusually favorable, and the nationalistic spirit almost unknown during the medieval period, the guilds flourished mightily. They were less powerful in France and Spain where the transition from feudalism to nationalism was more direct; or in Italy, where the urbanization of the nobles checked their influence from the beginning, and where the development of the great commercial empires of Venice, Florence, and Genoa favored commerce at the expense of manufacture. So uneven were these rates of development that joint-stock companies had already displaced the ancient guilds of Florence before the guild system reached its full development in England.

Unwin has traced the history of the guilds [4] and companies of London in admirable detail, and certain unfamiliar elements deserve to be emphasized. The guild in London was originally a religious fraternity of private citizens devoted to the cult of a patron saint, very much like the *cofradías* which still occupy an important place in Latin American life. Some of these fraternities were organized by parish, or by voluntary inclination; the membership of others was based on a common trade. The guild as an economic institution emerged very late. Not until the fourteenth century can the craft-guild be clearly recognized, and by that period, the interests of merchants and artisans were clearly opposed. From the very beginning of the system, occupational stratification was reflected in the superior privileges of the "greater misteries" and their tendency to dominate or even annex the "lesser misteries." By the time of the Tudors, the merchant guilds — in the form of livery companies — had achieved great wealth and influence, competing with the court in the sumptuousness of their feasts and the interior decoration of their halls. They had already ceased to fulfill many guild functions and in the next century the Crown practice of selling commercial monopolies put an end to their trade privileges. Those which outlasted the seventeenth century survived as honorific societies, some of which still exist today.

Although the English guild never achieved a dominant position in its own time, its vestigial survivals provided the background for the modern development of both unions and professional societies in the English-speaking world. This is in sharp contrast to the situation on the Continent, where the guilds came to be identified with the privileges and perquisites of the burgher aristocrats and where the revolutions which abolished absolute monarchy made a clean sweep of the ancient corporations.

Even in medieval times, journeymen's associations were not uncommon. Although they were principally ceremonial, they occasionally took collective action to improve working conditions, and even strikes were not unheard of. The first labor organizations in the modern sense were organized on the Continent in the seventeenth century. These were outside the guild organization, among skilled workmen whose principal grievance was the neglect by employers of journeymen's customary rights and privileges. According to McCabe and Lester:

Not only had the number of skilled workmen who had no expectation of rising from the wage-earning status increased, but the need for defensive organization to preserve the customary standards was becoming increasingly evident. The old statutory apprenticeship requirements were being more and more ignored, and the provisions on the statute books for the fixing of wages were fading into general nonobservance. Moreover, this increasing obsolescence of legal regulations was accompanied by a widening toleration by employers of organization among the wage-earning craftsmen. Through the eighteenth century an increasing number of associations of craftsmen dealt with their employers on the terms of employment and attempted to enforce the customary apprenticeship as a prerequisite to employment as a journeyman. When the legal prohibition of combinations among workmen was extended and tightened at the close of the eighteenth century, the movement for organization had developed sufficient strength to endure in spite of legal proscription and even instances of severe punishment. And after legal freedom to organize was granted in 1824 the labor movement in England grew rapidly.[5]

The New England colonies were founded while the guilds were still nominally active in England. It might have been thought that conditions in early New England were very suitable for a revival of the guild system. As Mumford [6] and other discerning commentators have pointed out, the New England township, with its representative theocracy, its sumptuary regulation and building controls, its highly developed local consciousness, and its "organic" responsibility for the complete lives of its citizens, was in some ways the archetype of medieval communities. As a matter of fact, a number of guilds are recorded in the early years and one formed by the colony shoemakers in 1648 seems to have been a typical craft-guild in all respects. In the long run, however, the guild system was not adapted to the American scene. The colonies were faced with a perennial surplus of resources and a shortage of labor which was always more or less acute. Any attempt to establish customary wages and working conditions was therefore foredoomed to failure. Indeed, most of the economic motives for the combination of producers were lacking. Until well into the nineteenth century, all but a small fraction of the American population were engaged in rural occupations, supplemented by domestic handicrafts. Bound labor in the North and Negro slavery in the South were the principal devices evolved to meet the labor shortage, and all attempts at organization by these servitors were crushed with ruthless severity.[7]

Not until after the Revolution were the first labor unions founded. Commons [8] identified the Federal Society of Journeymen Cordwainers, founded in Philadelphia in 1794, as the first union in the modern sense. (It was quickly followed by a trade association of shoe-manufacturing employers.) These early organizations in the skilled trades were congenial societies and political clubs as well as negotiating groups. Until the 1830s, they were each confined to a single locality.

The 1830s and the 1840s were years of ideological restlessness in the United States. The period saw the socialism of Owen and Fourier; the religious utopianism of Noyes, Joseph Smith, Rapp, and hundreds of other prophets; and the temperate utopianism of the Concord School, together with abolitionism and the idea of manifest destiny. The labor movement, still entirely insignificant, took on a political coloration which it has never entirely lost, and the first workingmen's parties were founded at about the same time as the first Owenite colonies.

In 1842, the decision of Chief Justice Shaw in the famous case of *Commonwealth v. Hunt* (Massachusetts) repudiated for the first time the legal argument with which these first unions had been sporadically pursued in the courts as criminal conspiracies. Previous to this, the American courts had been almost unanimous in condemning labor organizations. (In a famous opinion of 1835, the English Combination Act passed in the reign of George III, and *repealed* in 1824, had been cited as authority for the condemnation of collective bargaining as conspiracy.) The Shaw decision warrants quotation:

Stripped . . . of the qualifying epithets attached to the facts, the averment is this; that the defendants and others formed themselves into a society, and agreed not to work for any person who should employ any journeyman or other person, not a member of such society, after notice given him to discharge such workman. The manifest intent of the association is to induce all those engaged in the same occupation to become members of it. Such a purpose is not unlawful. It would give them a power which might be exerted for useful and honorable purposes, or for dangerous and pernicious ones. If the latter were the real and actual object, and susceptible of proof, it should have been specially charged . . .

Nor can we perceive that the objects of this association, whatever they may have been, were to be attained by criminal means. The means which they proposed to employ, as averred in this count, and which, as we are now to presume, were established by the proof, were, that they would not work for a person, who, after due notice, should employ a journeyman not a member of their society. Supposing the object of the association to be laudable and lawful, or at least not unlawful, are these means criminal? The case supposes that these persons are not bound by contract, but free to work for whom they please, or not to work, if they so prefer. In this state of things, we cannot perceive that it is criminal for men to agree together to exercise their own acknowledged rights, in such a manner as best to subserve their own interests.

From 1850 to the end of the Civil War, conditions were relatively favorable for labor organization, and the first national unions emerged at this time, centered in the highly skilled crafts: typographers, stonecutters, machinists, and blacksmiths, and a little later, bricklayers, carpenters, locomotive engineers, shoemakers, steel workers, and cigar-makers. This expansion coincided with the height of the westward movement, with uninterrupted prosperity, and with the labor shortage created by the war.

The period stands out as perhaps the most peaceful in the history of American labor relations. Collective bargaining of a modern character was established in industries, such as steel and railroads, in which twenty years later the presence of unions would be opposed by force of arms. It is startling to find, in a contract signed between Pittsburgh employers and the Sons of Vulcan as early as 1865, an agreement for a sliding scale of wage rates pegged to the price of steel.[9]

The international craft unions (so called because they claimed jurisdiction in Canada) continued through the subsequent period with varying fortunes, mostly unfavorable, and in 1881 they combined to form the American Federation of Labor under the leadership of Gompers and Strasser. It was not originally a mass movement. Not until 1900 did membership rise to a quarter of a million, and meanwhile, a number of more conspicuous episodes had occupied the labor scene.

Four distinct efforts were made between 1870 and 1910 to extend labor organization beyond the conservative, exclusive, and nonpolitical craft unions.

The first was the development soon after the Civil War of the National Labor Union, based upon the local cooperative associations established during the war. It was the first labor organization to unite distinct trades in the same federation, and it maintained a program of limited political objectives, together with a lively faith in producers' cooperatives. It disappeared within a few years — apparently because the national organization had no way of holding together the city centrals of which it was composed, and these, in turn, could not assure the stability of their constituent locals.

It was succeeded by a much more important movement — the Knights of Labor. This was a huge, undifferentiated society, organized on a locality basis, without reference to either craft or industrial lines, but with a hierarchy of local, state, regional, and national officers. It is difficult at this distance to assess the importance of the Knights of Labor. It stood somewhat outside of the mainstream of labor history, resembling at once a secret society, a political party, a revolutionary movement, and a federation of industrial unions. Even its size cannot be closely estimated. At the peak in 1887, paid-up membership included between 5 and 50 per cent of the labor force. The long-range objective was to enable labor as a whole to exert a concentrated influence on both local and national issues. It leaned heavily on the sympathetic strike, never engaged in large-scale negotiation, and dwindled rapidly after its defeats in the industrial warfare of the 1880s.

Another crucial effort was the attempt to expand the union nuclei left by the Civil War in the heavy industries — steel and iron, railroads, car-building, coal, and copper — and to establish industry-wide bargaining with the great concentrations of management which were making their first appearance. These were the days of the Haymarket Riot, the Pullman Massacre, the Pinkertons, and blanket injunctions. The strength of the unions was vastly unequal to the effort, the courts were uniformly unsympathetic, private armies were used to break strikes in Pennsylvania, and federal troops served the same purpose in Illinois. The industrial unions were decisively crushed.

This same period saw the growth of a number of political and quasi-political movements which were more or less linked with organized labor. The most important of these were the Populists, who were the first to attempt the political union of urban labor and the farm vote, never realized until the Roosevelt Era. Coxey's Army, Tillmanism, the founding of a Socialist party which gained some local successes, and the development of radical movements within the Democratic party were other signs of the time. It is likely that the election of William Jennings Bryan in 1896 or 1900 would have vastly accelerated the slow growth of the unions.

Not until after 1900 did any important revolutionary unions appear. The first center of syndicalism was in the Mountain States, where the Western Federation of Miners laid the groundwork for that curious organization the International Workers of the World, whose program was compounded out of intense class consciousness, faith in "one big union," a romantic conception of revolution, and a belief in violence. It endured with varying fortunes into the twenties, but never recovered from the penalties to which its objections to World War I exposed it. The I.W.W. was an extremely loose organization; its symbolic character is evidenced by the fact that those carrying the famous red card were ten or twenty times as numerous as the dues-paying members. It was essentially an organization of the unorganizable: the migratory workers, the bindle stiffs, the miners of the Mountain States, and the unskilled. It never had any substantial strength in industry, but it had a good deal to do with the creation of an indigenous form of class consciousness which survives today among the industrial unions.

The pattern for durable labor organizations was established by the Depression of 1893–97, which destroyed the Knights of Labor and the industrial unions in heavy industry. The old-line craft unions emerged intact, although much reduced in membership. Membership rose rapidly until 1904, when it was checked by powerful antiunion campaigns, resumed its rise in 1910, was briefly checked in the recession of 1914–15, and then received its greatest impetus in the war years. The rapid expansion of industry, the rising cost of living, the sharp demand for labor, the cessation of immigration, and the development of new industrial centers, all contributed to this result. Another crucial element was the sympathetic attitude of the Wilson administration, which invited the participation of labor leaders in the wartime agencies, encouraged organization in the establishments under its control, and through the War Labor Board — on which employers and labor were equally represented — enforced an industrial truce which was favorable to union expansion. This impetus continued through the postwar period, but the disappearance of government support and the postwar depression reduced union membership almost to its prewar level. In the later hectic prosperity of the twenties, the unions barely held their own. The climate of the times was favorable neither to labor organization nor to reform movements. The ideology of the businessman was more generally accepted than ever before or since: the Lynds found little disposition to question the open shop in Middletown — even on the wrong side of the tracks.[10]

The first years of the Great Depression weakened the unions still further, and by 1933, the gains of the previous twenty years had been lost. But the passage of the National Industrial Recovery Act opened a new phase in labor history, and gave to the federal government the central role in labor relations which it has held ever since. This sweeping change of policy was contained in the famous Section 7 (a):

Every code of fair competition, agreement, and license approved, prescribed, or issued under this title shall contain the following conditions: (1) That employees shall have the right to organize and bargain collectively through representatives of their own choosing, and shall be free from the interference, restraint, or coercion of employers of labor, or their agents, in the designation of such representatives or in self-organization or in other concerted activities for the purpose of collective bargaining or other mutual aid or protection; (2) that no employee and no one seeking employment shall be required as a condition of employment to join any company union or to refrain from joining, organizing, or assisting a labor organization of his own choosing . . .

The response was immediate. It will probably never be accurately known how many workers affiliated themselves, nominally at least, with labor organizations in the months after the passage of the act. Certainly the number was far greater than the increase recorded in the figures of paid-up membership. Nevertheless the law proved largely unenforceable, and the rights it affirmed were not universally accepted by employers. After the invalidation of the act in 1935, the Wagner Act was passed, further affirming the right to collective bargaining, defining unfair labor practices, and establishing an independent board with power to investigate complaints, supervise plant elections, issue orders, and arbitrate disputes. This statute did not come into full effect until the Supreme Court recognized its constitutionality two years later, but the movement toward organization of the mass-production industries had already begun. In 1936, the main group of industrial unions left the American Federation of Labor and set up the Committee (later the Congress) of Industrial Organizations to promote industrial unionism. By 1938, the new industrial unions had gained substantial membership in most of the key industries which had historically maintained an open-shop policy — automobile, steel, rubber, textile, electrical, and oil — and had extended industrial unionism on a small scale to a number of white-collar occupations, including journalists, chemists, office workers, and civil service employees.

By 1940, when the defense program opened another era favorable to labor organization, paid-up union membership had reached about 8 million. During the war years, aided by union-security agreements and favorable clauses in government contracts, the unions continued to grow in size and influence, although their ability to secure wage increases was severely limited by the "no-strike pledge" and the government's wage-stabilization policy. The first postwar year was marked by large-scale strikes for wage increases. Additional wage increases were secured without extensive strikes in 1947, and at the end of that year, total union membership stood at nearly twice the prewar figure.

The passage of the Taft-Hartley Act in 1947 limited the right of unions to insist on union membership, curtailed the scope of collective bargaining, and made unions liable for unfair practices. It also reorganized the federal labor agencies in a manner designed to be less favorable to labor. The right to join and maintain unions, and the definition of collective bargaining as the normal procedure in labor relations, remained unchanged. The influence of the unions did not appear to be immediately affected. Indeed, after 1948, two important innovations were introduced into collective bargaining. The first, for which the pattern was set by negotiations between General Motors and the United Automobile Workers, was the long-term contract, in which a no-strike agreement by the employees is matched by the employer's obligation to adjust wages to the cost of living without negotiation. The other innovation involved the extensive development of welfare and pension plans, operated under joint control but largely financed by management. Paid-up union membership at the end of 1952 was in the neighborhood of 16 million.

Our primary concern here is not with the vast area of labor relations, which has one of the most extensive literatures in the entire field of human behavior, but with the labor union as a form of social organization. In this, the sources are less satisfactory. There is an inexhaustible supply of constitutions, resolutions, programs, manifestoes, and partisan pronouncements, but only a handful of empirical studies, most of which are rather recent and of limited extent. In the sections which follow, we shall consider the general types of union organization, the forms of union activity, and the interior structure of unions. The latter subject — the most important from the standpoint of occupational behavior — has not been thoroughly studied and any conclusions will be highly tentative.

TYPES OF UNION ORGANIZATION

Unions may be classified in a number of ways, and in the absence of reliable information on their interior structure, an excessive ingenuity has been devoted to such taxonomies.

Labor economists have long cited Hoxie's definitions: *Business unions* are concerned primarily with the improvement of wages and working conditions; *uplift unions* are devoted to benevolent activities, self-improvement, and elaborate funerals; *revolutionary unions* are subversive of the existing government; *reform unions* aim at gradual social change to be achieved by legislation; *company unions* are dominated openly or covertly by employers.[11] The classification is useful in outlining the major functions which unions do fulfill; its weakness lies in the fact that it is unusual to find a union which falls cleanly into any one of the categories. Business unions usually have reform motives of one kind or another, and almost always engage in "uplift" activities, as do many company unions. Revolutionary unions are perfectly capable of such "business" activities as collective bargaining for wage increases.

Another classification much cited in textbooks is that of vertical and horizontal unionism. These terms have been much confused. As Yoder points out, the popular identification of craft unions as horizontal and industrial unions as vertical is ambiguous. Vertical unionism originally referred to the organization of labor by product, in such a way as to include all the related jobs from the extraction of the raw material to the finishing of the final product, while horizontal organization is limited to a single stage of production but may take in a variety of products. Thus, most unions are horizontal; the few notable exceptions (like the Carpenters and Joiners, which includes both lumberjacks and cabinetmakers) are found in production lines where some similarity of tools and processes obtains throughout the entire course of production.

Another classification, and one that can scarcely be evaded, is by affiliation. American labor is presently divided into two great federations, themselves composed of federations identified by trade or industry or both; a number of independent federations, notably the railway unions, which have always been separate; the United Mine Workers, who, after a stormy course from the A.F.L. to the C.I.O. and back again, severed connections with both; and the International Ladies Garment Workers Union, which also played a prominent part in the founding of the C.I.O. but later withdrew. In addition to the federations, there are a vast number of local unions — oriented by trade, by industry, or by employer, and often limited to a single plant. Among these are a considerable number in which employer influence is conspicuous, and which are often described as company unions. It should be noted, however, that the latter term is an epithet rather than a classification. No union ever admits to being a company union; and the term has been applied to employee-representation plans, benefit societies, athletic leagues, and other projects sponsored by management which strictly speaking are not unions at all. These had their greatest vogue in the twenties, when they were widely proposed by management in connection with open-shop campaigns, but many of them have survived, and many new ones have been developed, even in plants which are completely unionized.

The most familiar classification distinguishes craft, industrial, and white-collar unions. In theory, the craft union is limited to a single occupation, the industrial union to a single branch of industry, and the white-collar union to a single status level. In practice, these distinctions are much less definite than they appear. At one extreme are a few unions, principally in the building trades, explicitly and literally restricted to a single craft. At the other extreme are the giant unions which may cover almost the entire labor force of a heavy industry. In between are all sorts of overlapping arrangements.

Even the "pure" craft union often includes helpers, apprentices, and foremen. Many craft unions bring together a number of allied occupations in the same locals: painters and plasterers, teamsters and chauffeurs, machinists and foundrymen. The A.F.L. has long provided the device of the national labor union, which combines any number of crafts into a single local in communities too small to support separate craft unions. Then too, the definition of an occupation may be made sufficiently broad so that a powerful craft union expands its jurisdiction indefinitely. The Teamsters' Union has at times embraced all the trades connected with transportation, as well as others, such as grocery clerks, whose connection with transportation is tenuous. Finally, the definition of a craft may group under the same heading a large number of occupations which are by no means identical. The Musicians' Union represents symphony conductors, night-club entertainers, and church organists.

The pattern presented by industrial unions is no more consistent. In the first place, almost all the industrial unions have been forced to recognize the jurisdiction of old, tightly organized crafts, such as steamfitters and upholsterers, and to develop some sort of compromise arrangement with them. Double union membership is not unusual in this situation; it allows the industrial union to become the sole bargaining agent in a completely unionized shop, while the craft union preserves the right to negotiate informally on craft matters. This is awkward, but no more awkward than the development of a separate status for craftsmen, or their incorporation into a separate local of the industrial union.

On the other hand, it sometimes happens that an industry scarcely includes more than a single occupation — the longshoremen and the miners, for example — so that it becomes a matter of choice whether the organization should be based ostensibly on craft or on industrial lines. Industrial lines, at best, are not clearly defined. Many businesses cross them, and in some cases it has been advantageous to organize a union parallel to the employer's business rather than on an industrial basis. It is difficult to find any major industrial activity which cannot reasonably be considered as belonging to two or more industries; this may occur either because of horizontal relations in production (the manufacture of phonographs is closely bound up with that of radios) or vertical relations to a finished product (the making of automobile batteries belongs to both the auto-

193

mobile and the electrical industry). In the course of time a single job may be considered for union purposes as belonging to any of a dozen craft or industrial categories.

Finally, there are a number of instances in which a single industry, under single management, is conventionally divided into noncommunicating branches of labor, separately organized. The best known of these divisions is between operating and nonoperating personnel on the railroads. The Brotherhoods have always been limited to employees who actually ride the trains or are directly concerned with their movement. Maintenance men, roundhouse employees, and station personnel belong for all practical purposes to a separate industry. A similar distinction exists in the monolithic telephone industry between the manufacture of telephone equipment and its operation.

The C.I.O., when founded in 1936, represented a revolt of the industrial unions against the dominant philosophy of craft unionism in the American Federation of Labor. As many observers have pointed out, the principal function of the A.F.L. had been to safeguard the jurisdictions of its member unions against each other's encroachment. The sponsoring of industrial unionism, with its inevitable crossing of occupational lines, would have meant the abandonment of its major functions. This formulation is accurate, in general, but it ignores the inherent complexity of the matter and the difficulty of maintaining either craft or industrial unionism in pure form except in a few industries, such as construction, which happen to be specially suited to one or the other. Consequently, the A.F.L. still includes a substantial number of industrial unions, and the C.I.O. has developed new craft unions. On the local level, it is not unusual to find a C.I.O. local competing with an A.F.L. local in an identically defined jurisdiction; it even comes about from time to time that a C.I.O. craft union protests the infringement of its jurisdiction by an A.F.L. industrial union.

When all this is recognized, there remains a real distinction between two general types of union organization, which differ substantially in size, composition, structure, policy, standards, methods, political orientation, and terminology. Even though the distinction has been somewhat blurred in recent years, it continues to exert a strong influence, and the two labor federations represent in some fashion two polar approaches to labor organization. The best confirmation is perhaps found in the fact that what might be called the social pathology of unionism is quite different in the two cases: C.I.O. unions have been as rarely suspected of racketeering and gangster control as A.F.L. unions of being directed by Communists toward purely political ends.

It would perhaps be more accurate to speak of "restrictive" and "expansive" unionism than of craft and industrial unions. Whether we consider such "pure" types as the Master Steamfitters and the United Automobile Workers, or merely note the general differences of emphasis between the federations, a number of coherent patterns may be distinguished.

The restrictive union is composed of skilled workers who for one reason or another are not easily replaceable. Its first objective is to control admission to the occupation so that increases in wages or improvements in working conditions will not be negated by an increase in the supply of workers. In thus fixing the supply of labor, it usually assumes responsibility for its equitable distribution among employers. This, in turn, leads to a close concern with the performance of work, and to continuous efforts to standardize work output. These motives are reinforced by the union's concern with apprenticeship, and by the necessity of safeguarding the existing craft against technological change. In a previous chapter, we considered the way in which this tends to render the craftsman's relationship with his employer rather transitory, while strengthening at every point his relationship with the union.

It is in unions of this type that some of the terminology and ritual of the guilds survives, and the underlying situations have many points of similarity. What most threatens their structure is an uncontrolled increase in the labor supply. Thus, craft unions have often excluded women and Negroes and aliens, have sometimes limited their membership to native-born white Protestants, and in extreme cases have denied apprenticeship to all candidates not related to a member or not born in the locality. The political aspect of these sweeping restrictions largely disappeared when organized labor's opposition to mass immigration was enacted into law after World War I, but restrictions of this kind are still an important element in the disadvantaged position of minorities, including women, although they are giving way in the face of a more general support of minority rights by pro-labor political groups. Aside from this single national issue, restrictive unionism has long been celebrated for its indifference to organized politics. The much-quoted slogan of Gompers that "labor would reward its friends and punish its enemies at the polls" implies a policy of party neutrality, based on the theory that the restrictive union, with its local and particular interests, risks more than it can possibly gain by entering the political arena. This policy, too, has been considerably tempered in recent years, but its main outlines remain unaltered.

The expansive union draws its membership principally from the semi-skilled and the unskilled, for whom there can be no question of permanently restricting the supply of labor, and who are too numerous and mobile to aim at differential wages based on a local monopoly. The alternative strategy is to mass the strength of very large numbers against management, and to control the entire labor force of a plant or of an industry at a particular time. This is facilitated by the technological situation. The normal field of the expansive union is in mass-production industries, which have attained their present scale largely through the intensive rationalization and continuous rearrangement of jobs, thus leaving little room for the development of standardized and codified skills. Their scale of operation invariably involves a large fixed capital and heavy overhead charges, which make the strike particularly effective. The small employer can sometimes wait out a strike indefinitely. The history of restrictive unionism records at least one strike that lasted ten years, and innumerable occasions on which strikes were met with lockouts or the removal of a plant. The large-scale manufacturer seldom has these choices. Indeed, the whole national economy may be threatened by a protracted strike in a large-scale industry. When legislation and court action weakened the coercive devices which employers had customarily used against strikers, the potential power of the expansive unions was increased many times.

As far as membership is concerned, the clearest danger to an expansive union lies in the existence of a reserve labor force, from which labor can be drawn at bargain prices and from which strikebreakers may be recruited. The expansive union has not only favored the admission of women, Negroes, aliens, and migrants on equal terms; it has also advocated the elimination of differential wages in general.

For similar reasons, the expansive union cannot deny to outsiders the benefits it secures for its own members. To do so would be to create an artificial minority whose presence would provide management with a similar leverage as the existence of a "natural" minority. This circumstance decidedly weakens the individual worker's interest in keeping up his membership, or in participating in union affairs.

Whereas the restrictive union figures largely in the day-to-day employment of its members, the weight of the expansive union is designed for use at moments of crisis. The implications of this situation were discovered about 1935 after the first impetus of expansive organization was spent. It was found that membership figures could decline precipitously through "loss of interest." While the older restrictive union might collapse after a defeat, a successful strike tended to preserve it. The expansive unions, by contrast, lost membership rapidly after successful strikes or negotiations and they soon turned to two kinds of devices to offset this tendency.

The first was to enlist — or to compel — the cooperation of employers in maintaining union membership. This was done by providing that employment would terminate if union membership were abandoned (e.g., union shop, maintenance of membership clauses); by having dues deducted directly from the pay check by the employer (the check-off); or by developing welfare plans, particularly old-age and unemployment benefits, for which union membership was required.

The second device was the development of supplementary activities to maintain interest and informal participation. These went far beyond the conventional funeral attendance and the ladies' auxiliary of old-fashioned unionism. Expansive unions have run summer camps, produced plays, held dances and essay contests, built housing projects, organized night courses, operated hobby shops, formed cooperative stores, published thousands of newspapers, and experimented with any other interests which promised to appeal to their membership.

The political activities of the expansive union are equally variegated. There are several reasons. The restrictive union requires only a minimum of protection to enable it to exercise its effective monopoly of a necessary group of services — notably the right to organize, the right to strike, and freedom from violence — but the expansive union must operate within a framework established by legislation and by the current activities of law-enforcement agencies. Beyond the protections enumerated above, it requires the acceptance of collective bargaining by the employer, the accompanying procedures for designation of collective bargaining agents, and means of enforcement for the resulting contracts. In addition, there must be some way of checking the importation of strikebreakers by management, and a definite strategy for situations in which the interruption of production affects the general community.

A number of more remote political factors are also involved. Because very large numbers of employees are covered by negotiations in the basic industries, wage changes have some influence on the general price structure. For the same reason, wage negotiations affect the general standard of living through the cost of living and through changes in the average work week.

As a matter of fact, some coordination of effort among the expansive unions is regarded as desirable, and the pattern is now expressed in terms of "rounds" of wage increases, and "series" of welfare fund negotiations. Harbison and Dubin [12] have shown in detail why a power center tends to be established in a mass-production industry, so that negotiations between the most powerful employer and the most powerful union local set the pattern which the rest of the industry follows with minor variations. In the same way, the crucial and well-publicized negotiations which take place in the mass-production industries tend to set the pattern for the rest of the economy. A single contract negotiation in the automobile or the steel industry may exert a leverage entirely out of proportion to the number of union members involved, which is large to begin with.

The surveillance of the economy, with respect to the relationship between wages and prices, has come to be a function of the federal government, and in times of crisis, verges on direct control. As a highly interested arbiter, the government is capable of exerting a decisive influence in crucial negotiations and in the settlement of issues arising out of strikes. The expansive union may win more through politics than it can achieve directly at the negotiating table, and in any case, its fate is closely bound up with the attitude of administrative agencies and of legislatures. The involvement of expansive unions in politics appears therefore to be inevitable. Although the strong reaction developed in 1948 against the Political Action Committee of the C.I.O. led to a partial union withdrawal from national politics, the very existence of expansive unions depends upon continued political participation, which takes place in two ways: the use of strategic economic positions to influence the formulation of policy; and the attempt to weld the very large memberships of the expansive unions into coherent electoral blocs.

These processes have already produced a definite ideological pattern, which characterizes the expansive unions. While the attention of the restrictive union is usually focused on local issues and on particular incidents in labor relations, the membership and the leadership of the expansive union are continuously concerned with certain fixed issues on a national scale. The most important of these are the relation between wages and consumer prices, which provides a running index of labor's situation;

the relation between wage and profits, which indicates roughly but adequately the chance of securing concessions from management; and the trends of legislation, court decisions, and administrative action, which define the relative strength of management and labor at a given time.

The union member is thus trained to regard himself as belonging to a broad economic group whose interests are more or less uniform, and more or less consistently opposed to the interests of management. The vocabulary of expansive unionism is largely the vocabulary of class-conscious Marxism; such terms as "greedy bosses" and "slave-driving" are used in union publications so routinely as to lose most of their pejorative significance. This phenomenon is not unconnected with the presence, until recently, of an influential Communist minority in many of the expansive unions. Nonetheless, the underlying ideology is remarkably dissimilar to the orthodox class consciousness of Europe, and its leading themes are different. Perhaps the fundamental difference is that the economic theory implicit in expansive unionism is that of Keynes rather than that of Marx. The idea of an inevitably increasing exploitation of labor has virtually no currency in this system, where major emphasis is placed upon a continued increase of labor's distributive share. By the same token, the expansive union is vitally interested in a high level of production and in the general prosperity of the industry with which it is concerned. The only economic theorem which enjoys unquestioning acceptance is the one which states that increases in consumer purchasing power contribute to the increased productivity of the total system.

There are a variety of other reasons why the class-consciousness characteristic of expansive unionism is limited in effect to the consciousness of membership in an economic interest group. Some weight must be given to the prevailing emphasis on upward mobility in the United States, and the identification of expansive unionism with a steady increase of living standards. Over and above these is the practical exigency that a program designed to secure the political adherence of union members must be confined to the narrow range of objectives on which they can be brought to agree. The characteristic heterogeneity of the industrial force in mass-production industries, the wide geographical dispersion of heavy industries, and the lack of permanent identification either with a particular semiskilled occupation or with factory work in general, all tend to limit these objectives sharply. Recent elections have suggested that the political integration of organized labor is even less than has been supposed.

The white-collar unions need to be separately considered. Although they are not very important numerically, they represent a unique development in occupational organization, and have created a new framework of employee relations in a few fields.

The term *white-collar union* is hardly precise. It covers a variety of distinct situations, including the organization of wage earners doing non-manual work, of managerial and professional personnel, and of manual workers whose level of training and remuneration is so high that they are not generally identified with labor. It is used to describe unions of office and clerical workers, professional personnel in the government service, policemen and mail clerks, teachers, foremen in industry, actors, journalists, screenwriters, and commercial aviators.

Whether some of these should be regarded as unions is questionable. Even the terminology is not clear: many of these organizations are called associations, societies, guilds, or leagues; but they are no less likely to be affiliated with labor federations than those which call themselves unions. The identification with labor cannot be brushed aside. Although teaching is generally considered a learned profession, and is notable for the unusual stringency of community controls to which its members are subject, teachers' unions have repeatedly conducted successful and protracted strikes, complete with mass picketing, in the face of a long-standing prejudice against strikes by public employees.

Benevolent and protective associations of public employees have a long history in the United States; they have supported a variety of functions, ranging from pure congeniality to negotiations on working conditions, but their principal concern has usually been with retirement benefits, group insurance policies, assistance to widows and orphans, and funeral ceremonies. The early excursions of some of these societies into the field of collective bargaining were harshly discouraged, and Calvin Coolidge won national approval in 1909 for his suppression of the Boston policemen's strike.

Most of the existing white-collar unions were created in the wave of enthusiasm for unionization which followed the passage of the Wagner Act, and a number of the older societies were revitalized. The important developments may be briefly summarized.

The unionization of office and clerical workers tended to be successful wherever the conditions of office employment approached the impersonality and large-scale organization of the factory, especially where the drive for organization paralleled the progress of expansive unions in the same industry. A considerable number of these still survive and show no striking differences from other labor unions. Where these conditions did not exist, clerical unions tended to disappear rapidly.

Given the favorable attitudes toward labor which characterized the national administration and many local governments throughout this period, it is not surprising that office unions were especially conspicuous in government agencies. Although, in general, they recognized their inability to strike or to use other means of direct coercion, they were in many cases able to evolve a basis for negotiation, and their presence provoked many of the existing civil service agencies into action akin to collective bargaining.

The most significant development, by far, was the organization of unions in professional, quasi-professional, and technical occupations, which were in no sense professional societies, but which were directly concerned with wages and working conditions and used the conventional devices of negotiation, strikes, picketing, boycotts, and appeals to public opinion against their employers. In many cases — notably that of teachers and laboratory technicians — the professional society continued to exist parallel to the union without great conflict. Since these professions were almost entirely salaried, the regulation of fees and working conditions by the professional society had never assumed major proportions.

What sometimes gave the activities of these new unions a bizarre flavor was the fact that some of their members enjoyed very high incomes — especially motion picture actors and other entertainers — and in a few cases the entire occupation represented by a union was extraordinarily privileged. Considerable publicity was given to the statement of a labor leader who dismissed a strike of airline pilots in 1949 as a "quarrel between two sets of capitalists," and the public has seldom taken seriously the participation in union protests of entertainers with astronomical incomes.

Yet the motives which favored unionization of the fringe professions were substantial. In the case of teachers, nurses, librarians, laboratory technicians, chemists, and some groups of engineers, salaries tended consistently to lag far behind the cost of living and were generally considered to be disproportionately low in view of the specialized training required. Wherever the entire profession was on a salary basis, the conventional devices of the professional society for protecting the economic position of its members were inoperative. Precisely because of the individualization

201

of performance which marks the profession, members often lack security of employment without being able to command the payment of premiums for their particular services.

Almost the opposite situation exists in journalism and the entertainment occupations, where the great and irrational individualization of services makes it impossible to limit recruiting in any serious way, while the high rewards offered at the top of the occupation attract a horde of marginal competitors. Before the establishment of union control in these fields, the effect of this situation was sometimes to reduce the marginal wage to zero or less: young actors or reporters might pay the employer for the privilege of acquiring experience.

The two quite different situations represented have led to quite different results. With the passage of time, the unionization of salaried professionals, once regarded as a threat to professional status, has become respectable — especially where union activity has been followed by definite improvements in the terms of employment contracts. The previous absence of even informal pressure groups in some of these occupations seems to have left a considerable gap between the going salary rate and the maximum obtainable, so that even a weak teachers' union often finds its efforts crowned with immediate success. It would be misleading to pretend that white-collar unionism has changed the basic situation of the salaried professional very sharply; it remains a small-scale movement. However, with the acceptance of the principle that collective bargaining is consistent with professional dignity, it is not unlikely that a form of occupational organization midway between the professional society and the union may develop. Such a structure would be realistically related to the actual structure of the salaried professions.

For journalism and the various branches of entertainment, the essential problem is the establishment of a minimum wage, in order to prevent marginal competitors from disorganizing the occupation. There is no question of a standard wage, nor are there any particular problems of occupational solidarity, which is more than adequately realized by intensive informal association. Thus, the union tends to become a business office, supervising the execution of employment contracts, and if well enough established, it may even be able to substitute unilateral fixing of minimum fees for negotiation. Within its area of operation it is very powerful, but the scope of its activities is more narrowly restricted than that of any other type of occupational association.

THE INTERNAL STRUCTURE OF UNIONS

The basic pattern of formal union organization in the United States follows that of the American Federation of Labor, which has not changed materially in seventy years. The smallest unit is the *local,* which is a constituent part of a *national* union (usually designated as the *international*) from which it derives its charter and most of the policies and regulations under which it operates. The national unions are the autonomous components of the federation, from which they may withdraw at will, and in whose conventions they are represented in proportion to their membership. Except on questions of jurisdiction, such authority as the federation exercises is indirect and incidental. In addition to the national unions, there are a number of locals which are directly affiliated with the federation, either as emerging national unions which will achieve autonomy when several locals have been formed, or as collections of mixed trades in areas which cannot support separate locals. The federation is further divided into a small number of *departments,* which represent groups of related industries, and a large number of *city centrals* and *county centrals* which bring the locals within a community together on matters of common local interest.

This organization is essentially duplicated in the Congress of Industrial Organizations, except that in a few crucial centers, the national unions have permitted the growth of very large locals, themselves mass organizations, which are further subdivided into *sections* or *branches.* In most cities, the C.I.O. city central is separate from the A.F.L. city central and they are typically hostile to each other, although merger has occurred under certain circumstances.

Of the major organizations outside of the two federations, only two present significant modifications of these arrangements: the Railway Brotherhoods, who function as an informal federation without official existence, and the United Mine Workers, who insert the *district* as another level of organization between the national and the local.

The participation of most union members is limited to the local, which may range in size from half a dozen members to many thousands, and which may represent the intimate association of a handful of old cronies at one extreme or the mute impersonality of a reading public at the other. In addition to differences in size and in intensity of interaction, there are important structural variations.

The several kinds of functionaries in the local union have distinct roles. The business agent, or "walking delegate," is a permanent salaried official, usually but not always a past member of the occupation, who deals with both employers and employees as an official representative of the union. The shop steward is an employee who assumes responsibility for union affairs, especially for the collection of dues and the presentation of minor grievances, in the shop in which he himself works. His jurisdiction usually covers the same area as that of his foreman, so that in tightly organized plants, management is represented in each crew by the foreman and the union by a shop steward.

The officers of the union may be professional union functionaries, paid by the union for full-time supervision of its affairs, or union members who continue at their old jobs after election, and whose activity is voluntary and unpaid.

A special and important role is played by the professional organizer — the "outside agitator" of managerial propaganda — who is sent into the local situation by a national union to undertake the original formation of a union, or to organize a drive for expanded membership, or even, on occasion, to dissolve a recalcitrant local.

Some of these functions may be easily combined. The business agent is often an officer of the local; so are many shop stewards. The organizer of a new local may remain as business agent. Or the functions may be further subdivided. In large locals, the duties of business agent and shop steward may be shared among a considerable number of officials: educational directors, negotiating representatives, grievance investigators, plant representatives, city-central delegates, and so forth. The most important distinction is between the full-time union official and the workman who handles the business of the union in his spare time. Whether primary responsibility for union affairs will be entrusted to one or the other depends upon the centralization of authority in the national, the size of the local, and the way in which employers are organized. Although every possible variant of these factors can be found somewhere, it will be illuminating to compare again the type cases of the restrictive and the expansive union.

The restrictive union is usually of moderate size, and in the overwhelming majority of cases, all its routine affairs can be handled by a single business agent. Since the number of employers is considerable and their identity changeable, it is obviously necessary to have a paid representative. It is also the object of the restrictive union to control its own members in many ways — enforcing, for example, the prohibition against working on jobs in which material is obtained from boycotted suppliers. The business agent often assumes the role of arbiter between employer and employee; in the building trades, particularly, both may be union members and the business agent's ties with the employer may be as close as with the workman.

In the expansive union, the local often coincides with a single plant; and in any case, union organization usually follows that of the industry. Where the routine direction of the union is in the hands of a council of shop stewards, all of whom habitually negotiate with management in one way or another, it is feasible for the principal union representatives to be active employees. On the other hand, since the expansive local engages in a broad range of activities, the volume of its business may be very great.

The expansive union will be much more centralized. Although the charters of most locals of either type require that they seek permission from the national before calling a strike, the issues that confront the restrictive union are almost always local issues in which the national union has no particular motive for intervention. The expansive union, by contrast, is not concerned with only local affairs. Its objectives are linked to broad economic developments and, in theory at least, the strike should be reserved for use in negotiating campaigns which engage the entire industry.

The strength of a restrictive union may be measured by the degree of influence exerted by the business agent over both employers and employees in the enforcement of contracts and craft rules. It is thus to the interest of the national union to strengthen the business agents in every way possible, and this has been done by extending their personal authority and, in many cases, by granting them a permanent tenure which it is almost impossible for the members of the local to disturb. It may, for example, be stipulated that the business agent can be removed only by vote of a general membership meeting, when only the business agent himself is authorized to call one. This concentration of authority, together with the lack of responsibility to the local membership, facilitates abuses of power, of which bribe-taking and collusion with employers are the most common.

The effectiveness of an expansive union depends upon the extent to which its members will follow its direction in a crisis. For national organizations of this type, the main internal problem has always been the development of sufficient discipline to enable its representatives to negotiate on a large scale without interference from dissident locals or individuals, and to enforce its obligations under the resulting contract. This is not simply a matter of the locals following the national. It also involves the question of whether members will conform to the directives of the local to which they belong, but to which their ties are much weaker than in a craft union. It sometimes happens that local disagreements take on the character of organized revolt against the policy of the union. Wildcat strikes are sometimes called in specific protest against a contract or a procedure to which the membership has been committed with less than its full consent. Since any publicized dissidence weakens the bargaining power of the national union immediately, it has always been possible for a determined minority to exercise great influence by brandishing the threat of local resistance.

In each type of organization, authority tends to be concentrated at the points where significant negotiations are conducted. In spite of its nominal centralization, the restrictive union tends to be operated by a group of interrelated business agents who together control the national organization much more than they are controlled by it. The expansive union, on the other hand, is sharply hierarchical; there is a continuous extension of downward control and a continuous elaboration of the national headquarters until they compare in diversity of function to the managerial organizations with which they are matched. When fully developed, this control is expressed in a power of appointment and removal which extends down to the shop stewards. Here, however, it sustains a popular check. The effectiveness of the shop steward depends upon the cooperation he can evoke in his shop; there is no way of securing this support coercively in the long run.

A clear distinction should be made between the administration and the determination of policy. Both federations have annual county, state, and national conventions, and some national unions have their own system of conventions. It rests to a large extent with the professional leadership whether these conventions should be democratically chosen and free to express a consensus of the membership. In practice, active participation in local union affairs is so limited that even where the selection of delegates is by popular nomination and vote, the conventions tend to be representative of leadership factions, rather than of the rank and file. Yet, membership opinion often makes itself strongly felt, especially in the expansive unions, where important issues arising between conventions are sometimes submitted to a referendum of the membership.

The foregoing pages describe union structure in general terms. But any such discussion must take into account the great frequency with which changes in the structure, the functions, and the composition of labor organizations occur. Unlike the business organization which it faces, whose primary activities of production and marketing are continuous, the union is primarily organized for collective bargaining, which is an intermittent activity. Its size, shape, and form at any particular moment depend upon its orientation to the next crisis and to the last one. Although the bureaucratization of expansive unions, and the development of a vast amount of routine business having to do with grievance procedures, job classification, and welfare activities, have had some stabilizing influence, the history of any union is likely to be a series of sharply distinct phases.

Large-scale unionism is so recent an innovation in this country that we are more familiar with the introductory events in the typical union history than with the normal period which follows. Selekman [13] has traced the changing role of a labor organization from the *introductory period,* when it is regarded by management as a dangerous threat to be suppressed, through the *negotiation of the first agreement,* which establishes a modus vivendi, allows for the development of supplementary union activities, but at the same time decreases identification of members with the organization, through the *period of building joint relationships* (marked by further bureaucratization and the development of a set of consistent attitudes by both management and the union) to a further stage which involves the acceptance of the union as a permanent fact, and the development of joint administrative channels for the handling of grievances and the regular reopening of negotiations.

Even in this latter stage, the union remains an organization designed for industrial conflict, not for outings and bowling tournaments. What changes most drastically is the relationship of the individual member to the organization. In the early stages, when the union is struggling to establish itself, the new member joins after a personal choice, and sometimes at considerable risk. He is immediately involved in intensive participation; if his affiliation is serious, he will attempt to bring others into the fold. Conflict with fellow employees who oppose the union, and with management representatives who attempt to weaken it, helps to reinforce the sentiment of belonging to a close-knit and solidary group. Moreover, the early stages are usually marked by strikes, and here the area of participation is enormously widened — union activity touches the worker's family and his whole position in the community.

The establishment of the union on a permanent basis, and the development of what Selekman calls joint administrative channels with management, alter the entire character of the union as a form of association. In many instances, joining the union is incidental to the procedure of being employed, and union membership is maintained for the duration of employment with little or no effort on the part of the member. The union functionaries with whom he comes into contact are met as functionaries, exercising a certain power and enjoying a certain superiority. How their formal role of representing the worker will be perceived depends largely upon the accidents of personal relations — for example, the popularity of a foreman. They may easily come to be regarded as part of the intangible They to whom the manual worker is subject in so many ways.

Several other factors combine to weaken the intimacy of participation. As authority is concentrated in the business agents or in the national headquarters, the decisions taken in local meetings — which may have been crucial during the original organizing campaign — lose most of their importance, and the local may find little business before it. As the apparatus of negotiation becomes more effective, there is some tendency to eliminate the strike, with its direct involvements and experiences. Even where the use of the strike continues, it tends to be called on national or industry-wide issues. Strikes based on local grievances may be actively discouraged as part of the discipline necessary to maintain the bargaining position of the national union. Finally, the personnel of the local become increasingly specialized and increasingly remote from the shop floor.

The effectiveness of the union in securing wage increases and improvements in working conditions, and in protecting the worker against arbitrary action by management, is not diminished by these changes. On the contrary, they are the incidental effects of increasing stability.

There can be little doubt that membership in a union has a marked influence on social and political attitudes. On the other hand, it would appear that attitudes toward the union itself are characterized by ambivalence. The union is sometimes regarded as an agency outside the worker's sphere of action, and even outside his scrutiny. This is carried to an extreme in situations where the union is very large, where membership is an automatic consequence of employment, and where the working relationship between union and management is close. Archibald's study [14] of a wartime shipyard illustrated that, although attitudes toward the union were more favorable than toward management, the similarities were more striking than the differences.

Rose's study of participation in a successful and well-integrated union [15] leads him to the conclusion that, "In concrete terms, loyalty to the union does not mean disloyalty to the employer."

There are some striking resemblances between the institutional form of the fully developed union and that of the political party. Both command a considerable loyalty, capable of being completely mobilized at rare intervals, and operate during the interims with skeleton organizations manned by paid and specialized personnel with the assistance of a small number of volunteers. Both are compelled to view their membership as a public, and to maintain communication principally through newspapers, mass meetings, and other secondary means. The structural parallel can be pushed even further. There is a distinct similarity between the restrictive union with its permanent business agents, and the city machine, with its permanent ward bosses. The expansive union is closer to the national political party in its hierarchical organization and likewise relies upon the charismatic reputation of a few great spokesmen to hold the somewhat loose organization together.

This analogy is useful in showing why the modern union is typically an impersonal interest-group, rather than an intimate and spontaneous collectivity. Like all analogies it can be pushed too far. Union organization has a number of aspects for which no close parallel can be found in party politics; these center around the working relationship between organized labor and organized management.

Cooperation between labor and management is especially marked in a few industries where employers are financially weak and very numerous, so that the union may well be the strongest economic unit in the industry. The most notable example is the manufacture of women's clothing, where the union assumes the responsibility for the partial support of the industry, including market research, technical advice, advertising, campaigns to increase productivity, and even loans to weak employers. This has been widely heralded as an example of exceptionally good labor relations, but it seems to be dependent upon the special circumstances of the case. The same may be said of those few industries where a relatively weak company commands a secure market and is able to offer its employees a guaranteed annual wage and a share in ownership and profits.

Cooperation may take another, less favorably regarded, form in industries where employers are numerous and weak, but are subject to the influence of powerful or monopolistic suppliers in the preceding stage of production. This is a situation characteristic of construction, some forms of food processing, and a number of consumer services. Here cooperation may take the form of collusion to raise wages and profits simultaneously, to boycott new products, or to discriminate against competitors by withholding labor from them.

In the mass-production industries, the intervention of labor in management comes about in a different way. When negotiations cover a broad industrial sector, the financial position of the employer becomes a crucial factor in bargaining. This in turn depends largely on small variations in productivity. Thus, unions claim the right to be acquainted with management's books. When this is conceded, they tend to acquire an interest in increasing production. In addition, during the emergency periods which began in 1933, 1939, and 1950, labor and management in mass-production industries were in effect given joint responsibilities for maintaining production. This tendency has been sporadically resisted by management, which sees in it a fundamental encroachment on its prerogatives, and by labor as well, which fears that union leadership might become an arm of management. Yet the area of such cooperation appears to be slowly and surely expanding.

Current opinion is very sharply divided on the implications of cooperation and hostility in labor relations. The problem is highlighted by the single major study directly contrasting the two alternatives, in which Harbison and Dubin [16] compared the continuing conflict characterizing the relations of General Motors and the United Automobile Workers with the constructive relations obtaining between Studebaker and the same union at South Bend.

Speaking of labor-management relations in the automobile industry's power center, they noted that the size and prestige of giant organizations creates union concentrations of power, that bargaining leads to internal centralization of decision-making, that the day-to-day administration of the contract must be formal and legalistic, that the area of conflict overshadows the area of cooperation, and that issues usually have political overtones. They concluded tentatively that free collective bargaining was impossible in power centers because of the repercussions in the total economy.

At Studebaker, they observed the stability and security of the union, and the relatively informal management structure. Both sides maintained a "problem-solving" attitude toward labor problems and formal procedural devices seemed relatively unimportant. It was pointed out that labor relations had been greatly influenced by the tenuous competitive position of the company, and that they took place within the economic environment created by the larger automotive manufacturers.

Since the publication of the study in 1947, there has been a running controversy as to the interpretation of its findings. While many readers accept the assertion that the harmonious relations at Studebaker represent a superior and more desirable state of affairs, a number of critics have concluded not only that the conflict situation at General Motors was more advantageous (either to labor or to the economy at large) but that peaceful cooperation at Studebaker was only achieved by the mutual abandonment by management and labor of any real responsibility in their own jurisdictions, in favor of the pattern set by hostile interaction in Detroit.

In a similar vein, Sheppard [17] has vigorously criticized the point of view of Elton Mayo and his disciples who hold "that a fundamental identity of interests exists between the parties involved in industrial relations, and that this identity is increasingly interrupted by regrettable misunderstanding or breakdowns in communication." Tead has also pointed out the failure of the Mayo group to take into account "the role that may be played by labor unions in giving workers a total sense of security, self-respect, and opportunity to voice complaints and suggestions." [18]

Certainly, there is no justification in history or sociological theory for the belief that the pre-industrial or early industrial society was free of conflict, nor for the assumption that the existence of conflict tends to disintegrate social institutions. Indeed, it is impossible to conceive of the primordial social institution — the family — without large areas of institutionalized conflict. We need to know much more about the differences between the organized opposition of social groups with opposed interests, and the development of a climate of hostility which demoralizes an institution. That this relation is not a simple one is suggested by the fact that hostility between labor and management has been most marked when their relative positions were changing. The great anti-union campaigns sponsored by management in 1903–7 and in 1920–29 generated enough hostility to reduce the labor movement to a defensive remnant. Similarly, the encouragement of hostility toward management is the characteristic device of an organizing campaign; and its termination usually marks the firm establishment of the union. In any case, it is difficult to believe that an atmosphere of contentment is the goal of collective action in labor relations. The central purposes of any occupational association are to safeguard and enlarge the control of members over the conditions and rewards of work. The extent to which these ends can be achieved is determined in the long run by the distribution of political power and the state of the industrial arts as well as the outcome of particular struggles.

NOTES

[1] Frank E. Horack, "The Horseshoers' Strike of Philadelphia," *American Journal of Sociology*, vol. 8, November 1902.

[2] Jean Pierre Waltzing, *Etude Historique sur les Corporations Professionnelles Chez les Romains Depuis les Origines Jusqu'à la Chute de l'Empire d'Occident* (4 vols.; Louvain: C. Peters, 1895–1900).

[3] "Seven years seem anciently to have been, all over Europe, the usual term established for the duration of apprenticeships in the greater part of the incorporated trades. All such incorporations were anciently called universities: which indeed is the proper Latin name for any incorporation whatever. The university of smiths, the university of taylors, are expressions which we commonly meet with in the old charters of ancient towns. When those particular incorporations which are now peculiarly called universities were first established, the term of years, which it was necessary to study, in order to obtain the degree of master of arts, appears evidently to have been copied from the term of apprenticeship in common trades, of which the incorporations were much more ancient." *The Wealth of Nations*, Book I, Chapter 10, Part II.

[4] George Unwin, *The Gilds and Companies of London* (3rd ed.; London: George Allen & Unwin, 1938). The spellings (*guild, gild*) are equally correct, but *guild* is more frequently used in this country.

[5] David A. McCabe and Richard A. Lester, *Labor and Social Organization* (rev. ed.; Boston: D. C. Heath & Company, 1948), pp. 13–14.

[6] Lewis Mumford, *Sticks and Stones* (New York: Boni and Liveright, 1924). See Chapter I, "The Medieval Tradition."

[7] Richard B. Morris, *Government and Labor in Early America* (New York: Columbia University Press, 1946).

[8] John R. Commons, "American Shoemakers, 1648–1895," *Quarterly Journal of Economics*, vol. 24, November 1909.

[9] John A. Fitch, *The Steel Workers* (New York: Charities Publication Committee, 1910), part of The Pittsburgh Survey, edited by Paul Underwood Kellogg for the Russell Sage Foundation.

[10] Robert S. and Helen M. Lynd, *Middletown* (New York: Harcourt, Brace & Company, 1929), pp. 76–80.

[11] Robert F. Hoxie, *Trade Unionism in the United States* (New York: Appleton-Crofts, 1928).

[12] Frederick H. Harbison and Robert Dubin, *Patterns of Union-Management Relations* (Chicago: Science Research Associates, 1947).

[13] Benjamin M. Selekman, *Labor Relations and Human Relations* (New York: McGraw-Hill Book Company, 1947).

[14] Katharine Archibald, *Wartime Shipyard: A Study in Social Disunity* (Berkeley, Calif.: University of California Press, 1947), pp. 132–33: "Although the thousands of shipyard workers were enjoying wages and working conditions which manifestly were the product of years of union struggle, they saw no connection between the dues they paid and the benefits they received. On the contrary, it was commonly assumed that unions, like other businesses, existed for the benefit of owners and managers . . ."

[15] Arnold M. Rose, *Union Solidarity: Internal Cohesion of a Trade Union* (Minneapolis: University of Minnesota Press, 1952), p. 189.

[16] *Op. cit.*

[17] Harold L. Sheppard, "The Treatment of Unionism in 'Managerial Sociology'," *American Sociological Review,* vol. 14, April 1949. See also his unpublished doctoral dissertation, "Managerial Sociology: A Critical Commentary on the Mayo Influence in Industrial Sociology" (Madison: University of Wisconsin, 1948).

[18] Ordway Tead, "Review of Mayo's *Social Problems of an Industrial Civilization,*" *Survey Graphic,* vol. 35, May 1946, p. 180.

CHAPTER 9

VOCATIONAL CHOICE

"The probability that any particular person shall ever be qualified for the employment to which he is educated, is very different in different occupations."
ADAM SMITH

IN PREVIOUS chapters, we have considered the recruiting process as an activity of the occupational group. We have now to study it from the standpoint of the individual.

Regardless of the particular setting, occupational choice can be understood in terms of two theoretical limits. At one extreme, the occupation of the father determines that of the son, and no problems of individual choice are allowed to arise. At the other, occupational functions are rigorously allocated according to individual characteristics, as determined by testing and observation. The first situation is approximated in Hindu communities where the caste system has remained intact. The second situation is the one toward which our own society is thought to be moving.

The age at which occupational choices are made has a great deal to do with the kind of choices which are possible. If occupations — or at least occupational statuses — are inherited, the "choice" may be said to take place at birth. If they are allocated rationally, on the basis of aptitude and interest, the allocation can scarcely take place before adolescence.

Surprisingly little is known about occupational choice in our own or any other mobile society. Since a permanent occupational choice can only be identified after a lapse of years, it can only be studied retroactively, by which time the successive mental states in the choice process will seldom be recalled with any accuracy. Then too, error and accident often play a larger part than the subject himself is willing to concede.

Given this limitation, a comprehensive picture can best be obtained by examining in detail the several modes of selection by which people may be drawn into particular callings. Although we lack the data to measure the relative influence of these, we can be reasonably sure that the normal career is affected by all of them to some degree.

PARENTAL INFLUENCE

Direct inheritance of a father's occupation is nowhere uncommon, but as a matter of course, it will be most conspicuous in occupations requiring either capital investment or childhood participation. Both of these elements are typically found in farming, and almost all farmers are recruited from farmers' sons. Retail trade is another major occupation characterized by these same elements, although to a lesser degree, since retail investments are less stable and the participation by children in storekeeping tends to be much more limited than their participation in farm work.

Isolation is another factor which clearly promotes the inheritance of occupations. Farmers, miners, mill operatives, or fishermen are likely to be physically isolated in communities where very few new jobs are open to their sons. Physicians, army officers, clergymen, musicians, and policemen often inhabit psychologically isolated milieus which exercise some restriction on their children.

A moderate probability of occupational inheritance may be sufficient to establish rather strong expectations on the part of the family and the community. In the United States, occupational continuity of two generations is regarded as a tradition of some weight. In the extraordinary case of an occupation transmitted from father to son for five or six generations, the obligation to continue it may be very strongly felt. Even menial and disgraceful callings may assume this aura. Gilmore has traced the history of a begging family for five generations, noting that the members of each generation were systematically trained as beggars and acquired the appropriate attitudes and skills in childhood.[1]

Wherever expectations of this sort exist, the selection of a new career implies some revolt against parental authority. Indeed, the whole question is closely related to a broader theme — the projection of parental ambitions into the careers of their children. The projection of career goals may be viewed as an essential phase of middle-class mobility. It provides both a long-term incentive (to give my children what I never had myself) and a compensation for failure (my children's future is more important than my own). Almost all middle-class parents expect that their children will *not* select menial, unskilled, or semiskilled occupations, and a considerable proportion pursue the conscious goal of raising their children — through education — to a status higher than their own.

There are several reasons why this kind of projection can be emotionally destructive. When the interests and aptitudes of the individual plainly unfit him for the career on which his parents have set their hearts, the scene is set for maladjustment whether he follows their inclinations or his own. Equally unhappy situations arise from a man's failure to reach the level of achievement imposed by a parent, or to justify the failure to himself. Often enough, it is the parents who are victimized when their children do achieve higher status and reject them because of it.

These considerations obviously emphasize the inheritance of occupational levels rather than of particular occupations. The difference is important. There have been a number of studies of the inheritance of occupational level since Sorokin first outlined the principles of vertical mobility. But the inheritance of occupational level is different from the inheritance of particular occupations. In the one case, the subject's choice is determined by his parent's occupation. In the other, his possible choices are limited by the circumstances of his upbringing. Thus, the inheritance of occupational level is most appropriately considered in terms of the various mechanisms which operate to restrict the *range* of occupational choices.

FORMAL EDUCATION

The principal device for the limitation of occupational choice is the educational system. It does this in two ways: first, by forcing the student who embarks upon a long course of training to renounce other careers which also require extensive training; second, by excluding from training and eventually from the occupations themselves those students who lack either the intellectual qualities (such as intelligence, docility, aptitude) or the social characteristics (such as ethnic background, wealth, appropriate conduct, previous education) which happen to be required. The more strongly the educational system affects occupational choice, the more efficiently will it function in this way. Indeed, education cannot serve as a channel of vertical mobility unless it also serves to exclude those who are not educated in the appropriate way.

It is generally felt that exclusion on the basis of social characteristics works an injustice, especially where such characteristics as wealth pertain to the candidate's family more than to himself. From this it comes to be assumed that selection on the basis of intellectual qualities is entirely adequate.

This assumption is open to some question. The correlation between tests of mental ability and school achievement will seldom exceed $+.50$, even where a large battery of tests is used. Indeed, this limit has been so frequently encountered in studies of educational outcome that there is some reason to think that it cannot be significantly exceeded no matter how much the tests are improved. (Similar limits are found in other kinds of studies which have predicted individual performance or behavior from data available in advance. Predictions of happiness in marriage, or success on parole, also tend to show limits in the neighborhood of $r = .50$. The utility of such tests lies, of course, in the fact that they are predictive with a very high degree of accuracy for cases at the extremes. It is virtually certain that a boy with an I.Q. of 80 will not succeed in college, and that a prisoner in the highest percentile of a parole prediction scale will not violate his parole. The practical use of these tests, however, is seldom restricted in this rigorous way.)

The correlation between school grades and occupational achievement is of about the same order, and this limitation too probably reflects an underlying reality, rather than a weakness in the statistical operation. Success or failure in a job bears some resemblance to success or failure in the training for that job, but the resemblance is by no means an identity.

In sum, the selective process which precedes and accompanies formal educational training for a vocation is useful in eliminating the totally unfit — those who lack the fundamental abilities regarded as necessary for the occupational task. Beyond this narrow service, the selective process is of doubtful value to the individual. It is statistically certain that some considerable proportion of those eliminated would have been better practitioners than the average of those passed, unless all those capable of qualifying are automatically accepted.

It is probable, nevertheless, that recruitment through educational channels — not only for the professions but for desirable careers in business, government, and the arts — will be increasingly important in the future. However imperfect the educational machinery may be, it is in some sense responsive to the individual, and it rewards individual effort. For these reasons, it may be rationally preferred to those systems which assign occupations by purchase, inheritance, or chance.

Perhaps the most important features of any school system, regarded as a device for occupational distribution, are the age levels at which major choices must be made. In general, the earlier a choice must be made, the less equitable will be the eventual distribution of function and the less connection will there be between the individual's own interests and the occupational role chosen for him.

It is sad but inevitable that attempts to improve the educational process by careful counseling and by the establishment of pre-vocational sequences are likely to lower the age at which a decision must be made, and thereby substitute one form of maladjustment for another.

A series of important choices confronts the school child as early as the eighth grade, and a mistaken decision is often irrevocable. This is the point at which, in many large cities, pupils must choose whether to attend an academic or a "vocational" high school. The latter choice may effectively commit them to an occupation which does not require higher education. Within the academic high school, it is not uncommon for a choice to be exacted between college preparatory courses and those sequences which terminate with graduation from high school. The major choice, of course, occurs at graduation, with the decision as to whether to proceed to college. This may sometimes be delayed a year or two, but seldom longer. Finally — and this is likely to be a conclusive choice so far as occupations requiring advanced training are concerned — the student must usually decide no later than his third year of college whether he will pursue a particular professional curriculum.

There have been very few studies of how these decisions are made. In some cases, of course, the fixation of occupational interest occurs early and the child pursues a steady course into maturity without ever altering his goals. There is some evidence [2] that superior children are less liable to such early fixation. But for the vast majority, the serious choice of an occupation is made in adolescence.

The bases for decision are often trivial. A student decides to study law because he has gotten his highest grades in history courses, dislikes the idea of teaching, and knows that courses in history are required for entrance to law school. A grade school pupil elects the vocational high school because someone has told him that automobile mechanics get high wages. A high school sophomore transfers from the academic sequence to the clerical course to be with her best friend. The crucial decision to leave school and go to work may reflect the most casual dissatisfaction or the lure of a passing opportunity.

In general, the earlier a boy leaves school, the greater the number of occupations from which he is barred. Leaving before graduation from high school is an effective disqualification not only for the learned trades, but for many kinds of bureaucratic employment. It virtually guarantees a lifetime in manual work or in the insecure white-collar fringe. But the critical effect of the decision to leave school is obscured by two factors. First, the disqualification is not absolute. There remain a number of fields of strategic importance in which education confers no absolute advantage. This is true of small business, entertainment, politics, and sales. Second, the norms of formal education have risen so rapidly in this country that many persons still in the labor force entered their occupations under conditions totally different from those which are now in effect. Many practicing physicians, lawyers, and architects were trained by clerkship, and many others entered professional schools without the prerequisite of a high school diploma, let alone a college degree.

Within the educational system itself, endless dilemmas arise from the essential differences between general education and specific training. Occupational specialization has tended to multiply the vocational activities required of schools at all levels. The advocates of vocational training are often critical of any teaching which is not directly related to a future job. For instance, a recent work discussing the relation of college education to occupational adjustment has this to say: "In fact, even those who were concerned about their occupational future received little direction or guidance. Instead, they were frequently encouraged to concentrate in esoteric fields such as French Literature or Philosophy." [3] The reply of the humanists, as they protect the citadels of scholarly learning from conversion into job-training centers, tends to be more elegantly phrased, but no less dogmatic.

The argument cannot be simply resolved. It is often forgotten that the classical humanistic curriculum, founded solidly on Latin and Greek, was in fact vocational preparation, with its graduates destined at first for the pulpit, later for the learned professions of law and medicine, and still later for belles-lettres, politics, and business, but never for engineering, laboratory work, plant management, the graphic arts, social work, salesmanship, script writing, or embalming. It is still true of the European schools and universities which follow the conventional scheme of higher education that the majority of their graduates are destined for administrative, academic, or clerical posts for which the humanities are directly preparatory. Equally fundamental is the fact that acquaintance with the humanities was historically the hallmark of a social class with distinct privileges.

The democratization of education, especially the expansion of high schools after World War I, and of colleges and universities after World War II, represents the transfer of occupational selection from the marketplace to the schoolroom. Consequently, educational institutions must prepare their students for a much wider range of callings than formerly. Courses in restaurant management, embalming, and clothing design are taken for granted in the American university, where only a few decades ago their very existence would have been inconceivable.

As the processes of occupational selection are moved into the educational system, they take on an academic coloration. Intellectual competence becomes a requirement for many occupations in which dexterity or mere inclination were once sufficient. The humanities and the social sciences are considered essential for the well-rounded realtor or veterinarian. This has the effect of continually lengthening the curriculum, especially that part of it which precedes professional training. The effect is to lower the age of occupational choice *within* the educational institution and to raise the age at which the working career begins. The sophomore at a university finds himself already restricted to a particular group of occupations. If preparing for a course in business, he will be fairly well debarred from specialization in science or medicine. If his studies are centered in an agricultural field, he cannot, without considerable loss of time, turn to journalism or social work. Increasingly then, occupational choices are made at a time when the student is still remote from the world of work. They are made in terms of school requirements, which may call for quite different abilities and tastes from those which will be related to the eventual job.

Except for that tiny minority whose occupational choices are crystallized in childhood or early adolescence, choices occur at the points where they are built into the educational system. They cannot be evaded. Under the emerging system of occupational determination, complete passivity on the part of the student is itself a choice. If he does not elect the appropriate subjects in his early years of high school, he rejects in effect the occupations for which college training is required. If he omits the natural sciences in favor of the social sciences, he eliminates himself as a candidate for thousands of industrial jobs, and if he ignores both of them, he will never be qualified for the beginning ranks in the government service.

Increasingly, then, occupational choices are made in the schoolroom, under the impersonal pressure of the curriculum, and remote from many of the realities of the working situation. In these circumstances, it is hard for many people to choose at all and difficult for many to be certain of their choices once they have been made.

VOCATIONAL CHOICE

To meet the problems created by this situation, vocational guidance came into existence in connection with the public high school and has since become a major function of educational institutions at all levels in the United States. It may be studied as another mode of selection — closely related to, and interwoven with, formal education.

VOCATIONAL GUIDANCE

Vocational guidance consists of psychological measurement intended to discover the individual's interests and abilities; the presentation of vocational information; and a rather amorphous cluster of counseling functions which include fatherly advice, psychotherapy, curriculum planning, assistance in job hunting, and some kinds of training.

The primary activity is the measurement of the subject's interests and abilities. The measurement of interests is perhaps the more important of the two, partly because school achievement and nonvocational tests provide some prior measure of abilities, partly because the people most likely to be treated are those who cannot identify their own preferences, or who cannot adjust their wishes to reality.

Superficially, there is something absurd in giving an adolescent — or anyone else — a test of his interests. Interests, by definition, represent areas of high motivation. It might be maintained that anyone who is not already aware of his own interests, but must take an examination to determine what they are, is in fact devoid of any real interests. There is undoubtedly some truth in this argument. Those for whom interest measurement is designed are not usually characterized by powerful and well-defined motivations. However, the fact that occupational choices must often be made long before a career can be begun, and far from the environment of the occupation itself, necessarily reduces the intensity of interests. If a place in the world must be chosen by schoolboys who know neither the world nor themselves very well, it is perhaps reasonable that they take a pencil-and-paper test to discover their own inclinations.

The most frequently used of the interest tests is the Strong Vocational Interest Inventory designed in the 1920s by Edward K. Strong of Stanford University. The Inventory consists of some 400 questions, having to do with activities, preferences, sports and hobbies, general attitudes, personality traits, aspirations, and of course, direct occupational preferences. The responses are weighted and scored on a separate scale for each of nearly 50 different occupations, as well as on some miscellaneous scales

221

which measure such traits as maturity and masculinity. Since each occupational scale is merely a rescoring of the original answers, the number of scales which can be developed is limited only by the labor of standardization, which consists of giving the test to a sample of "successful" persons drawn from any occupation and assigning positive, negative, or neutral weights to each item in terms of the average response of the sample.

In spite of a great number of painstaking researches [4] on the Vocational Interest Inventory, which have consisted principally of correlating its component scales among themselves, the scales are of dubious validity. In spite of the variety of items included, most of the weight in the final score for any occupation is actually derived from direct statements of preference for the occupation itself and for allied activities.

The real utility of interest testing lies in two aspects of the method. First, since the tests can be used over and over again and standardized on any group whatever, they have distinct advantages of convenience and economy over the mere checking of occupational choices or statements of preference. Second, the use of a profile of vocational interests, in which occupations are grouped in terms of the empirical similarity of their scales, produces a reasonably smooth continuum, in which the subject can locate himself by *area*. We have discussed at great length the difficulties of occupational classification. This one, too, has certain marked deficiences, but as long as the scoring technic brings out some clustering of high and low scores on the profile, it becomes possible for the counselor to talk in terms of a type of occupation or of a kind of work. This provides the client with some sort of focused objective without actually specifying his choice.

The interest inventory is therefore a highly useful method for helping people to make up their minds. There is another irony here, however. Much of its effectiveness in hastening the crystallization of decisions is due to the misunderstanding of the students who take the test, and who almost inevitably regard it as a test of aptitude, capacity, or suitability. Whether interests are, in fact, closely related to aptitudes remains a moot point. There must be some correlation — if only because of the negative experiences sustained by those who undertake activities for which they lack the appropriate aptitudes. However, most occupations cannot be summed up in terms of a single aptitude, and even the measurement of single aptitudes is complicated by all sorts of difficulties, especially those which arise from the virtual impossibility of parceling out original aptitudes from the effects of learning.

The measurement of abilities or of aptitudes, which have been defined as "the ability to acquire a particular ability," has become one of the favorite indoor sports of educators, and is, in a sense, the hallmark of American pedagogy. The movement is surprisingly young; it dates only from the adaptation of Binet's intelligence tests in this country about forty years ago. At the present time, the summary description of the tests in current use occupies most of a fair-sized encyclopedia.[5] Most of them are easy to administer and score; their results are often highly reliable. There are tests of clerical aptitude and tone discrimination, of taste sensitivity and digital dexterity, of analogizing powers and mental maturity, as well as scores of tests which measure whole groups of capacities related to particular kinds of work.

Practically speaking, the most satisfactory and informative of these tests are those which are exceedingly general (e.g., the standard intelligence tests which measure a combination of factors including verbal ability, information, visualization, and numerical skill), or those which are exceedingly specific (e.g., measure the ability to discriminate musical pitches, or judgment of depth in the visual field). It is the very general and the very specific tests whch show the highest correlation with objective behavior. The explanation is probably that in one case everything accessible to pen-and-paper testing is being measured; in the other, the skill sought is clearly known and easily observed.

Validity in intermediate cases is much less satisfactory. Thorndike reports the use of a Mechanical Aptitude Test which would not measure mechanical aptitude, and of a Clerical Aptitude Test which *did* measure mechanical aptitude.[6] Low validity is normal for devices of this kind, and there is probably not much that can be done about it. The difficulty is analytical rather than methodological. The builder of a test begins with a rather clear-cut idea of what qualities and activities are necessary in clerical work. As he proceeds, he discovers that clerical work has relatively few special characteristics by which it can be distinguished from other human activities of similar difficulty. Hence, he is likely to emerge either with a clerical test that shows no particular relation to clerical performance, or with one which measures mechanical dexterity or social insight better than efficiency in office work.

It has therefore become a cardinal principle of vocational guidance not to rely upon a single test, but to aim at valid results through the use of a battery of related tests. It is not unusual for a battery of vocational tests to occupy two full days. Whether this actually does lead to greater validity in counseling depends on the application of certain general principles of statistical interpretation.

Aptitude tests are subject to the limitation cited earlier in this chapter: the predictability of behavior from background factors seldom exceeds a Pearsonian correlation of $r = +.50$. There is also a further limitation, arising from the loose relationship between whatever aptitude is measured and the actual criteria of occupational performance. An intermediate test score — or a whole series of them — tells us literally nothing about what the individual may do. That is, conspicuous success and absolute failure are both reasonably probable when the predictive score stands somewhere near the midpoint of the scale. It is only at the extremes of the distribution that determination becomes relatively great. This arises from the fact that both variables are normally distributed and may be seen graphically in the pointed oval which appears on the scatter diagram representing the linear relationship between moderately correlated variables. A very high score on one variable will seldom be accompanied by a very low score on the other, and vice versa. Test batteries may therefore be legitimately used in two quite different ways: first, to find and eliminate those candidates with a high probability of failure (having a very low score on *any* predictive test); second, to select those with a high probability of success (having very high scores on *all* predictive tests). What constitutes a very high or a very low score for this purpose depends upon the predictivity of the test, but however this is computed, it remains true that the administration of an aptitude or background test to the average subject must inevitably produce inconclusive results, and that the multiplication of intermediate scores on each of a battery of tests merely substantiates our ignorance of the subject's future.

To the extent that this limitation is overlooked, the vocational counselor becomes a crystal-gazer, using the statistical findings as flexible arguments to support whatever hunches he arrives at by other routes.

The second major function of the vocational counselor — the presentation of vocational information — is beset with fewer theoretical problems, but is no less difficult in practice. An entire book has recently been devoted to summarizing the major sources of occupational information.[7] Occupational descriptions on an industry-wide basis are issued by the United States Employment Service, and individual occupational booklets are available for more than a hundred occupations. Occupational monographs

and leaflets are issued in a continuous stream by the United States Office
of Education, the Department of Agriculture, and the Women's Bureau of
the Department of Labor. The field is large enough to provide profitable
opportunities for private information services. The best known are the
occupational monographs of Science Research Associates, the Careers
Research Monographs of the Institute for Research, the occupational ab-
stracts of Occupation Index, Incorporated, the curriculum subject monographs prepared at Ohio State University, the vocational guidance
monographs of the Commonwealth Book Company and those of the
Quarrie Corporation. Altogether, an imposing list.

For current trends, there are the industry descriptions of the United
States Employment Service, the *Monthly Labor Review* published by the
Bureau of Labor Statistics, and the current serial publications prepared by
some of the companies which publish occupational monographs. The
coverage of the best of these monographs is accurately reflected in the
National Vocational Guidance Association's "Content of a Good Occupational Monograph," which presents the following outline:

    I. History of the Occupation
    II. Importance of the Occupation and Its Relation to Society
    III. Number of Workers Engaged in Occupation
    IV. Need for Workers — Trends
    V. Duties
    VI. Qualifications
    VII. Preparation
    VIII. Methods of Entering
    IX. Length of Time before Skill Is Attained
    X. Advancement
    XI. Related Occupations to Which Job May Lead
    XII. Earnings
    XIII. Hours
    XIV. Regularity of Employment
    XV. Health and Accident Hazards
    XVI. Organizations
    XVII. Typical Places of Employment
    XVIII. Supplementary Information [8]

The strengths as well as the weaknesses embodied in the current framework of occupational description for guidance purposes will be seen rather
clearly on examination of the outline.

A large body of reliable and unbiased reference material is available
for most of the familiar callings with respect to labor market factors, pre-

requisites, and working conditions. Within a given range, rational selection is entirely possible and this conduces not only to individual adjustment, but to the ironing out of inequalities and incongruities in the distribution of the labor force itself.

The weaknesses of this information tend to lie outside of the monographs and bulletins themselves.[9] They arise from the fact that occupational information is necessarily focused on occupations which have large populations and simple and stable conditions, and which permit immediate entry under known terms. Almost inevitably, these involve work for large-scale enterprises or government departments. The counselor may tend to neglect many of the opportunities which do not conform to the specifications for inclusion in occupational monographs. This is not a fundamental deficiency, however. While the information available for vocational guidance sometimes leaves a good deal to be desired, it is becoming increasingly adequate in providing the high school or college student, or the unadjusted adult worker, with the knowledge he requires to enlarge his vocational opportunities.

Whether the choice of an occupation is made with or without the benefit of guidance, putting the choice into effect involves some elements of personal planning which depend directly upon the information available. Quite often, the function of the counselor is limited to assisting the realization of a decision made in a more spontaneous fashion. Even where no occupational decision is made in advance of vocational guidance, the counselor will soon become aware of general preferences for certain kinds of work rather than others, and of fixed rejections which will not ordinarily be altered.

DEVELOPMENT OF PROJECTIVE
PATTERNS OF CHOICE

The choice of occupation, viewed as a subjective process and as part of the achievement of maturity, has been the subject of a recent interdisciplinary study at Columbia University.[10] The basic elements in the general theory of occupational choice presented by the study are these: "it is a process; the process is largely irreversible; compromise is an essential aspect of every choice."

By *process,* these authors mean a developmental sequence which extends over a long time. They divide the occupational choice process into three periods: the period of fantasy choice, extending from early childhood to puberty, the period of tentative choices in early adolescence, and the period of realistic choices which follows sooner or later.

"In the fantasy period," they point out, "the youngster thinks about an occupation in terms of his wish to be an adult." He chooses the most spectacular and unchildlike roles which come into his ken: cowboy, railroad engineer, policeman, explorer, doctor, and baseball player are entirely typical choices. Lawyer, accountant, lathe operator, store manager, teacher, technician, or salesman would be rather unusual choices. Fantasy choices are made in terms of pleasurable activity, not as adjustments to reality.

"The tentative period is characterized by the individual's recognition of the problem of deciding on a future occupation." What characterizes this period as tentative is that choices are still made in terms of subjective factors without much concession to reality. Choices made during this period are serious, in the sense that they have some symbolic relationship with the future, but they are seldom translated directly into any effective activity.

The realistic period is that in which a choice is finally made with the intention of realizing it in actuality. It is characterized by the difficult compromise between the aspirations of the individual and the opportunities offered in his environment.

The period of tentative choices is further subdivided by these authors into interest, capacity, value, and transition stages — so called from the general themes which condition occupational ambitions at each stage. The period of realistic choices is broken down into the stages of exploration, crystallization, and specification, the last of which involves specialization and planning *within* an occupational field.

The empirical work undertaken in connection with this study was rather limited and inconclusive. We shall do better to consider this presentation of periods and stages, not as a set of findings, but as a hypothesis about individual development. As such it takes the place of a considerable number of vague psychoanalytical pronouncements (e.g., many adolescents sublimate their sadistic impulses by turning to surgery, excessive emphasis on bladder training accounts for an interest in hydraulic engineering) and a variety of naively conceived studies which have quizzed children about their occupational choices or asked adults to recall their childhood orientation to work.

It is unlikely that all, or even many, individuals pass through each of these periods and stages in a set order and at a regular rate. Nevertheless, there are certain fixed elements which seem to characterize the projective aspect of occupational choice:

1. Crystallization of choice may take place in isolated instances at any age whatever. Thus, musically gifted children in musically oriented families may be said to show "crystallization" of choice before entering kindergarten. At the other end of the age scale, it is not unusual to find men who have gone through an entire working life, and into retirement, without ever making an emotional commitment to a particular calling.

2. In general, the time at which commitments are made will depend upon cultural norms, rather than upon the strength of individual motivations.

3. Fantasy choices are highly stylized and stereotyped and — if this can fairly be applied to any doings of children — unimaginative. Their demonstrated significance for future behavior is nil.

The period of tentative choices is, above all, a period of increasing self-awareness. For those with limited and specific talents in a privileged environment, it constitutes a phase of preliminary adjustment to the adult world. For the superior, for the handicapped, and for the versatile, the choices made at this time have little meaning except that they turn attention in one general direction rather than another, and lead the person to make fixed judgments about himself which, true or false, become the basis for future activity.

4. Realistic choices typically involve the abandonment of old aspirations in favor of more limited objectives. This is, in some sense, only a temporary abandonment. With the crystallization of occupational choice, the youth looks around for the means which lie at hand, and these are initially humble. But crystallizations of this sort are often impermanent. Closer acquaintance with the occupational milieu may eventually re-create some of the conditions of the transition stage. In other words, the realistic choice is not — especially for the mobile middle-class functionary — the final period of development as far as occupational projections are concerned. Instead, a continuous process of alternately lowering and raising goals will be initiated. Not until late in his career will the average man be able to sum up his total expectations with some degree of finality and measure them against his remaining aspirations so as to arrive at a permanent sense of frustration, a permanent glow of complacency, or an irregular oscillation from one to the other.

NOTES

[1] Harlan W. Gilmore, "Five Generations of a Begging Family," *American Journal of Sociology,* vol. 37, March 1932, pp. 768–74.

[2] David MacKaye, "The Fixation of Vocational Interest," *American Journal of Sociology,* vol. 33, November 1927.

[3] Eli Ginzberg, Sol W. Ginsburg, Sidney Axelrad, and John L. Herma, *Occupational Choice: An Approach to a General Theory* (New York: Columbia University Press, 1951), p. 13.

[4] Edward K. Strong, Jr., *Vocational Interests of Men and Women* (Stanford, Calif.: Stanford University Press, 1943), contains a summary to that date.

[5] Oscar J. Kaplan, editor, *Encyclopedia of Vocational Guidance* (2 vols.; New York: Philosophical Library, 1948).

[6] Edward L. Thorndike and others, *Prediction of Vocational Success* (New York: The Commonwealth Fund, 1934).

[7] Carroll L. Shartle, *Occupational Information: Its Development and Application* (New York: Prentice-Hall, 1946).

[8] Occupational Research Section, National Vocational Guidance, Inc., "Content of a Good Occupational Monograph — The Basic Outline," *Occupations,* vol. 19, October 1940, pp. 20–23.

[9] Although they have also been criticized for unreadability and white-collar bias. See Arthur H. Brayfield and Grace T. Mickelson, "Disparities in Occupational Information Coverage," *Occupations,* April 1951; Arthur H. Brayfield and Patricia Aepli Reed, "How Readable Are Occupational Information Booklets?" *Journal of Applied Psychology,* vol. 34, no. 5, October 1950.

[10] Ginzberg, Ginsburg, Axelrad, and Herma, *Occupational Choice: An Approach to a General Theory,* p. 186.

CHAPTER 10

OCCUPATIONS OF WOMEN

Worker Factors	Per Cent of Occupations
Male required	79
Female required	11
Either sex	10

UNITED STATES EMPLOYMENT SERVICE

IN A previous chapter, a contrast was drawn between the occupational distributions of male and female workers according to the census classification. These need further examination. As of 1950, more than a quarter of the employed women were clerical workers, about a fifth were factory operatives, and a tenth were engaged in each of four categories: saleswomen, domestic servants, other service workers, professional and semi-professional workers, in all of which women were proportionately more numerous than men. Table B in the Appendix illustrates the concentration of women in a few occupations, and it may be useful to summarize their place in each of the major occupational groups.

Most of the women in the professions are nurses, teachers, social workers, and librarians. Nursing, social work, and library work are monopolized by women, except for certain specialties and administrative posts. Teaching in the elementary schools is women's work (with significant consequences for the American personality); high school teaching is rather evenly divided, but women are nearly excluded from advanced teaching, even women's colleges being largely staffed by men.

The entry of women into the other professions was widely heralded about two generations ago. Women physicians had made a place for themselves soon after the Civil War, and the first woman judge was appointed about the turn of the century. In recent decades, this movement has come to a standstill. The proportion of women students in the major professional schools is slightly less than it was in 1910. Women practitioners limit themselves for the most part to specialties where most of their clients are women (pediatrics, divorce litigation, remodeling, domestic science teaching) or

230

to those completely removed from public contact (laboratory and library work). It appears that the influence of women in the professional societies has declined.

In the semiprofessional categories, women figure almost equally with men in entertainment and the arts; they predominate in certain occupations which are ancillary to a major profession, such as dental hygienist, but are almost unrepresented in the technical trades.

The number of women enumerated as farmers and farm managers is very small: less than 5 per cent of all rural proprietors. Most of them are widows or unmarried daughters who have inherited a family farm and continue to operate it. This is usually a temporary status. The woman farmer is likely to marry or to sell her farm as soon as possible. Here again, women have lost ground since the turn of the century, although it must always be remembered in discussing the farm population that no clear distinction can be made between domestic activities and farm work. There is no way of guessing how many women really operate farms whose nominal male operator is absent, disabled, or incompetent.

There are proportionately nearly half as many women as men among proprietors, managers, and officials. They are for the most part the owners or operators of small retail businesses, or the occupants of minor administrative posts involving clerical duties. Women are effectively barred from the higher reaches of industrial management. The three largest manufacturing corporations in the United States do not have a single woman as director, or in a major executive position. Even in political positions, where the power of the female half of the electorate is feared, it is not usual to give more than token representation to women. Thus, in 1953, the United States had 12 women members of Congress out of 531 senators and representatives and one ambassador out of 73 envoys.

The number of women exceeds the number of men both absolutely and proportionately among clerical and kindred workers. A whole cluster of occupations associated with the conduct of affairs in the modern office is reserved exclusively to women. Male clerical workers are employed only under special conditions, as on the factory floor, or where the job has an element of technical qualification, as in a lumber yard. Otherwise, the work which consists of answering the telephone, directing visitors, opening mail, making transcripts, typing letters and other documents, preparing bills and statements, and keeping the files is women's work. With the increasing standardization of communication procedures, it becomes diffi-

231

cult for any organized activity from a creamery to a political campaign to operate without an office, and increasingly rare for an office to be maintained without the full complement of useful and ritual gestures.

Women outnumber men proportionately, but not absolutely, in retail sales, but the census enumeration is probably invalid, because of the confusion of male retail employees with canvassers and traveling salesmen — two large groups with whom they have little in common. It is probable that there are more women than men directly engaged in retail sales, and that their number is increasing faster. The prevailing pattern is that salesmen serve male customers, and saleswomen serve female customers. Where the customers are mixed in gender, the sales force follows the majority. An exception is made for very heavy or very valuable commodities, which are commonly sold by men. A whole set of folkways is developed on the basis of these principles. Thus, in a normally organized department store, there will be men in the sports-goods department, women to sell curtains and dishware, men to sell hardware, women to sell books, but men to sell wedding silver and furniture. Since most shoppers are women, the enforcement of these curious principles leads increasingly to a female sales force. It is only recently, for example, that men have been partly displaced from women's shoe departments.

The number of women employed as craftsmen, foremen, and kindred workers is almost negligible. The woman craftsman is a curiosity. Every skilled trade — including blacksmithing — has a tiny representation of women who indulge a self-conscious eccentricity by following what is regarded as a man's calling. For all practical purposes, the crafts are reserved to men. The women in the foreman category are mostly forewomen in factories employing women machine operators. At least half of them are found in textile manufacture.

The proportions of each sex employed as operatives and kindred workers are identical, and this is the only category of which this may be said. On the whole, the principles determining the sex of factory employees are more complex than those for a sales force, and they owe even more to custom and to historical accident. By and large, it is the practice of the industry rather than the policy of each employer which determines whether employment should be limited to one sex or the other, whether both should be employed in the same plant, and if so, whether crews should be mixed or segregated. In theory, men are preferred for jobs which are dirty, strenuous, or mobile, and Americans abroad are profoundly shocked to see women engaged in coal mining although many women's jobs in this country exhibit similar elements. In theory, women are preferred for work which is precise, delicate, or especially monotonous, but as often as not, these are rationalizations after the fact. Any job for which only women are employed is likely to be classified as delicate, or even as monotonous, because it is women's work. Where a mixed working force is employed, as in the manufacture of electrical apparatus, and even where crews are mixed in sex, as in the shoe industry, jobs continue to be separated, and a hard and fast line is drawn between men's work and women's work. Under the modern attitudes which apply to the employment of women, this is inevitable. The possibility that the distinction is based upon attitudes rather than upon technical requirements is suggested by the fact that what is woman's work in one shoe factory may be man's work in another, and vice versa. There is a real reluctance, however, to employ both sexes together at the same work, even in such casually organized industries as canning.

The occupational category in which men are most heavily outnumbered is that of domestic service, where there are ten to fifteen times more women. Domestic servants are somewhat more numerous than the census figures indicate. Housemaids are not ordinarily reported for income tax or social security purposes, and they tend to conceal their paid employment when questioned. Perhaps a million housemaids, working approximately full time but living in their own households, reported themselves as housewives not otherwise employed in 1950. This is generally thought to be the lowest rung of legitimate employment for women. Wherever a large underprivileged population is present, there is some tendency for other women to avoid domestic service entirely. Except for a small number of governesses, companions, housekeepers, and others who are socially distinct from servants as presently identified, the occupation is reserved to Negro women throughout most of the South,[1] divided between Negro women and slum dwellers of recent foreign extraction in the northern metropolitan centers, and elsewhere confined to special populations from the wrong side of the tracks. Only in rather isolated rural districts is domestic service quite free of disgrace.

The number of women laborers is negligible. Those counted as farmhands are for the most part family members who work under a salary arrangement for one reason or another, or are so declared to the census-taker. The number of women who earn their living by sexual activity is not known. It appears to be much less than it was a generation ago, when the few occupational studies made [2] suggested that a large proportion of shopgirls, waitresses, and machine operators also engaged in occasional prostitution.

The remaining occupational category is marked by even greater concentration than most of the others. Although there are scores of occupations for "service workers, except domestic and protective," the majority of women in this group are employed in restaurants and beauty shops. No other type of industrial or commercial establishment has enjoyed such rapid and sustained growth as these. As institutions, both the restaurant and the *salon de coiffure* were originally patterned after European models staffed by men. The expensive and elegant establishment still has male personnel. This has a depressing influence upon the occupations involved: chef, pastry chef, waitress, hairdresser, and so forth. Though staffed predominantly by women, and regarded as characteristically female occupations, their upper reaches are closed to women.

Even this very brief summary suggests that certain trends have been much exaggerated. Given the changes in the economy since 1900, and the extremely rapid urbanization of the population, the increase in the proportion of women employed from 20.4 per cent in 1900 to 28.5 per cent in 1950 is very modest, though the proportion of urban women permanently employed outside the home appears to have unequivocally increased.

The assumed progress toward occupational equality between the sexes becomes, upon closer examination, a change in the forms of inequality. Thus, the principle of equal pay for equal work is often officially accepted and embodied in wage scales at about the time that it becomes effectively meaningless — because of a sharpening of job segregation (as in clerical work) or because of a system which provides rapid promotion for men only (as in school teaching).

It is very unlikely that the proportion of women employed will sustain any marked long-term increase so long as the contemporary family structure remains intact, and the role of housewife continues to be the leading role for adult women. Occupational inequality is guaranteed by customs and folkways which differentiate the careers of women from those of men, and it may be well to examine in some detail the special conditions of female employment.

1. The occupational careers of women are not normally continuous. It is the normal expectation that a man will be at work or seeking work

from the termination of his schooling until his death or retirement. This is not the expectation for women, and in fact only a small minority of those employed remain in the labor force throughout their mature years. Except among the wealthy, women are expected to work in the interval — if there is one — between the termination of their schooling and marriage. They may continue to work until the birth of their first child. Thereafter, they are likely to return to the labor force in case of financial need, divorce or early widowhood, a national emergency, or excessive leisure. In general, the higher the class status, the higher the probability that work will be interrupted at marriage, and the lower the chance that women will return to the labor force after the birth of children. Nevertheless, the intermittent career pattern is typical of all socioeconomic levels, with the partial exception of the highest and the lowest.

2. Most employed men support the family group to which they belong, but most employed women are secondary breadwinners. Either their earnings are used only for their own support, or they supplement the earnings of parents, husband, or other family members. The pressures toward wage discrimination created by this situation are both economic and psychological. Women can often, without any real disadvantage, accept wages too low to support a family, and may even be able to afford luxuries at a wage rate which implies poverty for a male employee. As we have seen, considerations of need always enter more or less into the determination of wages; it is perceived as right and just that, needing less, women workers receive less. For the same reasons, women are not as likely to press for wage increases, even when adequately organized and led.

3. Women tend to be residentially immobile. More precisely, their residence tends to be determined by the occupational exigencies of the principal breadwinner if they belong to a household, and by nonoccupational considerations if they live alone. This becomes increasingly true with increasing age. It is possible to recruit clerical workers from a distance for Washington agencies, and with strong inducements, some migration of female factory workers can be arranged, but those involved are unmarried girls. This immobility is a particular disadvantage on the higher occupational levels, where almost all positions involve the possibility of a change of residence, and in private bureaucracies, which attach particular emphasis to experience in different parts of the organization.

4. In any woman's occupation, a considerable proportion of the qualified workers in a given area will be out of the labor force at a given moment.

These constitute a reserve whose presence is always felt. There are always a considerable number of women in any community who can be attracted into paid employment. Indeed, this is the principal device by which the swift increases of industrial manpower in 1941–42 and 1950–51 were supported. Curiously, it would appear that this reserve is mobilized at both extremes of the business cycle: at the low point, unemployment and low wages drive housewives into the labor market out of sheer necessity. At the high point they are drawn in by the attractive conditions offered.

Under no circumstances has the reserve of employable women been fully mobilized. Thus, it is almost impossible for a woman's occupation to be effectively monopolized by the incumbents. Any occupation with a large proportion of female workers is vulnerable. In the economist's language, the elasticity of supply is very great. Employers are always able to find substitute workers without much difficulty. Improvements in working conditions are followed by increased competition for jobs, and all the usual ways of raising wages — including strikes — are relatively ineffective. Only where such occupations are merged administratively or organizationally with male occupations controlling critical skills are they likely to avoid the threat posed by the permanent labor reserve.

4. Women are everywhere confronted with a vast network of special statutes, rules, and regulations — some designed for their protection, some intended to reduce their effectiveness as competitors, and some adroitly contrived for both purposes at once. Most of the states, and many cities, have enacted legislation to limit the hours of women's work, to forbid or restrain night work, to prohibit their holding jobs which are especially strenuous, to require higher standards of health and hygiene in shops employing women, to permit or to require a reasonable adaptation to the requirements of pregnancy, and so forth down to regulations specifying the way in which women's occupations shall be designated in Help Wanted advertisements. The requirements are now far behind current practice in many areas, and these laws are falling into disuse, but they seem to have been largely responsible for the disappearance of the fantastically harsh working conditions imposed upon women half a century ago, and described by Annie Marion MacLean in the earliest issues of the *American Journal of Sociology*.[3] On the other hand, they impose a sort of penalty upon employers who choose to hire women in place of men, and it is for this reason that feminists have recently advocated the abolition of all protective legislation of this type.

Another kind of formal discrimination is represented by civil service requirements, statements of company policy, union bylaws, and the entrance qualifications of professional schools, all of which exclude women gratuitously from many types of employment and from many posts for which they might be perfectly qualified. Finally, there are the bans on the employment of married women — most familiar in teaching and nursing — and the rules relating to nepotism and seniority in most large organizations.

Some sort of limitation on the simultaneous employment of close relatives — particularly husband and wife — is a feature of almost all public bureaucracies, and of many private enterprises as well. The motive of limiting competition by women who are well placed to compete effectively undoubtedly plays a part in these policies, together with the desire to prevent favoritism and the growth of family cliques. As is often the case where a weak ideal is confronted with a strong practical interest, the suppression of nepotism is least effective where it matters most. But in teaching, and in certain kinds of technical and managerial work, it may put an effective stop to the career of a woman who marries one of her colleagues.

Seniority rules have more general implications. Since they are usually written in such a way as to give great weight to continuity of employment, they are certain to place women at a disadvantage. Even where allowance is made for maternity, the life cycle does not allow women to compete successfully with men in terms of occupational continuity. The increasing emphasis upon seniority in industry, and in bureaucratic employment, is thus an additional barrier to the working woman.

These are the structural elements which differentiate the occupational position of women so clearly from that of men. Taken by themselves, they may account for the failure of the feminine emancipation in other domains to be extended to the working world. To understand the high concentration of women in a few occupational categories, however, it is necessary to bring many other facts into the picture. Women are barred from four out of every five occupational functions, not because of incapacity or technical unsuitability, but because the attitudes which govern interpersonal relationships in our culture sanction only a few working relationships between men and women, and prohibit all the others on grounds that have nothing to do with technology. For the moment, it will be convenient to discuss these attitudes as if they were held only by men. We shall consider later the extent to which they are sustained or undermined by women.

237

There are two central themes: (1) that it is disgraceful for a man to be directly subordinated to a woman, except in family or sexual relationships; (2) that intimate groups, except those based on family or sexual ties, should be composed of either sex but never of both.

The evidence for the existence of these themes is scattered through the literature. A specially explicit and elegant formulation is found in W. H. Whyte's study of the restaurant industry.[4] A considerable amount of statistical material emerges from the work done with Clifford Kirkpatrick's belief-pattern scale of feminism.[5] The case records of every major investigation in industrial sociology contain a mass of relevant details. Yet, it cannot be denied that the distribution of these attitudes in the population at large has never been directly checked. We are forced to adopt a technique of the social anthropologists, which is to assert the universality of a cultural theme on the basis of personal observation, introspection, and what might be called circumstantial evidence in the literature. When labeled, and when used sparingly, this has been an effective method. Its principal fault is that the analyst cannot invite the reader to check the process by which he arrived at his own certainty that the theme deserves as much emphasis as he gives it.

The matter is further complicated by the fact that neither of these themes is an isolated statement, or even an article of belief. They are rather the least common denominators of a large number of beliefs, prejudices, habitual reactions, ways of perceiving, and opinions, which are highly developed and ramified.

The psychoanalysts, and more recently such sociologists as Waller and Parsons and very notably the anthropologist Margaret Mead, have sketched out the implications of the female control to which the young male in our culture is subject from birth to about the middle of adolescence.[6] Some of the consequences, like the association of goodness with femininity, do not particularly concern us here. What is significant in this connection is that emancipation from female dominance is associated for men with the achievement of maturity and full adult status. This is further reinforced by a pattern of sexual behavior which emphasizes male dominance, and a family system which — in emotional terms — vests some of the disciplinary functions lost by the mother in the wife. The refusal to be subordinate to women thus appears both as an assertion of essential masculinity, and as compensation for a degree of continued subordination within the family.

The insistence that intimate groups developed in the working situation and elsewhere outside of the family be composed of the same sex has equally profound roots. From the time when the early adolescent is taught to scorn those of his fellows who associate with the opposite sex in the classic terms of "sissy" or "tomboy," a good deal of opprobrium is associated with any emotionally weighted relationships between the sexes which do not have explicit sexual connotations. Especially in the male group, which tends to reject overtly, if superficially, the official morality sponsored by women in the family, there is a culturally recognized atmosphere which symbolizes the exclusion of women. The use of tabooed words, the fostering of sports and other interests which women do not share, and participation in activities which women are intended to disapprove of — hard drinking, gambling, practical jokes, and sexual essays of various kinds — all suggest that the adult male group is to a large extent engaged in a reaction *against* feminine influence, and therefore cannot tolerate the presence of women without changing its character entirely.

There is another and quite different set of factors which must be taken into account. Practically speaking, it may be predicted that sexual or quasi-sexual relationships of some importance will develop in most mixed working groups. Insofar as this introduces extraneous conflicts, it represents a direct threat to the group. Indirectly, by arousing the interest and sometimes the intervention of outsiders, including wives and husbands, it poses an additional threat and disturbs the carefully guarded separation between home and work which figures so largely in the psychic economy of the modern breadwinner.

No one has ever traced these two themes through the occupational structure. All that can be done here is to indicate briefly some of their major consequences. In a hierarchy, men accept women superiors with great reluctance. This objection is so strong that the problem hardly arises in industrial plants. The idea of placing a woman foreman over a male crew is regarded as intrinsically ridiculous. In white-collar work, and particularly in well-organized bureaucracies, the issue is not evaded so easily, but it is nevertheless evaded. The majority of women at supervisory levels are found to have only women subordinates, or to be engaged in technical or staff jobs which require little authority to be exercised. Women supervisors may be used in charge of training sections, where the status of their subordinates is temporary, or in connection with a highly routinized operation like a mail service where morale can be more or less disregarded. An occasional highly gifted woman may be used in an authoritative position where the number of her direct subordinates is small, and where the nature of the job requires little cooperation with executives on the same level. This appears to be part of the special situation of the department store buyer. Even in the case of these exceptions the essential problem remains. A woman supervisor cannot ordinarily command the loyalty of male subordinates, who will resent her on principle and reject her authority almost spontaneously. Thus, it is highly unlikely that she will be able to supervise effectively. Many private bureaucracies avoid this problem by refusing to hire women above the clerical level. Public agencies and other large-scale institutions contrive less graceful escapes, which often involve flat discrimination.

In sum, it may be said that the main channels of vertical mobility in organized employment are not open to women. Even in the professions, a comparable situation exists. Josephine Williams has studied women physicians as a minority group within the profession.[7] The reluctance of men to serve women colleagues as assistants makes it almost impossible for a woman to practice surgery or to supervise a hospital. Even more forcible considerations keep the few women magistrates in the lower reaches of the judiciary. They are usually relegated to courts of domestic relations or juvenile delinquency where the role of attorneys is relatively slight, and where the judge does not need to exercise any real authority over her professional colleagues before the bar. It is curious that acting is the only highly specialized field in which men and women seem to be substantially equal in all respects — it being also the only one in which the exercise of direct authority is never called for. Producing and directing, in spite of the fact that they fall within the same general framework, are occupations normally barred to women, although a few actresses of overwhelming prestige have engaged in them. All in all, it seems likely that the ban on the exercise of direct authority by women over male subordinates of comparable social status (the schoolteacher may give orders to the janitor with no violation of this principle) is about as effective as might be expected if the two sexes were closed castes.

Whyte suggests a more precise terminology, introduced by Chapple in his scheme for the statistical measurement of social interaction.[8] He directs our attention to the "initiation of action." This, of course, is the principal function of the supervisor in his relation with a subordinate, and it also arises at many other points in the working situation. Thus, it is the customer who initiates action for the salesclerk and the policeman for the traffic offender. In any cooperative relationship of equals, it is periodically the function of each to initiate action for the others. It may not be farfetched to speak of a generalized cultural resistance by men to action initiated for them by women to whom they are not related emotionally. One of the several illustrations given by Whyte will provide a better idea of what is involved.

In several of the restaurants studied, only the waitresses circulate among the tables but any drinks ordered at the tables are prepared by the male bartenders. The waitress takes the customer's order, and in turn orders the drink from the bartender. This was found to be a point of friction and of delay, except in those cases where the bartender had reorganized the situation so that the waitress was no longer in the position of initiating action for him. One bartender, for example, classified all orders in piles according to the type of drink, and prepared them in batches. Whyte shows rather convincingly that in the usual case, the bartender reacted to his interactional subordination by overt resistance, which ranged from surliness to sabotage. He also shows that this problem did not exist when employees initiated action for others of the same sex, or when men initiated action for women.

Similar considerations apply to the relationship between professional and client, when the practitioner is a woman and the client a man, and explain why policewomen are usually unable to direct traffic successfully. Perhaps the most typical situation in industry is that in which female inspectors are assigned to check the work of male employees. Inspection is usually monotonous, often delicate, and seldom strenuous, and therefore likely to be classified as women's work. There are certain advantages too in having a degree of social isolation between the inspectors and other workers. For these reasons, the experiment has been tried hundreds of times. It fails with high consistency. Either the women inspectors succeed in doing their job of initiating action for the men on the production line and create a severe problem of morale, or they are unable to oppose the resistance offered and the inspection becomes ineffective.

Another of the major consequences of the attitudes we have outlined is that a group of male workers will almost invariably oppose the introduction of a woman into their midst. The reasons are apparent, and double-edged. In the case of privileged occupations, the presence of women is felt to weaken the cohesiveness of the group and to diminish its offensive and defensive strength. In the case of underprivileged occupations, pride in the virile character of the work and involvement in its antifeminine culture usually compensate in some measure for the absence of more tangible rewards. Here women represent even more of a threat; their first appearance alters the environment in a drastic way and is resented accordingly.

There is another difficulty of a practical sort. If a number of women are introduced at once, their arrival is felt as a sort of invasion, and requires serious readjustments on the part of the men. If only one woman is employed, the necessary adaptations to her presence appear excessive to everyone concerned, including immediate changes in verbal habits, dress, and comportment, and potential changes in the organization of the group.

What adjustments take place after the introduction has been accomplished depends upon a number of factors, of which the size and previous cohesiveness of the group are perhaps the most important. In a highly cohesive group, one or two women will be either effectively isolated or treated — by special exception — as if they were men. This latter adjustment is regarded as the successful one, but it is evidently a rather delicate and insecure arrangement. If the women are more numerous, they are likely to form a group apart, having the minimum of spatial and social contacts with the men. In more casually organized working situations, the position of the single woman is likely to be both unstable and emotionally charged, so that she will usually find it intolerable after a short time. Where numbers are more evenly balanced, the sex groups will be somewhat isolated from each other but will probably show enough hostility to make any permanent accommodation difficult.

A related problem arises throughout the occupational world, but especially at the higher levels, when women are placed in posts which require coordinate cooperation with men. In a collegial body, such as a board of directors, a staff conference, or an administrative committee, the atmosphere of formality and the short duration of contact facilitate cooperation without reference to sex roles. But where the cooperating group is informally organized, where contacts are more or less continuous, and especially where the relations between equals (two parallel department heads, for example) are personalized, we encounter once more the barriers which hinder men and women from free mutual participation. In this connection, the most difficult problem is the organization of conflict. Here again, the relevant motivations are a curious melange of childhood conditioning, economic interests, and conventional rules.

Coordinate statuses in any social structure do not always imply absolute equality, but they do imply the possibility of mutual aggression, which is always more restricted between superiors and subordinates. As a matter of fact, overt competition, shading by degrees into hostility and active conflict, is often expected and even mildly approved between persons who occupy parallel positions in large organizations. The more closely the organization approaches the pyramidal structure of the perfect bureaucracy, the more will these patterns of opposition be institutionalized, since promotion is impossible except by the exclusion of colleagues.

Now it may fairly be observed that the training of boys in childhood and adolescence includes the severe prohibition of "fighting with girls." The derivative forms of hostility are tolerated only between boys. This is the case in all social classes, and the taboo is founded upon still deeper inhibitions which arise from the Oedipus theme. Aggression by males toward females assumes an emotional charge which differentiates it sharply from the socially sponsored aggression which is normally associated with economic competition.

In short, occupational competition between men and women is complicated by the feelings of guilt aroused in the men, and the fact that both sexes have been systematically trained to avoid competition in those terms. But the problem goes further.

Occupational competition rests explicitly upon the evaluation of individual performance. It is true, of course, that the standards of judgment are often irrational, and that extraneous factors (e.g., "personality") are often allowed to weigh heavily. The fact remains that in individualized jobs, there is a continuous process of evaluation, in which both productivity and conformity are taken into account. Men are prepared for this competition by the circumstances of their late childhood and adolescent experience, which systematically inculcates the appropriate techniques for weighing efficiency against conformity, and for sustaining the impact of adverse judgments. But, as many students of the culture have found, the early experience of women is designed to prepare them for their family roles, and for the critical courtship era which largely determines their lifetime situation.

The difference may be roughly indicated in these terms: Men are trained to derive their principal ego-satisfactions from competitive performance and from the favorable opinions of their fellows. Women tend to find permanent gratifications in their own personal characteristics and in the

243

responses of affectional relationships. As thus stated, the distinction is grossly oversimplified. It is nevertheless of paramount importance, and may be illustrated in many different ways. For example, the appearance of a woman is always a major factor in her occupational relationships. Similarly, the occupationally successful woman enjoys only a limited ego security compared with her male colleague; her claims to recognition are always checked by the quasi-sacred values attached to the role of the housewife. This is a favorite theme of popular fiction; and the conflict in the story is typically resolved by the transformation of the female executive or professional woman into a contented housewife.

No positive values whatever are attached to spinsterhood within the accepted framework of roles. The spinster is regarded as having failed in the essential effort of women: to find a husband and raise a family. This bias has perhaps been strengthened in recent years by the popularization of psychoanalytic ideas on the suppression of sexual impulses, whose effect has been to increase the suspicion in which permanent virgins are held. Since most environments still effectively taboo any overt claims to sexual achievement on the part of unmarried women, the middle-aged spinster is sociologically a virgin, and subject to all the penalties of that state.

The combination of an occupational role with the role of wife and mother is perhaps the only way out of this impasse for the women who attempt to follow a serious occupational career. The principal objection is that it is seldom fully practicable. The interruptions occasioned by pregnancy, the care of small children, and miscellaneous family emergencies create an almost hopeless set of handicaps in competition with male workers. As a matter of fact, the superimposition of household duties upon the normal working day implies more than normal energy if it is to be indefinitely continued, and tends to limit this alternative to women of extraordinary talents.

Parsons has indicated the other factors which limit the occupational participation of the married woman, even in those cases where the presence of a female relative in the home, or some other special circumstance, makes it especially feasible. The system of motivations which ties the male breadwinner to his family obligations implies the elimination of competitive pressures within the family. The existing system of class stratification with its strong current of upward mobility requires that members of a family household have identical status. Both of these conditions are threatened by the serious involvement of the wife in the occupational world. Not only will the emotional support she offers to her husband be diminished; she may injure both his self-respect and his formal status by achieving higher occupational status. When the actual domestic economy contradicts the assumptions upon which the family organization is based, it is possible for successful individual adjustments to be made but the probabilities of conflict and confusion of roles are vastly increased.

In sum, while the system retains sufficient flexibility to allow a number of real choices to women who insist on genuine occupational activity, the practical difficulties are of such a nature that only under exceptional circumstances can women pursue a vocation on substantially the same terms as men.

In this light, it is easy to see why certain occupations have been reserved to women and why they are barred by custom or administrative practice from the vast majority of those for which they might qualify. It is possible to predict the characteristics of an occupation suited to women under the conditions we have just described.

Given the intermittent character of female employment, a woman's occupation must be one in which employment is typically by short term, in which the gain in skill achieved by continuous experience is slight, in which interchangeability is very high, and in which the loss of skill during long periods of inactivity is relatively small. Note how closely the occupations of elementary teacher, nurse, librarian, shop clerk, typist, sewing-machine operator, and waitress conform to these criteria.

Given the attitudes which hedge the exercise of authority by women, a woman's job must be one which does not involve the subordination of adult males, or any close participation with male workers doing parallel jobs. The only large-scale exception occurs where male workers advance through the ranks of a predominantly female occupation to positions of authority more or less reserved to them. This is conspicuously the case in elementary teaching, social work, and library work, and in many offices. The tendency to deny authority to women is so strong that even in such predominantly female occupations, there is an organized effort to find male candidates for supervisory functions. For the male social worker or stenographer, advancement is virtually automatic.

Finally, it is characteristic of women's occupations that they cannot be effectively monopolized. Some of them demand a high level of general education with little specific training. In others, employment is intermittent and sporadic, or else the elasticity of demand is very great. Clerical work illustrates the first situation, restaurant work the second, and door-to-door canvassing the third. Teaching, nursing, and the other auxiliary professions do require substantial training, but it is notable that in the absence of fully qualified personnel, untrained teachers, nurses, librarians, or social workers are readily substituted. Indeed, in some areas a librarian or social worker with the appropriate professional background is still something of a curiosity.

Occupation by occupation, unorganizability appears both as the cause and the effect of a preponderance of women. Well-organized occupations have usually been able to prevent the entry of women and have done so, for reasons previously outlined. The occupations which women are able to enter freely are those which have low prestige and poor working conditions or are associated in some way with home and housework. All the conditions which put women workers at a disadvantage limit their organizability. Above all, discontinuity of employment is fatal to the development of occupational solidarity. The same attitudes and prejudices which keep women out of supervisory positions also limit their ability to develop strong leadership for negotiation and collective bargaining.

NOTES

[1] Current trends have been summarized in a recent study in these terms: "The nonfarm South now participates fully in the nation-wide sharp decline of servants. Previously, servant use in the Deep South spread far down the income scale, manifesting a 'caste' rather than a 'class' incidence. A greater proportionate decrease in white, over Negro, servants, is shown in both North and South. Servant frequencies are closely but imperfectly related to Negro population; the South, both farm and nonfarm, is extremely diverse in its servant use. The waning of the servant, a key feature of traditional southern life, manifests the shift from familistic toward impersonal and equalitarian culture traits." C. Arnold Anderson and Mary Jean Bowman, "The Vanishing Servant and the Contemporary Status System of the American South," *American Journal of Sociology*, vol. 54, no. 3, November 1953, p. 215.

[2] Frances R. Donovan, *The Woman Who Waits* (Boston: Richard G. Badger, 1920); Annie Marion MacLean: "Life in the Pennsylvania Coal Fields with Particular Reference to Women," *American Journal of Sociology*, vol. 14, November 1908, pp. 329–51; "The Sweat Shop in Summer," *American Journal of Sociology*, vol. 9, November 1903, pp. 289–309; "Two Weeks in Department Stores," *American Journal of Sociology*, vol. 4, May 1899, pp. 121–41; "With Oregon Hop Pickers," *American Journal of Sociology*, vol. 15, July 1909, pp. 83–95.

[3] *Ibid.*

[4] William Foote Whyte, "The Social Structure of the Restaurant," *American Journal of Sociology*, vol. 54, January 1949, pp. 302–10; *Human Relations in the Restaurant Industry* (New York: McGraw-Hill Book Company, 1948).

[5] See Clifford Kirkpatrick, "The Measurement of Ethical Inconsistency in Marriage," *International Journal of Ethics*, vol. 46, July 1936.

[6] Margaret Mead, *And Keep Your Powder Dry* (New York: William Morrow & Company, 1942).

[7] Josephine J. Williams, "Patients and Prejudice: Lay Attitudes towards Women Physicians," *American Journal of Sociology*, vol. 51, January 1946.

[8] Eliot D. Chapple (with the collaboration of Conrad M. Arensberg), "Measuring Human Relations: An Introduction to the Study of the Interaction of Individuals," *Genetic Psychology Monographs*, vol. 22, no. 1, February 1940.

CHAPTER 11

OCCUPATION AND FAMILY

> Broadly speaking, there is no sector of our society where the dominant patterns stand in sharper contrast to those of the occupational world than in the family.   TALCOTT PARSONS

IN ALL societies, the family system and the occupational system are closely related. The family prepares the individual for work and it is the immediate beneficiary of his labor. The working group is often coincident with the family circle and even where it is not, the work required by housekeeping engages a large part of the population. Yet occupational institutions are not identical with family institutions even among primitive people, and in the urbanized, secular, middle-class culture of today, the values of the two systems are often in sharp conflict.

Throughout historic times, the effective family unit has usually been larger than the single household, and the household has usually been composed of more than one set of parents and children. A family unit of this kind is called an extended family, although the forms which it exhibits are not identical in all cultures. The polygynous Moslem household, the Hindu joint family, the Chinese great family, the American farm family of the eighteenth century, are quite different in detail, and the roles which they sustain do not much resemble each other. Moreover, at any given time and place, the family system will vary from class to class.

In general, it would appear that the extension of the effective kinship group and of the household increases with social status. The maintenance of a family compound in China requires considerable wealth, and most Moslems are necessarily limited to one wife. This tendency is not affected by the differential birth rate. The essential element of the extended family is not its inclusion of a larger population, but of a wider circle of relations and dependents. The Chinese great family often includes four generations under one roof, together with their wives, nephews, uncles, and cousins, as well as the servants and their relatives. The Moslem family group extends in theory — and sometimes in practice — to fourth cousins on the maternal side, and sixth cousins by paternal descent, with whom intermarriage is barred by the Koran.

Whatever its form, the extended family has certain consequences for the working lives of its members. It is best adapted to the family enterprise, closed to outsiders and based on inherited skills and secrets. The usual form of family enterprise has been a farm. However, if the forms of economic activity are stable, there is no reason why a commercial establishment, an artisan's shop, or even a factory may not be organized in this way. It is normal for small industry in China and India, fairly common in Western Europe, and not unheard of in the United States.

The extended family implies occupational immobility, based in turn on residential immobility. The family derives its status and its economic privileges from a network of local associations, even when it is not directly tied to the land. Any mobility threatens the existence of the extended family, but it may withstand a certain amount of occupational diversification if it retains its territorial stability. As Mandelbaum comments on the Hindu joint family:

When a man gets a job in a factory and earns his pay independently of the efforts of his parent and brothers, he is not so prone to turn over his earnings to the common family fund as was the case when he and his brothers worked the soil together. Nor is the physician who begins to enjoy the returns from a practice which he himself has established so apt to merge his career with the fortunes of the whole family as was the case when the livelihood of all members of the joint family was derived from the yield of ancestral property or, say, from the joint services of the men of the family as temple priests.

The bonds of the joint family, though weakened in this manner, are rarely severed completely. Both factory worker and physician will generally remit something to the joint family, for typically some members of the group remain in the ancestral village, and carry on the old family patterns. And both will feel that their real home is not in the city but in the joint household of the village; here the tutelary deities of the family are worshipped by all the members, and here each member, physician and worker alike, is likely to return for religious festivals and social occasions.[1]

The extended family is usually characterized as patriarchal. In the model patriarchal family, authority is centered in the general father, usually but not always the oldest active male; age enjoys an overwhelming prestige, typically supported by supernatural sanctions; and women are relegated to a subordinate position, being considered in the extreme case simply as movable property. The continuity between generations is very strong, dead ancestors are ceremonially venerated, and the hand of tradition regulates the conduct of family affairs at every point.

All these features are seldom found together in a single culture. Women are seldom as thoroughly subordinated as the Victorian anthropologists supposed. Even where their legal status is low, they tend to acquire enough informal influence to mitigate the disadvantage. Then too, the cultural norm of respect for the aged cuts across the norm of male superiority. In the Hindu family, where young women are harshly treated by their husband's relatives, old women often rule the entire clan. Most important, it is only in upper-class families, numerically few in any society, that women are excluded from the work organization, and in their occupational functions women are likely to enjoy substantial equality with their husbands.

There are two other ways in which the necessities of work limit the patriarchal pattern. Where the economic base will not support very large households in the same place, the continuity of generations is certain to be interrupted. In Islam, with its high incidence of nomadic activities, it is normal for marriage to be followed by the establishment of a separate household, and even in China, the growth of a sub-family beyond the point where it can be accommodated in the parental house leads to an eventual division of the kinship group. Wherever the form of organization allows younger members of the family to develop a marked occupational superiority over the general father, there is some tendency for the patriarchal authority to be limited, even though the posture of respect is maintained. In the Hindu family, which has developed special adaptations for many kinds of productive activity, all the males of the family are nominal equals in the ownership of family property. In China, the head of the family may retire from that role before his death, or delegate his powers to a son.

Wherever it still exists, even in the heart of the most isolated and traditional cultures, the patriarchal family is subject to disorganization as the traditional sanctions crumble under the influence of modern secularization. The essential process is the one described by Mandelbaum in the selection just quoted. Members of the family become factory workers or doctors. Attracted by the higher rewards offered, they abandon the traditional family occupation for one related to secular technics. In this situation the extended family is incapable of providing them with the appropriate training, or with the material and emotional security furnished before, and they soon rebel against its demands for loyalty, conformity, and support.

The incompatibility between the extended family and the modern organization of work appears to be fundamental. The traditional household is inherently inefficient as a productive unit. A review of its characteristics shows why this must be so. Workers are selected by chance, and those incapable of good performance are continued in the occupation. The marginal labor of children, invalids, and the aged is used. Technical improvements are opposed as violations of customary ways. The keeping of internal accounts is limited by lack of skill, lack of necessity, and the nonmonetary character of internal transaction. Specialization is limited by the relatively small population, as is the division and subdivision of operations. Since training is informal, there is no channel for the importation of new skills. Both the location and size of the establishment are fixed and cannot readily be adapted to changes in sources of supply, in resources, or in external markets.

Needless to say, the criterion of efficiency cannot be legitimately applied to the functions of the family in general. For many modern commentators, the large enfolding family, with its internal cohesion and its barriers against the outside world, represents a lost paradise to which we must somehow return. The idea has been made commonplace to a whole generation of readers by Pearl Buck, and it has a certain currency in psychological literature.

Given the inefficiency of the family as a productive unit, the question naturally arises as to why it was not displaced earlier in history. There are a number of special conditions which favor the family enterprise. If communication and transportation are so limited that all production must be consumed on the spot, most of its disadvantages disappear. If the conduct of the enterprise depends upon the maintenance of secrecy, or upon a high degree of mutual confidence, there are few guarantees as effective as the bonds of kinship. In the few trades still held secret — bell-casting, gondola-making, certain kinds of perfumery [2] — the family organization of production has remained almost unchanged since the Middle Ages. In many parts of the world, brokerage houses and other establishments engaged in the speculative branches of commerce still tend to be family affairs, based on the necessity for internal solidarity in matters of trust.

It will be noted that until quite recently these special conditions were the conditions of production everywhere. Markets were overwhelmingly local, most useful skills were carefully guarded, and there were few convenient devices for enforcing contracts between strangers.

251

One further condition which favors the family enterprise should be emphasized. Where the location of a productive establishment is permanently fixed and its expansion is permanently limited, there is no way for competing forms of organization to enter. Family enterprises persist in significant numbers in the two places where this condition is approximately fulfilled: general farms and neighborhood retail stores. With the evolution of new devices — machinery appropriate for large-scale cultivation, and the bulk-purchasing and distribution system of the chain store — these two remaining strongholds are slowly giving way.

These considerations help to explain the principle previously noted: within each cultural system, the degree of extension of the family is a function of social status. Exceptions to this principle may occur where two different family systems are mixed by migration or assimilation. It may happen temporarily that a lower class composed largely of immigrants shows wider kinship circles than the dominant groups. In the same way, a patriarchal pattern may persist in the rural environment long after it has disappeared among the urban population.

Otherwise, this status effect may be readily observed in any society, including our own. On the highest levels, the kinship group may even be international (as evidenced by the Almanach de Gotha or the New York Social Register) and it is customary to acknowledge the remotest degrees of relationship. At the other extreme, as Frazier has shown for the lower-class Negro family,[3] there is a tendency for the family to be reduced to mother and children, with even the father excluded. Indeed, one of the significant discoveries of recent research has been that of the continued existence of the extended family as a social reality among the upper classes of New England and southern communities and the appearance of the attenuated maternal family among the underprivileged.[4]

A moment's reflection will show the basis of this regularity. The essence of the extended family is continuity; once disorganized and dispersed, it can never be put back together again. It can achieve continuity only by providing for its members in a continuous fashion, which implies both economic security and the maintenance of status. This program is only feasible if the family's resources are sufficient to meet crises. Practically, this has always meant that the extended family is founded on the possession of property or of such intangible equivalents as an occupational monopoly. The Chinese great family disintegrates among the landless; the joint family among low-caste Indians does not survive the technological obsolescence of an hereditary trade. In all societies, the higher the class the more likely will it be to command resources in both goods and privileges, and the more secure will be its possessions. Indeed, this statement is tautological since status may be defined in terms of social reward.

When we come to the modern urban middle-class family, we are immediately struck by the reduction of the extended family to a household group consisting of parents and young children, with vague and undifferentiated ties to a larger circle of "relatives." No distinction is made between paternal and maternal relations, and very little between those related by consanguinity and those by marriage. The outer boundary of the kinship circle [5] excludes cousins beyond the first degree, and the mores do not require the maintenance of any active kinship relationship at all, except with one's own parents, children, and siblings. The household itself is partly dissolved at the maturity of the children, who are expected to establish separate households in which to raise their own children. No other relative, not even a widowed parent, has any unconditional right of entry into the household. As Parsons remarks, "It is difficult to see that emphasis on the solidarity of kinship groups could be whittled down much farther without breaking up the family system altogether." [6]

It is important to realize that the "middle class" to whom this system refers are not the bourgeoisie of nineteenth-century Europe, who used to be identified (and still are to some extent) as those who owned sufficient property to ensure their subsistence without working. The term *middle class* is now used to denote the large and expanding section of the urban population who do no manual labor, follow the norms of respectability, are educated beyond the legal minimum, are actively concerned with personal advancement, and are ordinarily able to devote part of their income to display. The high standard of living which characterizes this group is typically founded on occupational income and not on inherited property or privilege.

This middle class maintains a set of cultural values which are its most essential characteristic, and which are capable of being partially accepted under current conditions by manual workers and the owners of productive property. The dominant theme is the emphasis upon personal achievement, and the belief that social rewards are — or should be — distributed in proportion to individual merit, as measured by the performance of occupational tasks. As Mead has pointed out, virtue comes to be identified with success, and success itself as the outcome of a competition, in which the determining factor is the participant's eagerness to compete and his perseverance in the face of obstacles.[7] Merton summarizes the system in these terms: "Thus the culture enjoins the acceptance of three cultural axioms: first, all should strive for the same lofty goals, since these are open to all; second, present seeming failure is but a way station to ultimate success; and third, genuine failure consists only in the lessening or withdrawal of ambition." [8]

It is highly doubtful whether any substantial proportion of the middle class would give unqualified assent to these axioms, as baldly stated. Merton himself follows with an analysis of the deviant responses of those who reject either the cultural goals or the institutionalized means of arriving at them, which he discusses under the headings of Innovation, Ritualism, Retreatism, and Rebellion. Nearly thirty years ago, the Lynds found that the mythology of competitive success was not accepted without demur in Middletown. In the interim, the alternative goal of "security" has become increasingly respectable. Nevertheless, so long as wealth continues to be the essential measure of social status in our society, and occupational mobility continues at a level which allows the individual a rather wide range of choice in his wealth-getting activities, it is hardly possible to exaggerate the cultural insistence upon competitive behavior, which makes itself felt before the growing child has learned to talk. As Parsons points out:

Equally important to effective socialization in our society is the maintenance by the individual of a certain level of anxiety with regard to the attainment of the required behavior for his status. This socialized anxiety plays a major role in propelling him along that cultural route prescribed by his family, school, and later by adult society at his cultural level. The development of adaptive, socialized anxiety in middle-status life is all the more essential because the social and prestige rewards of this status must necessarily be postponed during the prolonged training of the child and adolescent for high skills and complex responsibilities. . . .

With regard to upward status-mobility, in the sense of climbing the "democratic ladder," furthermore, this anxiety motivation is entirely realistic and rational in our kind of society. It is experienced both as an urge to flee from the deprivations of low status and as a pull toward the greater biological and social security of high-status persons.[9]

In this context, certain inconsistencies between the occupational system and the family system are immediately apparent. These too have been brilliantly analyzed by Parsons, who points out that in the occupational system, "Roles are organized about standards of competence or effectiveness in performing a definite function." One is judged in his occupational role by impersonal and objective standards. The expectations of the role are linked to the "technical content" of the function, and irrelevant elements are excluded. The elements of occupational performance are subject to a continuous process of rational criticism and improvement. "This is fundamentally incompatible with any traditionalized system of norms of behavior — the rightness of behavior is judged by its objective efficiency not by its conformity with models of the past."

But if these norms are to function, it is essential that the individual be free to change his status on the basis of his occupational performance, and there must be some way of segregating this sector of his life from those which involve incompatible attitudes and standards. The patterns of the family institution are sharply opposed to those just described. The family is a solidary group, whose functions rest on customary ways of behaving and are highly charged with emotional significance. Status is determined by age, sex, and biological affiliation, rather than by objective standards of performance, which do not exist.

According to Parsons, "this problem of structural compatibility is solved in the United States by making sure that in the type case only one member of the effective kinship unit, the conjugal family, plays a fully competitive role in the occupational system." He points out that the family role of the husband and father is clearly segregated from his occupational role. His residence is separated from his place of work, and the mechanism of the conjugal family frees him from the hampering ties of the extended family and leaves him free for status mobility based on his occupational performance. Moreover, the emancipation of the conjugal family from the larger kinship unit and the limitation of occupational participation to one member — in a general way — make possible the residential mobility which is also essential to the functioning of the occupational system.

The matter may be looked at from the opposite standpoint. The family system, and particularly the marriage relationship which is the core of the conjugal family, must be protected against the threat represented by the occupational system. "As a structurally unsupported relationship resting largely on emotional attraction, it must be protected against the kind of stresses that go with severe competition for prestige between the members." Thus, Parsons concludes, it is necessary that married women be excluded from full participation in the occupational system, in order that direct competition for prestige not take place between husband and wife. He suggests, therefore, that in spite of certain contrary tendencies, such as increasing educational equality, the segregation of sex roles tends to sharpen in contemporary society.

In the light of the same consideration, Parsons says, "It follows further that parents and dependent children must be equals in class status." If they were not, it would be impossible for family life to retain its intimate and solidary character, and the institution would be destroyed by internal competition for prestige.

The dilemma posed by the total pattern is this: mobility of status is a fundamental norm of the occupational system. This means that class status is freely determined by occupational performance as rationally evaluated. For the reasons just given, however, the class status of parents and their children must be the same. The children of upper-class groups will of course enter the occupational competition on more favorable terms, and their status will not be determined by occupational performance alone. "This," says Parsons, "is the point at which the most obvious limitations on full realization of the ideal of equality of opportunity become evident. But analysis of the problems of social structure involved makes it quite clear that perfect realization of this ideal would be fundamentally incompatible with the existence of a functioning family system."

This theory sets out in sharp relief the essential elements involved in the complex relationship between family institutions and occupational institutions. Like most theories which maintain the inevitability of a status quo, it confers a somewhat inflexible character on the historical sequence which preceded the existing state of affairs. If we assume a hypothetical situation in which perfect equality of opportunity existed, then the intersection of the two systems would, according to the theory, produce some degree of inequality in the next generation. Historically, the contrary has occurred. Starting with almost perfect inequality in the pre-industrial occupational system, we have arrived at a situation in which substantial equality of opportunity exists for large sectors of the population, even though perfect equality is nowhere achieved. Parsons seems to believe that this process has reached an institutional barrier and can go no further:

This is by no means to say that very important adjustments are not possible. Above all, the specially talented youth of the lower-class and lower-income groups can, by special measures, be given opportunities fully commensurate with their abilities. Many such adjustments may well be of great importance, but it is scarcely conceivable that the main lines of the present situation could be altered without consequences fatal to the total of our unique society.[10]

There is an interior contradiction here which leads to another difficulty. The conjugal family is viewed as the product of a gradual and continuous reduction imposed by occupational institutions, and it is suggested that any further reduction would destroy the family entirely. But if the occupational system has become increasingly dominant, then the achievement of social status on an individualized and rationalized basis has become increasingly predominant in the same measure. From this it would follow that the class system in the United States had reached its point of minimum development. This assumption is contradicted by the findings of several dozen studies of class structure, all of which show a more-than-minimum organization of social classes.

Several reasons may be suggested why Parsons' theory, which obviously takes account of the principal elements of the situation, leads us to this untenable conclusion.

In the first place, there is really no fixed rule about the extent to which superior class status will confer an advantage in occupational competition. It cannot be demonstrated, a priori, that it must necessarily convey any advantage at all. As recently as 1900, higher education was effectively limited to the children of upper-middle-class and upper-class families. While perhaps half of those qualified to do superior college work are still excluded on financial or social grounds, there has been a strong, steady tendency toward the removal of such bars, with the consequence that the college population becomes progressively more representative.[11] In this crucial area, the effect of family status upon subsequent occupational competition has been much diminished.

Similarly, bureaucratization tends to reduce the effect of initial status upon the individual's subsequent career. This is due in part to the impersonality of bureaucratic standards and partly to the systematic efforts which are made to repress nepotism. Most important perhaps is the requirement that all candidates for a given kind of advancement enter the system at the same point. It is possible to find bureaucratic systems where superior family status is a neutral factor, and others where by reason of a peculiar variant of class consciousness [12] it is a positive disadvantage. Here again, the effect of family status upon competitive position appears to be declining, although it is by no means negligible.

257

Finally, it cannot be too much stressed that the *mythos* of a culture and the institutions of the corresponding society are not identical. According to the *mythos* summarized by Merton, occupational competition should be rational, continuous, and unlimited. The relevant institutions do not allow it to be any of these. Thus, the incompatibility between the occupational and family systems in operation is not really as sharp as Parsons' theoretical analysis would lead us to suppose.

As we have seen, emotional and affective elements do enter into the work life. The evaluation of workers is always based — at least in part — on the same qualities which figure in the family role, although these may not have the same value for occupational purposes. In many situations, factors irrelevant to functional performance are dominant in the evaluation of performance. A Negro salesman or poet may be identified primarily as the representative of a minority. Even the impersonal evaluation of his efficiency is usually conditioned by the color of his skin. Moreover, rational evaluation of performance is not necessarily alien to the scale of familial values. For a foreman, a teacher, or a private secretary, the quality of personal relations is a major component of efficiency. Then too, there are large sectors of the occupational world where no attempt at rational evaluation is made, either because the method is inapplicable (as in the case of actors) or because individual performance cannot be isolated (as in a railway mail crew) or because acceptance and rejection are frankly based on other grounds (as in politics) or because the individual has a vested right in his function (as in any monopolized activity).

Competition is not continuous either. In any bureaucratic system, the continuity of competition will be limited in two ways: by the imposition of time limits which control the maximum rate of advancement, and by the recognition of terminal positions from which no advancement is ordinarily possible. Where educational and experience requirements are steeply graded, it may happen that the overwhelming majority of all employees occupy positions from which they do not expect to be promoted.

In a less formal way, the same thing is true of almost all middle-class occupations, the exceptions being those which are speculative and hazardous and which do not ordinarily confer secure status. The individual career will be marked by periods of acute competition, especially in early stages, but there will be other periods in which there is no expectation of abrupt change. Moreover, as the earlier discussion of career curves suggested, it is only the most fortunate competitors who are able to maintain upward mobility to the very end of their working lives. In most cases, the peak of the curve is reached long before.

Least of all is competition unlimited. The most superficial examination of the occupational system reveals its division into more or less isolated compartments. Within these, the rules of the game do not usually permit open competition for unlimited status, but restrict the possibilities for any given position in a very definite way.

One further complication should be taken into account. The family system is relatively stable; even in periods of rapid social change, family patterns have considerable continuity from each generation to the next. Even such a drastic readjustment as the twentieth-century increase in divorce appears to be linked to a regular trend. The divorce rate predictions made by Willcox in 1888 [13] were essentially correct for the entire period through 1950. The occupational structure, however, is far less durable. Any contemporary description of it suffers in two ways. In the first place, although the great tendency of industrial society has been *toward* occupational mobility, the special conditions created in the United States by the existence of the frontier allowed a high degree of occupational freedom at the very beginning of our industrial history, which was later withdrawn with the closing of the frontier and the stabilization of the ratio between population and resources. Thus, it is always a little difficult to determine whether we are rushing headlong toward an egalitarian society of technicians, or toward a society made up of almost unchangeable castes.

Another problem of description is created by the fluctuations of the business cycle. These have become progressively more violent for nearly a century and a half, culminating in the unprecedented depression of the thirties and the unprecedented prosperity of the forties. There is hardly any essential identity between the occupational system as it might have been described in 1933 and the system as it appeared twenty years later. The first of these eras was marked by downward mobility on a huge scale and by the collapse or depreciation of conventional controls, including the controlling ideologies. The second was characterized by a level of economic security never before achieved in any nation, widespread upward mobility, and, at the same time, the concentration of economic power on a scale not previously known.

With the foregoing qualifications in mind, we may find it pertinent to examine the relation between occupation and family under two major

259

headings: (1) the role of the housewife and (2) the effect of occupational goals and symbols on the raising of children.

THE ROLE OF THE HOUSEWIFE

At the end of 1950, there were 57 million females over 14 years of age in the United States, of whom 16 million were in the labor force and 32 million were engaged in housekeeping, the remainder being in school or unable to work. The long-term trend toward the increasing employment of women has been much exaggerated. As early as 1880, 23 per cent of adult women were working for wages, and between 1880 and 1950, the proportion of women in the labor force increased only from 15.5 to 28.5. We know very little about the changes in the composition of the female labor force over the seventy-year period. It seems certain that a larger proportion of the women employed in 1880 were permanent workers who remained in the labor force from maturity to retirement. By 1950, with a higher proportion married and the virtual disappearance of family employment in mills and factories, the highest incidence of paid employment among the female population was in the age group 18–19: 52 per cent were in the labor force. Thirty-five per cent in the age group 25–34 were employed (this represents most of the childbearing group), and 29 per cent in the age group 55–64.

The paid occupations of women outside the home were considered in the preceding chapter. All of them taken together involve a smaller population than are found in the single occupation of "housewife." Indeed, if we consider keeping house as an occupation, then it is by far the most important occupation, there being now more than four times as many housewives as farmers.[14]

In the normal family type the husband is gainfully employed, the wife keeps house, the children are either at home or in school, and the household includes no relatives, dependents, or servants. Families of this type comprise more than half of the total households, and most of the others are essentially the same except for the departure of the children at maturity, or the loss of one parent by death or divorce.

Keeping house is in many ways the most singular of all occupations, as will be seen from a brief review of its elements.

SELECTIVE QUALIFICATIONS

This occupation is the only one which shows approximately the same distribution of intelligence and of all aptitudes as the general population.

OCCUPATION AND FAMILY

One of the reasons for the widespread maladjustment of housewives may be inferred from the circumstance that the same job requirements are imposed on morons and on women of superior intelligence. There is no age requirement either. Girls of ten years and upwards may be able to keep house competently; and it is frequently done by women in their eighties.

TRAINING

Historically, adolescent girls learned the technics of keeping house by informal apprenticeship with their mothers. In earlier times, the range of such technics was considerably wider and included the details of a number of household industries: dressmaking, preserving, baking, pickling, wine-making, candle-making, upholstery, and pharmacy, among others. Because of the romantic aura which surrounds everything connected with obsolete family institutions, it is quite impossible to determine whether the technical superiority imputed to our grandmothers is real or mythical. In at least two respects, the legend will bear immediate correction. The households of that departed era were larger, and in the middle and upper classes invariably included servants. Thus, there was room for a degree of specialization which is quite impossible for the isolated housewife of today. Secondly, the household industries were never very important in urban families, except under primitive conditions. In other parts of the world, where the household is still large and where fewer productive activities have been transferred to chain stores and factories, it is the servants who are both skilled and specialized, while the mistress of the house is expected to limit her activities to supervision. This is the case in the prosperous classes. For the poor, in Latin America or in the Orient, the problem of housekeeping is simplified by the paucity of house furnishings and the lack of resources for household industry.

The housewife of today still typically owes most of her direct training to her mother, but the extent of this training is sharply limited. Girls are now in school at the ages when such instruction is appropriate, and the school emphasizes a range of extracurricular activities in the specialized teen-age culture which are far away from housework. Consciously and unconsciously, the adolescent girl is engaged in preparation for the crucial competition of the courtship years, which will determine not only her subsequent career, but also the social status which she will assume. It is literally true that in most cases she cannot know in advance the kind of house she will be expected to keep. In the meantime, such formal training

261

as she receives is mostly for the paid occupation which she will follow briefly until marriage, and to which she may return sporadically in later years. High school curriculums and even college curriculums usually include a few courses on cooking and allied matters, but these are essentially meant as symbolic gestures, and are no more likely to train housewives than the shop courses offered to boys under similar conditions are likely to produce skilled carpenters. Full-scale training in home economics or household management is limited to correctional institutions, schools for the retarded, and a few colleges of agriculture.

JOB COMPONENTS

The housekeeping complex in the fullest sense includes a vast range of technics ranging from knitting to interior decorating, and from contraception to topiary gardening — all of which are included in the literature of the trade. There are three activities, however, which essentially define the housewife's job, and these occupy most of her working time: food preparation, cleaning, and child care. Food preparation includes the purchase, storage, preservation, cooking, serving, and clearing of food. Cleaning includes dusting, sweeping, polishing, waxing, straightening, airing, washing, drying, and so forth. Child care involves a general responsibility for the health, comfort, and good behavior of children. The marked variation in work load which characterizes the housewife's career pattern is largely due to changes in the child-care component.

To understand the interrelation of these job components, it may be illuminating to trace the "typical" career pattern of the housewife; we must, of course, recognize that any such construction is highly artificial and merely highlights those problems which develop in sequence.

The housewife's career normally begins at marriage. At this point, the job includes only food preparation and cleaning, which are accomplished under favorable conditions. The household includes only two persons, the equipment is usually new, and the husband is expected to lend his active cooperation. The housewife's job is so light that it can easily be combined with full-time outside employment, and this is done in about three out of five new marriages. This is typically a learning phase, in which the new housewife acquires necessary skills by instruction, trial and error, and study. If she does not have an outside job, she will be tempted to develop her role in an elaborate way, and to set up very high standards which she will not be able to maintain later on.

The second phase begins with the birth of a child, which works a drastic change in the housewife's situation. In the demographically typical case, she herself came from a family of no more than three children, born fairly close together, and therefore had no opportunity to acquire the skills associated with child care by early example. Further, for reasons rather too complex to explore here, the entire pattern of middle-class child-raising is marked by strong anxiety feelings centered on the child. This anxiety can only be held in check if the baby is raised by the most perfected technic available. The mainstay of the housewife's special literature is the provision of timely advice to mothers. The manufacture of clothing, furniture and micellaneous devices for babies is a major industry, and few medical specialties are more profitable than pediatrics. The presence of this elaborate apparatus to prevent or mitigate errors in child-raising technic reassures the housewife, but at the same time strengthens the basis of her anxiety and strengthens the elements of compulsive ritual which are already present. Moreover, the whole complex — like any dynamic culture complex — tends to expand by continually accepting innovations, and each of the activities involved in child care has a tendency to grow increasingly complicated. It is not unusual for the feeding of a very small baby to require more time, effort, and equipment than the feeding of the rest of the household.

The phase of very intensive care ordinarily lasts until the child enters school, somewhere between the age of three and six. There is a tendency for this age to be steadily reduced, but it has probably attained a natural minimum with nursery schools which admit pupils at the age of two. There follows a phase of still intensive care, broken now by the absence of the child for considerable periods. At the age of ten or thereabouts, the child ceases to require extensive help and surveillance in daily routines, and becomes rather similar to an adult in housekeeping requirements.

The period of child care normally lasts between ten and twenty years, and this latter figure is seldom exceeded in families of three children or less. It is characterized by a diminishing work load in the final years. The maximum work load is usually reached when there are two or more children who simultaneously require the very intensive care of infancy. In general, succeeding children require less of the mother's time, because of greater experience, lessened anxiety, and the help offered by older children.

The appearance of the first child changes the occupational role of the mother so completely as to constitute a social emergency. The relatively simple tasks of food preparation and cleaning are increased by those of child care, and it becomes necessary to coordinate the day's work in predetermined sequences, which represents a much higher level of effort than formerly. In addition, the housewife's day is extended around the clock. Even if the number of working hours remains within reasonable limits, this new schedule obliges her to organize leisure in an unfamiliar pattern. Where she had previously enjoyed much greater freedom than her husband in the disposition of her time and energies, she now finds herself with much less. This reversal takes place at the same time as many other emotional readjustments, of which the most significant is the displacement of the wife's predominant emotional attachment from the husband to the child.

The culture provides a number of alternative adaptations. The simplest adjustment occurs where the wife withdraws into the role of housewife, conserving her energy by abandoning other roles and interests (including sexual ones). She may also, or alternately, lower the standards of performance for food preparation and cleaning in order to meet the demands of child care. Indeed, such a reduction almost always occurs in some measure.

A small minority of women revolt against the work schedule and seek outside employment as soon as the child is old enough to be turned over to a relative or servant. A more common pattern, and one increasingly accepted in these days of the forty-hour week, is the recruitment of the husband to take over part of the housewife's duties. Starting with a joint responsibility for the care of the infant, the husband often comes to assume his share of food preparation and cleaning as well. This division is usually abandoned later on; in some cases the husband must purchase his release from housework by providing the appropriate labor-saving devices for his wife. In other cases, the husband continues to participate actively in the responsibilities of his wife's role. This may have the effect of enabling her to resume other forms of social participation including employment, or it may, on the contrary, simply accelerate the occupational crisis which is characteristic of the next phase.

Somewhere between the ages of thirty and fifty (under forty for the woman marrying at the urban median age and having the median number of children) with her youngest child approaching adolescence, the housewife finds that her work load has sharply declined. She may find herself almost without occupation, and unable in most cases to add another occupational function to her work as housewife. The motive to do so is not very strong in the middle-income groups. Family income is likely to be approaching its maximum at this time. There are only a few serious occupations which are freely open to women; most of these require a training which it is either too late to acquire or which has already been half-forgotten. In the lower-income groups, women return to wage-earning jobs in great number. In upper-class circles, they are provided instead with a wide range of substitute activities: self-improvement, welfare, entertainment, civic improvement, and Culture — whose principal function in the social structure is to reinforce existing status divisions. The importance of the organizations developed by upper-class women as occupational substitutes is conspicuous in Middletown, Yankee City, Southerntown, Elmtown, Plainville, and the other lightly camouflaged communities which have been anatomized by social surveys.

In the older pattern of the extended family, this period was merely a short interim, succeeded by the arrangement of the children's marriages, and the assumption of new functions as a grandmother. Today, the intervention of the grandmother is reserved for occasional crises. The functions of the housewife continue to decline in scope and in importance, and she is placed in virtual retirement before her husband has passed the middle of his working life. In the typical case she outlives him, being younger to begin with and having a longer life span besides, so that the role of housewife may keep her in partial idleness for half a century.

This situation is mitigated in several ways. In the normal course of events, crises of various sorts create opportunities for the semiretired housewife to resume the full functions of the role, at least temporarily. The effect of the maturity, marriage, and departure of the children in a middle-income family is often to raise the status of the family considerably, since the same income which formerly supported the complete family is now available to the parents alone. This rise in status may permit a much higher level of community participation than the family has been accustomed to and introduce a number of activities — travel, systematic hobbies, amateur work in the arts — which are often very felicitous occupational substitutes.

Withal, the general situation is highly unfavorable for the housewife in her middle years. In a culture which attaches extreme importance to striving and to individual productivity, the housewife at fifty is typically idle, with no economic need for employment but with a pressing psychological need to justify herself. At the least, she is constrained to give an appearance of difficulty to a job which has long since ceased to require serious attention or effort. Generally speaking, this group of women, with their unused energy transposed in various neurotic themes, are the most conspicuously maladjusted segment of the population.

OCCUPATIONAL INSTITUTIONS

By its informality, its irrationality, and its cultural importance, the whole situation of the housewife stands in violent contrast to the rest of the occupational system. With the passage of time, housewives have come to be the only large group in the population engaged in the same activity, and their work and working conditions have become ever more the same with urbanization and with the diffusion of middle-class values. On the technical side, the transfer of household industries to outside agencies, the reduction of the housekeeping arts to a few essential technics, the distribution of identical household machinery everywhere in the country, and above all, the development of the communications network focused on the housewife as consumer and principal domestic purchaser, all these have created an occupational culture of remarkable uniformity in which not only the technics but the values are effectively standardized. This identity of métier transcends class lines and regional boundaries. It is very different from the specialization which distributes the rest of the adult population into partially insulated compartments.

The system of motivation attached to the work of the housewife bears no resemblance to any other. Considering the whole range of income and status, there is a sense in which it may be said that the remuneration of a housewife is in inverse ratio to the effort demanded of her. Obviously, it is easier to keep house under conditions of affluence, but the matter is more specific than that. The higher the family's status, the fewer, in general, the children, and the more assistance will be provided to the wife by way of paid help and labor-saving devices. Moreover, although there have been no studies of the distribution of family income between husband and wife, it is probable that with higher income, a higher proportion is spent by the wife. Because of the orientation of the whole machinery of retail marketing toward women purchasers, the possible expansion of women's demands for goods and services — at a given class level — is much greater than for men. It is a rare banker who spends more than five or six times as much for his clothes as his barber. His wife might easily spend fifty or sixty times as much as the barber's wife.

This circumstance reinforces the mechanism of indirect competition, according to which the wife is expected to maintain pressure on her husband to pursue his occupational advancement without flagging. When the effort is successful, incentives are developed quite impersonally through the medium of a rising family budget. When the husband does not succeed in progressively raising the family's status, the wife's sentiments of frustration are likely to be especially acute in view of the fact that she has the larger stake in the matter but cannot intervene directly. Angell's study of families under the impact of the Depression illustrated very clearly the hostility and conflict which resulted from the breakdown of indirect competition.[15]

Another anomaly in the system of remuneration is the premium attached to inefficiency. This comes about in several ways. Numerous observers have recorded a dichotomization of the feminine role in our culture.[16] There is a recognized contrast between the Glamour Girl and the Good Woman. Neither of these is clearly dominant; indeed one of the principal sources of cultural confusion in the family pattern is the expectation that both parts be played at the same time. Nevertheless, incompetence as a housewife may help sustain the wife's claim to personal attractiveness.

Another way in which inefficiency is often rewarded arises from the circumstance that household technology is highly dynamic. No customary standards are available to determine the appropriate provision of labor-saving devices at any income level, the share of family income devoted to household expenses, or even the amount of housework to be required from the husband. Such allocations are made according to apparent need, so that the inefficient housewife probably receives more favorable consideration in all these respects.

The work load of the housewife is likely to be out of balance at typical stages. The highly efficient worker may well be emotionally harassed by her lack of usefulness when underemployed and by her inability to maintain her standards of performance when overworked. Since high efficiency is usually coupled with strong internal compulsions in our culture, the psychological penalties of efficiency may be quite heavy.

There is another ambivalence inherent in the culture which contributes to the uncertainty of the housewife's role, as it is presently defined. Among the vestiges of the pre-industrial class structure which still influence the evaluation of occupational functions is the special degradation associated with domestic service. This is especially notable in the United States where only the most disadvantaged minorities have been unable to obtain employment in other fields. The household servant is stereotyped as a Negro or as an unassimilated foreigner. Yet, strictly speaking, the economic functions of the housewife are interchangeable with those of the domestic servant, and literal substitution is usually possible. To avoid this menial identification (which is insupportable under the general requirement that the class status of all members of the conjugal family be the same) it is necessary to attach great importance to the difference in emotional quality between the work of the housewife and that of the servant. This device is not entirely successful. The technically sophisticated middle-class housewife continues to be aware of the identity, and to question whether household drudgery (literally, servant's work) is the best occupational expression she can achieve. The contrast between the highly valued activities engaged in by her husband — manipulation of symbols and personal contacts — and her own work becomes increasingly invidious as they ascend the social scale. On the other hand, the emotional aura surrounding housework is so intensified by this manner of regarding it that any rationalization of functions (the establishment of cooperative kitchens in housing projects, for example) is seriously hampered. The most curious consequence is that the housewife who wishes to effect a substitution, by hiring a servant and taking on the outside employment for which she is qualified, is likely to sustain both guilt feelings and criticism from others, in terms of the belief that no real substitution is possible. It seems rather unjust, but the housewife who employs a servant in order to assure her own leisure is not penalized in this way. Her continued presence in the household guarantees the emotional values.

It is impossible to analyze the occupational situation of the housewife without giving careful attention to the place of the domestic servant in the family pattern. While scholars describing the evolution of the modern family discuss with pleasing unanimity the disappearance of the domestic servant, the major studies of occupational trends [17] show that the proportion of servants in the labor force seems to have increased slightly through the last three generations. The explanation appears to be that the typical middle-class family (*middle class* is still used in the sense defined above) of 1870 had at least one domestic servant; that of 1950 does not. But in the interim, the proportion of middle-class families has increased enormously. A very rough index of this increase may be derived from the change in the number of adolescents graduating from high school: from 16,000 in 1870 to 1,199,000 in 1950.[18]

Outside of the United States, and a few other high-wage areas such as Switzerland, the middle-class family is still characterized by the presence of servants. It would appear that the closer the median income of a population approaches the level of minimum subsistence, the greater will be the number of servants. In France and Italy, the family capable of maintaining the housewife at home and not requiring her wages is usually capable of providing her with a servant. In Latin America, even families in which the wife must work can afford servants, if the wife earns more than the very low local minimum. It is not at all unusual for a woman employed as a maid in an upper-class Latin American family to keep a servant of her own at home.

In the advanced industrial countries, a given amount of labor produces more goods with each passing year, but there is no corresponding increase in the production of personal services. The comfortable position of the middle-class family rests essentially upon the enhanced production of goods; its income is not sufficient to purchase large quantities of labor. By the same process, labor becomes too valuable to be casually wasted. Thus, even aside from such supporting factors as the diminishing size of families and of family dwellings, the servantless household is a result of the same industrial progress which raises the general standard of living.

The labor of the housewife is also too valuable to be wasted. The provision of more and more household machinery — washing machines, vacuum cleaners, deep freezers, and so forth — increases her productivity in the technical sense, but, like the parallel process in industry, tends to decrease the personal skill required, and therefore tends to reduce the probability that the job will be satisfying for women who possess more talents than are necessary for semiskilled machine operation.

To this complex problem — with its emotional stresses and its real waste of human resources — there is no ready solution.

THE OCCUPATIONAL SYSTEM AND CHILD-RAISING

The degree to which the family system and the occupational system are effectively segregated is most clearly seen in connection with the occupational initiation of children. In most forms of the extended family, the transition from childhood to adulthood is explicit and ceremonial, but occupational maturity is achieved gradually. The process of initiation begins very early in life. The child is able to observe the work activities of his father, his uncles, and his older brothers as soon as he is able to walk. He imitates them in his play, and is able to assist in minor ways long before any question of skill is involved. Thus, a boy of ten or twelve has years of experience and familiarization behind him. The values and habits of the occupation are assimilated painlessly and formal instruction by an elder completes a training which is already extensive.

As might be expected, the situation is reversed in our own system, where family roles are dependent upon occupational function, rather than vice versa. With the separation of home from place of work, the child has very little opportunity to observe and imitate his father's work. Moreover, with the specialization of occupational functions, work becomes much more difficult for a child to understand. If it has to do with the manipulation of symbols, it has too abstract and passive a character to be comprehensible or even interesting. If it has to do with mechanized production, it cannot be understood without reference to a whole system of complex processes. Moreover, with the fragmentation of labor, the growing child is less able to understand the occupational system as a whole. For the few dozen trades which were the whole technology when Benjamin Franklin's father led him by the hand to observe them, there have been substituted the many thousands of specialties which no child can hope to know in a familiar way. Even for the child of the farmer, the policeman, or the grocer, the world of work is shrouded in mystery.

The situation of girls is generally thought to be more favorable, in that they can observe, mimic, and take part in the household activities which will engage most of them as adults. It is possible for them to assimilate the basic attitudes and some of the skills of housework, which the boys are forced to reject as part of their preparation for man's estate.

A more crucial problem is created by the family's explicit function in our society of preparing its children for upward occupational mobility. This often means that the goals of achievement are set with reference to the parents' own history. The child is expected not only to surpass his parents occupationally, but to accomplish this in just those areas where they were frustrated. Thus, we have the familiar story of the parent with professional or artistic ambitions which are transferred to the careers of his children, and the equally familiar theme of *escape* — from the factory, the mine, or retail business.

It is very difficult to disentangle the specifically occupational elements in this pattern. We may note that in our society the performance of children, from earliest infancy, has some effect upon the status of their parents. There is nothing extraordinary about this phenomenon; it occurs in many societies. In India or China, the bearing of a male child is crucial in securing the rights and privileges of the mother. Its subsequent health, appearance, and conduct add to or detract from her essential status. In the same way, the American family with well-behaved or talented children receives a moderate amount of local recognition, which matters most in the neighborhood circle of the mother, but is mildly gratifying to all concerned. On the other hand, the possibility of losing face through the disgrace of children is less marked in the conjugal family than formerly under the extended family. The conjugal family is mobile in both time and space. A crime, an illegitimate baby, a mental deficiency, no longer form part of a permanent community record as they formerly did. The occupational career of a son is much more clearly separated from that of his father than it would have been in the days of the family enterprise.

It might even be suggested that the occupational outcomes of children's careers now have fewer direct consequences for the parental family than ever before. Strictly speaking, the economic interest of parents in the "success" of their children has been much diminished. At the same time, the symbolic value of their achievements may have been increased.

The matter is too complex to be thoroughly explored here; any detailed consideration would soon lead us far afield from the question of occupational influences. We might usefully consider, instead, the two extreme points of the process by which the newborn infant is assimilated to the adult society: the beginning of infancy and the termination of adolescence.

The introduction of the first child into the household changes the occupation of the mother drastically and, as we have seen, for the worse, in terms of fatigue and working conditions. The father, at the same time, is deprived in a number of ways. His income is no longer sufficient to maintain the same standard of living; he must therefore — except in the unusual case of a family living markedly below its income — either accept a reduction in living standards, or contrive by one means or another to improve his income. Except for the occupationally favored, mobility is significantly reduced by the presence of an infant. The father may be forced to retain an inferior position from which he might otherwise escape, for fear of the consequences of unemployment or even of insecure employment. In general terms, he will be less free to take occupational risks, and his chances of wealth and promotion will be measurably reduced. This disadvantage is supposed to be made up by the greater necessity under which he will henceforth work, but this necessity is itself felt as a coercive and menacing aspect of the social situation.

The curious thing about our family system is that no corresponding economic advantage is gained by the having of children. In traditional family systems, children had a potential value as laborers which began to be realized at the age of eight or nine. In some places — eighteenth-century England or modern Japan — they could be sold for more than the cost of their raising. In any case, a numerous progeny has almost everywhere been the most effective form of insurance against unemployment, disability, and old age. Then too, there were often no technics for avoiding conception without abandoning marital relations. Making the best of this situation implied the reduction of the costs of child-raising to a minimum, in sharp contrast to the present tendency to maximize the cost by insisting on a higher level of medical care, nutrition, clothing, and entertainment for the children than their parents are able to command for themselves.

The having of children appears to be, in large measure, an independent cultural value which competes successfully with the whole ideology of occupational success. Some years ago, it appeared that the median size of the family was declining rapidly, but this trend has disappeared. The number of very large families continues to decline, but so does the proportion of childless families. In certain urban, middle-class, high-income groups, there is a definite return to the pattern of the numerous family with three to six children. This tendency is sufficiently definite to establish that further urbanization and the spread of the middle-class conjugal family will not of themselves lead to any precipitous fall in the birth rate.

If the having of children has become an independent value, it is none-theless in real conflict with those values which sustain the occupational system. For both parents, the occupational disadvantages occasioned by their children may be offset by the complex satisfactions provided by the parental role, or even by the permanent expansion of their daily activities. But in the ordinary case, the occupational disadvantage is never directly offset. Indeed, it may grow heavier with the passage of time; freedom of occupational choice becomes increasingly limited with the appearance of each successive child, and the heaviest direct expense may be incurred during the adolescence of the children rather than in their infancy.

This would appear to be the contribution of the occupational system to the network of organized anxieties which constitute the parent-child relation in our society. The parent is aware of the "sacrifices" he has made in accepting substantial occupational handicaps as the penalty for having children. This realization is one of several reasons for the ambivalence of parents toward their children. Its corollary is the resentment which may be felt by the child when he discovers that his parent's failure to achieve a higher status affects him directly in the ferocious social competition of the adolescent world and in his vocational chances as an adult.

The principal consequence of this anxiety is what Margaret Mead has called "conditional love." [19] The child is made to feel that the emotional support he receives from his parents is provided as a reward for good conduct and performance, and may be withdrawn whenever he ceases to conform to the standards which have been set for him. According to some theorists, this experience develops the habit of pursuing competitive goals and at the same time provides the emotional flexibility which will enable the child, when grown, to endure the insecurities of a modern economy.

This does not quite explain why so much emphasis is placed by parents upon achievement of a quasi-occupational sort — in schoolwork, sports and hobbies, and part-time employment. Fundamentally, the fact remains that the child's occupational future is usually not of paramount interest to the parent. There is the further paradox that while the parent is likely to gain from some slight improvement in his children's status compared to his own, he is likely to sustain an emotional loss if their mobility is great enough to carry them into another social class, and so inhibit subsequent communication.

Arnold Green [20] and others have laid great stress on the projection of parental ambitions into the careers of children. There can be no doubt that this is a familiar cultural theme, yet it hardly seems adequate to account for the powerful stress on achievement in activities related to work which is maintained all the way through childhood and youth. It has been suggested that what this half-playful competition offers to the adults who participate vicariously is a model of the real world with the characteristic inequities removed and with the stakes lowered. The potato race at the nursery school is operated in much closer conformity to the principles of

273

pure competition than the insurance business, and the loser doesn't go home hungry. Thus, the child's world offers the adult a sort of refuge and relaxation from the inconsistent goals by which he lives. This theory is ingenious, but like most explanations of its kind, it can be neither confirmed nor disproved.

If we turn our attention to the part played by the family in occupational placement, we discover a major institutional change which is still taking place in the substitution of impersonal records and formal procedures of certification for personal recommendation and the direct ties of kinship or acquaintance. Throughout human history, nepotism and inheritance have been the normal devices for filling all social positions except the most disadvantageous. The right to cultivate the soil — on whatever terms — has ordinarily been inherited, together with the occupancy of most commercial establishments, down to market stalls. The right to fill an employment has sometimes been inherited, as in the case of the eighteenth-century bureaucracy, or the seventeenth-century craft union. More frequently, it was obtained by purchase; even apprenticeships to the menial trades had to be paid for. Those posts which remained open were the subject of friendly intercession. It is significant that the statutes creating the Military Academy at West Point provided that appointments be filled — in effect — by nepotism, and that most congressmen, in recent years, have chosen to substitute on their own initiative the impersonal procedure of an open examination.

It would be manifestly absurd to deny the continuing importance of nepotism and inheritance as means of distributing social privilege. An examination of the ways in which they function will illustrate, nonetheless, the gradual reduction of the area in which these traditional safeguards of the extended family are effective.

For all professional and technical work, for the public bureaucracies and for most of the fully developed industrial bureaucracies, for most of the older skilled trades and especially for the mechanical specialties, education is the only channel of initiation and either a specific educational requirement, or a minimum level of educational preparation is set. For the remaining employments, education beyond the legal minimum usually confers some advantage, as in farming or retail business.

The unequal ability of the family to provide for the education of its children has become the principal means by which status inequalities are expressed in occupational initiation. It is true, too, that somewhat more than simple family income may be involved. In the older colleges and universities, admission is partly a matter of family lineage. It is not customary to refuse admission to the children or grandchildren of alumni, or to apply uniform scholastic standards to members of minority groups seeking entry. The tendency to preserve the ancient criteria of collegiate acceptability (students at Harvard in the eighteenth century were seated at table according to the "rank" of their families) is even more characteristic of the private preparatory schools, which are frankly engaged in the marketing of class distinctions. However, except in a few odd institutions of learning which combine social prestige with academic incompetence, the systems of grading and evaluating students are more or less incorruptible. Since more rigid standards are applied at the outset to those without family connections, and especially to those with the negative prestige of the wrong race, religion, or region, they tend to be more competent — considered as a group — and to receive more than a proportionate share of honors for intellectual performance. There is even a tendency for the grading system to eliminate a large number of those admitted on the basis of family status, and thus to increase the proportion of "outsiders" during the course of each college generation.

Yet, it is the specific function of colleges of the Ivy League type to recruit candidates for the upper class, and specifically for positions in industrial and commercial oligarchies. State universities and colleges with a local sphere perform the same function for their areas, but with much less specialization, and much less effectively. This recruitment is competitive, but the relevant competition is not in terms of scholastic achievement. Parallel to the official mechanism of evaluation, which confers grades, Phi Beta Kappa keys, and degrees, is the system of student associations — partly embodied in fraternities, eating clubs, and honorary societies, partly a matter of informal understandings. It is by achieving status in this parallel system that the student may gain a privileged occupational position, especially in such fields as banking, brokerage, foreign service, journalism, and the nonbureaucratized branches of manufacturing.

The most important component of status in this parallel system is family position. Personal qualities, athletic reputation, and even scholastic achievement figure with different weightings in the total, but the system is essentially a means of transferring parental status. Where the social prestige of the institution is great, and its academic standards very high, a curious cleavage takes place in the student world between the insiders, for whom the campus is a complex hierarchy, and the outsiders, whose participation is limited to the formal system of courses, public entertainments, and open meetings. This division has never been sharp outside of a few historic institutions, which specialize in status ceremonials. It appears to be weakening everywhere as the whole framework of higher education expands, as scholarships and other financial aids reduce the emphasis on family income in determining eligibility, and as military service tends increasingly to interrupt the continuity of the post-adolescent career. The time is long past when the revolt of student societies against the democratization program of a university president could become an issue in national politics.

Recent studies, especially those of Hollingshead,[21] have emphasized the high school period as the transitional stage between the protected home environment of the child and the merciless occupational world faced by the adult. Parsons sums up the essential features of this "youth culture":

It involves a kind of esoteric culture sharply differentiated from that of adults rather than a stage of approximation to adult behavior. Irresponsibility and a compulsive conformity coupled with a certain peculiar hedonism — the orientation of life to the goal of having a good time — seem to be its primary characteristics. Driving automobiles at excessively high speeds is a good example of the first; insistence on being clothed exactly like everybody else, of the second.

The fundamental relations to the social structure of the family are fairly simple. Our family system places the child in a position where his security depends on an intense emotional relationship to a few people, notably the mother; but at the same time it requires him to break these ties to a large extent in setting up his own independent family, and to do so on the basis of emotional attraction to a marriage partner. Broadly speaking, the element of revolt and the assertion of independence from adults may be interpreted as a means of our young people's achieving this necessary emotional independence of the family of orientation. Since their earlier dependence is so real and intense, drastic measures, as it were, are psychologically necessary in order that they achieve emancipation. At the same time, the need for dependence is very great and cannot be satisfied within the family circle. This need therefore tends to be transferred to the group of their age peers, which thus acquires a compulsive intensity of solidarity . . . [22]

This arrangement has some curious consequences for occupational initiation. It means that occupational interests are almost completely subordinated to the ego motivations and sexual concerns of the teen-age group at just the time when the first occupational decisions are being made.

During the middle years of high school, the decisions on whether to leave high school for a job, or to finish high school, or to seek technical training, or to go on to college are usually taken. At this time too, the direction of occupational interest is supposed to be determined, in a general way. Although the specific vocational choices made are subject to change, they often turn out to be permanent.

The significant effect of the youth culture and its typical involvements is to neutralize these decisions almost completely. In other terms, the adolescent — faced simultaneously with the necessity for adjusting to adult sexual roles and for deciding on a vocational career — is seen to devote most of his attention to the problems which touch his ego and his emotions more immediately. His first steps toward an adult job are taken without excessive concern, and often without much interest.

The interposition of this special culture between childhood and maturity further weakens the primitive continuity of generations from the occupational standpoint. In the typical case, the boy or girl is emotionally isolated from his parents for a considerable time, during which identification with them is consistently rejected. There is in this situation a considerable inducement not to follow the occupation of the father, if that has been in question. Whatever occupational decisions are necessary are likely to be taken without seeking parental approval or in opposition to adult judgment. Finally, the first serious employment is likely to occur toward the end of this vaguely defined period. The family is not invited to participate in the experience, or kept well enough informed to exert much influence upon it.

Needless to say, these are merely tendencies, contradicted in thousands of specific instances. What may reasonably be maintained is that the existence of the youth culture, with its characteristic isolation of adolescents within their own tribal circle, contributes strongly to the discontinuity of occupational experience from one generation to the next.

The inheritance of property or of privilege illustrates further changes which have altered both family and occupational institutions. In former times, all positions except those of simple laborers were tinged with considerations of inheritance. In farming and in the operation of business establishments, the normal mode of acquiring an occupational position was through a family succession. The skilled trades and the liberal professions often involved property inheritance too — a blacksmith shop, a doctor's practice, a law library, a set of machine tools. Besides these, the son of the artisan or the professional received a free apprenticeship, a friendly introduction to his father's colleagues, and a measure of formal assistance. Sometimes the right to practice in a particular locality was inherited directly.

In societies which retain their traditional character, the occupational structure must provide for two situations which arise frequently: that of the fully adult heir who must spend a large part of his maturity waiting for his father's death or retirement and that of the younger son, for whom some other employment must be found. The specific character of peasant societies in modern Europe rests largely upon these two accommodations. Where primogeniture governs, as in most of the northern countries, the stage is set for migrations, which may be seasonal, annual, or permanent, but which all provide alternative work for younger sons and for waiting heirs. Where Roman law prevails and property is divided evenly among the heirs, there is a tendency for the population to be limited by celibacy, late marriage, and birth control, in the effort to check the gradual decline of living standards which results from continual subdivision of farms. In both cases, the details of familial roles, the mutual responsibilities of family members, and even their daily preoccupations will be much tinged by the question of eventual inheritance. Similar considerations apply — if in a less uniform manner — to commercial classes founded on the possession of modest establishments, which nevertheless maintain their proprietors in a situation of comfort and prestige inaccessible to the simple wage worker.

Here too, recent modifications in the social structure have contributed to the discontinuity between generations. With the specialization of occupations, property has ceased to be as closely associated with occupational functions; and at the same time, has become more mobile and more abstract. Except in very wealthy families, whose wealth may be associated with a privileged position in a particular industry or in a local region, the form in which wealth is inherited has ceased to be very important. The inheritance of heirlooms, of family dwellings, of family farms, and of family businesses, is simplified by the easy convertibility of wealth, and the complete separation of the filial and the parental household. It is not uncommon for the retiring farmer to sell the family farm so that his children will be able to set themselves up in farming somewhere else. The inheritance of small retail businesses has become the exception rather than the rule. The heir is unlikely to be in the same trade, and even when he is, will often have established himself in another place, from which there is no reason for him to move.

With the continued exception of the great fortunes, it is possible to trace the emergence of an entirely new pattern of inheritance, under which the parental contribution of property is made at the moment that the children establish their independent household rather than at death. This shift has come about for evident reasons. Society at large no longer defends the right of aged parents to claim maintenance from their active children. At the same time, various factors in the economy have reduced the average age at retirement and extended the period of inactivity which follows. It is no longer expected that the farmer or the shopkeeper will remain active until physically disabled. Yet it is necessary for him to provide for his own support during his old age; his children are not expected to assume the responsibility. It is usually necessary to liquidate his property, and convert it into cash savings or some form of actuarial savings in order to guarantee a standard of living for retirement. Once this has been done, any surplus may be immediately conveyed to the children who are likely to stand in greatest need of assistance soon after marriage. The conventional pattern of inheritance no longer suits the convenience of either generation. The emerging pattern is based upon the discontinuity of occupational experience, which it reinforces in turn.

NOTES

[1] David Mandelbaum, "The Family in India," in *The Family: Its Function and Destiny*, edited by R. N. Anshen (New York: Harper and Brothers, 1949), p. 95.

[2] Trade secrets are easily penetrated with the resources of a modern laboratory; all the secret skills which remain are addressed to a very limited market.

[3] E. Franklin Frazier, *The Negro Family in the United States* (Chicago: University of Chicago Press, 1934).

[4] August B. Hollingshead, "Class Differences in Family Stability," *Annals of the American Academy of Political and Social Science*, vol. 272, November 1950.

[5] See Talcott Parsons, "The Social Structure of the Family," in *The Family: Its Function and Destiny*, edited by R. N. Anshen, pp. 173ff.

[6] *Ibid.*, p. 196.

[7] Margaret Mead, *And Keep Your Powder Dry* (New York: William Morrow & Company, 1942).

[8] Robert K. Merton, "Social Structure and Anomie," in *The Family: Its Function and Destiny*, edited by R. N. Anshen, p. 235.

[9] Parsons, "The Social Structure of the Family," pp. 190–94.

[10] *Ibid.*, p. 196.

[11] See Leila Calhoun Deasy and C. Arnold Anderson, "Selectivity in the University: A Study of the Influence of Social Status on Enrollment," *Journal of Higher Education*, vol. 24, March 1953.

[12] As Whyte remarked succinctly in his notable article on "The Wives of Manage-

ment," *Fortune,* October 1951: "The Bryn Mawr accent can be absolute death for a [husband's] career in some midwestern corporations."

[13] These are summarized, together with the achieved rates, in W. F. Willcox, *Studies in American Demography* (Ithaca, N.Y.: Cornell University Press, 1940), pp. 343ff.

[14] "Women have always worked and have always made contributions that could be counted as part of the nation's gross national product, if it were so desired. In the past their work was carried on in the home to a greater extent than at present. Baking and other food preparation, the making and washing of clothes, the making of certain home furnishings such as draperies and curtains, and other such production of goods and services can be carried on in either the home or the factory. When carried on in the home, they do not enter into the computation of the gross national product; the persons who carry them on receive no pay and are not counted as 'workers.' When the same services are performed by persons who receive pay, they are counted as part of the gross national product and the persons who perform them are counted as workers.

"Margaret Reid, in discussing the economies of household production, defined household production as '. . . those unpaid activities which are carried on, by and for the members (of the household), which activities might be replaced by market goods, or paid services, if circumstances such as income, market conditions, and personal inclinations, permit the service being delegated to someone outside the household group.'

"The above definition of household production could have been applied to the activities carried on by women during the past decades. If all who carried on such activities had been listed as workers, or 'gainfully occupied,' the proportion of women who could have been designated in the working force possibly would have been as great as that of men, and may have shown little if any change over time." A. J. Jaffe and Charles D. Stewart, *Manpower Resources and Utilization* (New York: John Wiley & Sons, 1951), pp. 163–65.

[15] Robert C. Angell, *The Family Encounters the Depression* (New York: Charles Scribner's Sons, 1936).

[16] See Mirra Komarovsky, "Cultural Contradictions and Sex Roles," *American Journal of Sociology,* vol. 52, November 1946, and Paul Wallin, "Cultural Contradictions and Sex Roles: A Repeat Study," *American Sociological Review,* vol. 15, April 1950.

[17] Alba M. Edwards, *Comparative Occupational Statistics for the United States, 1870–1940* (Washington, D.C.: Bureau of the Census, 1943).

[18] U.S. Office of Education.

[19] Margaret Mead, *op. cit.,* pp. 89–93.

[20] Arnold Green, "The Middle-Class Male Child and Neurosis," *American Sociological Review,* vol. 11, February 1946.

[21] August B. Hollingshead, *Elmtown's Youth* (New York: John Wiley & Sons, 1949).

[22] Parsons, "The Social Structure of the Family," p. 196.

CHAPTER 12

WORKING CONDITIONS

"While, as to wealth, no citizen should be rich enough to be able to buy another, and none poor enough to be forced to sell himself . . ."

JEAN JACQUES ROUSSEAU

THE social consequences of the division of labor are closely related to the rapid and continuous improvement in productivity which has taken place in recent times. This improvement has long been estimated to amount to about 3 per cent compounded annually for the American economy as a whole. It is a familiar fact that there are extreme variations in the improvement of output from one kind of production to another and that these variations have important social consequences. They arise not only from differences in technological development but also from the circumstance that some kinds of labor are much less divisible than others.

Musical composers, as a group, do not increase their production by 3 per cent a year, nor does their capacity increase regularly from small sonatas to long symphonies. Indeed, because arts develop from crafts, the history of a fine art tends to be marked by a diminishing volume of individual productivity. The maximum creative output seems to occur at the point where each art achieves a climactic form but where its working traditions still pertain to the artisan's workshop rather than the artist's studio. No serious artist of the present day has attempted to rival the output of Bach or Titian or Lope de Vega.

Jean Fourastié, whose recent work on mechanization and human welfare represents the first great step in half a century in the study of living standards and their relation to economic progress, points out that since a man's haircut has required about fifteen minutes for the last three centuries, the price of haircuts has remained in a fixed relationship with wages throughout that time, varying between two thirds and three thirds of the hourly wage rate of barbers. The difference, such as it is, depends on the luxury of the establishment.

In contrast, he traces the decline in the labor involved in the production of a mirror of four square meters, from the equivalent of 40,000 man-hours in 1702 to 6900 man-hours in 1845, 1000 man-hours in 1862, 200 man-hours in 1905, and slightly over 100 man-hours today. "Thus," he writes, "one can understand that economic evolution involves the progressive reduction of the price of goods subject to technical progress in comparison with goods whose technical improvement is less or absent. Goods or services which have not benefited from any technical innovations since 1700 must necessarily cost as much (in hourly wage units) today as under Louis XIV." [1]

He goes on to propose that the disparities in living levels among the regions of the world may be attributed to differences in the rate of technical progress, that these will be reflected in the price of commodities, and that the commodities whose production has been subject to the most improvement will show the greatest variations in price (measured in hourly wage units) from one area to another. These expectations appear to be borne out by the facts.

Improvements in living levels must depend ultimately on improvements in production, since in the long run there can be no increase in the consumption of a commodity without an equivalent increase in its production. Although the ownership of large stocks of gold or of an efficient marauding army may for a short time enable a community to consume a good deal more than it produces (or to live on less than it produces if its neighbor has the army), consumption must equal production in the long run within any complete system, and products must be consumed in about the same proportion as they are produced. If half of all productive effort goes into the growing of food, then about half of all wages will be paid for agricultural labor, and about half of all expenditures will be for alimentation.

Any material change in the level of living or the style of life in a community will necessarily involve important occupational redistributions. If automobiles replace horses, there will have to be more garage mechanics and fewer stableboys. If there is a shift from a diet of turnips and rutabagas to butter and cream, there will have to be some shift of population away from turnip-growing and a shift of either population or other resources into dairy farming. If, as has actually happened in the Western world since 1700, cereals are reduced from the major component of all consumption to a small fraction of the food consumed, which in turn is now only a fraction of total consumption, then a major movement of labor takes place from the production of cereals to the production of other commodities like can openers and vocational counseling and electric power.

Scholars are not entirely in agreement as to the changes which have taken place in levels of living. Zimmerman, in the course of a careful review of the early budget studies which appeared in great numbers toward the beginning of the eighteenth century,[2] concludes:

. . . the picture of the economic standard of living in western countries at the end of the seventeenth century looks strangely familiar to us at the present time in spite of the fact that this period was supposed to be one of great misery . . . The general content of consumption seems to have been rather varied as far as diet is concerned, ranging from bread, biscuits, pastry and pudding through lamb, pigs, pork, venison, kid, bacon, and conies to pickles, confectionaries, jellies and sweetmeats. Similar studies by Mandeville in 1718 and Joseph Massie in 1756 corroborate the conception that there was a considerable variation in the items in the consumer's basket. Whereas the common people did not ordinarily consume foreign wines, arrack, rum, brandy, coffee, tea, chocolate or foreign manufactured silks, linen and cotton in large quantities, nevertheless they had their locally made malts, hops, beer, cider, gin, and woolen clothing . . .[3]

Fourastié, however, writes:

The situation of the average man in the traditional epoch of humanity, prior to 1800, might be summed up in the following terms. The purchasing power of the working classes depended essentially on atmospheric conditions (from year to year) and the level of living of a working family by head by day oscillated between a maximum of two and one-half to three pounds of grain in the best years and an exceedingly low minimum, which even well into the eighteenth century, often sank below the level of a pound of bread. To grasp the meaning of this level of living, it is sufficient to remind oneself that aside from all niceties of the division of calories into proteins, carbohydrates and so forth, two and one-half pounds of bread represents 3,000 calories, or almost exactly the average physiological minimum . . . Thus, in economies of the type which prevailed in France and practically speaking, in the entire world, before 1800, the per capita consumption of goods and therefore the average national production, were lower than the physiological minimum. It is essential to remember that under these conditions, consumption, and therefore production, had to be essentially made up of the cereals. In effect, any large scale production of meat was necessarily prevented by the fact that the production of meat requires from five to ten times as much agricultural land as the growing of cereals in order to obtain an equal number of calories . . .[4]

It is probable that Zimmerman overestimates the proportion of the pre-industrial population living above the minimum subsistence level of the urban and rural laborers, and that Fourastié somewhat underestimates the same groups. It is certain, however, that before 1700 the production of cereals represented the major share of the total production even in the richest countries of the world, and that there simply could not have been any ample supply of other commodities to distribute. As late as 1849, one third of the national income of the United States was realized by agriculture. A century later, in 1949, the net value added by agriculture was less than 8 per cent of the national income, although the value of agricultural production was more than twenty times as great. During the same century, the proportion of the labor force engaged in agriculture declined from 64 per cent to about 16 per cent of those gainfully occupied.[5]

Whether or not it can be demonstrated that most of our ancestors sustained life on a diet of local grains, meagerly supplemented by other foods regarded as luxuries, it is certain that this situation prevails in many parts of the world today, and it is said that the average daily ration of the Hindu would cost seven cents in the United States.

This alteration in the patterns of production and consumption means that in advanced economies most human labor is now performed in order to obtain other commodities than food or drink. It represents a profound alteration in the human condition, closely related to the phenomena of aggregation, differentiation, and rationalization, with which our discussion began.

Whether the gain in tangible wealth made possible by these trends is worth the loss in intangible values is a scientifically pointless question, although probably worth raising anyway. Much of what passes for sociological literature consists of sermons of protest against the uprooting of old beliefs and the emancipation of the secularized urban dweller from the tight control of the primordial village community in which most of the men who ever lived have passed their lives. Whether anomie, organized neurosis, and loss of the sense of purpose and rightness in the universe are balanced by the increase of comfort and the multiplication of minor pleasures, is a question whose answer depends on the personality of the critic, or even on his mood. It is unfortunate that skepticism about the advantages of material progress has often turned into doubt about its existence. No account of the modern social scene can be reasonably complete or tolerably accurate if it does not give prominence to the process whereby the modern worker obtains more and more return for less and less effort.

The diminution of effort can be seen at several points. First, in the gradual disappearance of jobs which are very strenuous or especially disagreeable. Any work process requiring the lifting of heavy loads, unaided locomotion over long distances, unusually sustained alertness, exposure to environmental extremes, or conspicuous social abasement, is almost certain to be undergoing mechanization. Increases in mechanical energy used tend to outrun gains in production by a wide margin and to represent the diminution of the effort needed in particular work situations.[6]

There would also appear to be some tendency to rely upon relatively mild forms of authority, and to abandon direct coercion as a means of getting work done. Although behavior in the assembly-line factory may be rigorously controlled, it is done by means of impersonal devices. Slavery, contract servitude, personal apprenticeship, child labor, agricultural peonage, and forced labor of all kinds seem to be inconsistent with mechanization. Slave labor camps are technically, as well as morally, regressive.

The most important way in which effort has been diminished is in the drastic reductions of the working day, week, and year which have taken place in the last half-century. In 1953, the average workweek in manufacturing was just under 40 hours. In 1920, it was ten hours more, and in 1900, fragmentary figures indicate a manufacturing workweek in the neighborhood of 60 hours. This in turn represented a considerable decline from the 11- or 12-hour day and the minimum six-day week which prevailed before the Civil War. In some industries, the decline has been even sharper. The average workweek in the steel industry declined from 66 to 38 hours in the 40 years from 1913 to 1953.[7] The over-all figures are spectacular. The average number of hours worked per week in manufacturing and commerce has decreased somewhat more in the past half-century than it could possibly have decreased throughout prior historic time, since the practical maximum for the workweek over any long period is only about 75 hours. It is equally important to note that the fully employed worker now spends more of his time at leisure than at work.

Of course, the phenomenon is not quite as simple as it may appear. The first factories in the modern sense — the infamous textile factories of England and New England — operated on a work year of 3500 to 4000 hours, ten to twelve hours a day through all the days of the year, with an occasional holiday or a half-Sunday allowed if the machinery could be stopped without difficulty. This schedule developed out of agriculture, where steady work from sunup to sundown was common in many places, although never universal. But a schedule which was harsh in the fields became savagely cruel in the factory. The rhythm of the seasons diversifies the work of the farmer, and the coming of winter gives him a period of relative leisure. Most important, the man who works in a field will, except under the worst slaveries, be somewhat free to dispose of his time, to stop and rest, talk to a neighbor, admire a passing girl, or quench his thirst. There is no such freedom in a cotton mill, and for a hundred years or so after the Industrial Revolution, industrial operators were made to work harder than free men had ever worked before. The factory schedules of 1810 are bloodcurdling — children coming to work at six in the morning, getting fifteen minutes off for lunch, and another fifteen for dinner, released by the closing whistle at 8 P.M. Then, very slowly at first, and later much faster, the curtailment of the workweek began, and its end is by no means in sight.

Although increasing wages and decreasing hours are observed to go hand in hand, they represent forces which tend in opposite directions. Increasing wages are made possible by real increases in production. Decreasing hours represent a diminution of production — a sacrifice of output for leisure. In a sense, leisure has become the most important product in our economy, since it accounts for about 40 per cent of the available labor power. Recent increases in productivity have been taken partly in the form of goods and services, and partly in the form of disposable leisure.

There is a good deal of evidence that the trend toward fewer hours of work is not limited to factory employment. Bureaucratic hours have declined in the same way and at about the same rate. There are strong indications that independent professional workers work fewer hours than formerly, as do artists, detectives, railroad engineers, and sideshow performers. Some of the sharpest changes have taken place in occupations formerly established on a round-the-clock basis; many hospital nurses and sailors, for example, have had their working time reduced by more than half in the last two decades.

It is often alleged that the long working day represents a loss of efficiency, and this is certainly true of callings which demand unusual alertness, like piloting an airplane, or which demand spontaneity, like most of the arts. In some cases, considerations of efficiency may even have had something to do with the reduction of hours, but the argument for the greater efficiency of shorter hours is more often a rationalization after the fact.

It is surprising that the reduction of working time has not been more often discussed as a factor offsetting the stresses and pressures of status competition. This becomes particularly significant as the size of the literate and technically trained groups in the labor force increases. Again, we find ourselves dealing with a fairly unified process, and it may be well to attempt a single restatement.

In an economy which permits technical progress, the continuously advancing division of labor allows output in the production and processing of materials to increase at an accelerating rate. At the same time, the necessity for large-scale organization to maintain a highly ramified division of labor leads to the diversion of more and more labor into functions of communication, record-keeping, and control, which are essential to production but whose productivity cannot be increased at a constant rate and may indeed be totally uncertain. As Thorstein Veblen observed:

The typewriter is, no doubt, a good and serviceable contrivance for the expedition of a voluminous correspondence, but there is also no reasonable doubt but its introduction has appreciably more than doubled the volume of correspondence necessary to carry on a given volume of business, or that it has quadrupled the necessary cost of such correspondence . . . The largest secure result of these various modern contrivances designed to facilitate and abridge travel and communication appears to be an increase of the volume of traffic per unit of outcome, acceleration of the pace and heightening of the tension at which the traffic is carried on, and a consequent increase of nervous disorders and shortening of the effective working life of those engaged in this traffic. But in these matters invention is the mother of necessity, and within the scope of these contrivances for facilitating and abridging labour there is no alternative, and life is not offered on any other terms.[8]

In time, however, these functions too are rationalized and mechanized (as in the introduction of machines to copy typescript or automatic telephone exchanges) and there is a further displacement of workers toward nondivisible services which seem to be incapable of continuous improvements in productivity. These range from psychoanalysis to serving a meal. All of them occasionally develop improvements in technic. Even the barber cited earlier as the performer of an unchanging service is aided by electric clippers. Improvements of this type, however, do not consistently and steadily reduce the amount of time and effort required for a unit of output. Indeed, they are likely to lead to increases in time and effort by raising qualitative standards of performance. Student counseling, for example, usually begins as a casual and easily executed function and becomes more difficult, expensive, and time-consuming with each improvement of technic.

Even if large-scale organization did not sustain the demand for quasi-creative functions of this kind, the increasing productivity of the total system leads to a demand for more nondivisible services in at least three ways: by evolving new auxiliary functions to cope with the machinery of production, by increasing wages and thereby broadening the demand for many kinds of service formerly restricted to a small elite, and by the invention of new forms of human activity. The first might be illustrated by the development of high-speed computers of the Eniac variety and their attendant experts, the second by the increasing predisposition to college attendance on the part of adolescents from low-income families, the third by the rapid growth of television occupations.

Projected into the indefinite future, these trends shape themselves into a kind of science-fiction utopia, in which hydroponic farms and cybernetic factories grind out a stream of scientifically tailored products with automatic zeal and in any quantity desired, while human labor is mostly engaged in creative services. Like many dreams based on the assumption of technical progress, this one is inherently reasonable. The transitions which have taken place in this country since 1890 are in many ways quite as drastic as these would be. The predictions require only the assumption of continued technical progress, which is still tenable in 1954, although it can hardly be taken for granted.

The first hazard is the possibility that weapons of fission or fusion will soon put a final stop to the civilization of machines and great cities. Another possibility is the stultification of technology by economic or political disasters along the lines of the Great Depression or the Third Reich. Finally, and much less precise, are the threats posed by regional inequalities in development. Despite the wide acceptance which has been given to the goal of economic development for backward areas, it is very difficult to say what their full industrialization would imply, and even more difficult to determine whether it is theoretically possible to bring the local economies of the whole world to the same technical level without developing a single planetary culture.[9]

Even with these reservations, the utopia of automatic production is inherently plausible. Indeed, the situation of the United States today, in which poverty has come to mean the absence of status symbols rather than hunger and physical misery, is awesomely favorable when measured against the budgetary experience of previous generations or the contemporary experience of most of the people living on the other continents.

Yet it is unduly simple to imagine that the achievement of permanent prosperity implies a solution to all the problems which arise in human interaction. The institutional forms of the division of labor, as we have seen, are limited in variety. They change slowly and reluctantly. The privileges of guilds, the formalism of bureaucracies, the isolation of transient workers, the jealousy of cliques in the large work group, the intrigues of the cloister and the courthouse, and the contradiction between mobility and security are likely to remain in one form or another as long as human nature is not fundamentally altered. Technology and the material elements of culture can be continuously improved under favorable conditions, and the improvement can be measured in quantitative terms. Social institutions can be perfected by stabilization — a fact recognized by philosophers from Plato to Pogo — but stabilization requires the prohibition of disturbing innovations, including the prohibition of material progress. Most hopeful men feel that social institutions can also be improved through change, but the improvement can hardly ever be measured in quantitative terms It is at best a slow spiral, which presents such problems as the relation between generations, or the maintenance of order, or the coordination of work, in many new lights but forever in the same categories.

NOTES

[1] Jean Fourastié, *Machinisme et Bien-Etre* (Paris: Les Editions de Minuit, 1951), pp. 125ff. See also his *Le Grand Espoir du Vingtième Siècle* (2nd ed.; Paris: Presses Universitaires de France, 1950).

[2] Especially the tracts of Gregory King, Daniel Defoe, Charles D'Avenant, and the Project du Dîxme Royale of Vauban. Both Zimmerman and Fourastié give excellent bibliographies in the works cited above.

[3] C. C. Zimmerman, *Consumption and Standards of Living* (New York: D. Van Nostrand Company, 1936), p. 364.

[4] Fourastié, *Machinisme et Bien-Etre*, p. 35. My translation.

[5] Bureau of the Census, *Historical Statistics of the United States, 1789–1945* (Washington, D.C.: Government Printing Office, 1949), Series A 154–164 and Series D 1–10; and *Statistical Abstract of the United States* (Washington, D.C.: Government Printing Office, 1951), pp. 178 and 263.

[6] Effort, in the sense in which it is used here, should not be confused with the reaction to incentives built into the social framework of a job. The eager junior executive may be driven by excessively sharp incentives and may develop violent psychosomatic symptoms to show his resistance, but the literal demands made upon him are unlikely to require a muscular or neurological output which approaches the physiological maximum.

[7] Bureau of the Census, *Historical Statistics of the United States,* Series D, and *Monthly Labor Review,* June 1953.

[8] Thorstein Veblen, *The Instinct of Workmanship* (New York: The Macmillan Company, 1914), p. 315.

[9] Some observers believe that acceptance of industrialization necessarily implies the acceptance of societal patterns which are dominant in Western industrialized society. See George A. Theodorson, "Acceptance of Industrialization and Its Attendant Consequences for the Social Patterns of Non-Western Societies," *American Sociological Review,* vol. 18, no. 5, October 1953.

APPENDIX, BIBLIOGRAPHY, AND INDEXES

APPENDIX

A BRIEF STATISTICAL DESCRIPTION OF THE AMERICAN LABOR FORCE

ALTHOUGH some information on the economic activities of the population has been collected at each decennial census but one since 1820, the categories have been frequently changed and it is only since 1940 that periodic reports on the labor force have been issued, so that it is not ordinarily possible to analyze long-term trends with much assurance.[1]

The labor force as now defined by the Bureau of Census includes all persons employed for pay or profit, all those who work at least 15 hours a week without pay in a family, farm, or business, employed persons who are absent from work because of vacation, illness, strikes, lockouts, bad weather, or temporary layoff, and all unemployed persons who are looking for work or who would be looking for work except for interfering factors. Persons over 14 outside the labor force fall into three groups: homemakers, students, and others. The "others" include institutional inmates, permanently disabled and retired workers, and persons of leisure.

In May 1953, the population 14 years of age and over was distributed as shown in Table A. Of the 48.4 million adults not in the labor force, 72 per cent were engaged in keeping house and 15 per cent were at school.

The census classification of occupations follows a double scheme: each person is classified both under an occupation and under an industry. As of April 1950, the distribution of the civilian labor force into the occupational categories was as shown in Table B.

Like all occupational distributions taken at a given moment in time, the foregoing figures reflect both long-term trends and short-term fluctuations. The distribution in 1950 was subject to the influence of the cold war, a decade of full employment, high marriage and birth rates, and a variety of other short-term factors. In general, the effect of full employment is to exaggerate the effects of aggregation, differentiation, and rationalization. Unemployment has the contrary effect and encourages regression to earlier types of occupational distribution, as when hand labor is substituted for machinery in the construction of public works, or the supply of domestic servants increases.

Even without background information and closer analysis of the occupational classification, some interesting conclusions may be drawn from Table B. It will be noted that farmers, farm managers, farm foremen, and farm laborers

---

[1] The principal source for information on occupational trends in the United States is Alba M. Edwards, *Comparative Occupation Statistics for the United States, 1870–1940* (Washington, D.C.: Government Printing Office, 1943).

THE SOCIOLOGY OF WORK

Table A. The American Labor Force, May 1953

Employment Status of Civilians	Number
Civilian noninstitutional population	*111,398,000*
In civilian labor force	62,964,000
Employed	61,658,000
At work	59,676,000
35 hours or more	50,334,000
15–34 hours	7,186,000
1–14 hours	2,156,000
With a job but not at work	1,982,000
Unemployed	1,306,000
Not in the labor force	48,434,000

Source: Adapted from Bureau of the Census, *Current Population Reports*, Series P-57, No. 131

Table B. Functional Distribution of the Civilian Labor Force, April 1950

Major Occupation Group	Number (in Thousands)			Percentage Distribution		
	Total	Male	Female	Total	Male	Female
Total employed	*58,668*	*41,492*	*17,176*	*100.0*	*100.0*	*100.0*
Professional and semiprofessional workers	4,457	2,595	1,862	7.6	6.3	10.8
Farmers and farm managers ...	4,596	4,343	253	7.8	10.5	1.5
Proprietors, managers, and officials, except farm	6,379	5,438	941	10.9	13.1	5.5
Clerical and kindred workers ..	7,657	3,118	4,539	13.1	7.5	26.4
Salesmen and saleswomen	3,887	2,371	1,516	6.6	5.7	8.8
Craftsmen, foremen, and kindred workers	7,500	7,319	181	12.8	17.6	1.1
Operatives and kindred workers	11,930	8,715	3,215	20.3	21.0	18.7
Domestic service workers	1,923	152	1,771	3.3	0.4	10.3
Service workers, except domestic	4,773	2,605	2,168	8.1	6.3	12.6
Farm laborers and foremen ...	2,424	1,761	663	4.1	4.2	3.9
Laborers, except farm and mine	3,142	3,074	68	5.4	7.4	0.4

Source: Adapted from Bureau of the Census, *Current Population Reports*, Series P-57, No. 94.

together form only 11.9 per cent of the labor force, that only one out of five workers is "unskilled" (even on the careless assumption that all service workers can be so characterized), and that almost half of the people in the labor force are not engaged in the direct production of goods. It will also be seen how sharply the occupational distribution of women differs from that of men — the percentages being totally dissimilar except for operatives and farm laborers.

THE GROWTH OF THE LABOR FORCE

In the last half-century, the growth of the labor force has tended to outrun the growth in population, although at a slackening rate (see Table C).

Durand [2] gives two principal explanations: the increasing labor force participation of women, and the decreasing proportion of young children in the population, which is a function both of the diminished birth rate and of the aging of the population. Both of these factors are related to urbanization, and in countries more urbanized than the United States the rate of female employment has long exceeded the American average. As far back as 1881, the proportion of women gainfully employed in Great Britain exceeded the current figure (30.2 per cent) for the United States. The same is true of France as far back as the statistics extend.

On the other hand, the proportion of adult males in the labor force has fallen since 1890. There is a marked tendency for young men to enter the labor force at a later age, and for old men to withdraw from it earlier. Statutory restrictions on child labor and public sentiment against it have virtually terminated the employment of children under 14, except in certain farming areas. The lengthening duration of formal education also defers the entry of both boys and girls into the labor force (see Table D).

At the other end of the working span, the tendency toward earlier retirement is equally marked. The growth of pension, insurance, social security, and other retirement plans has had a marked effect. Involuntary retirement is also important. Maximum hiring ages have in some cases been brought down to age 40 for ordinary industrial employment, and it is virtually impossible for men over 50 to secure new employment in many of the more mobile occupations.[3] It is significant that the census records a steady increase in the proportion of older men who report themselves or are reported as "unable to work." In a survey by the Social Security Board of men receiving old age benefits in 1941 and 1942, only about 5 per cent reported that they stopped working voluntarily while in good health. Yet as Table E shows, more than half the male population is retired by age 65. The further increase of both voluntary and involuntary retirement at all ages over 50 is probable. To a considerable extent, devices for voluntary retirement are adjustments to the social problems which have been created by the decreasing employability of the aged.

PARTICIPATION IN THE LABOR FORCE

Unlike other demographic attributes which are enumerated in population censuses, the employment status of an individual is a relatively variable characteristic. As noted earlier, occupational identification is very stable and definite on some levels and only transitory on others. Much the same is true of participation in the labor force.

The 1940 census for the first time disclosed the work record of all experienced workers for an entire year. Only 52 per cent had worked the full year, and 19 per cent had not worked as much as six months. In a sense 1939 was a median year. Although these figures would have been considerably higher in

---

[2] John D. Durand, *The Labor Force in the United States, 1890–1960* (New York: Social Science Research Council, 1948).

[3] For an excellent summary of the problem of premature retirement see Jaffe and Stewart, pp. 364ff. One of the best empirical studies is Marvin D. Dunnette and Wayne K. Kirchner, "Utilization of Older Employees in Minnesota," *Business News Notes*, University of Minnesota, no. 7, February 1953.

Table C. Labor Force and Population, 1900–1950

Year	Total Population	Labor Force	Percentage of Population
1900	75,995,000	27,640,000	36.4
1920	105,711,000	40,282,000	38.1
1930	122,775,000	47,404,000	38.6
1940	131,669,000	53,299,000	40.5
1950	150,696,000	59,592,000	39.5

Table D. Estimated Number and Percentage of Children from 10 to 15 Years of Age in the Working Force of the United States, 1870–1950

Date	Number in the Working Force (in Thousands)			Percentage of Workers in Age Group 10–15		
	Total	Male	Female	Total	Male	Female
1870	765	565	200	13.2	19.3	7.0
1880	1,118	825	293	16.8	24.4	9.0
1890	1,504	1,095	409	18.1	25.9	10.0
1900	1,750	1,264	486	18.2	26.1	10.2
1910	1,622	1,188	434	15.0	21.7	8.1
1920	1,417	1,058	359	11.3	16.8	5.8
1930	667	461	206	4.7	6.4	2.9
1940	250	196	54	1.8	2.7	0.8
1947	640	470	170	5.0	7.2	2.7
1950	709	528	181	5.3	7.8	2.8

Table E. Working Force Participation Rates for Older Persons in the United States, 1890–1950

Age	Percentage of Population in Working Force						
	1890	1920	1930	1940	1945	1947	1950
Both Sexes							
Total 45 years and over	50.4	50.8	50.1	48.6	54.0	52.1	52.5
45–54 years	55.0	58.7	58.5	59.9	66.8	63.8	65.5
55–64 years	52.1	52.6	52.4	52.5	57.9	57.1	56.7
65 years and over ...	38.7	31.7	30.7	24.6	28.7	27.3	26.8
Male							
Total 45 years and over	87.1	83.4	82.6	78.8	82.2	82.0	77.9
45–54 years	93.9	93.6	93.9	93.7	97.1	95.9	96.1
55–64 years	89.0	86.5	86.6	85.6	87.8	90.4	86.4
65 years and over ...	68.2	55.6	54.0	43.3	49.7	48.4	46.1
Female							
Total 45 years and over	11.1	14.4	15.4	17.7	26.1	23.0	26.5
45–54 years	12.5	17.9	19.7	24.2	36.2	32.3	37.1
55–64 years	11.5	14.4	15.3	17.8	27.2	23.5	27.6
65 years and over ...	7.6	7.3	7.3	6.7	9.3	8.1	9.7

Source: A. J. Jaffe and Charles D. Stewart, *Manpower Resources and Utilization* (New York: John Wiley & Sons, 1951).

the early years of the Depression, and considerably lower in the postwar period, the full-time employment of the full-time labor force is still an unknown and unlikely condition.

Sample surveys by the Bureau of the Census in 1948 and 1949 provide a clearer picture of the extent to which participation in the labor force is temporary, intermittent, or partial. The average number of women employed in 1948 was only 78 per cent of the total number who worked for pay or profit during the year. Among men, the average number working was 92 per cent of the number who worked at some time during the year.

Most of the seasonal fluctuation in the labor force is attributable to the occasional employment of people who are primarily students or housewives, and to the continuous shifting of a sizable population between farm and non-farm work. About 2 million students and some 3 million housewives had paid work experience in 1948. Almost 3 million farm workers also engaged in some other type of paid work during the year. Another numerous group alternated between the operation of an independent business and paid employment.

A survey taken in the first week of May 1953 showed about 9.3 million persons working part time. About 2 million of these worked less than 15 hours in the survey week. There are a variety of factors like illness, bad weather, slack of work, and job turnover which help to account for this partial employment, but the principal factor, at least in times of full employment, is involvement in keeping house or attending school.

THE FUNCTIONAL DISTRIBUTION OF THE LABOR FORCE

There are a variety of ways in which the functional distribution of the labor force can be analyzed to elicit trends. The simplest approach is to compare the relative populations engaged in various industries or occupations over a substantial period of time. It is also theoretically possible to examine the proportions engaged in manual labor and white-collar work, or to compare the group engaged directly in production with those engaged in such auxiliary functions as inspection, record-keeping, selling, advertising, and transportation. There would be considerable interest in an analysis of the changing ratio of subordinates to supervisors, or of the relative size of illicit, illegal, and parasitic occupations, and even in more abstract classifications, such as might divide the labor force into those persons who handle tools and materials, those engaged in manipulating symbols, and those occupied with human relationships. In practice, it is barely possible to compare the major industrial divisions and occupational groups from one period to another, and finer conclusions must rely upon inference or upon the illustrative evidence of a few occupational groups whose history can be traced in some detail. Even such a basic distinction as that between skilled and unskilled manual workers turns out to be a rough approximation obtained by arbitrarily classing certain types of employment into the category which fits some of the persons employed. Where the classification of occupations happens to be relatively simple — as in distinguishing between farming and stenography — the major changes may be determined with relative ease. Where classification offers more complex problems, as in the enumeration of machinists apart from machine-tenders, certain questions must remain unanswered.

Table F shows the trends in occupational changes in major industrial divisions over a fifty-year period. By and large, these were continuous and consistent. The precipitous decline in agriculture and allied occupations was almost precisely compensated by the increases in transportation, clerical service, and public employment. The proportions engaged in manufacturing and domestic and personal service have scarcely varied at all. Professional services have increased at a diminishing rate. The only suggestion of a complex trend is in mining, where the rapid increase in the latter part of the nineteenth century, as the demand for coal and iron accelerated, was followed by a substantial decrease as technological improvements, market instability, and a dearth of new resources restricted employment.

On closer analysis, it appears that these proportions mask almost as many trends as they reveal. During this long period of America's growth to industrial maturity, manufacturing production increased about 2000 per cent [4] and dozens of major industries were born. This development created enormous demands for manpower, but at the same time the mechanization of production and the displacement of human energy from actual production to auxiliary functions kept the manufacturing force from outstripping the growth of the population by any wide margin.

Similarly, the fairly constant proportions of the labor force engaged in domestic and personal service mask a tremendous shift of household functions to public restaurants, laundries, and other commercial service facilities. The

Table F. Changes in the Industrial Distribution of the Labor Force, 1910–1950

Industrial Groupings, 1910	Percentage of Labor Force	Industrial Groupings, 1950	Percentage of Labor Force
Agriculture	37.5	Manufacturing	25.3
Manufacturing and mechanical industries	24.8	Service industries	21.6
		Wholesale and retail trade	18.6
Trade	10.6	Agriculture	12.8
Domestic and personal service	9.7	Transportation, communication, and other public utilities	7.6
Transportation and communication	6.7	Construction	6.2
Professional service	4.1	All other industries	4.7
Clerical occupations	2.5	Mining	1.7
Extraction of minerals	2.4	Industry not reported	1.5
Public service	1.0		
Forestry and fishing	0.7		

surprisingly modest growth of professional services involves an intricate history of increasing demand limited by occupational barriers, the extension of training, and the partial mechanization of some of the professions. In both of these categories, the entrance of women in increasing numbers enabled many

[4] This is based on Table 909, *Statistical Abstract of the United States,* 1950.

occupations to flourish without attracting any substantial number of recruits from other fields.

Table G illustrates the trends in the functional divisions of the labor force from 1910 to 1950. Here the groups are more heterogeneous, and the trends are less explicit. Farm owners and tenants are included among the proprietors; farm laborers are found among the unskilled. It is therefore not surprising that these groups show conspicuous declines. The clerical group is reasonably

Table G. The Functional Distribution of the Labor Force,
1900–1950 (in Percentage)

Kinds of Workers	1910	1920	1930	1940	1950
Professional persons	4.4	5.0	6.1	6.5	7.5
Proprietors, managers, and officials	23.0	22.3	19.9	17.8	16.3
Clerks and kindred workers	10.2	13.8	16.3	17.2	20.2
Skilled workers and foremen	11.7	13.5	12.9	11.7	13.8
Semiskilled workers	14.7	16.1	16.4	21.0	22.4
Unskilled workers	36.0	29.4	28.4	25.9	19.8

homogeneous. Again we note the sharp increase, distinctly accelerating after 1930. The relative stability in the proportions of both skilled and semi-skilled workers is more difficult to interpret. The analysis of trend is complicated by several effects: the decline of some traditional crafts, the corresponding increase in some of the less definite factory crafts, and the upgrading of unskilled labor in many industries to functions which are really semiskilled. These factors tend toward an understatement of the numbers now in each group.

Tables H and I illustrate the essential complexity of the matter. It will be seen that no two of the industrial divisions have similar occupational distributions. Indeed, the contrast among industrial divisions is far more marked than the contrast between 1910 and 1940 in any one division. The danger of assuming that trends in the industrial structure are good indexes of changes in the total occupational structure is rather vividly illustrated by this chart. Note, for example, that the increase in service workers in manufacturing — about which so much has been written —is an almost negligible component in the growth of the service occupations, and that the increase in professional workers in manufacturing far exceeds the increase of professional workers engaged in direct professional services. The variation in occupational and industrial environments which arises from totally different distributions of workers from one industrial division to another can scarcely be exaggerated. Even fields so closely related from the technical standpoint as manufacturing and construction are totally dissimilar with respect to occupational distribution. This dissimilarity may help to explain why managerial technics, labor unions, and informal organizations in these two areas show hardly any resemblance to each other.

Even so elaborate a classification as that shown in Tables H and I falls somewhat short of realistically presenting the kinds of work actually done in

299

Table H. Percentage Distribution of Occupational Groups by Industry in 1910 and 1940

Industry Group	Total		Professional and Semi-professional Workers		Proprietors, Managers, Officials		Clerical and Sales Workers		Craftsmen and Foremen		Operatives		Service Workers		Laborers	
	1910	1940	1910	1940	1910	1940	1910	1940	1910	1940	1910	1940	1910	1940	1910	1940
Total, all industries ...	100.0	100.0	100.0	100.0	100.0	100.0	100.0	100.0	100.0	100.0	100.0	100.0	100.0	100.0	100.0	100.0
Agriculture, forestry, & fishery ...	31.1	19.1	...	0.6	70.5	58.1	0.1	0.2	0.1	0.2	0.0	0.5	...	0.1	54.6	53.2
Mining ...	2.8	2.1	0.4	0.5	0.3	0.4	0.4	0.5	2.0	2.4	16.7	8.5	...	0.1	...	0.0
Construction ...	6.1	4.6	0.0	1.9	2.0	1.3	0.4	0.7	33.2	24.1	0.8	1.9	0.0	0.2	6.7	7.3
Manufacturing ...	20.5	23.8	3.4	9.6	4.1	5.2	12.9	20.1	40.6	40.9	54.7	55.9	0.4	3.0	21.5	24.0
Transportation, communication, & other public utilities ...	8.6	7.0	0.7	2.6	2.4	2.4	13.6	9.9	13.3	10.7	10.3	11.8	1.1	2.0	14.1	7.5
Wholesale & retail trade ...	11.7	16.9	0.1	3.5	16.7	23.0	51.8	38.3	2.6	7.4	4.9	12.4	9.2	16.7	1.9	3.8
Finance, insurance, & real estate ...	1.6	3.3	0.0	0.5	1.1	2.9	10.9	12.8	0.1	0.6	0.0	0.2	2.5	3.3	0.1	0.4
Business & repair services ...	0.8	1.9	...	1.0	0.2	1.2	...	1.5	4.9	9.2	0.9	1.1	0.1	0.5	0.0	0.7
Personal services ...	9.7	9.0	1.3	2.5	0.9	1.4	1.9	1.7	2.2	1.9	11.1	5.6	74.5	54.8	0.5	1.3
Amusement, recreation, & related services ...	0.5	0.9	6.1	3.1	0.4	0.8	0.1	0.7	0.2	0.3	0.1	0.4	0.5	1.8	0.1	0.4
Professional & related services ...	4.7	7.5	87.2	69.1	0.1	0.6	2.2	5.0	0.3	0.9	0.4	1.0	3.6	8.0	0.1	0.4
Government ...	1.9	3.9	0.8	5.1	1.3	2.7	5.7	8.6	0.5	1.4	0.1	0.7	8.1	9.5	0.4	1.0

Source: *Industrial and Occupational Trends in National Employment*, Research Report No. 11, Industrial Research Department, Wharton School of Finance and Commerce, University of Pennsylvania, 1949. Reprinted by permission.

Table I. Percentage Distribution of Industry Groups by Occupation of Employed Workers in 1910 and 1940

Industry Group	Total		Professional and Semi-professional Workers		Proprietors, Managers, Officials		Clerical and Sales Workers		Craftsmen and Foremen		Operatives		Service Workers		Laborers	
	1910	1940	1910	1940	1910	1940	1910	1940	1910	1940	1910	1940	1910	1940	1910	1940
Total, all industries ...	*100.0*	*100.0*	*4.5*	*7.5*	*24.6*	*19.9*	*10.1*	*16.5*	*11.4*	*11.3*	*14.5*	*18.7*	*9.8*	*12.5*	*25.1*	*13.6*
Agriculture, forestry, & fishery	100.0	100.0	...	0.2	55.8	60.8	0.0	0.2	0.1	0.2	0.0	0.5	...	0.1	44.1	38.0
Mining	100.0	100.0	0.7	1.9	2.5	3.4	1.4	3.7	8.4	13.1	87.0	76.9	...	0.8	...	0.2
Construction	100.0	100.0	0.0	3.1	8.1	5.7	0.7	2.7	61.9	58.9	1.9	7.8	0.0	0.4	27.4	21.4
Manufacturing	100.0	100.0	0.7	3.0	4.9	4.4	6.4	14.0	22.7	19.4	38.8	43.9	0.2	1.6	26.3	13.7
Transportation, communication, & other public utilities	100.0	100.0	0.4	2.7	6.8	7.0	16.0	23.3	17.6	17.4	17.2	31.4	1.3	3.6	40.7	14.6
Wholesale & retail trade	100.0	100.0	0.1	1.6	35.0	27.1	44.7	37.4	2.5	4.9	6.1	13.7	7.6	12.3	4.0	3.0
Finance, insurance, & real estate	100.0	100.0	0.1	1.2	16.5	17.6	67.1	64.1	0.4	2.0	0.4	1.0	14.5	12.5	1.0	1.6
Business & repair services	100.0	100.0	...	3.8	6.1	11.9	...	12.8	73.1	53.2	17.4	10.4	1.8	2.9	1.6	5.0
Personal services	100.0	100.0	0.6	2.1	2.4	3.1	1.9	3.0	2.6	2.4	16.5	11.5	74.8	75.8	1.2	2.0
Amusement, recreation, & related services ...	100.0	100.0	56.1	26.1	20.2	17.3	2.4	12.5	3.5	3.7	3.8	9.1	9.1	25.3	4.9	6.0
Professional & related services	100.0	100.0	84.2	69.4	0.7	1.7	4.8	11.0	0.6	1.4	1.3	2.5	7.6	13.3	0.8	0.7
Government	100.0	100.0	1.8	9.7	16.3	13.4	30.6	35.9	2.8	4.1	0.6	3.2	42.2	30.1	5.7	3.5

Source: *Industrial and Occupational Trends in National Employment*, Research Report No. 11, Industrial Research Department, Wharton School of Finance and Commerce, University of Pennsylvania, 1949. Reprinted by permission.

each section of the economy. There have been a number of efforts to develop functional classifications which would get at the matter more directly. A step in this direction was achieved by Bingham, who classified occupations into six occupational groups as follows:

1. *Primary production* of raw materials, as in agriculture, mining, lumbering, and fishing.

2. *Processing,* or converting raw materials into tools, clothing, food, and consumption goods.

3. *Transporting* raw and finished products from where they originate to the ultimate consumer.

4. *Trading* or merchandising and financing the exchange of goods.

5. *Administering* and managing the enterprises concerned with these functions.

6. *Serving,* in functions other than the above, consumers' personal needs, as for health, education, religion, recreation, and other forms of professional and personal service.

The changes in these functional groups over the same period of 1910 to 1940 have been striking. While primary production and processing now occupy proportionately fewer workers than in 1910, transportation, service, and trading have outrun the growth of population, and the "administrative" population has grown even faster than the volume of goods produced.

Occasional attempts have also been made to demonstrate the upgrading of the entire population in terms of skill and training. To the extent that increasing formal education, and the disappearance of most of the jobs calling for simple muscular effort, are involved in this sort of upgrading, there can be no doubt of a general trend. To demonstrate such a trend in detail on the higher occupational levels requires a finer precision in occupational analysis than has yet been achieved on a national basis. It might be supposed a priori that the tendency toward continued differentiation would not only reduce the number of persons in unskilled occupations, but also destroy some of the traditional clusters of skills associated with undifferentiated crafts, and this appears to be the case. There is a good deal of evidence to suggest a migration out of most of the older skilled trades, at the same time that the population of the least skillful occupational groups has been steadily depleted.

BIBLIOGRAPHY

Chapter 1. The Assignment of Work

Alpert, Harry. *Emile Durkheim and His Sociology*. Studies in History, Economics, and Public Law, No. 445. New York: Columbia University Press, 1939.

Becker, Howard. "Constructive Typology," in *Contemporary Social Theory*, edited by H. E. Barnes and H. Becker. New York: Appleton-Century, 1940.

Buxton, L. H. Dudley. *Primitive Labor*. London: Methuen & Co., 1924.

Carr-Saunders, A. M., and P. A. Wilson. *The Professions*. Oxford: The Clarendon Press, 1933.

Davis, Kingsley, and Wilbert Moore. "Some Principles of Stratification," *American Sociological Review*, vol. 10, no. 2 (April 1945).

Dawson, Carl A., and Warner E. Gettys. *An Introduction to Sociology*. 3rd edition. New York: The Ronald Press, 1948. Chapter 17.

Firth, Raymond. *Primitive Economics of the New Zealand Maori*. New York: E. P. Dutton & Co., 1929.

Firth, Raymond. *Primitive Polynesian Economy*. London: George Routledge & Sons, 1939.

Firth, Raymond. *We, the Tikopia*. London: George Allen & Unwin, 1936.

Gervasi, Frank. *Big Government: The Meaning and Purpose of the Hoover Commission Report*. New York: Whittlesey House, 1949.

Gurvitch, Georges, editor. *Industrialisation et Technocratie: Recueil de la Première Semaine Sociologique*. Paris: Librairie Armand Colin, 1949.

Herbertson, A. J., and F. D. Herbertson. *Man and His Work: An Introduction to Human Geography*. 2nd edition. London: Black, 1902.

Herskovitz, Melville J., *Economic Anthropology*. New York: Alfred A. Knopf, 1952.

Hiller, E. T. *Social Relations and Structures: A Study in Principles of Sociology*. New York: Harper and Brothers, 1947.

Hobhouse, L. T., G. C. Wheeler, and M. Ginsberg. *The Material Culture and Social Institutions of the Simpler Peoples: An Essay in Correlation*. London: Chapman & Hall, 1930.

Malinowski, Bronislaw. *Argonauts of the Western Pacific: An Account of Native Enterprise and Adventures in the Archipelagoes of Melanesian New Guinea*. London: George Routledge & Sons, 1932.

Moore, Wilbert E. *Industrialization and Labor: Social Aspects of Economic Development*. Ithaca, N.Y.: Cornell University Press, 1951.

Murdock, George P. *Our Primitive Contemporaries*. New York: The Macmillan Company, 1926.

North, Cecil Clare. *Social Differentiation*. Chapel Hill, N.C.: University of North Carolina Press, 1926.

OSS Assessment Staff. *Assessment of Men*. New York: Rinehart & Company, 1948.

Ramos, Guerreiro. *A Sociologia Industrial: Formação, Tendencias Atuais*. Rio de Janeiro: Published privately, 1952.

Redfield, Robert. *The Folk Culture of Yucatan*. Chicago: University of Chicago Press, 1941.

Renard, G. *Life and Work in Prehistoric Times*. Translated by R. T. Clark. New York: Alfred A. Knopf, 1929.

Renard, G., and G. Weulersse. *Life and Work in Modern Europe*. New York: Alfred A. Knopf, 1926.

Roethlisberger, F. J., and William J. Dickson, assisted by Harold A. Wright. *Management and the Worker*. Cambridge, Mass.: Harvard University Press, 1950.

Salz, Arthur. "Occupation," *Encyclopedia of the Social Sciences*, Vol. 11, 1933.

Spackman, William Frederick. *An Analysis of the Occupations of the People* . . . London: published by the author, 1847.

Spykman, Nicholas J. *The Social Theory of Georg Simmel*. Chicago: University of Chicago Press, 1925.

Thompson, Warren S. "It Was Not Always So," in Elmer T. Peterson, editor, *Cities Are Abnormal*. Norman, Okla.: University of Oklahoma Press, 1946.

Thurnwald, Richard. *Economics in Primitive Communities*. London: Oxford University Press, 1932.

Timasheff, N. S. "Business and the Professions in Liberal Fascist and Communist Society," *American Journal of Sociology*, vol. 45, no. 6 (May 1940).

Unwin, George. *The Gilds and Companies of London*. 3rd edition. London: George Allen & Unwin, 1938.

Viljoen, Stephen. *The Economics of Primitive People*. London: P. S. King & Son, 1936.

Viteles, Morris S. *Motivation and Morale in Industry*. New York: W. W. Norton & Company, 1953.

Vuillemin, Jules. *L'Etre et Le Travail*. Paris: Presses Universitaires de France, 1949.

Weber, Max. *Das Antique Judentum*. Vol. III of *Gesammelte Aufsätze zur Religionssoziologie*. Tübingen: Mohr, 1923.

Yang, Martin C. *A Chinese Village: Taitou, Shantung Province*. London: International Library of Sociology and Social Reconstruction, 1947.

Chapter 2. Occupational Status

Anderson, C. Arnold, and Mary Jean Bowman. "A Typology of Societies," *Rural Sociology*, vol. 16, no. 3 (September 1951).

Anderson, W. A. "The Occupational Attitudes of College Men," *Journal of Social Psychology*, vol. 5 (1934).

Beckman, R. O. "A New Scale for Gauging Occupational Rank," *Personnel Journal*, vol. 13 (September 1934).

Baudler, Lucille, and Donald G. Paterson. "Social Status of Women's Occupations," *Occupations*, vol. 26, no. 7 (April 1948).

Bingham, Walter Van Dyke. *Aptitudes and Aptitude Testing*. 12th edition. New York: Published for the National Occupational Conference by Harper and Brothers, 1937.

Bogardus, Emory. "Occupational Distance," *Sociology and Social Research*, vol. 13, no. 1 (September–October 1928).

Centers, Richard. *The Psychology of Social Classes*. Princeton, N.J.: Princeton University Press, 1949.

Centers, Richard. "Social Class, Occupation, and Imputed Belief," *American Journal of Sociology*, vol. 58, no. 6 (May 1953).

Christensen, T. E. "The Dictionary Classification of AGCT Scores for Selected Civilian Occupations," *Occupations*, vol. 25, no. 2 (November 1946).

Clark, Robert E. "Psychoses, Income, and Occupational Prestige," *American Journal of Sociology*, vol. 54, no. 5 (March 1949).

Clark, Robert E. "The Relationship of Schizophrenia to Occupational Income and Occupational Prestige," *American Sociological Review*, vol. 13, no. 3 (June 1948).

Counts, George S. "The Social Status of Occupations: A Problem in Vocational Guidance," *School Review*, vol. 33 (January 1925).

Crafts, Leland W., and others. "The Abilities and Personality Traits of Different Occupational Groups," Chapter XVI in *Recent Experiments in Psychology*. New York: McGraw-Hill Book Company, 1938.

Davis, Edwin W. "Aids to Occupational Research," *Occupations*, vol. 3, no. 6 (March 1935).

Davis, Jerome. "Testing the Social Attitudes of Children in the Government Schools in Russia," *American Journal of Sociology*, vol. 32, no. 6 (May 1927).

Davis, Kingsley. *Human Society*. New York: The Macmillan Company, 1949. Chapter IV, "The Organization of Statuses."

Deeg, Maethel E., and Donald G. Paterson. "Changes in Social Status of Occupations," *Occupations*, vol. 25, no. 4 (January 1947).

Duncan, H. G., and W. L. Duncan. "Attitudes of College Students toward Professions," *Journal of Educational Sociology*, vol. 9 (December 1935).

Edwards, Alba M. *Comparative Occupational Statistics for the United States, 1870–1940*. Washington, D.C.: Government Printing Office, 1943.

Evans, Kenneth, Vernon Hughs, and Logan Wilson. "A Comparison of Occupational Attitudes," *Sociology and Social Research*, vol. 21, no. 2 (November–December 1936).

Fryer, Douglas. "Occupational-Intelligence Standards," *School and Society*, vol. 16 (1922).

Fuson, William M. "Research Note: Occupations of Functional Psychotics," *American Journal of Sociology*, vol. 48, no. 5 (March 1943).

Goodenough, F. L., and J. E. Anderson. *Experimental Child Study*. New York: Century Company, 1931. Revised in 1948 by Katherine Nikolaisen and others; issued in mimeographed form.

Harrell, T. W. and M. S. "Army General Classification Test Scores for Civilian Occupations," *Educational and Psychological Measurement*, vol. 5 (1945).

Hartmann, G. W. "The Relative Social Prestige of Representative Medical Specialties," *Journal of Applied Psychology*, vol. 20 (1936).

Hatch, David L., and Mary A. Hatch. "Criteria of Social Status as Derived from Marriage Announcements in the New York Times," *American Sociological Review*, vol. 12, no. 4 (August 1947).

Hatt, Paul K. "Occupation and Social Stratifications," *American Journal of Sociology*, vol. 55, no. 6 (May 1950).

Kavanaugh, Nelson. "New Terms for Occupational Roles," *Occupations*, vol. 20, no. 4 (January 1942).

Lehman, Harvey C., and Stuart M. Stoke. "Occupational Intelligence in the Army, a Postscript," *American Journal of Sociology*, vol. 36, no. 1 (July 1930).

Lehman, Harvey C., and P. A. Witty. "Further Study of the Social Status of Occupations," *Journal of Educational Sociology*, vol. 5 (1931).

Lorge, Irving, and Ralph Blau. "Broad Occupational Groupings by Intelligence Levels," *Occupations*, vol. 20 (March 1942).

McCormick, Thomas C., and Melvin S. Brooks. "Occupational Birth and Marriage Rates, Wisconsin, 1920–1936," *American Sociological Review*, vol. 6, no. 6 (December 1941).

McMillan, Robert T. "Voting Differentials of Rural Farm and Non-Farm Populations," *Southwestern Journal*, vol. 1, no. 2 (1944).

Menger, C. "The Social Status of Occupations for Women," *Teachers College Record*, vol. 33 (1932).

Murphy, Gardner, Lois Barclay Murphy, and Theodore M. Newcomb. *Experimental Social Psychology: An Interpretation of Research upon the Socialization of the Individual*. Revised edition. New York: Harper and Brothers, 1937.

Pond, M. "Occupations, Intelligence, Age and Schooling," *Personnel Journal,* vol. 11 (1933).

Radcliffe-Brown, A. R. "On the Concept of Function in Social Science," *American Anthropologist,* vol. 37, no. 3 (July–September 1935).

Redmon, Edward J. "Class Stratification in Industry," *Sociology and Social Research,* vol. 33, no. 3 (January–February 1949).

Rodnick, David. "Status Values among Railroad Men," *Social Forces,* vol. 20, no. 1 (October 1941).

Sauvy, Alfred. *Economie et Population.* Volume I in *Théorie Generale de la Population.* Paris: Presses Universitaires de France, 1952.

Sims, V. M. *The Measurement of Socio-Economic Status.* (Thesis, Yale, 1926.) Bloomington, Ill.: Public School Publishing Company, 1928.

Smith, Mapheus. "An Empirical Scale of Prestige Status of Occupations," *American Sociological Review,* vol. 8, no. 2 (April 1943).

Smith, Mapheus. "Occupational Differentials in Physical Status," *American Sociological Review,* vol. 12, no. 1 (February 1948).

Smith, Mapheus. "Proposals for Making a Scale of Status of Occupations," *Sociology and Social Research,* vol. 20, no. 1 (September 1935).

Spengler, Joseph J. "Changes in Income Distribution and Social Stratification: A Note," *American Journal of Sociology,* vol. 54, no. 3 (November 1953).

Stevens, R. B. "The Attitudes of College Women toward Women's Vocations," *Journal of Applied Psychology,* vol. 24 (1940).

Super, Donald. *Appraising Vocational Fitness.* New York: Harper and Brothers, 1949.

Taussig, F. W. *Principles of Economics.* New York: The Macmillan Company, 1939. Volume 2, Chapter 52.

Terman, L. M., editor. *Mental and Physical Traits of a Thousand Gifted Children.* Volume I in *Genetic Studies of Genius.* 2nd edition. Stanford, Calif.: Stanford University Press, 1926.

Tietze, Christopher. "Differential Reproduction in the United States . . . Paternity Rate for Occupational Classes among the Urban White Population," *American Journal of Sociology,* vol. 49, no. 3 (November 1943).

Trabue, Marion R. "Functional Classification of Occupations," *Occupations,* vol. 15, no. 2 (November 1936).

Welch, Maryon K. "The Ranking of Occupations on the Basis of Social Status," *Occupations,* vol. 26, no. 4 (January 1949).

Williams, Robin M., Jr. *American Society: A Sociological Interpretation.* New York: Alfred A. Knopf, 1952.

Yerkes, R. M., editor. "Psychological Examining in the U.S. Army," *Memoirs of the National Academy of Science,* vol. 15 (1921).

Chapter 3. Vertical Mobility

Adams, Stuart. "Regional Differences in Vertical Mobility in a High Status Occupation," *American Sociological Review,* vol. 15, no. 2 (April 1950).

Baudler, Lucille, and Donald G. Paterson. "Social Status of Women's Occupations," *Occupations,* vol. 26, no. 7 (April 1948).

Becker, Howard S. "The Career of the Chicago Public Schoolteacher," *American Journal of Sociology,* vol. 57, no. 5 (March 1952).

Bernard, William S. "Cultural Determinants of Naturalization," *American Sociological Review,* vol. 1, no. 6 (December 1936).

Beynon, Erdmann Doane. "Occupational Succession of Hungarians in Detroit," *American Journal of Sociology,* vol. 39, no. 5 (March 1934).

Bingham, Walter V. "Abilities and Opportunities," *Occupations,* vol. 12, no. 6 (February 1934).

Caldwell, Morris Gilmore. "The Economic Status of Families of Delinquent Boys in Wisconsin," *American Journal of Sociology,* vol. 37, no. 2 (September 1931).

Carr-Saunders, A. M., and D. Caradog Jones. *A Survey of the Social Structure of England and Wales: as Illustrated by Statistics.* 2nd edition. Oxford: The Clarendon Press, 1937.

Centers, Richard. "Occupational Mobility of Urban Occupational Strata," *American Sociological Review,* vol. 13, no. 2 (April 1948).

Chevallier, Gabriel. *Les Héritiers Euffe.* Paris: Presses Universitaires de France, 1945.

Chinoy, Ely. "The Tradition of Opportunity and the Aspirations of Automobile Workers," *American Journal of Sociology,* vol. 57, no. 5 (March 1952).

Davidson, Percy E., and Dewey Anderson. *Occupational Mobility in an American Community.* Stanford, Calif.: Stanford University Press, 1937.

Dublin, Louis I., and Alfred J. Lotka. *The Money Value of a Man.* Revised edition. New York: The Ronald Press, 1946.

Dunnette, Marvin D., and Wayne K. Kirchner. "Utilization of Older Employees in Minnesota," *Business News Notes,* University of Minnesota, no. 7, February 1953.

Form, William H., and Delbert C. Miller. "Occupational Career Pattern as a Sociological Instrument," *American Journal of Sociology,* vol. 54, no. 4 (January 1949).

Form, William H. "Status Stratification in a Planned Community," *American Sociological Review,* vol. 10, no. 5 (October 1945).

Hall, Oswald. "The Informal Organization of the Medical Profession," *Canadian Journal of Economics and Political Science,* vol. 12, no. 1 (February 1946).

Hall, Oswald. "The Stages of a Medical Career," *American Journal of Sociology,* vol. 53, no. 5 (January 1948).

Hall, Oswald. "Types of Medical Careers," *American Journal of Sociology,* vol. 55, no. 3 (November 1949).

Homans, George C. *The Human Group.* New York: Harper and Brothers, 1951.

Lehman, Harvey C. "The Age of Eminent Leaders: Then and Now," *American Journal of Sociology,* vol. 52, no. 4 (January 1947).

LePlay, Pierre Guillaume Frederic. *Les Ouvriers Européens.* 2nd edition. Tours: A. Mame et fils, etc., 1877–79. (Vol. 1, 1879.)

Lewis, Roy, and Angus Maude. *The English Middle Classes.* New York: Alfred A. Knopf, 1950.

Lewis, Sinclair. *Babbitt.* New York: Harcourt, Brace & Company, 1922.

Lynd, Robert S., and Helen M. Lynd. *Middletown.* New York: Harcourt, Brace & Company, 1929.

Macdonald, Margherita, Carson McGuire, and Robert J. Havighurst. "Leisure Activities and the Socio-Economic Status of Children," *American Journal of Sociology,* vol. 54, no. 6 (May 1949).

Miller, Delbert C., and William H. Form. *Industrial Sociology: An Introduction to the Sociology of Work Relations.* New York: Harper and Brothers, 1951.

Mills, C. Wright. "The Middle Classes in Middle-Sized Cities," *American Sociological Review,* vol. 11, no. 5 (October 1946).

Mills, C. Wright. *White Collar: The American Middle Classes.* New York: Oxford University Press, 1951.

Moore, Wilbert E. *Industrial Relations and the Social Order.* New York: The Macmillan Company, 1946.

Mullan, Hugh, M.D. "The Regular Service Myth," *American Journal of Sociology,* vol. 53, no. 4 (January 1948).

O'Grady, John. "The Trade Union — the Old Man," *American Journal of Sociology,* vol. 23, no. 3 (November 1917).

Pancoast, Omar, Jr. *Occupational Mobility*. New York: Columbia University Press, 1941.

President's Commission on Higher Education. *Higher Education for American Democracy*. New York: Harper and Brothers, 1947.

Reymert, Martin L., and John Frings. "Children's Intelligence in Relation to Occupation of Father," *American Journal of Sociology*, vol. 41, no. 3 (November 1936).

Rogoff, Natalie. "Recent Trends in Occupational Mobility." Unpublished Ph.D. thesis, University of Chicago Libraries, 1950.

Schneider, Joseph. "The Definition of Eminence and the Social Origins of Famous English Men of Genius," *American Sociological Review*, vol. 3, no. 6 (December 1938).

Schneider, Joseph. "Social Origins and Fame: The United States and England," *American Sociological Review*, vol. 10, no. 1 (February 1945).

Smith, Mapheus. "University Student Intelligence and Occupation of Father," *American Sociological Review*, vol. 7, no. 6 (December 1942).

Sorokin, Pitirim A. *Social Mobility*. New York: Harper and Brothers, 1927.

Sorokin, Pitirim A. *Society, Culture and Personality: Their Structure and Dynamics*. New York: Harper and Brothers, 1947.

Terman, Lewis M., editor. *Mental and Physical Traits of a Thousand Gifted Children*. Volume I in *Genetic Studies of Genius*. 2nd edition. Stanford, Calif.: Stanford University Press, 1926.

Terman, Lewis M., and others. *The Gifted Child Grows Up*. Volume IV in *Genetic Studies of Genius*. Stanford, Calif.: Stanford University Press, 1947.

Thorndike, Edward L., and others. *Prediction of Vocational Success*. New York: The Commonwealth Fund, 1934.

Visher, Stephen S. "Environmental Backgrounds of Leading American Scientists," *American Sociological Review*, vol. 13, no. 1 (February 1948).

Visher, Stephen S. "Occupations as Shown in Who's Who," *American Journal of Sociology*, vol. 30, no. 5 (March 1925).

Warner, W. Lloyd, Robert J. Havighurst, and Martin B. Loeb. *Who Shall Be Educated?* New York: Harper and Brothers, 1944.

Wilson, Logan. *The Academic Man: A Study in the Sociology of a Profession*. New York: Oxford University Press, 1942.

Winston, Sanford. "Bio-Social Characteristics of American Inventors," *American Sociological Review*, vol. 2, no. 6 (December 1937).

Wolfle, Dael. "Intellectual Resources," *Scientific American*, vol. 185, no. 3 (September 1951).

Chapter 4. Other Mobilities

Abbott, E. "Women in Industry: The Manufacture of Boots and Shoes," *American Journal of Sociology*, vol. 15, no. 3 (November 1909).

Anderson, Nels. *The Hobo: The Sociology of the Homeless Man*. Chicago: University of Chicago Press, 1923.

Anderson, Nels. *Men on the Move*. Chicago: University of Chicago Press, 1940.

Archibald, Katherine. *Wartime Shipyard: A Study in Social Disunity*. Berkeley, Calif.: University of California Press, 1947.

Becker, Howard S. "Some Contingencies of the Professional Dance Musician's Career," *Human Organization*, vol. 12, no. 1, Spring 1953.

Bureau of Labor Statistics, *Handbook of Labor Statistics*. Washington, D.C.: Government Printing Office, 1950.

Caplow, Theodore. "Transiency as a Cultural Pattern," *American Sociological Review*, vol. 5, no. 5 (October 1940).

Cottrell, W. Fred. *The Railroader*. Stanford, Calif.: Stanford University Press, 1940.

Davidson, Percy E., and H. Dewey Anderson. *Occupational Mobility in an American Community*. Stanford, Calif.: Stanford University Press, 1937.

Dinkel, Robert. "Factors Underlying the Location of Physicians within Indiana," *American Sociological Review*, vol. 11, no. 1 (February 1946).

Federal Writers' Project. *These Are Our Lives*. Chapel Hill, N.C.: University of North Carolina Press, 1939.

Freedman, Ronald, and Amos Hawley. "Education and Occupation of Migrants in the Depression," *American Journal of Sociology*, vol. 56, no. 2 (September 1950).

Freedman, Ronald, and Amos Hawley. "Migration and Occupational Mobility in the Depression," *American Journal of Sociology*, vol. 55, no. 2 (September 1949).

Gillin, John L. "Vagrancy and Begging," *American Journal of Sociology*, vol. 35, no. 3 (November 1929).

Hagood, Margaret, and Louis Ducoff. "Some Measurement and Research Problems Arising from Sociological Aspects of a Full Employment Policy," *American Sociological Review*, vol. 11, no. 5 (October 1946).

Hayner, Norman. "Taming the Lumberjack," *American Sociological Review*, vol. 10, no. 2 (April 1945).

Healey, James C. *Foc's'le and Glory-Hole: A Study of the Merchant Seaman and His Occupation*. New York: Merchant Marine Publishers Association, 1936.

Joy, Arness. "Note on the Changes of Residence of Families of American Business and Professional Men," *American Journal of Sociology*, vol. 33, no. 4 (January 1928).

Katona, George, and James N. Morgan. *Industrial Mobility in Michigan*. Ann Arbor, Mich.: Survey Research Center, 1951.

Lipset, Seymour M., and Reinhard Bendix. "Social Mobility and Occupational Career Patterns," *American Journal of Sociology*, vol. 57, no. 5 (March 1952).

McWilliams, Carey. *Factories in the Field: The Story of Migratory Farm Labor in California*. Boston: Little, Brown & Company, 1939.

Mayo, Elton, and George F. F. Lombard. "Teamwork and Labor Turnover in the Aircraft Industry of Southern California," *Harvard University Business Research Studies*, no. 32 (October 1944).

Nelson, Lowry. "Distribution, Age and Mobility of Minnesota Physicians, 1912–1936," *American Sociological Review*, vol. 7, no. 6 (December 1942).

Noland, E. William. "An Application of Scaling to an Industrial Problem," *American Sociological Review*, vol. 10, no. 5 (October 1945).

Noland, E. William. "Worker Attitudes and Industrial Absenteeism: A Statistical Appraisal," *American Sociological Review*, vol. 10, no. 4 (August 1945).

Ravelstein, E. G. "The Laws of Migration," *Journal of the Royal Statistical Society*, vol. 52 (June 1889).

Rodehaver, Myles W., and Luke M. Smith. "Migration and Occupational Structure: the Clergy," *Social Forces*, vol. 29, no. 4 (May 1951).

Shih, Kuo-Heng. *China Enters the Machine Age: A Study of Labor in Chinese War Industry*. Edited and translated by Hsiao-Tung Fei and Francis L. K. Hsu. Cambridge, Mass.: Harvard University Press, 1944.

Shryock, Henry, Jr., and Hope Tisdale Eldridge. "Internal Migration in Peace and War," *American Sociological Review*, vol. 12, no. 1 (February 1947).

Sorokin, Pitirim A. *Social Mobility*. New York: Harper and Brothers, 1927.

Stouffer, Samuel A. "Intervening Opportunities: A Theory relating Mobility and Distance," *American Sociological Review*, vol. 5, no. 6 (December 1940).

Sutherland, Edwin H., editor. *The Professional Thief, by a Professional Thief*. Chicago: University of Chicago Press, 1937.

Thorndike, Edward L., and others. *Prediction of Vocational Success*. New York: The Commonwealth Fund, 1934.

Veblen, Thorstein. *The Instinct of Workmanship and the State of the Industrial Arts*. New York: The Macmillan Company, 1914.

Whyte, William Foote. *Street Corner Society: The Social Structure of an Italian Slum*. Chicago: University of Chicago Press, 1943.

Chapter 5. Occupational Institutions

Barnard, Chester I. *The Functions of the Executive*. Cambridge, Mass.: Harvard University Press, 1947.

Barnard, Chester I. *Organization and Management: Selected Papers*. Cambridge, Mass.: Harvard University Press, 1948.

Baur, E. Jackson. "The Function of Ceremony in the Advertising Business," *Social Forces*, vol. 27, no. 4 (May 1949).

Caplow, Theodore. "The Criteria of Organizational Success," *Social Forces*, vol. 32, no. 1 (October 1953).

Chamberlain, Neil W. *Management in Motion*. New Haven, Conn.: Labor and Management Center, Yale University, 1950.

Clark, Harold F. *Economic Theory and Correct Occupational Distribution*. New York: Bureau of Publications, Teachers College, Columbia University, 1931.

Douglas, Paul H. "Occupational Versus Proportional Representation," *American Journal of Sociology*, vol. 29, no. 2 (September 1923).

Dubin, Robert. "Decision-Making by Management in Industrial Relations," *American Journal of Sociology*, vol. 54, no. 4 (January 1949).

Dubin, Robert. *Human Relation in Administration*. New York: Prentice-Hall, 1951.

Dublin, Louis I., and Alfred J. Lotka. *The Money Value of a Man*. Revised edition. New York: The Ronald Press, 1946.

Durkheim, Emile. *On the Division of Labor in Society*. Translated by George Simpson. New York: The Macmillan Company, 1933.

Gold, Ray. "Janitors Versus Tenants: A Status-Income Dilemma," *American Journal of Sociology*, vol. 57, no. 5 (March 1952).

Goode, William J., and Irving Fowler. "Incentive Factors in a Low Morale Plant," *American Sociological Review*, vol. 14, no. 5 (October 1949).

Hall, Oswald. "The Stages of a Medical Career," *American Journal of Sociology*, vol. 53, no. 5 (March 1948).

Hastings, E. C., and P. W. Hutson. "State Regulation of Occupational Activity," *Occupations*, vol. 20, no. 4 (January 1942).

Henry, William E. "The Business Executive: The Psychodynamics of a Social Role," *American Journal of Sociology*, vol. 54, no. 4 (January 1949).

Hollingshead, August B. "Behavior Systems as a Field for Research," *American Sociological Review*, vol. 4, no. 6 (December 1939).

Homans, George C. *The Human Group*. New York: Harper and Brothers, 1951.

Hughes, Everett C. "Institutional Office and the Person," *American Journal of Sociology*, vol. 43, no. 3 (November 1937).

Hughes, Everett C. "The Sociological Study of Work: An Editorial Foreword," *American Journal of Sociology*, vol. 57, no. 5 (March 1952).

Mayo, Elton. Foreword to E. J. Roethlisberger, *Management and Morale*. Cambridge, Mass.: Harvard University Press, 1941.

Miller, Delbert C. "The Social Factors of the Work Situation," *American Sociological Review*, vol. 11, no. 3 (June 1946).

Park, R. E. Introduction to Frances R. Donovan, *The Saleslady*. Chicago: University of Chicago Press, 1929.

Pirenne, Henri. *Medieval Cities: Their Origins and the Revival of Trade*. Princeton, N.J.: Princeton University Press, 1925.

Roethlisberger, F. J., and William J. Dickson, assisted by Harold A. Wright. *Management and the Worker.* Cambridge, Mass.: Harvard University Press, 1946.

Roy, Donald. "Quota Restriction and Goldbricking in a Machine Shop," *American Journal of Sociology,* vol. 57, no. 5 (March 1952).

Stewart, Cecil. *A Prospect of Cities.* New York: Longmans, Green & Company, 1953.

Thorner, Isidor. "Pharmacy: the Functional Significance of an Institutional Pattern," *Social Forces,* vol. 20, no. 3 (March 1942).

Turner, Ralph H. "The Navy Disbursing Officer as a Bureaucrat," *American Sociological Review,* vol. 12, no. 3 (June 1947).

Chapter 6. Occupational Ideologies

Anderson, Dewey, and Percy E. Davidson. *Ballots and the Democratic Class Struggle: A Study in the Background of Political Education.* Stanford, Calif.: Stanford University Press, 1943.

Arnold, Thurman W. *The Folklore of Capitalism.* New Haven, Conn.: Yale University Press, 1937.

Bardet, Gaston. *Le Nouvel Urbanisme.* Paris: V. Freal, 1948.

Barthuli, Effie F. "Occupational Attitudes of Dentists," *Sociology and Social Research,* vol. 20, no. 6 (July–August 1936).

Bogardus, Emory. "Personality and Occupational Attitudes," *Sociology and Social Research,* vol. 12, no. 1 (September–October 1927).

Briggs, Arthur E. "Social Distance between Lawyers and Doctors," *Sociology and Social Research,* vol. 13, no. 2 (November–December 1928).

Brown, Esther Lucile. *Lawyers and the Promotion of Justice.* New York: Russell Sage Foundation, 1938.

Brown, Esther Lucile. *Social Work as a Profession.* New York: Russell Sage Foundation, 1936.

Carr-Saunders, A. M., and P. A. Wilson. *The Professions.* Oxford: The Clarendon Press, 1933.

Centers, Richard. "The American Class Structure: A Psychological Analysis," in Theodore M. Newcomb and Eugene L. Hartley, editors, *Readings in Social Psychology.* New York: Henry Holt & Company, 1947.

Chapman, Stanley H. "The Minister, Professional Man of the Church," *Social Forces,* vol. 23, no. 2 (December 1944).

Chapple, Eliot D., with the collaboration of Conrad M. Arensberg. "Measuring Human Relations: An Introduction to the Study of the Interaction of Individuals," *Genetic Psychology Monographs,* vol. 22, no. 1 (February 1940).

Clark, Harold F. *Life Earnings in Selected Occupations in the United States.* New York: Harper and Brothers, 1937.

Dalton, Melville. "The Industrial Rate-Buster: A Characterization," *Applied Anthropology,* vol. 7, no. 9 (Winter 1948).

Davis, Allison. "The Motivation of the Underprivileged Worker," *ETC* (A Review of General Semantics), vol. 3, no. 4 (Summer 1946).

DeMan, Henri. *Joy in Work.* Translated by Eden and Cedar Paul from *Der Kampf um die Arbeitsfreude* (Jena, 1927). New York: Henry Holt & Company, 1929.

Desenberg, Bernard N. "Occupational Attitudes of Taxi Dancers," *Sociology and Social Research,* vol. 25, no. 3 (January–February 1941).

Dickson, M. G. "The Factory Worker's Philosophy," *Sociological Review* (British), vol. 28, no. 3 (July 1936).

Fiske, E. R. *The Veterans' Best Opportunities.* New York: Duell, Sloan & Pearce, 1946.

Gilmore, Harlan W. "Five Generations of a Begging Family," *American Journal of Sociology,* vol. 37, no. 5 (March 1932).

Gilmore, Harlan W. "Types of Begging," *Sociology and Social Research,* vol. 14, no. 6 (July–August 1930).

Henderson, Charles. "Business Men and Social Theorists," *American Journal of Sociology,* vol. 1, no. 4 (January 1896).

Hoppock, Robert. *Job Satisfaction.* New York: Harper and Brothers, 1935.

Jones, Alfred Winslow. *Life, Liberty, and Property.* Philadelphia: J. B. Lippincott Company, 1941.

Kriesberg, Louis. "The Retail Furrier: Concepts of Security and Success," *American Journal of Sociology,* vol. 57, no. 5 (March 1952).

Komarovsky, Mirra. "The Voluntary Associations of Urban Dwellers," *American Sociological Review,* vol. 2, no. 6 (December 1946).

Langerock, Hubert. "Professionalism: A Study in Professional Deformation," *American Journal of Sociology,* vol. 21, no. 1 (July 1915).

McMillan, Robert T. "Voting Differentials of Rural Farm and Non-Farm Populations," *Southwestern Journal,* vol. 1, no. 2, 1944.

Marquand, John P. *Point of No Return.* New York: Bantam Books, 1952.

Moore, Arthur. *The Farmer and the Rest of Us.* Boston: Little, Brown & Company, 1945.

Nimkoff, Meyer F. "Personality Problems of Beggars," *Sociology and Social Research,* vol. 12, no. 5 (May–June 1928).

Park, Robert. "Industrial Fatigue and Group Morale," *American Journal of Sociology,* vol. 40, no. 3 (November 1934).

Roethlisberger, F. J. *Management and Morale.* Cambridge, Mass.: Harvard University Press, 1941.

Rosten, Leo C. *Hollywood: The Movie Colony, the Movie Makers.* New York: Harcourt, Brace & Company, 1941.

Rosten, Leo C. *The Washington Correspondents.* New York: Harcourt, Brace & Company, 1937.

Roucek, Joseph S. "Social Attitudes of the Prison Warden," *Sociology and Social Research,* vol. 21 (September–October 1936).

Roucek, Joseph S. "The Sociology of the Diplomat," *Social Science,* vol. 14, no. 4 (October 1939).

Roucek, Joseph S. "The Sociology of the Nurse," *Sociology and Social Research,* vol. 24, no. 6 (July–August 1940).

Roucek, Joseph S. "The Sociology of the Prison Guard," *Sociology and Social Research,* vol. 20, no. 2 (November–December 1935).

Sheppard, Harold L. "The Treatment of Unionism in 'Managerial Sociology'," *American Sociological Review,* vol. 14, no. 2 (April 1949). See also his unpublished doctoral dissertation, "Managerial Sociology: A Critical Commentary on the Mayo Influence in Industrial Sociology," University of Wisconsin, 1948.

Sutherland, Edwin H., editor. *The Professional Thief, by a Professional Thief.* Chicago: University of Chicago Press, 1937.

Tilgher, Adriano. *Work: What It Has Meant to Men through the Ages.* Translated by Dorothy Canfield Fisher from *Homo Faber.* New York: Harcourt, Brace & Company, 1930.

Warren, Roland L. "The Naval Reserve Officer: A Study in Assimilation," *American Sociological Review,* vol. 11, no. 2 (April 1946).

Weinberg, S. Kirson, and Henry Arond. "The Occupational Culture of the Boxer," *American Journal of Sociology,* vol. 57, no. 5 (March 1952).

Whyte, William Foote. *Human Relations in the Restaurant Industry.* New York: McGraw-Hill Book Company, 1948.

Whyte, William Foote. "The Social Structure of the Restaurant," *American Journal of Sociology,* vol. 54, no. 4 (January 1949).

Wilson, Logan. *The Academic Man: A Study in the Sociology of a Profession.* New York: Oxford University Press, 1942.

BIBLIOGRAPHY

Chapter 7. Sociology of the Labor Market

Anderson, C. Arnold. "Soviet Russia and the Nature of Society," *Southwestern Social Science Quarterly,* vol. 33, no. 2 (September 1952).

Barnard, Chester I. *Functions of the Executive.* Cambridge, Mass.: Harvard University Press, 1938.

Barnard, Chester I. "Functions and Pathology of Status Systems in Formal Organizations," in W. F. Whyte, editor, *Industry and Society.* New York: McGraw-Hill Book Company, 1946.

Bendix, Reinhard. "Bureaucracy: The Problem and Its Setting," *American Sociological Review,* vol. 12, no. 5 (October 1947).

Bendix, Reinhard. *Higher Civil Servants in American Society.* Boulder: University of Colorado Studies, 1949.

Clark, Harold F. *Economic Theory and Correct Occupational Distribution.* New York: Bureau of Publications, Teachers College, Columbia University, 1931.

Clark, Harold F. *Life Earnings in Selected Occupations in the United States.* New York: Harper and Brothers, 1937.

Colean, Miles. *American Housing: Problems and Prospects.* New York: The Twentieth Century Fund, 1944.

Committee on Labor Market Research of the Social Science Research Council, *Memorandum on University Research Programs in the Field of Labor,* Washington, D.C.: Social Science Research Council, 1949.

Commons, John R. *Myself.* New York: The Macmillan Company, 1934.

Davis, Kingsley. "The Sociology of Prostitution," *American Sociological Review,* vol. 2, no. 5 (October 1937).

Dewors, Richard E. "Custom and Contract; a Functional Analysis of the Wage System in the Atlantic Fisheries," *American Sociological Review,* vol. 13, no. 1 (February 1948).

Dorcus, R. M., and M. H. Jones. *Handbook of Employee Selection.* New York: McGraw-Hill Book Company, 1950.

Dreyfuss, Carl. *Occupation and Ideology of the Salaried Employee.* Translated by Eva Abramovitch. Vol. 1. Mimeographed. New York: WPA and Department of Social Science. Columbia University, 1938.

Dubin, Robert. *Human Relation in Administration.* New York: Prentice-Hall, 1951.

Frazier, Franklin. "Occupational Classes among Negroes in Cities," *American Journal of Sociology,* vol. 35, no. 4 (January 1930).

Gardner, Burleigh B. *Human Relations in Industry.* Homewood, Ill.: Richard D. Irwin, 1945.

Ginzberg, Eli. *The Labor Leader.* New York: The Macmillan Company, 1948.

Hall, O. Milton. "How Occupational Trends Are Studied," *Occupations,* vol. 12, no. 6 (February 1934).

Hall, Oswald. "The Informal Organization of the Medical Profession," *Canadian Journal of Economics and Political Science,* vol. 12, no. 1 (February 1946).

Hall, Oswald. "The Stages of a Medical Career," *American Journal of Sociology,* vol. 53, no. 5 (January 1948).

Hall, Oswald. "Types of Medical Careers," *American Journal of Sociology,* vol. 55, no. 3 (November 1949).

Harbison, Frederick H., and Robert Dubin. *Patterns of Union-Management Relations.* Chicago: Science Research Associates, 1947.

Hollingshead, A. B. "Ingroup Membership and Academic Selection," *American Sociological Review,* vol. 3, no. 6 (December 1938).

Hughes, Everett. "The Knitting of Racial Groups in Industry," *American Sociological Review,* vol. 11, no. 5 (October 1946).

Jaques, Elliott. *The Changing Culture of a Factory.* New York: The Dryden Press, 1952.

Katona, George. *Psychological Analysis of Economic Behavior.* New York: McGraw-Hill Book Company, 1951.

Kotschnig, Walter M. *Unemployment in the Learned Professions: An International Study of Occupational and Educational Planning.* London: Oxford University Press, 1937.

Lee, Rose Hum. "Occupational Invasion, Succession, and Accommodation of the Chinese of Butte, Montana," *American Journal of Sociology,* vol. 55, no. 1 (July 1949).

Long, C. D. "Professors' Salaries and Inflation," *Bulletin of the American Association of University Professors,* vol. 38, no. 4 (Winter 1952–53).

Malthus, Thomas Robert. *First Essay on Population.* London, 1798.

Merton, Robert K. "Role of the Intellectual in Public Bureaucracy," *Social Forces,* vol. 23, no. 4 (May 1945).

Merton, Robert K., and others. *Reader in Bureaucracy.* Glencoe, Ill.: The Free Press, 1952.

Miller, William. *Men in Business: Essays in the History of Entrepreneurship.* Cambridge, Mass.: Harvard University Press, 1952.

Moore, Wilbert E. *Industrial Relations and the Social Order.* New York: The Macmillan Company, 1946.

Morris, Richard B. *Government and Labor in Early America.* New York: Columbia University Press, 1946.

Neumann, John Von, and Oskar Morganstern. *Theory of Games and Economic Behavior.* Princeton, N.J.: Princeton University Press, 1947.

Odaka, Kunio. "An Iron Workers' Community in Japan: A Study in the Sociology of Industrial Groups," *American Sociological Review,* vol. 15, no. 2 (April 1950).

Parsons, Talcott. *Structure of Social Action.* New York: McGraw-Hill Book Company, 1937.

Pigors, Paul, and Charles A. Myers. *Personnel Administration: a Point of View and a Method.* New York: McGraw-Hill Book Company, 1947.

Reissman, Leonard. "A Study of Role Conceptions in Bureaucracy," *Social Forces,* vol. 27, no. 3 (March 1949).

Sayles, Leonard R., and George Strauss. "Conflicts within the Local Union," *Harvard Business Review,* vol. 30, no. 6 (November–December 1952).

Selznick, Philip. "An Approach to a Theory of Bureaucracy," *American Sociological Review,* vol. 8, no. 1 (February 1943).

Selznick, Philip. "Foundations of the Theory of Organization," *American Sociological Review,* vol. 13, no. 1 (February 1948).

Smith, Adam. *An Inquiry into the Nature and Causes of the Wealth of Nations.* 4th edition. London: A. Strahan and T. Cadell, 1786.

Survey of Current Business: "Incomes of Physicians, Dentists and Lawyers," vol. 32, no. 7, July 1952; "Income of Physicians," vol. 31, no. 7, July 1951; "Income of Lawyers," vol. 29, no. 8, August 1949.

Taussig, F. W. *Principles of Economics.* New York: The Macmillan Company, 1939. Vol. 2.

Tawney, Richard Henry. *The Acquisitive Society.* New York: Harcourt, Brace & Company, 1920.

Vogt, P. L. "Functional Industrial Relationships and the Wage Rate," *American Journal of Sociology,* vol. 19, no. 6 (May 1914).

Warner, W. Lloyd, and J. O. Low. *The Social System of the Modern Factory,* subtitled *The Strike: a Social Analysis.* Vol. IV in Yankee City Series. New Haven, Conn.: Yale University Press, 1947.

Whyte, William Foote, editor. *Industry and Society.* New York: McGraw-Hill Book Company, 1946.

Wilson, Logan, and Harlan Gilmore. "White Employees and Negro Workers," *American Sociological Review,* vol. 8, no. 6 (December 1943).

Yoder, Dale, Donald G. Paterson, Herbert G. Heneman, Jr., and others. *Local Labor Market Research.* Minneapolis: Industrial Relations Center, University of Minnesota, 1948.

Yoder, Dale. *Manpower Economics and Labor Problems.* New York: McGraw-Hill Book Company, 1939.

Chapter 8. The Labor Union as an Occupational Association

Anderson, C. Arnold. "Sociological Elements in Economic Restrictionism," *American Sociological Review,* vol. 9, no. 4 (August 1944).

Archibald, Katherine. *Wartime Shipyard: a Study in Social Disunity.* Berkeley, Calif.: University of California Press, 1947.

Boyle, James E. "The Union Label," *American Journal of Sociology,* vol. 9, no. 1 (July 1903).

Commons, John R. "American Shoemakers, 1648–1895," *Quarterly Journal of Economics,* vol. 24, no. 1 (November 1909).

Dennis, Wayne, and others. *Current Trends in Industrial Psychology.* Pittsburgh, Pa.: University of Pittsburgh Press, 1949.

Fitch, John A. *The Steel Workers.* New York: Charities Publication Committee, 1910. Part of The Pittsburgh Survey, edited by Paul Underwood Kellogg for the Russell Sage Foundation.

Galenson, Walter. *Labor in Norway.* Cambridge, Mass.: Harvard University Press, 1949.

Gouldner, Alvin W. "Attitudes of 'Progressive' Trade Union Leaders," *American Journal of Sociology,* vol. 52, no. 5 (March 1947).

Greer, Thomas H. *American Social Reform Movements: Their Pattern Since 1865.* New York: Prentice-Hall, 1949.

Harbison, Frederick H. "Some Reflections on a Theory of Labor-Management Relations," *Journal of Political Economy,* vol. 54, no. 1 (February 1946).

Harbison, Frederick H., and Robert Dubin. *Patterns of Union-Management Relations.* Chicago: Science Research Associates, 1947.

Hardy, Jack. *The Clothingworkers: A Study of the Conditions and Struggles in the Needle Trades.* New York: International Publishers Co., 1935.

Horack, Frank E. "The Horseshoers' Strike of Philadelphia," *American Journal of Sociology,* vol. 8, no. 3 (November 1902).

Hoxie, Robert F. *Trade Unionism in the United States.* New York: Appleton-Crofts, 1928.

Industrial Relations Center, University of Minnesota. *The Industrial Relations Five-Foot Shelf.* Minneapolis: University of Minnesota Press, 1947.

Kornhauser, William. "The Negro Union Official: A Study of Sponsorship and Control," *American Journal of Sociology,* vol. 57, no. 5 (March 1952).

Lynd, Robert S., and Helen M. Lynd. *Middletown.* New York: Harcourt, Brace & Company, 1929.

McCabe, David A., and Richard A. Lester. *Labor and Social Organization.* Revised edition. Boston: D. C. Heath and Company, 1948.

McIsaac, Archibald M. *The Order of Railroad Telegraphers.* Princeton, N.J.: Princeton University Press, 1933.

Merton, Robert. "The Machine, the Worker, and the Engineer," *Science,* vol. 105, no. 2714 (January 1947).

Millis, Harry A., and Royal E. Montgomery. *Organized Labor.* New York: McGraw-Hill Book Company, 1945.

Moore, Wilbert E. *Industrial Relations and the Social Order.* New York: The Macmillan Company, 1946.

Morgan, John J. B. "Why Men Strike," *American Journal of Sociology*, vol. 26, no. 2 (September 1920).

Morris, Richard B. *Government and Labor in Early America.* New York: Columbia University Press, 1946.

Mumford, Lewis. *Sticks and Stones: A Study of American Architecture and Civilization.* New York: Boni and Liveright, 1924.

National Institute of Industrial Psychology. *The Foreman: A Study of Supervision in British Industry.* London: Staples, 1951.

Peterson, Florence. *American Labor Unions.* New York: Harper and Brothers, 1945.

Rose, Arnold M. *Union Solidarity: Internal Cohesion of a Trade Union.* Minneapolis: University of Minnesota Press, 1952.

Scott, Jerome F., and George C. Homans. "Reflections on the Wildcat Strikes," *American Sociological Review*, vol. 12, no. 3 (June 1947).

Selekman, Benjamin M. *Labor Relations and Human Relations.* New York: McGraw-Hill Book Company, 1947.

Sheppard, Harold L. "The Treatment of Unionism in 'Managerial Sociology'," *American Sociological Review*, vol. 14, no. 2 (April 1949). See also his unpublished doctoral dissertation, "Managerial Sociology: A Critical Commentary on the Mayo Influence in Industrial Sociology," University of Wisconsin, 1948.

Smith, Adam. *The Wealth of Nations,* Book I. 1776.

Starr, Mark. "Role of Union Organization," in W. F. Whyte, editor, *Industry and Society.* New York: McGraw-Hill Book Company, 1946.

Strauss, George, and Leonard R. Sayles. "The Unpaid Local Leader," *Harvard Business Review*, vol. 30, no. 3 (May–June 1952).

Tead, Ordway. "Review of Mayo's *Social Problems of an Industrial Civilization,*" *Survey Graphic*, vol. 35, no. 5 (May 1946).

Unwin, George. *The Gilds and Companies of London.* 3rd edition. London: George Allen & Unwin, 1938.

Waltzing, Jean Pierre. *Etude Historique sur les Corporations Professionnelles Chez les Romains Depuis des Origines Jusqu'à la Chute de l'Empire d'Occident.* Four volumes. Louvain, Belgium: C. Peters, 1895–1900.

Warner, W. Lloyd, and J. O. Low. *The Social System of the Modern Factory,* subtitled *The Strike: A Social Analysis.* Vol. IV in Yankee City Series. New Haven, Conn.: Yale University Press, 1947.

Wray, Donald E. "Marginal Men of Industry: The Foremen," *American Journal of Sociology*, vol. 54, no. 4 (January 1949).

Yoder, Dale. *Labor Economics and Labor Problems.* New York: McGraw-Hill Book Company, 1950.

Chapter 9. Vocational Choice

Bell, Howard M. *Youth Tell Their Story.* Washington, D.C.: American Council on Education, 1938.

Bingham, Walter V. "Abilities and Opportunities," *Occupations*, vol. 12, no. 6 (February 1934).

Bingham, Walter V. *Aptitudes and Aptitude Testing.* 12th edition. New York: Published for the National Occupational Conference by Harper and Brothers, 1937.

Brayfield, Arthur H., and Grace T. Mickelson. "Disparities in Occupational Information Coverage," *Occupations*, April 1951.

Brayfield, Arthur H., and Patricia Aepli Reed. "How Readable Are Occupational Information Booklets?" *Journal of Applied Psychology*, vol. 34, no. 5 (October 1950).

BIBLIOGRAPHY

Bureau of Labor Statistics, United States Department of Labor. *Occupational Data for Counselors.* Bulletin no. 817, February 1945.

Chinoy, Ely. "The Tradition of Opportunity and the Aspirations of Automobile Workers," *American Journal of Sociology,* vol. 57, no. 5 (March 1952).

Chyatte, Conrad. "Personality Traits of Professional Actors," *Occupations,* vol. 27, no. 4 (January 1949).

Clark, Carroll D., and Noel P. Gist. "Intelligence as a Factor in Occupational Choice," *American Sociological Review,* vol. 3, no. 5 (October 1938).

Clark, Harold F. *Economic Theory and Correct Occupational Distribution.* New York: Bureau of Publications, Teachers College, Columbia University, 1931.

Crawford, Albert Beecher, and Stuart Holmes Clement, editors. *The Choice of an Occupation.* New Haven, Conn.: Department of Personnel Study, Yale University, 1932.

Davis, Edwin W. "Aids to Occupational Research," *Occupations,* vol. 3, no. 6 (March 1935).

Dodge, A. F. "What Are the Personality Traits of Successful Clerical Workers?" *Journal of Applied Psychology,* vol. 24, no. 5 (October 1940).

Fiske, E. R. *The Veterans' Best Opportunities.* New York: Duell, Sloan & Pearce, 1946.

Form, William H., and Delbert C. Miller. "Occupational Career Pattern as a Sociological Instrument," *American Journal of Sociology,* vol. 54, no. 4 (January 1949).

Froehlich, Clifford P., and John G. Darley. *Studying Students: Guidance Methods of Individual Analysis.* Chicago: Science Research Associates, 1952.

Gilmore, Harlan W. "Five Generations of a Begging Family," *American Journal of Sociology,* vol. 37, no. 5 (March 1932).

Ginzberg, Eli, and others. *Occupational Choice: An Approach to a General Theory.* New York: Columbia University Press, 1951.

Gist, Noel P., C. T. Pihlblad, and C. L. Gregory. "Scholastic Achievement and Occupation," *American Sociological Review,* vol. 7, no. 6 (December 1942).

Greenberg, Walter. "A Bibliography of Occupational Monographs Available through the Federal Government," *Occupations,* vol. 25, no. 7 (April 1947).

Kaplan, Oscar J., editor. *Encyclopedia of Vocational Guidance.* New York: Philosophical Library, 1948.

Keller, Albert G. "The Working Boy," *American Journal of Sociology,* vol. 2, no. 3 (November 1896).

Landis, Paul H. *Social Control: Social Organization and Disorganization in Process.* Philadelphia: J. B. Lippincott Company, 1939.

MacKaye, David. "The Fixation of Vocational Interest," *American Journal of Sociology,* vol. 33, no. 3 (November 1927).

Manson, Grace E. *Occupational Interests and Personality Requirements of Women in Business and the Professions.* Vol. 3. Ann Arbor, Mich.: Bureau of Business Research, University of Michigan, 1931.

Myers, Charles S. *Industrial Psychology.* New York: The People's Institute Publishing Company, 1925.

Occupational Research Section, National Vocational Guidance, Inc. "Content of a Good Occupational Monograph — the Basic Outline," *Occupations,* vol. 19, no. 1 (October 1940).

Paterson, Donald G., and C. Harold Stone. "Dissatisfaction with Life Work Among Adult Workers," *Occupations,* vol. 21, no. 3 (November 1942).

President's Commission on Higher Education. *Higher Education for American Democracy.* New York: Harper and Brothers, 1947.

Science Research Associates. *Occupational Briefs on America's Major Job Fields.* Chicago: Science Research Associates, 1946.

THE SOCIOLOGY OF WORK

Shartle, Carroll L. *Occupational Information: Its Development and Application.* New York: Prentice-Hall, 1946.

Steiner, M. E. "The Search for Occupational Personalities," *Personnel*, vol. 29, no. 4 (January 1953).

Strong, Edward K., Jr. *Vocational Interests of Men and Women.* Stanford, Calif.: Stanford University Press, 1943.

Terman, Lewis M., and others. *The Gifted Child Grows Up.* Vol. IV in *Genetic Studies of Genius.* Stanford, Calif.: Stanford University Press, 1947.

Thorndike, Edward L., and others. *Prediction of Vocational Success.* New York: The Commonwealth Fund, 1934.

Waller, Willard. *The Sociology of Teaching.* New York: John Wiley & Sons, 1932.

Warner, W. Lloyd, Robert J. Havighurst, and Martin B. Loeb. *Who Shall Be Educated?* New York: Harper and Brothers, 1944.

Woods, E. B. "Social Waste of Unguided Personal Ability," *American Journal of Sociology,* vol. 19, no. 3 (November 1913).

Zimand, Gertrude Folks. "The Changing Picture of Child Labor," *The Annals of the American Academy of Political and Social Science,* vol. 236 (November 1944).

Chapter 10. The Occupations of Women

Abbott, Grace. "The Midwife in Chicago," *American Journal of Sociology,* vol. 20, no. 5 (March 1915).

Addams, Jane. "A Belated Industry," *American Journal of Sociology,* vol. 1, no. 5 (March 1896).

Anderson, C. Arnold and Mary Jean Bowman. "The Vanishing Servant and the Contemporary Status System of the American South," *American Journal of Sociology,* vol. 59, no. 3 (November 1953).

Baudler, Lucille, and Donald G. Paterson. "Social Status of Women's Occupations," *Occupations,* vol. 26, no. 7 (April 1948).

Beard, Mary R. *Woman as Force in History: A Study in Traditions and Realities.* New York: The Macmillan Company, 1946.

Breckinridge, S. P. "The Activities of Women Outside the Home," in *Recent Social Trends in the United States.* New York: McGraw-Hill Book Company, 1934.

Chapple, Eliot D., with the collaboration of Conrad M. Arensberg. "Measuring Human Relations: An Introduction to the Study of the Interaction of Individuals," *Genetic Psychology Monographs,* vol. 22, no. 1 (February 1940).

Clark, Alice. *Working Life of Women in the Seventeenth Century.* New York: Harcourt, Brace & Company, 1920.

Devereux, George, and Florence R. Weiner. "The Occupational Status of Nurses," *American Sociological Review,* vol. 15, no. 4 (August 1950).

Donovan, Frances R. *The Saleslady.* Chicago: University of Chicago Press, 1929.

Donovan, Frances R. *The Schoolma'am.* New York: Frederick A. Stokes Company, 1938.

Donovan, Frances R. *The Woman Who Waits.* Boston: Richard G. Badger, 1920.

Horton, Mildred McAfee. "Women in the United States Navy," *American Journal of Sociology,* vol. 51, no. 5 (March 1946).

Kingsbury, Susan M. "The Relation of Women to Industry," *Publications of the American Sociological Society,* vol. 15, (1920).

Kirkpatrick, Clifford. "The Measurement of Ethical Inconsistency in Marriage," *International Journal of Ethics,* vol. 46, no. 4 (July 1936).

MacLean, Annie Marion. "Life in the Pennsylvania Coal Fields with Particular Reference to Women," *American Journal of Sociology,* vol. 14, no. 3 (November 1908).

318

MacLean, Annie Marion. "The Sweat Shop in Summer," *American Journal of Sociology*, vol. 9, no. 3 (November 1903).

MacLean, Annie Marion. "Two Weeks in Department Stores," *American Journal of Sociology*, vol. 4, no. 6 (May 1899).

MacLean, Annie Marion. "With Oregon Hop Pickers," *American Journal of Sociology*, vol. 15, no. 1 (July 1909).

Mead, Margaret. *And Keep Your Powder Dry*. New York: William Morrow & Company, 1942.

Park, R. E. Introduction to Frances R. Donovan, *The Saleslady*. Chicago: University of Chicago Press, 1929.

Tharp, B. B. "Vocational Interests of Eminent Women of Today," *American Journal of Sociology*, vol. 39, no. 3 (November 1933).

Weatherly, U. G. "Access of Women to Industrial Occupations," *American Journal of Sociology*, vol. 14, no. 6 (May 1909).

Whyte, William Foote. *Human Relations in the Restaurant Industry*. New York: McGraw-Hill Book Company, 1948.

Whyte, William Foote. "The Social Structure of the Restaurant," *American Journal of Sociology*, vol. 54, no. 4 (January 1949).

Williams, Josephine J. "Patients and Prejudice: Lay Attitudes towards Women Physicians," *American Journal of Sociology*, vol. 51, no. 4 (January 1946).

Chapter 11. Occupation and Family

Anderson, W. A. "Family Social Participation and Social Status Self-ratings," *American Sociological Review*, vol. 11, no. 3 (June 1946).

Angell, Robert C. *The Family Encounters the Depression*. New York: Charles Scribner's Sons, 1936.

Anshen, Ruth Nanda, editor. *The Family, Its Function and Destiny*. Science of Culture Series, Vol. V. New York: Harper and Brothers, 1949.

Byington, Margaret F. "The Family in a Typical Mill Town," *American Journal of Sociology*, vol. 14, no. 5 (March 1909).

Centers, Richard. "Marital Selection and Occupational Strata," *American Journal of Sociology*, vol. 54, no. 6 (May 1949).

Conrad, Laetitia. "Differential Depression Effects on Families of Laborers, Farmers and the Business Class," *American Journal of Sociology*, vol. 44, no. 4 (January 1939).

Deasy, Leila Calhoun, and C. Arnold Anderson. "Selectivity in the University: A Study of the Influence of Social Status on Enrollment," *Journal of Higher Education*, vol. 24, no. 3 (March 1953).

Durand, John D. "Married Women in the Labor Force," *American Journal of Sociology*, vol. 52, no. 3 (November 1946).

Edwards, Alba M. *Comparative Occupation Statistics for the United States, 1870–1940*. Washington, D.C.: Government Printing Office, 1943.

Elliott, Mabel A., and Frances E. Merrill. *Social Disorganization*. Revised edition. New York: Harper and Brothers, 1941.

Fitch, John A. *The Steel Workers*. New York: Charities Publication Committee, 1910. Part of The Pittsburgh Survey, edited by Paul Underwood Kellogg for the Russell Sage Foundation.

Frazier, E. Franklin. *The Negro Family in the United States*. Chicago: University of Chicago Press, 1934.

Glick, Paul C. "Family Life and Full Employment," *American Journal of Sociology*, vol. 54, no. 6 (May 1949).

Green, Arnold. "The Middle-Class Male Child and Neurosis," *American Sociological Review*, vol. 11, no. 1 (February 1946).

Hergt, Kathleen, and J. R. Shannon. "Marriage vs. Careers — and Fame," *Occupations*, vol. 16, no. 9 (June 1938).

Hollingshead, August B. "Class Difference in Family Stability," *Annals of the American Academy of Political and Social Science*, vol. 272 (November 1950).

Hollingshead, August B. *Elmtown's Youth*. New York: John Wiley & Sons, 1949.

Hunt, T. C. "Occupational Status and Marriage Selection," *American Sociological Review*, vol. 5, no. 4 (August 1940).

Jaffe, A. J., and Charles D. Stewart. *Manpower Resources and Utilization: Principles of Working Force Analysis*. New York: John Wiley & Sons, 1951.

Komarovsky, Mirra. "Cultural Contradictions and Sex Roles," *American Journal of Sociology*, vol. 52, no. 3 (November 1946).

Lewis, Roy, and Angus Maude. *The English Middle Classes*. New York: Alfred A. Knopf, 1950.

Locke, Harvey J., and Muriel Mackeprang. "Marital Adjustment and the Employed Wife," *American Journal of Sociology*, vol. 54, no. 6 (May 1949).

MacLean, Annie Marion. "Life in the Pennsylvania Coal Fields with Particular Reference to Women," *American Journal of Sociology*, vol. 14, no. 3 (November 1908).

Mandelbaum, David. "The Family in India." In R. N. Anshen, editor, *The Family: Its Function and Destiny*. New York: Harper and Brothers, 1949.

Marvin, Donald M. "Occupational Propinquity as a Factor in Marriage Selection," *Publications of the American Statistical Association*. Vol. 16. 1918–19.

Mead, Margaret. *And Keep Your Powder Dry*. New York: William Morrow & Company, 1942.

Merton, Robert K. "Social Structure and Anomie." In R. N. Anshen, editor, *The Family: Its Function and Destiny*. New York: Harper and Brothers, 1949.

Nimkoff, Meyer. "Occupational Factors and Marriage," *American Journal of Sociology*, vol. 49, no. 3 (November 1943).

Parsons, Talcott. "Age and Sex in the Social Structure of the United States," *American Sociological Review*, vol. 7, no. 5 (October 1942).

Parsons, Talcott. "The Social Structure of the Family." In R. N. Anshen, editor, *The Family: Its Function and Destiny*. New York: Harper and Brothers, 1949.

Riemer, Svend. "Maladjustment to the Family Home," *American Sociological Review*, vol. 10, no. 5 (October 1945).

Whyte, William. "The Wives of Management," *Fortune*, October 1951.

Willcox, W. F. *Studies in American Demography*. Ithaca, N.Y.: Cornell University Press, 1940.

Zimand, Gertrude Folks. "The Changing Picture of Child Labor," *Annals of the American Academy of Political and Social Science*, vol. 236 (November 1944).

Chapter 12. Working Conditions

Auten, Nellie. "Sweating System in the Garment Trades of Chicago," *American Journal of Sociology*, vol. 6, no. 5 (March 1901).

Blakey, Roy G., William Weinfeld, James E. Dugan, and Alex L. Hart. *Analyses of Minnesota Incomes, 1938–39*. Minneapolis: University of Minnesota Press, 1944.

Blumer, Herbert. "Sociological Theory in Industrial Relations," *American Sociological Review*, vol. 12, no. 3 (June 1947).

Bushnell, Charles. "Some Social Aspects of the Chicago Stock Yards," *American Journal of Sociology*, vol. 7, no. 2–5 (September 1901–March 1902).

Dublin, Louis I., and Robert J. Vane. *Causes of Death by Occupation*, Bulletin No. 507 of the United States Bureau of Labor Statistics. Washington, D.C.: Government Printing Office, 1930.

Engels, Frederick. *The Condition of the Working Class in England in 1844*. Translated by F. K. Wischnewestzky. London: George Allen & Unwin, 1892.

BIBLIOGRAPHY

Foley, J. P., Jr. *An Experimental Study of the Effect of Occupational Experience upon Motor Speed and Preferential Tempo.* Archives of Psychology, No. 219, November 1937.

Foley, J. P., Jr. "The Occupational Conditioning of Preferential Auditory Tempo: A Contribution toward an Empirical Theory of Esthetics," *Journal of Social Psychology,* vol. 12 (August 1940).

Fourastié, Jean. *Le Grand Espoir du Vingtième Siècle.* 2nd edition. Paris: Presses Universitaires de France, 1950.

Fourastié, Jean. *Machinisme et Bien-Etre.* Paris: Les Editions de Minuit, 1951.

Friedmann, Georges. *Où Va Le Travail Humain.* Paris: Librairie Gallimard, 1950.

Hunt, Elizabeth Pinney. *Arthur Young on Industry and Economics.* Being excerpts from Arthur Young's observations on the state of manufactures and his economic opinions on problems related to contemporary industry in England. Bryn Mawr, 1926.

King, Willford Isbell. *The Wealth and Income of the People of the United States.* New York: The Macmillan Company, 1922.

Lastrucci, Carlo L. "The Status and Significance of Occupational Research," *American Sociological Review,* vol. 11, no. 1 (February 1946).

Meadows, Paul. *The Culture of Industrial Man.* Lincoln, Nebr.: University of Nebraska Press, 1950.

Moore, Wilbert E. "Industrial Sociology: Status and Prospects," *American Sociological Review,* vol. 13, no. 4 (August 1948).

Mumford, Lewis. *Technics and Civilization.* New York: Harcourt, Brace & Company, 1934.

Pangburn, Weaver. "The Worker's Leisure and His Individuality," *American Journal of Sociology,* vol. 27, no. 4 (January 1922).

Peterson, Florence. *Survey of Labor Economics.* New York: Harper and Brothers, 1947.

Siegfried, Andre. *America Comes of Age.* Translated by H. H. Hemming and Doris Hemming. New York: Harcourt, Brace & Company, 1927.

Simmel, Georg. "The Sociology of Sociability," *American Journal of Sociology,* vol. 55, no. 3 (November 1949). Translated by Everett C. Hughes.

Theodorson, George A. "Acceptance of Industrialization and Its Attendant Consequences for the Social Patterns of Non-Western Societies," *American Sociological Review,* vol. 18, no. 5 (October 1953).

Zimmerman, Carle C. *Consumption and Standards of Living.* New York: D. Van Nostrand Company, 1936.

Appendix. A Brief Statistical Description of the American Labor Force

Bickham, Martin H. "The American Labor Market," *American Journal of Sociology,* vol. 43, no. 4 (January 1938).

Bureau of the Census. *Statistical Abstract of the United States.* Washington, D.C.: Government Printing Office, 1950.

Christensen, Thomas E. "Dictionary Classification of the AGCT Scores for Selected Civilian Occupations," *Occupations,* vol. 25, no. 3 (December 1946).

Durand, John D. *The Labor Force in the United States, 1890–1960.* New York: Social Science Research Council, 1948.

Edwards, Alba M. *Comparative Occupation Statistics for the United States, 1870–1940.* Washington, D.C.: Government Printing Office, 1943.

Gillen, Paul Bates. *The Distribution of Occupations as a City Yardstick.* New York: King's Crown Press, 1951.

THE SOCIOLOGY OF WORK

Hauser, Philip M. "The Labor Force and Gainful Workers — Concept, Measurement, and Comparability," *American Journal of Sociology,* vol. 54, no. 4 (January 1949).

Hurlin, Ralph G., and Meredith B. Givens. "Shifting Occupational Patterns," in *Recent Social Trends in the United States.* New York: McGraw-Hill Book Company, 1934.

Jaffe, A. J., and Charles D. Stewart. *Manpower Resources and Utilization: Principles of Working Force Analysis.* New York: John Wiley & Sons, 1951.

Kitson, Harry D. "Distribution of Workers in Selected Occupations," *Occupations,* vol. 25, no. 3 (December 1946).

Landis, Paul H. *Population Problems: A Cultural Interpretation.* New York: American Book Company, 1943.

Lebergott, Stanley. Comment on "Discrimination against Older Workers in Industry," *American Journal of Sociology,* vol. 51, no. 4 (January 1946).

Ogburn, William, and Clark Tibbitts. "Occupations," *American Journal of Sociology,* vol. 34, no. 6 (May 1929).

Pollak, Otto. "Discrimination against Older Workers in Industry," *American Journal of Sociology,* vol. 50, no. 2 (September 1944).

Wolfbein, S. L., and A. J. Jaffe. "Demographic Factors in Labor Force Growth," *American Sociological Review,* vol. 11, no. 4 (August 1946).

Wolman, Leo, and Gustav Peck. "Labor Groups in the Social Structure," in *Recent Social Trends in the United States.* New York: McGraw-Hill Book Company, 1934.

"The Workers," *Fortune,* vol. 21, no. 2 (February 1940).

Woytinsky, W. S. *Labor in the United States: Basic Statistics for Social Security.* Washington, D.C.: Committee on Social Security, Social Science Research Council, 1938.

OCCUPATIONAL INDEX

Accountant, 38, 50, 51, 59, 135, 139, 147, 170, 227
Acid chamberman, 134
Acrobat, 45
Actor, 35, 52, 124, 200, 201, 202, 258
Actuary, 63
Administrative consultant, 33
Anesthetist, 79
Architect, 6, 52, 77, 102, 110, 170, 219
Artist, 36, 50, 52, 63, 65, 286
Auctioneer, 34, 149
Auditor, 50, 52
Auto mechanic, 51
Aviator, 34, 200, 201

Baker, 78
Banker, 34, 35, 40, 41, 54, 56, 65, 112
Barber, 36, 48, 50, 55, 281, 287
Bartender, 48, 51, 241
Baseball player, 227
Beautician, 48
Beggar, 124, 215
Bell caster, 76, 251
Bellboy, 48
Bill collector, 135
Blacksmith, 35, 55, 186, 232
Blueprinter, 135
Boilermaker, 164
Bookkeeper, 50, 54
Bootblack, 32, 36, 48
Bottle-maker, 138
Boxer, 124
Bricklayer, 36, 52, 104, 136, 164, 186
Broker, 34, 63, 66, 148
Building inspector, 62
Butcher, 36, 37, 46, 51, 102
Buyer, 39, 68, 240

Cabinetmaker, 51, 63, 143, 192
Cameraman, 164
Candy-maker, 82, 84
Canvasser, 34, 232
Caretaker, 135
Carpenter, 35, 38, 44, 51, 54, 56, 62, 63, 102, 134, 136, 143, 164, 186, 192
Cartoonist, 67
Cashier, 50
Cesspool cleaner, 47
Chauffeur, 48, 51, 52, 54, 193

Chef, 34, 36, 38, 48, 76, 134, 143, 234
Chemist, 34, 50, 170, 190, 201
Chimney sweep, 47
Chiropodist, 42, 48
Cigar-maker, 186
Circus performer, 76
Clergyman, 44, 53, 54, 79, 90, 11, 215
Coal-carrier, 47
Composer, 281
Conductor, symphony, 52, 193
Copyreader, 143
Coremaker, 31
Counterman, 32
Cowboy, 227
Criminal, 32, 96, 97, 98, 124
Croupier, 76

Dental hygienist, 231
Dentist, 49, 52, 62, 102
Detective, 286
Diplomat, 61, 98, 124, 231
Ditch digger, 55, 56
Draftsman 50, 52, 62
Dry cleaner, 164

Editor, 36, 38, 47, 102
Electrician, 35, 41, 50, 53, 54, 56, 63, 102, 136, 164, 165, 169
Engineer, 50, 51, 53, 135, 139, 164, 201
Engraver, 164
Entertainer, 63, 65, 93
Etcher, 45
Evangelist, 67
Executive, 48, 60
Explorer, 227

Farmer, 6, 32, 35, 37, 38, 40, 41, 42, 52, 54, 62, 65, 124, 214, 231, 270
Farmhand, 51, 148, 172
Filling-station operator, 102, 135
Fireman, 42, 53
Fisherman, 215
Foreman, 35, 42, 50, 74, 168, 169, 200, 232, 258
Fortuneteller, 41
Foundryman, 193
Freight-handler, 172
Furnace tender, 135
Furrier, 138

Gambler, 41
Garage mechanic, 282
Gardener, 38, 52
Glue-maker, 47
Gondola-maker, 251
Governess, 48, 233
Grocer, 46, 54, 62, 102, 270
Group dynamicist, 134

Hairdresser, 42, 234
Hod carrier, 55
Horseshoer, 181
Hostler, 47
Housekeeper, 48, 233
Huckster, 30
Hunter, 30
Hypnotist, 30, 35

Iceman, 137
Inspector, 50, 85, 241
Insurance agent, 41, 56

Jailkeeper, 35
Janitor, 32, 36, 53, 55, 135, 240
Jazz musician, 61, 95, 97, 98, 164
Joiner, 192
Journalist, 35, 50, 52, 65, 68, 124, 134, 135, 138, 139, 190, 200
Judge, 12, 40, 52, 230, 240
Junk dealer, 47, 139

Laboratory technician, 53, 62, 201
Lacemaker, 12
Lathe operator, 227
Lawyer, 50, 54, 62, 102, 110, 126, 135, 147, 219, 227, 240
Legislator, 52
Librarian, 34, 35, 38, 78, 201, 230, 245, 246
Lineman, 60
Linotyper, 45, 164
Locomotive engineer, 36, 54, 59, 113, 135, 186, 227, 286
Locomotive fireman, 59
Longshoreman, 53, 193
Lumberjack, 51, 124, 192

Machine operator, 32, 43, 44, 45, 50, 68, 172, 234, 245
Machinist, 35, 36, 50, 54, 63, 186, 193
Mail clerk, 45, 200
Manufacturer, 35, 40, 62, 133
Marine, 42
Market research investigator, 36
Mason, 62, 63, 102, 107, 136, 164, 165, 169
Masseur, 48
Mechanic, 38, 50, 63, 135, 218
Mechanical engineer, 62
Medical technologist, 139

Metal finisher, 78
Midwife, 60
Millwright, 63, 84, 135, 164, 215
Miner, 46, 51, 53, 55, 101, 145, 193, 215
Missionary, 54
Molder, 51
Movie projectionist, 45, 106, 138
Movie star, 67, 130
Musician, symphony, 35, 37, 67, 98, 124, 215

Nurse, 48, 60, 201, 230, 245, 246, 286

Officer, 54, 59, 105, 124, 148, 215
Oil-well gun perforator, 134
Organist, 193

Painter, 51, 107, 136, 164, 193
Pawnbroker, 35
Peddler, 6
Pharmacist, 14, 38, 50, 124, 148
Philosopher, 134
Photographer, 50
Physician, 14, 31, 38, 49, 54, 56, 60, 77, 102, 106, 110, 124, 126, 135, 138, 170, 172, 215, 219, 227, 250
Pianist, 149
Piano tuner, 52
Pipe fitter, 51
Plant pathologist, 63
Plasterer, 78, 107, 164, 193
Plumber, 36, 50, 54, 63, 164, 169
Poet, 111, 258
Policeman, 32, 42, 46, 54, 62, 113, 133, 134, 200, 215, 227, 241, 270
Politician, 44, 63, 65, 67
Porter, 36, 48
Post office clerk, 133
Postman, 54, 135, 136
Potter, 95, 97, 98, 164
Printer, 36, 50, 164
Professor, 36, 54, 64, 124, 134, 170
Promotor, 66
Prostitute, 40, 41
Public-opinion analyst, 33, 36, 39
Purchasing agent, 50

Radio operator, 138, 164
Ragpicker, 65
Railway conductor, 53, 54
Railway worker, 61, 96–97, 98, 124
Resort-keeper, 35
Restaurant worker, 48, 53
Riveter, 51
Roofer, 63, 164, 165

Sailor, 134, 138, 286
Salesman, 32, 38, 50, 54, 56, 62, 63, 65, 66, 67, 84, 135, 143, 148, 176, 227, 232, 241, 245, 258

Sanitary engineer, 47
Scholar, 133
Scientist, 22
Sculptor, 111
Secretary, 258
Seismic observer, 134
Servant, 32, 34, 42, 48, 62, 148, 172
Sewer cleaner, 46, 145
Sheetmetal worker, 165
Sheriff, 34
Shiprigger, 137
Shipyard worker, 124
Shoemaker, 185, 186
Sideshow performer, 286
Sign painter, 34
Snowplow driver, 135
Social worker, 170, 245, 246
Soldier, 12, 54
Stableboy, 282
Stagehand, 164
Steamfitter, 63, 102, 164, 169, 193
Steamship captain, 34
Steel ladler, 35
Steelworker, 124, 186
Stenographer, 36, 39, 50, 101, 245
Stonemason, 35, 186
Street cleaner, 41, 46, 55
Stripteaser, 42
Symphony conductor, 52, 193
Symphony musician, 35, 37, 67, 98, 124, 215

Tailor, 38, 54
Tanner, 47
Taxi-dancer, 124
Taxi driver, 48
Teacher, 35, 36, 38, 44, 50, 53, 54, 56, 78, 111, 124, 129, 135, 200, 201, 202, 227, 230, 245, 246, 258
Teamster, 51, 55, 193
Theater usher, 35
Tinker, 12
Tool and die maker, 50, 63
Toymaker, 60
Traffic manager, 33
Tree surgeon, 135
Truck driver, 36, 51, 145
Typist, 34, 36, 43, 50, 62, 245
Typographer, 54, 186

Undertaker, 47, 135, 139
Upholsterer, 51, 193

Vitrifier, 32

Waiter, 35, 48, 55, 59, 101, 124, 234, 241, 245
Ward heeler, 41
Watchmaker, 38, 50, 62
Weaver, 12, 50, 105
Welder, 51
Writer, 65, 67, 200

Zoo keeper, 79

GENERAL INDEX

Aggregation, 19–21
American Federation of Labor, 187, 190, 192, 193, 194: organization of, 203
American Journal of Sociology, 236
American Revolution, 185
Anderson, Dewey, 61, 62
Anderson, F. L., 34
Anderson, Nels, 91
Anderson, W. A., 40
Angell, Robert C., 267
Aptitude tests, 223–24
Archibald, Katherine, 86, 208
Army Alpha Test, 31, 38, 49
Army General Classification Test, 38, 49

Bach, Johann Sebastian, 281
Balzac, Honoré, 69
Bardet, Gaston, 128
Barr scale, 35, 37, 38, 49
Baudler, Lucille, 39
Becker, Howard, 12
Beckman, R. O., 34, 42
Bentham, Jeremy, 145
Bergson, Henri, 133
Binet test, 223
Birth-rate, 20
Blau, Ralph, 38
British Labour Party, 182
Bryan, William Jennings, 188
Buck, Pearl, 251
Building trades: recruiting, 102; involvement, 107–8; control of occupational behavior, 114
Bureaucracy, 149–55, 289: and assigned position, 31; in the factory, 44; and seniority, 74; definition of, 149; and unions, 168; and professions, 170; in the expansive union, 207; and women, 237; and the family, 257, 274; and hours, 286

Carr-Saunders, A. M., 14, 135
Centers, Richard, 36, 42
Chapple, Eliot D., 240
Chinese family, 248, 249, 250
Christensen, T. E., 38
Clark, Harold F., 106: and comparison of salaries, 104; quoted, 143

Clerical Aptitude Test, 223
Clerical work: qualifications for, 85; and migration, 90
Commons, John R., 185: on institutional economics, 4
Commonwealth Book Company, 225
Commonwealth v. Hunt, and first legal support of unions, 186
Concord School, 185
Congress of Industrial Organizations, 162, 190, 192, 194, 198, 203
Cooperation: medieval and modern, 27; between labor and management, 209–11; between men and women in working situation, 242–43
Cottrell, W. Fred, 96, 137
Counts, George S., 53: and first occupational prestige test, 32; quoted, 39, 40
Coxey's Army, 188
Craft union, compared with industrial union, 192–94. *See also* Unions
Crafts: involvement, 108; evaluation of merit, 111–12; coercion, 120; occupational folkways, 126–27; occupational attitudes, 131; stereotypes, 135–36; market for, 164–69; women in, 232

Davidson, Percy E., 61, 62
Davis, Kingsley, 40
Deeg, M. E., 39, 56
Depression, 162, 189, 288: and the family, 267
Dickson, William J., 112
Differentiation, 21–24: related to training, 27
Division of labor, 4, 10–19 *passim*
Dos Passos, John, 69
Dreyfuss, Carl, on German business in the 1920s, 155
Dubin, Robert, 158, 198, 210
Dublin, Louis I., 106
Durkheim, Emile: thesis on division of labor, 4; and occupational associations, 102

Economic theory: and the "just price" in modern and medieval times, 131; and wage levels, 142

Education: and occupational choice, 216–21; and the family, 257, 274–75

Edwards, Alba, 33, 42, 48, 93

Eighteenth century, mechanical looms in, 105

Elmtown, 265

English Combination Act, 186

Essay on Population, 142

Ethnology, and social functionalism, 7

Expansive union: as compared with restrictive union, 196–99; organization of, 205–7. *See also* Unions

Factory work: and migration, 90; recruiting, 103; involvement, 108; evaluation of merit, 112; control of occupational behavior, 115–17; coercion, 120; occupational folkways, 127–28; occupational attitudes, 131; stereotypes, 136; decrease in hours, 285–86. *See also* Wages

Family: monopoly of an occupation, 14; compared with occupational systems, 18; patriarchal types of, 248–51

Federal Society of Journeymen Cordwainers, first union in modern sense, 185

Federal Writers' Project, 82

Firth, Raymond: on division of labor, 10–12; on ritual among the Maori, 15; on remuneration in Tikopia, 17

Form, William H.: on mobility, 61, 63, 64; and occupational inheritance, 77

Fourastié, Jean: on wages and haircuts, 281; on hours and mirrors, 282; quoted on nutrition in *1800*, 283

Fourier, François Marie Charles, 146, 185

Franklin, Benjamin, 270

Frazier, E. Franklin, 252

Fryer, Douglas, and Army Alpha Test, 38

Galton, Francis, 5, 77

Geddes, Patrick, 5

General Motors, 158, 191, 210, 211

G.I. Bill of Rights, 79, 138

Gilmore, Harlan W., 215

Gompers, Samuel, 187, 195

Goodenough, F. L., and Minnesota Occupational Scale, 34

Grapes of Wrath, 174

Green, Arnold, 273

Guilds: definition of, 14; ceremonial convocations of, 16; and secret understandings, 23; rise and fall of in medieval Europe, 182–84

Guttman, Louis, 56

Hall, Oswald, and medical careers, 64

Hanseatic League, 13

Harbison, Frederick H., 157, 198, 210

Harrell, T. W. and M. S., 38, 39

Hartmann, G. W., 40

Hatt, Paul, 56, 57

Haymarket Riot, 188

Hershey Company, 158

Hiller, E. T., 12

Hindu: caste system as type of union, 182; family, 248, 249, 250; diet, 284

Hippocrates, Oath of, analysis, 114

Hobohemia, 91–95

Hollingshead, August B., 276

Homans, George C., 71

Hoppock, Robert, 133

Hormel Company, 158

Horseshoers Local No. 6, strike of, 181

Housewife: selective qualifications, 260–61; training, 261–62; job components, 262–64; work cycle, 262–66; and incentive, 266–67

Hoxie, Robert F., definition of unions, 191

Hughes, E. C., quoted, 101

Hunt, William C., 33: first classification of occupations, 31

Incentive, monetary, 146–47

Industrial psychology, 5

Industrial Revolution: and effect on redistribution of occupations, 19–20; and supervision, 23

Industrial sociology, 6

Industrial unions, compared with craft union, 193–94. *See also* Unions

Instinct of Workmanship, The, quoted, 85

Intelligence tests, 49–51, 216–17, 223. *See also* Army Alpha Test, Army General Classification Test

International Ladies Garment Workers, 192

International Workers of the World, 94, 188

Iron Law, Ricardo on supply and demand, 142

Just Price, 131, 144, 167

Keynes, John, 142, 199

Kirkpatrick, Clifford, 238

Knights of Labor, 187, 188

Labor market, 9, 175–77

Lehman, Harvey C., 40, 49

Lester, ichard, quoted, 184–85

Lewis, Sinclair, 69

Lope de Vega, 281

Lorge, Irving, comparison of Barr scores and Army Alpha Test, 38

Lotka, Alfred J., 106

Low, J. O., 160

Lynd, Robert S. and Helen M., 7, 64, 189, 254

McCabe, David, quoted, 184–85
MacLean, Annie Marion, 236
McWilliams, Carey, 92
Malinowski, Bronislaw, quoted, 17
Malthus, Thomas, 142
Mandelbaum, David, on Hindu family, 249, 250
Maori: division of labor, 10–12; ritual, 15
Marshall, Alfred, 142
Marx, Carl, 142, 199
Master Steamfitters Union, 195
Mayans, and remuneration, 16
Mayo, Elton, 211
Mead, Margaret, 147, 238, 253, 273
Mechanical Aptitude Test, 223
Menger, C., 40
Merton, Robert, quoted, 254, 258
Middle Ages, 79, 117, 166, 182–84, 251, 254
Middletown, 7, 189, 265
Migration, 60, 88–91, 235
Migratory worker, 91–98, 289
Miller, Delbert C.: and mobility, 61, 63, 64; and occupational inheritance, 77
Minnesota Occupational Scale, 34–35, 48
Mobility, and the family, 249, 271–72
Money Value of a Man, The, 106
Monthly Labor Review (United States Bureau of Labor Statistics), 225
Moore, Wilbert E., and seniority, 74
Morganstern, Oskar, 162
Morris, Richard B., 144
Moslem family, 248
Mumford, Lewis, 5, 185
Mythos, 258
National Industrial Recovery Act, quoted, 189
National Labor Union, 187
National Opinion Research Center, 56
National Vocational Guidance Association, 225
Negro: lower-class family organization of, 252; evaluation of work, 258; as servant, 268
Nepotism, 71: as a recruiting control, 105; and women's work, 237; and the family, 274
New England colonies, and guilds, 185
Noyes, J. H., 185

Oath of Hippocrates, analysis, 114
Occupation Index, Incorporated, 225
Occupational attitudes, formation of, 130–33
Occupational choice: parental influence, 215–16, 272; development of projective patterns of choice, 226–28
Occupational classification, 21, 22
Occupational control, contrasted with coercion, 120–21
Occupational folkways, 124–30

Occupational inheritance, 75–80
Occupational institutions, changes in, 137–40
Occupational scales, history of, 31–32
Occupational stereotype, 134–37
Owen, Robert, 185–86

Pancoast, Omar, Jr., 106
Panurge, 54
Park, R. E., and occupational associations, 102
Parsons, Talcott, 238, 244: quoted, 253, 254, 276; analysis of the family and occupations, 254–57, 258
Paterson, D. G., 39, 56
Performance, evaluation of, 110–13
Pirenne, Henri, and market regulations, 117
Plainville, 265
Plato, 289
Pogo, 289
Political Action Committee, 198
Pond, M., 38
Populists, 188
Pre-industrial society, and cooperation, 211
Preliterate society, remuneration in, 16
President's Commission on Higher Education, 79
Prestige scales, 39–41, 52–57
Professional organizer, 204
Professionalization, 170–72
Professions: and mobility, 64; earning curve, 75; occupational inheritance, 77; age of traditions, 101; manner of recruiting, 102–3; involvement, 106–7; evaluation of merit, 110–11; manner of control, 114; coercion, 120; occupational folkways, 124–26; occupational attitudes, 131; stereotypes, 135; market for, 170–72; and women, 230, 240; hours, 286
Prostitution, 233, 234
Psychometric scales, 36–39
Pullman Massacre, 188

Quarrie Corporation, 225

Railway Brotherhood, 203
Rappites, 185
Rationalization, 24–25
Ravenstein, E. G., 88
Recruiting: manner of, 102–6; in a bureaucracy, 151
Redfield, Robert, 16
Restrictive union: compared with expansive union, 195–99; organization of, 204–5. *See also* Unions
Retail trades: lack of recruiting controls, 103; involvement, 109; evaluation of merit, 112; control of occupational be-

havior, 117–19; coercion, 120; stereotypes, 136
Ricardo, David, 142
Ritual, 15, 16
Robinson, James Harvey, 5
Rodehaver, Myles W., 90
Roethlisberger, F. J., 112, 134
Romains, Jules, 69
Roman corporations, as embryonic unions, 182
Romany gypsies, as type of professional transient, 91
Roosevelt, Theodore, 188
Rose, Arnold, 208
Rosten, Leo C., 130, 147
Rountree, B. S., 75
Rule Book, and effect on control of trades, 115
Russia: use of Counts' scale in, 40; and wages, 146

Sayles, Leonard R., quoted, 163
Scales, see Army Alpha Test, Army General Classification Test, Minnesota Occupational Scale, Prestige scales, Psychometric scales, Socioeconomic scales, Strong Vocational Test
Schneider, Joseph, 77
Science Research Associates, 225
Scientific Management, 5
Selekman, Benjamin, 207
Self-employment, alleged superiority of, 45
Semiskilled manual work, 64, 74, 84–87, 157–64
Seniority, 73–75: evaluation of, 106–10; in a bureaucracy, 151; and wage structure, 164
Service trades, 64: and inheritance, 77; and women, 233; and middle-class family, 269
Shaw, Chief Justice, quoted, 186
Sheppard, Harold L., 211
Shop steward, as union representative, 204–6
Simmel, Georg, 25
Sims, V. M., 40
Slavery, as device to meet labor shortage, 185
Smith, Adam, 143
Smith, Joseph, 185
Smith, Mapheus, 40, 90
Socioeconomic scales, 31, 33–36, 42–49
Sons of Vulcan, 187
Sorokin, Pitirim, 59, 75
South Bend, Ind., 210
Southerntown, 265
Steinbeck, John, 174
Stevens, R. B., 40
Stokes, Stuart M., 49
Stouffer, Samuel, 88

Stranger, role of, 12, 13
Strauss, George, quoted, 163
Strikes, 198, 205–8: first analyzed, 181; in history of unions, 188; during World War II, 190–91; and the expansive union, 196; by the white-collar union, 200–1
Strong, Edward K., 221
Strong Vocational Interest Inventory, 221, 222
Studebaker, 210, 211
Sumner, William Graham, 7
Superannuation, 93
Supreme Court, and constitutionality of Wagner Act, 190
Sutherland, Edwin H., 96

Taft-Hartley Act, 190
Taussig, F. W., 40
Tawney, Richard H., quoted, 146
Tead, Ordway, 211
Teamsters' Union, 193
Tenure, in a bureaucracy, 151
Terman, L. M., 78: quoted, 37
Theory of Games, 162
Third Reich, 288
Thompson, Warren S., 20
Thorndike, Edward L., 223: and prediction of vocational success, 78
Thurnwald, Richard, 10
Tikopia, 9, 16, 17
Tilgher, Adriano, 132
Tillmanism, 188
Titian, 281
Todas, 16
Tolstoi, Leo, 69
Transient labor, 91–98, 289
Trobrianders, and remuneration, 17

Unions: controls exerted by, 103–16; expansion of, 157–58; and wages, 161–63; historical summary, 182–91; classifications of, 191–202; internal structure of, 203–12
United Automobile Workers, 158, 191, 195, 210
United Mine Workers, 192, 203
United States Bureau of Labor Statistics: and turnover rates, 87; and wage cuts, 152; industry descriptions in the Monthly Labor Review, 225
United States Bureau of the Census: first classification of occupations, 31; under Alba Edwards, 33
United States Department of Agriculture, 225
United States Employment Service, 224, 225
United States Office of Education, 225
United States Women's Bureau of the Department of Labor, 225

Unskilled labor, 64; earning curve, 75; wages, 143; market for, 172–75

Unwin, George, 16: description of medieval guilds of London, 183–84

Veblen, Thorstein: institutional economics, 4; quoted, 85, 287

Vertical mobility, definition of, 59. *See also* Mobility

Visher, Stephen S., 77

Vocational guidance, 221–26

Vocational interest tests, 221–22

Vocational literature, 224–25

Von Neumann, John, 162

Wages, 142–46: assessment of, 148; in a bureaucracy, 151–55; for factory work, 158–64; for crafts, 166; for common labor, 174; definition of, 177–78; and expansive union, 198; and white-collar union, 201–2; for women, 234–35

Wagner Act, 162, 190, 200

Waller, Willard, 238

Waltzing, Jean Pierre, 182

War Labor Board, during World War I, 189

Warner, W. Lloyd, 64, 160

Wealth of Nations, 4

Weber, Max, 12

Welch, Maryon K., 40

Western Electric Study, 6, 22, 134

Western Federation of Miners, 188

White-collar work: ascribed superiority of, 43; semiskilled, 64; training, 84; professionalization, 138, 139; and unions, 190, 200–2; women in, 239

Whyte, William F., 134

Whyte, William H., 238, 240, 241

Willcox, W. F., 259

Williams, Josephine, 240

Wilson, Logan, 64, 134

Wilson, Woodrow, unions during administration of, 189

Witty, P. A., 40

Works Progress Administration, market for common labor under, 173

World War I, 181, 188, 195, 219

World War II, 20, 181, 219

Wright, Carroll, 33

Yankee City, 265

Yankeetown, 160

Yerkes, R. M., 31, 36

Yoder, Dale, 191

Zimmerman, C. C., quoted, 283

51795